Economic Morality and Jewish Law

Economic Morality and Jewish Law

AARON LEVINE

OXFORD
UNIVERSITY PRESS

OXFORD
UNIVERSITY PRESS

Oxford University Press, Inc., publishes works that further
Oxford University's objective of excellence
in research, scholarship, and education.

Oxford New York
Auckland Cape Town Dar es Salaam Hong Kong Karachi
Kuala Lumpur Madrid Melbourne Mexico City Nairobi
New Delhi Shanghai Taipei Toronto

With offices in
Argentina Austria Brazil Chile Czech Republic France Greece
Guatemala Hungary Italy Japan Poland Portugal Singapore
South Korea Switzerland Thailand Turkey Ukraine Vietnam

Published by Oxford University Press, Inc.
198 Madison Avenue, New York, NY 10016

www.oup.com

Library of Congress Cataloging-in-Publication Data
Levine, Aaron.
Economic morality and Jewish law / Aaron Levine.
p. cm.
Includes bibliographical references and index.
ISBN 978-0-19-982686-5 (cloth : alk. paper) 1. Mishpat Ivri—Economic aspects.
2. Economics—Religious aspects—Judaism. 3. Law and economics. 4. Law and ethics.
5. Jewish ethics. I. Title.
KBM524.145.L48 2012
296.3′64—dc23 2012004775

9 8 7 6 5 4 3 2 1

Printed in the United States of America
on acid-free paper

CONTENTS

PREFACE

The central theme of *Economic Morality and Jewish Law* is a consideration of the criterion used to evaluate the worthiness of an economic action or initiative, whether by a private citizen or the government. In this regard, we compare the relevant criterion for standard welfare economics and Jewish law.

Espousing what philosophers would call a consequentialist ethical system, welfare economics evaluates the worthiness of an economic action based on whether the action would increase the wealth of society in the long run. This criterion is also called the Kaldor-Hicks criterion. Provided the law does not prohibit the action, consideration of the ethics of the action never enters the picture. What counts are outcomes, not means or intentions. Moreover, the criterion for deciding whether the law should prohibit a particular action in the first place is whether the prohibition would increase society's wealth in the long run.

Consideration of the worthiness of an action based on Kaldor-Hicks holds even if the matter at issue is enacting a law that would save human lives. This is so because proponents of Kaldor-Hicks are quite willing to assign an economic value to human life. Once a value for human life is set, cost–benefit analysis takes over to decide whether the economic benefits of saving human lives outweigh the economic benefits society would be required to forgo if the legislation were enacted.

In sharp contrast to the consequentialist philosophy of standard welfare economics, Jewish law espouses a deontological system of ethics. Within this ethical system, the worthiness of an action is evaluated based not only on its impact on one's opposite number and third parties, but also on the character of the initiator of the action. Specifically, if an action is deemed to debilitate the character of the initiator, the action might be prohibited, despite its neutral effect on others. For Jewish law, the determination of the worthiness of an action is all a matter of discovering the applicable rule in Judaism's code of ethics.

The concept of economic morality as used in welfare economics and in Jewish law serves as the analytic framework for introducing the various chapters of this book.

The intended audience for this book is one who has been exposed to economic theory. It is my hope that the references in the chapter headings to topics such as the Coase theorem, price controls, the lemons problem, and short selling will immediately pique the curiosity of students of economics, as these topics are encountered in various undergraduate courses.

It is the objective of this volume to introduce what for many readers will be a new perspective on familiar economic issues. Notwithstanding the very different approaches Jewish law and welfare economics take with regard to the criterion for evaluating the worthiness of an economic action, we will show that for certain issues, there is a remarkable bottom-line convergence between the two systems.

ACKNOWLEDGMENTS

This volume is the product of research conducted by Rabbi Dr. Aaron Levine in recent years on the interface between economics and Jewish law. After the manuscript was completed and accepted for publication by Oxford University Press, the author passed away in April 2011 on the first day of Passover, one day before his sixty-fifth birthday.

Earlier versions of certain portions of this work appeared in prior publications. An earlier version of Chapter 2 was published in *Mitokh Ha-Ohel: Essays on the Weekly Parashah from the Rabbis and Professors of Yeshiva University*, eds. Rabbi Daniel Z. Feldman and Stuart W. Halpern (New York: Maggid Books, 2010), 71–85. Chapter 4 is adapted from "Price Controls in Jewish Law: An Efficiency Analysis," *Diné Israel* 23 (2005): 1–52. Chapter 5 is an expansion and elaboration of "Reviving Yehoshua ben Gamla's Vision for Torah Education," *Hakirah* 6 (Summer 2008): 57–86. With some variations, Chapter 6 was first published as "Aspects of the Lemons Problem as Treated in Jewish Law," *Journal of Law and Religion* 23, no. 2 (2008): 379–424; Chapter 7 as "The Living Wage and Jewish Law," *Tradition* 41, no. 4 (Winter 2008): 8–32; and Chapter 8 as "Short Selling and Jewish Law," *Tradition* 43, no. 1 (Spring 2010): 56–77.

Dr. Levine presented an earlier version of Chapter 3, "The Coase Theorem as Treated in Jewish Law," at a conference sponsored by DePaul University College of Law Center for Jewish Law & Judaic Studies on May 13, 2010. Financial support for the conference was provided by the Jack Miller Center for Teaching America's Founding Principles and History.

For nearly four decades, Yeshiva University was the author's professional home. Our profound gratitude to Rabbi Dr. Norman Lamm, former President and now Chancellor of Yeshiva University and Rosh Yeshiva of the Rabbi Isaac Elchanan Theological Seminary, for his steadfast encouragement of the author's scholarship and the many kindnesses he extended to him over the years. From 1980 to 2000, the author published four books in Dr. Lamm's series, *The Jewish Library of Law and Ethics*.

Under the visionary leadership of President Richard M. Joel, the administration and faculty of Yeshiva University continued to foster an environment conducive to scholarship and intellectual growth. We thank the author's distinguished and devoted colleagues, Rabbi Shalom Carmy, Rabbi Dr. Joshua Krausz, Rabbi Dani Rapp, and Rabbi Yona Reiss, for the special interest they took in the author's work. To Dr. Elias Grivoyannis, our debt of gratitude for his generosity of spirit and for always going the extra mile. Our heartfelt appreciation to Dr. Fred Sugarman, Associate Dean of Yeshiva College, for his warm friendship and assistance with administrative matters. For the many amenities furnished to the author to facilitate his research, we kindly acknowledge Pearl Berger, Dean of University Libraries, and the staff of the libraries of Yeshiva University.

Our sincere thanks to Leon M. Metzger, a close friend of the author for twenty-five years. Drawing upon his expertise in finance and economics, extensive experience as an arbitrator in Jewish courts, and superb editorial skills, Professor Metzger helped enhance many of the author's published works by offering insightful comments and suggestions on manuscript drafts.

To the production team at Oxford University Press, we extend a special note of gratitude for skillfully shepherding this volume through the publication process. We gratefully acknowledge Terry Vaughn, Executive Editor, who displayed a singular appreciation for the author's work; Catherine L. Rae, Assistant Editor; Pamela Hanley, Production Editor; Kiruthika Govindaraju, Project Manager; and Wendy Walker, Copy Editor.

We salute Efraim, the author's son, for his expertise, dedication, and resourceful technical assistance.

Our debt of thanks to Dr. Michael Szenberg, Distinguished Professor of Economics, Pace University, for his enthusiastic encouragement and support of the publication of this work.

We will always remember the loyalty and nobility of character of Shalom Lamm, prominent businessman, historian, and former student of the author.

Until the very last day of his life, Dr. Levine demonstrated an extraordinary work ethic and indefatigable spirit. In that connection, we would like to express our appreciation to his physician, the esteemed Dr. Eileen M. O'Reilly. With sensitivity and humility, Dr. O'Reilly cheered on the author's accomplishments, particularly the publication of *The Oxford Handbook of Judaism and Economics* (Oxford University Press, 2010), for which Dr. Levine served as Editor and contributing author.

And last and foremost, to Aliza. Your prodigious undertaking and its impeccable execution, in all its variegated dimensions, remain the greatest tribute to your father's memory.

Family of Aaron Levine

Economic Morality and Jewish Law

INTRODUCTION

Scope of this Work

In his classical ethical work, *Mesilat Yesharim*, R. Moses Hayyim Luzzatto (*Ramhal*, Italy, 1707–1746) devotes an entire chapter to the concept of *mishkal ha-hasidut* (weighing saintliness). This concept means that we cannot rely on our instincts to decide whether a contemplated action is meritorious. Instead, we must weigh each deed against its expected result and the circumstances surrounding its performance. Only then can we decide to proceed with or abandon the action.

This calculation is not a matter of subjectivism. Rather, it must be arrived at through the knowledge of God's wisdom. In this vein, R. Luzzatto quotes Proverbs 2:6: "God gives wisdom; from His mouth stems knowledge and understanding."[1]

For the purpose of our work, we will cast the theological concept of "weighing saintliness" in modern economic terms. Our term of choice here is "economic morality." By "economic morality" we mean judging the propriety of an action by first conducting a comprehensive review of its ramifications and then testing those ramifications against a particular value system.

The major thrust of this work is a study of economic morality as it relates to both individual morality and public issues. Specifically, our focus will be to compare how welfare economics and Jewish law deal with economic morality in relation to a number of issues.

Our first task will be to delineate the normative theory behind the concept of economic morality for both welfare economics and Jewish law. These discussions will provide us with an analytic framework to introduce the issues addressed in this work.

Welfare Economics and Economic Morality

ORIGINS OF THE IDEOLOGY OF WELFARE ECONOMICS

Welfare economics' approach to economic morality is founded on the work of the father of modern economics, Adam Smith. Rejecting the widely held eighteenth-century idea that every action motivated by private gain is intrinsically adverse to the interests of society as a whole, Smith elevated the self-interest motive to the category of a virtue. Admiration for this impulse of human nature took on several dimensions. Most basically, it was recognized that only by appealing to man's self-interest can we hope for the satisfaction of our material wants. As Adam Smith put it:

> It is not from the benevolence of the butcher, the brewer, or the baker, that we expect our dinner, but from their regard to their own interest. We address ourselves, not to their humanity but to their self-love; and never talk to them of our own necessities but of their advantages.[2]

In a broader sense, it is the profit motive that assures us that production decisions and occupational choices are made on the basis of the individual's assessment of society's hierarchy of preferences.

The doctrine of "spontaneous harmony" represents another dimension of classical economic theory's admiration for the self-interest motive. This doctrine teaches that private interests are essentially consistent and harmonious with social welfare. Intending only their own good, men are led by an "invisible hand" to further social ends.

Adam Smith illustrated the workings of this doctrine in his critique of eighteenth-century English university education. Universities in his time were heavily endowed, and most teachers derived their incomes entirely from these endowments. The result was that the donees' income bore no relationship to their proficiency as either teachers or scholars. A compensatory system that would both promote pedagogical skill and scholarship and ferret out professional incompetence was needed. Replacing the endowment scheme with a system that funded teachers' salaries directly from student tuition payments would, according to Smith, accomplish this end. Hence, in his view, appealing to the self-interest motive would accomplish the socially desirable goal of improving education.[3]

The underlying thesis of the doctrine of spontaneous harmony is that the interest of the community is simply the sum of the interests of its members. Each man, if left alone, will seek to maximize his own wealth; therefore, all men, if unimpeded, will maximize aggregate wealth.

Economic freedom is the essential feature of the free enterprise ethic: Consumers buy what they want, businessmen produce what they can sell, and laborers work for whomever pays most.

Why do economic freedom and decentralized decision making not produce chaos in the allocation of society's resources? The workings of the price mechanism provide the answer. In an unregulated marketplace, price will rise when demand exceeds supply at the prevailing norm. This increase in price is the result of competitive bidding among demanders to secure the available supply. Similarly, when supply exceeds demand at the prevailing norm, competition among sellers to liquidate their inventories will depress price.

Differences in price act as a powerful stimulus for resource owners to expand output in those areas where supply is scarce relative to demand, and to limit output where the situation is in reverse.

Within the free enterprise model, abnormal profits in any particular industry would be a transient phenomenon. Alert resource owners would switch to the more profitable industry. With supply increasing relative to demand, prices and profit margins would be expected to fall in the advantaged area. Simultaneously, the decrease in supply in the disadvantaged sectors, other things equal, would tend to increase prices and profit margins there. These adjustments thus tend to narrow the original differential.

Though the free enterprise model allows man's selfish nature full expression, market forces, paradoxically, harness the selfish motive to serve the interests of society. Business establishments are deterred from furnishing adulterated or shoddy goods by the fear that customers may shift their patronage to rivals. Likewise, enterprises that fail to protect their labor force against accidents or industrial disease, or that work their employees unusually hard, are penalized by the refusal of workers to work for them except at a higher wage than other employers pay.

The growing complexity of production, marketing, and sales in the modern commercial markets has not dampened the enthusiasm of those who believe in the efficiency of the marketplace as a self-regulating mechanism against fraud. While individuals might not be capable of judging the quality of complex products, specialists capable of making such assessments certainly exist. The success of these specialists, such as large retailers and other middlemen, hinges heavily upon the reputation of reliability they establish among their customers.

WELFARE ECONOMICS AND THE ROLE FOR GOVERNMENT

The salient feature of voluntary exchange is that mutual advantage drives the parties to conduct their exchange. Specifically, if the exchange did not make each party better off, it would not have taken place. Voluntary exchange hence presumably maximizes society's wealth. This apparently leads to the proposition that government's role in the economy should be confined to ensuring that its citizens enjoy maximum economic freedom to engage in voluntary exchange. Welfare economics, however, recognizes that society will not attain wealth maximization unless government is assigned a role beyond ensuring economic freedom for its citizens. In what follows, we will consider a number of situations where wealth maximization for society is elusive without government intervention.

Pure Public Good Case

Goods sold in the marketplace exhibit two features: rivalry and excludability. Rivalry means that *A*'s consumption of a unit of a good precludes the possibility that *B* can consume that same unit. Excludability means that the seller is capable of directly excluding all those who do not pay for the good.

The presence of rivalry and excludability is what creates the possibility for a seller to make a profit in the sale of a good. If these two features are absent, the economic good will not be produced, even if the good is a preferred item in a consumer's budget. The latter example of marketplace failure is called the pure public good case.

Illustrating the pure public good case is the provision of national defense. Chapter 6 of this volume details this example of marketplace failure.

Positive and Negative Externalities

Another instance of marketplace failure, where government involvement can potentially enhance economic efficiency, is when the production of a good generates costs or benefits to third parties for which no compensation is paid. These uncompensated side effects are referred to in the economic literature as externalities. Chapter 3 presents a number of instances of this phenomenon.

Monopoly

The optimizing conditions that proceed from voluntary exchange presume that the good or service exchanged is produced under competitive conditions. Recall that within the framework of a competitive marketplace, price tends towards equilibrium. At the equilibrium price, the number of units demanded equals the number of units offered for sale. Accordingly, the additional value or utility consumers place on the last unit offered for sale is equal to the additional cost producers incur in producing this last unit. From a macroeconomic standpoint, if all markets are organized on a competitive basis, society's resources are allocated in a manner that maximizes its utility or wealth.

Suppose markets are not organized on a competitive basis, but instead one or a few sellers dominate each market. If a seller has monopoly power, he can dictate the price for his good. The higher the price he charges, however, the fewer units he will sell. Another constraint the monopolist faces is that, for practical reasons, he must charge all his customers the same price. Consequently, the marginal revenue the monopolist earns on the last unit he sells will always be less than the price he charges for that unit. Let's use the data of Table I.1 to illustrate this important point:

Table I.1 **Marginal Revenue of Monopolist**

P *(Price)*	**Qd** *(Quantity demanded over three months)*	**TR** *(Total Revenue; P × Qd)*	**MR** *(Additional revenue earned on last unit sold)*
$10	5	$50	n/a
$8	10	$80	$6
$6	15	$90	$2

Assume the monopolist is initially charging $10 for his product and selling five units over a given time period, say three months. His total revenue is $50 (i.e., $10 × 5). If the monopolist lowers his price to $8 per unit, he can sell 10 units over the same time period. At the lower price of $8, the monopolist's total revenue increases from $50 to $80. The $30 increase in total revenue is spread over the additional five units sold. This results in an increase in revenue of $6 for the last unit sold (i.e., $30/5). Because all customers must pay the new price of $8 per unit, including those five customers who are willing to pay $10 per unit, the marginal revenue the monopolist earns on the last unit sold is always less than the per-unit price he is currently charging.

If the monopolist is a profit maximizer, he will expand his output to the point where the marginal revenue he earns on the last unit sold equals the extra cost (i.e., marginal cost) he incurs by producing the last unit. Let's make use of Figure I.1 to illustrate this point and, most importantly, show why the monopolist's profit-maximizing price-output selection is not optimal from the standpoint of society.

In Figure I.1, marginal cost equals marginal revenue at point *a*, where $Q = 15$. At that Q, the price the monopolist will charge will be the highest price the market will bear, which is $6 (point *b*). Given that the $6 price represents the extra benefit or marginal utility society derives from the last unit bought, this price is optimal from a societal standpoint only if the marginal cost of producing the last unit is also $6. But at $Q = 15$, the marginal cost of producing the last unit is only $2. Because $P > MC$ at $Q = 15$, society would gain if Q would be expanded until $MC = P$. The optimal level of output is thus point *c*, where $Q = 30$.

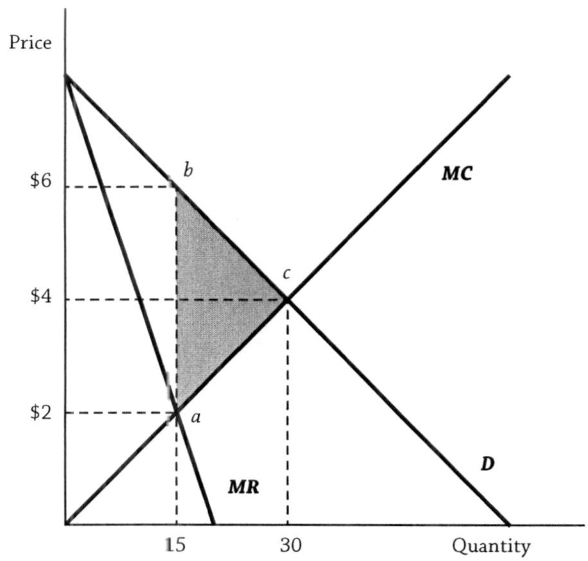

Figure I.1 Profit-Maximizing Output Level of Monopolist

From a societal perspective, the Q the profit-maximizing monopolist chooses is below the optimal level. This loss is referred to as the "deadweight loss" from monopoly. In Figure I.1, the deadweight loss is represented by the shaded area, *abc*. Government intervention here thus has the potential of improving the efficiency of the marketplace and moving society to a higher level of income.

WELFARE ECONOMICS AND THE PHILOSOPHY OF CONSEQUENTIALISM

Welfare economics adopts what philosophers would label a consequentialist approach to morality. Under that approach, what matters is not means or intentions, but rather outcomes. Specifically, for welfare economics, the measure for evaluating the worthiness of an economic action is whether the action would increase society's wealth in the long run. If the action promotes wealth maximization, it is worthy, even if the increase in wealth makes some people economically worse off. What matters therefore is how the action affects the aggregate level of income, regardless of whether the distribution of income among the members of society will change. Surprisingly, as we shall see, an action that entails moral failure is tolerated provided that the long-term result is wealth maximization.

Welfare economics makes the maximization of wealth the goal of economic public policy and government regulation. A restrictive form of this approach to social choice is the Pareto optimality criterion. Under that criterion, government action is not justified unless it offers the reasonable prospect of improving the economic well-being of at least one person without reducing the economic well-being of anyone else. If improvement for *A* can be accomplished only by reducing the welfare of *B*, the status quo must remain intact.

Since government action will almost invariably entail gains for some but losses for others, the Pareto rule is too austere to be of any operational use. A less stringent efficiency criterion, called the Kaldor-Hicks criterion, has accordingly been advanced as an appropriate guidepost for government action.[4] This criterion dictates that decision makers assess a proposed policy in terms of the value the gainers would assign to their gains and the amount of compensation the losers would demand to agree to implementation of the policy. If the gains exceed the losses in monetary value, the proposal is considered to enhance society's wealth and should therefore be adopted. This method of monetizing gains and losses to determine whether aggregate wealth would increase is known in the economic literature as the "willingness to pay" method.[5]

Kaldor-Hicks does not require the gainers to actually compensate the losers. Nevertheless, any proposal that meets the Kaldor-Hicks criterion has the potential to enhance the well-being of the losers in the long run even if the losers are not compensated at the time the proposal is adopted. This result obtains because the increase in *aggregate* income that satisfaction of the Kaldor-Hicks criterion makes possible sets into motion a series of rounds of spending and income creation. Called the "multiplier effect," this expansionary process results regardless of how the original gainers choose to divide their newfound increment in income between saving and spending.

To illustrate the multiplier effect, suppose G, the gainer, decides to spend the increment on P_1's product. G's spending then increases P_1's income. P_1, in turn, spends his newfound income on a purchase of P_2's product. P_2's income then increases. Since in each successive round of income creation some portion of the increment is saved, the expansionary process must eventually end. Suppose, however, that G opts to save the new increment in his income. Because G's action, other things equal, increases the supply of loanable funds relative to demand, G's saving lowers the borrowing cost for P_1. P_1's consequent increased borrowing will then enable him to make his extra purchases from P_2, setting into motion the multiplier effect described above.[6]

KALDOR-HICKS AS A SELF-SUFFICIENT CRITERION FOR PUBLIC POLICY

Kaldor-Hicks focuses on wealth maximization as the criterion for public policy but ignores distributional consequences. At times, ignoring the distributional consequences of a policy yields a result that many would regard as repugnant. A case in point is that on the basis of Kaldor-Hicks, a policymaker would recommend that toxic waste be dumped in lesser-developed countries without paying compensation. The rationale for this approach is that the value the gainers place on the outcome exceeds the compensation the losers would demand to allow the dumping to occur.[7]

Consideration that achieving economic efficiency does not necessarily also comport with societal notions of fairness led both Kaldor and Hicks to conclude that efficiency considerations are not the whole story for public policy. In their view, the economist's contribution for public policy works best if efficiency considerations are kept separate from distributional considerations, as economists have no particular expertise in addressing the distributional issues that arise in public policymaking.[8]

In a similar vein, Richard Posner, a leading scholar in the field of law and economics, acknowledges the limits of economic analysis in arriving at judicial decisions. First he notes that the common law is best explained as a system of maximizing the wealth of society by achieving an efficient allocation of resources. To be sure, the same cannot be said of statutory and constitutional law, but economic concerns and analysis permeate these branches of law as well.

Posner then posits that the economic approach to law will often manifest an element of justice. Consider the case where V is shot by a careless hunter, H. The concern of the opposing lawyers in the case will be whether the cost of the injury should be shifted from V to H. The judge, by contrast, will be concerned not only with the case at hand, but also with establishing legal precedent for future cases. For example, if the judge rules in favor of *H* even though *H* was careless, the judgment might lead to future careless behavior by other hunters. The judge must therefore be concerned with establishing proper incentives and deterrents to prevent future accidents.

Deciding a case or evaluating the worthiness of a policy based on whether it fosters maximization of society's wealth in the long run ignores the distributional consequences of the law or policy. Consequently, similar to Kaldor and Hicks, Posner ultimately concludes that notions of justice entail more than a concern only with efficiency.[9]

WELFARE ECONOMICS AND PUBLIC POLICY

Kaldor-Hicks provides the substance for the consequentialist criteria of welfare economics. To illustrate the various implications of the consequentialist approach in deciding matters of public policy, we take up three issues.

The first issue is an examination of a number of proposals relating to the regulation of advertising. The proposals we examine implicitly adopt Kaldor-Hicks. Under these proposals, the worthiness of a promotional technique that is permitted under current law is unquestioned as long as the stratagem fosters maximization of society's wealth in the long run. Consideration of the moral dimension of the stratagem never enters the analysis.

Beyond ignoring the moral dimension of a commercial practice when the law does not prohibit the practice, welfare economics explicitly invokes economic efficiency as the criterion for determining whether the practice should be regulated altogether. Illustrating the efficiency approach to regulation is our second issue, whether the government should regulate insider trading.

The third issue is whether the government should prohibit cell phone use while driving. The economic treatment of this issue demonstrates, as in the matter of insider trading, that welfare economics relies solely on cost–benefit analysis in deciding whether a practice should be subject to government regulation. Moreover, this example will show that cost–benefit analysis extends even to the point of assigning a value to human life.

Regulation of Advertising

The Federal Trade Commission (FTC) will not regulate a deceptive advertisement unless the claim is also material. In simple terms, this means that the claim must be important rather than trivial to consumers. The FTC requires that the deception be likely to affect consumers' choice of, or conduct regarding, a product.[10]

In today's legal environment, the FTC regards every explicit claim in an advertisement as material.[11] Accordingly, if an explicit claim is found to be false, the advertisement will be presumed to be deceptive. The FTC provides no practical guidance on how this presumption can be rebutted.

Professor Ivan Preston is very critical of the FTC's approach in this matter. He argues that a claim should not automatically be presumed to be material simply because it is explicit. Indeed, some claims are made only to distinguish the identities of similar products, even though the claimed feature has no bearing on consumer decision making. Moreover, he asserts, the burden of proving materiality should be borne by the FTC. In Preston's opinion, advertisers should be permitted to use a claim unless the claim is proven to be deceptive and material. Short of shifting the burden of proof of materiality to the FTC, Preston feels that the FTC should, at the very least, provide firms with methodological guidance on how to disprove materiality.

Preston suggests the contours of a test that would determine materiality. He proposes that the relevant factor in determining the materiality of a deceptive claim should not be whether the claim is likely to affect consumer behavior, but rather whether the deceptive claim is more likely than a true claim to affect consumer behavior. If consumers would take the same action regardless of whether the claim is true or false, the deceptive claim should not be regarded as material.

To illustrate, suppose *S* sells an item that is displayed in a showroom and advertises its price as $80. When customers come to the showroom, they are told that the ad is a mistake and the price is really $90. If the same number of customers would visit the showroom regardless of whether the advertised price is $80 or $90, the falsely advertised price should not be regarded as material. Certainly, Preston tells us, there would be little public interest in regulating this false claim.[12] Kaldor-Hicks would likely be in agreement with Preston's analysis.

Kaldor-Hicks bears on another consideration in the regulation of advertising, one raised by Professor Richard Craswell. Because Kaldor-Hicks is essentially a cost–benefit criterion, it would perhaps endorse Professor Craswell's notion that a materially false advertising claim is sometimes acceptable.

In this regard, Craswell points out that an advertising message that makes a misleading claim may at the same time convey useful information to the consumer. For example, suppose a manufacturer of storm windows claims that its windows can save homeowners "up to 85%" of their heating bill. The evidence shows that the claim may be literally true, in the sense that 85% may be the upper limit on the savings attainable by a homeowner with an extremely poorly insulated house. However, the evidence also shows that most homeowners can expect to save only 40% to 50% at the very most. Within the current regulatory environment, the storm window ad would be regarded as misleading because the ad incorrectly implies that an average consumer has a reasonable likelihood of obtaining a savings of 85%.[13]

In Craswell's opinion, the judgment that the ad is misleading should not be the end of the analysis. Instead, it should be recognized that the ad contains some useful information about the savings in fuel bills that one can expect from installing storm windows. Correcting the ad so that the false impression is eliminated might create new false impressions or entirely obscure the message that the installation of storm windows will lead to savings.

In evaluating the ad, the criterion the FTC should use, according to Craswell, is: "An advertisement is legally deceptive if and only if it leaves some consumers holding a false belief about a product, and the ad could be cost-effectively changed to reduce the resulting injury."[14] This approach requires comparing the ad with possible alternative ads.

According to Craswell, the most important factor in evaluating deceptive advertising is not the aggregate level of injury caused by the deception, but the extent to which that injury can be reduced. For example, if 10% of consumers hold a false belief about a product, but the evidence shows that at least 10% would hold that same false belief despite a misleading ad about the product, Craswell asserts that there is no point in ordering the ad to be corrected.

In another example, Craswell considers a case of two misleading ads that generate equally serious misconceptions. The first ad deceives 20% of its audience, and the addition of qualifying language would reduce that percentage to 10%. The second ad deceives 30% of its audience, but 25% would still be deceived even if the ad were corrected. The first ad, in Craswell's view, presents the stronger case for government intervention, even though the injury it causes is smaller in absolute numbers.[15]

Let's also consider the possibility that Kaldor-Hicks would embrace Professor Paul Rubin's proposal that allowing deceptive advertising to go unchallenged can at times result in a clear-cut long-term gain for the consumer. Rubin provides a number of illustrations:

1. Suppose a firm advertises a product as "Regularly $50, now $25." If $50 is not the regular price of the product, the ad is deceptive. Despite the possible deception here, the FTC rarely challenges deceptive claims regarding price because it recognizes that any advertisement that emphasizes prices is likely to lead to lower prices. Consumers hence gain in the long run from the deceptive ad.[16]

2. In the mid-1980s, fierce competition began among food producers in claiming that their products were low in cholesterol. Some producers that were making these claims were in fact producing products low in cholesterol, but their products were made with palm and coconut oils that had the same harmful effects as cholesterol. To be sure, drawing attention to their products' low level of cholesterol while at the same time hiding their tropical oil content was a deceptive health claim. But the deception worked to foster a long-term gain in welfare for the consumer. Competition for the patronage of health-conscious consumers led other firms to advertise that their products were not only low in cholesterol, but also did not contain tropical oils. Indicative of the substantial benefit society reaped in the long term from the original deceptive claims of producers of products that were low in cholesterol but high in tropical oil was that imports of palm oil fell 44% from 1986 to 1987.[17]

Insider Trading

Over the past 40 years, discussions in the literature of economics and law regarding insider trading have centered on whether lifting the ban on insider trading would promote wealth maximization for society. Over this entire time, Professor Henry

Manne has argued for the legalization of insider trading on efficiency grounds. Manne's original argument was that legalizing insider trading allows managers to profit from their efforts on behalf of the firm without having to negotiate with owners of the firm. When managers believe that their entrepreneurial activities will enhance the value of their firm, they can invest in their company's shares at their discretion. Having acquired an interest in the future course of their firm's share price, managers will concentrate their efforts on behalf of their firm to ensure that its programs will succeed and the resulting enhanced performance be disclosed.[18]

While this argument met many objections,[19] and Manne himself eventually abandoned this line of reasoning,[20] the efficiency approach remains very viable in the literature.[21] Manne himself has recently come up with a new efficiency argument for legalizing insider trading. In Manne's view, insider trading is a very useful means of improving the flow of corporate information to decision makers and thereby signaling to them that the proposals they are considering are good or bad ideas.[22]

Another argument why legalizing insider trading would improve the efficiency of the capital markets has been advanced by Professor Macey. He suggests that insider trading can be more effective than whistle-blowing in signaling to the capital markets that corporate wrongdoing is afoot.[23]

Banning Cell Phone Use While Driving

To illustrate how far welfare economics goes in invoking wealth maximization as the criterion for public policy issues, we consider our third issue, whether cell phones should be banned for motorists. We draw our example from Edgar K. Browning and Mark A. Zupan's 10th edition of *Microeconomics: Theory & Applications*.[24]

In Browning and Zupan's discussion of whether cell phone use while driving should be banned, the authors first note that of the 41,000 people who die annually in the United States in all car accidents, several hundred people die because of accidents precipitated by cell phone use. In reaction to the cell phone-related death toll, a growing number of states and municipalities are considering either banning the use of cell phones while driving, or requiring drivers to use a hands-free device in conjunction with a cell phone.

But there are a significant number of positive externalities to consider. For example, the use of cell phones while driving may keep drivers from falling asleep and thereby prevent accidents. Permitting drivers to use cell phones also enables drivers to notify relevant parties when they are running late for a meeting, thus obviating the need to speed up to avoid being late. Moreover, a motorist involved in or witnessing an accident can use a cell phone to summon help.

Finally, Browning and Zupan invoke the economic concept of consumer surplus to show the benefit of allowing drivers to use their cell phones while driving. Consumer surplus is the excess of the price a consumer is willing to pay for something over the price that is actually paid. The authors note that the estimated total annual consumer surplus associated with being able to make phone calls while driving is well over $50 billion.[25]

In deciding on government policy with respect to allowing the use of cell phones while driving, economic studies have simplified the choices to be considered with the finding that the use of hand-held cell phones while driving has no significant effect on car accidents.[26]

Based on the very significant direct and external benefits society reaps from allowing drivers to use their cell phones while driving, Browning and Zupan conclude that "leading studies indicate that banning cellular phone usage by motorists is a bad idea."[27]

From the standpoint of Kaldor-Hicks, Browning and Zupan's treatment is incomplete. What is missing is the assignment of a value to human life. Once this value is fixed, the cost–benefit calculus for the issue of banning cell phone use while driving can be quantified. Arguing in favor of the ban is the economic value of saving several hundred lives. Arguing against the ban is the external benefit society reaps by allowing cell phone use while driving.

Assigning a value to human life is nothing new or innovative as far as welfare economics is concerned. Consider that U.S. federal agencies such as the Consumer Product Safety Commission and the Environmental Protection Agency use the concept of the "value of statistical life" (VSL) in making regulatory decisions. VSL is an estimate of the monetary benefits of preventing the death of an unidentified person. It is the maximum amount that government agencies will pay to save a life. Current VSL estimates are determined by society's willingness to pay to eliminate private health risks.[28]

As a practical matter, researchers extrapolate willingness to pay by conducting compensating wage studies and contingent valuation studies. Compensating wage studies determine the amount of income necessary to convince workers to accept increased on-the-job health risks. For example, elephant handlers at the Philadelphia Zoo receive an extra $1,000 per year because of the dangerous nature of their job. Contingent valuation studies use surveys to directly ask consumers how much they are willing to pay for a certain good, and are thus designed to reveal the respondents' preference for risk. Based on these two valuation methodologies, major government agencies today typically place a dollar value on a statistical life in the range of $5 million to $6 million.[29]

Let's apply the VSL technique to the issue of whether cell phone use while driving should be banned. Recall that several hundred motor vehicle deaths per year can be attributed to driver use of cell phones. For purposes of our analysis, let's use a conservative estimate of 200 for the number of lives that could be saved each year if cell phone use while driving were banned. If we assign a value of $6 million to each life saved, the benefit of banning cell phone use while driving would be $1.2 billion per year. That figure is dwarfed by the $50 billion of consumer surplus consumers now enjoy by the use of cell phones while diving. Cost–benefit analysis therefore indicates that cell phone use while driving should not be banned.

Reinforcing the above conclusion is the recognition that some motorists will continue to use their cell phones while driving despite a ban on this practice. Compliance with the ban will depend to a large extent on the resources that the government is willing to devote to enforcing the ban. If a certain degree of non-compliance can be expected when the ban is in place, legislating a ban against the practice will not save 200 lives per annum. Moreover, motorists who refuse to comply with the ban will generate external benefits to society. These considerations only reinforce the conclusion that instituting a ban is "bad" policy from the standpoint of welfare economics.

Economic Morality and Jewish Law

JEWISH LAW AND DEONTOLOGICAL PHILOSOPHY

In sharp contrast to welfare economics, Jewish law espouses what philosophers would call a deontological ethical system. Under that system, the moral rightness or wrongness of an action depends on its intrinsic qualities, and not, as in consequentialism, on the nature of its consequences.[30] For Jewish law, it is all a matter of discovering the rule that applies to the situation at hand. The measure of the worthiness of an economic action is whether the action satisfies Jewish law's moral code, which prohibits the infliction of harm on one's fellow even if the harmful action would maximize society's wealth in the long run.

In this section, we illustrate the deontological nature of Jewish business ethics with two examples. The first is the code of ethics relating to the prohibition against falsehood. We then take up the rules Jewish law imposes on an obligator.

Prohibition Against Falsehood

Falsehood is prohibited even when it causes no harm.[31] This stringency, as R. Dov Berish Gottlieb (*Yad ha-Ketanah*, Poland, 1740–1796) points out, proceeds from an analysis of the wording employed in the Biblical source of the prohibition: "Distance yourself from a false word" (Exodus 23:7). Instead of prohibiting the speaking of falsehood, the Torah bids us to distance ourselves from a false word. The terms "distance" and "word" signify that a lie is prohibited even if it does not deceive someone or cause harm.[32]

Notwithstanding the stringency of the prohibition against lying, falsehood is permitted when the motive of the speaker is to end conflict. The permissibility of uttering such a lie, called the *darkhei shalom* (lit., ways of peace) lie, however, is subject to many qualifications:

1. One caveat, enunciated by R. Israel Meir ha-Kohen Kagan (*Hafetz Hayyim*, Radin, 1838–1933), is that lying to promote peace is permissible only when the objective cannot be achieved without lying.[33] R. Nahum Yavruv (Israel, contemp.), basing his opinion on R. Hayyim Kanievsky (Israel, contemp.), avers that even if

considerable toil and effort must be exerted to achieve peace without lying, that route is preferable to lying.[34]

2. The *darkhei shalom* motive, in the opinion of R. Yavruv, legitimizes the telling of a lie, even if the one who tells the lie realizes that the lie will eventually be exposed and the peace it achieves will dissipate. This is so because telling a lie to achieve temporary peace is also legitimate. Nonetheless, if the peacemaker assesses that when the lie is exposed, the discord that it ended will re-emerge in an exacerbated form, *darkhei shalom* does not permit the telling of the lie.[35]

3. According to R. Judah b. Samuel he-Hasid (Regensburg, ca. 1150–1217) et al., a *darkhei shalom* lie is permitted only concerning a past event. Uttering falsehood regarding matters of the present or future, by contrast, is prohibited.[36] The reason for this distinction is that, compared to lying about the past, lying about the present or future is more likely to habituate a person to lie.[37]

Another school of thought, led by Maimonides (*Rambam*, Egypt, 1135–1204), makes no distinction between a lie that relates to a past event and a lie that relates to the present or future. If the motive is *darkhei shalom*, a lie is permissible, regardless of whether it relates to the past, present, or future.[38]

Noting the dispute among the authorities, R. Yavruv posits that the stringent view is sufficiently well established that we should conduct ourselves in accordance with this view in the first instance. In difficult circumstances, we may follow the lenient view. Even under difficult circumstances, however, the use of ambiguities is preferred to outright lies.[39]

4. Lying for the purpose of ending discord, according to R. Solomon b. Jehiel Luria (*Maharshal*, Poland, 1510–1573), is permitted only when the *darkei shalom* setting requires a one-time lie. If attaining peace is possible only if a lie is repeated again and again, the lie is not permitted.[40] The basis for this stringency is that repeated lies will accustom the peacemaker to lie.[41]

5. In his treatment of the prohibitions of lying and deception, R. Jonah b. Abraham Gerondi (*Rabbeinu Yonah*, Spain, ca. 1200–1263) categorizes liars by order of severity into nine groups.[42] In the fourth group, R. Jonah places a person who lies because he "loves falsehood."[43] If someone "loves falsehood," telling a lie, even for the purpose of achieving peace, is prohibited.[44]

Duties of an Obligator

The richness of the deontological system of Jewish law can be seen in its treatment of an individual, *A*, who refuses to make good on a commitment he made to *B*. Depending on the circumstances, *A* may face legal consequences or moral sanctions for not making good on his commitment.

If an individual verbalizes a commitment, he must sincerely intend to carry it out. Making an insincere commitment violates Jewish law's moral code.[45]

In Jewish law, a commitment reaches its highest level when it is consummated through a formal symbolic act, called a *kinyan*. To effect a *kinyan*, the Sages instituted different symbolic acts for a variety of transactions.[46]

One symbolic act that is effectively an all-purpose *kinyan* is a *kinyan sudar* (lit., acquisition by means of a kerchief). Conceptually, it is symbolic barter. In a *kinyan sudar*, *B* hands his kerchief to *S*. By lifting the kerchief, *S* acquires ownership of it and thereby commits himself to his end of the deal.[47]

Once a *kinyan* is executed,[48] the Jewish court will, if necessary, intervene to ensure that *S* makes good on his end of the deal. One exception is that in a labor contract, where a worker obligates himself to perform only a specific task, the court will not use coercion to ensure specific performance by the worker, as an individual may not be forced to work against his will.[49] Nonetheless, the reneging worker will be subject to penalties.[50] In the case of a public servant, however, inexcusable refusal on the part of the worker to execute his public duties may subject him to a judicial order to remain on the job until he supplies a replacement worker.[51]

The reason a *kinyan* generates an ironclad duty to make good on a commitment to perform a specific task, according to R. Shalom Albeck, is that when a transaction advances to the stage of a *kinyan*, it is objectively evident that each party to the transaction has irrevocably resolved to make good on his end of the deal.[52]

Let's now move to the other extreme of the moral-legal spectrum. Suppose *A* resolves in his heart to give *B* a gift of a specific amount of money, but does not verbalize this resolve. Here, Jewish law says that it would be a matter of moral duty for the God-fearing person to follow through on this resolve of the heart.[53]

For a commitment to carry with it moral sanctions if the obligator does not follow through, the commitment must be verbalized. Suppose *S* and *B* reach a verbal agreement on all the details of their commercial transaction, including price. The agreement calls for *S* to deliver a specific item, say, a sweater, to *B* at a specific price. No money has yet passed hands from *B* to *S*. If at this juncture either *S* or *B* reneges on the deal, the reneging party is called untrustworthy (*mehusar emunah*).[54] Nonetheless, if the price of the good increased or the circumstances of the seller changed since the time the parties reached their original agreement, the seller is free of the moral sanction of being called untrustworthy. Similarly, if the price of the good declined or the buyer's circumstances changed, the buyer is not considered untrustworthy.[55]

A variation of the case above occurs when, in addition to *B* and *S* having reached a verbal agreement on all the particulars regarding the sweater, *B* gave *S* a deposit. The circumstance that the parties agreed on all the terms and that the transaction advanced to the point where *B* made a deposit generates expectations that the transaction will become binding. In that case, if one of the parties reneges, the reneging party incurs the judicial imprecation: "He who punished the generation of the Flood (*dor ha-mabbul*) and the generation of the Dispersion (*dor haflagah*), will exact payment from he who does not stand by his word."[56]

Charitable pledges not only generate a moral duty to make good on the pledge, but carry legal consequences as well. Once verbalized, a pledge to charity is subject to judicial enforcement.[57]

The consequences facing one who reneges on a verbal commitment to make a gift takes into account whether the obligee relied on the commitment. Thus, if *A* commits to give *B* a small gift, reneging on this commitment brands *A mehusar emunah* because *B* certainly relied on this commitment and fully expected to receive the gift. But suppose *A* promises *B* that he will confer a largess upon him. Given the extraordinary nature of *A*'s promise, *B* does not rely on *A* fulfilling his promise. Because *B* does not rely on *A*'s promise, *A* may subsequently retract his promise without being considered *mehusar emunah*.[58]

POLICIES DESIGNED TO MAXIMIZE WEALTH: A MORAL TEST

Once it is recognized that Jewish law espouses a deontological ethical system, policies designed to maximize wealth must be put to a moral test before they can be validated under Jewish law. With this end in mind, let's test the three issues referred to earlier that welfare economics analyzes in terms of efficiency.

Moral Test—Regulation of Advertising

Let's first take up Preston's proposals regarding how the FTC should address the issue of materiality in deceptive advertising. Preston's proposal that the onus of proving that an advertiser's claim is material should be placed on the FTC amounts to saying that the advertiser should be allowed to rely on his own judgment in determining whether he violates the law against deception.

Jewish law would reject Preston's proposal. Under Jewish law, the determination of whether an advertisement is deceptive is not based on the judgment of the advertiser, but rather whether the target group perceives the claim to be misleading. Towards this end, before releasing an ad to the public, the advertiser would be required to pilot test the advertisement to ensure that the reasonable man would not be misled. Statistically, this translates into a requirement that no more than 10% to 15% of those exposed to the pilot test be deceived.[59]

Moreover, Preston's consequentialist test for materiality is totally unacceptable from the standpoint of Jewish law. The fact that the same number of customers would visit the showroom regardless of whether the ad quoted a price of $80 or $90 does not give the seller the right to advertise the item at $80. For one, the deliberate lie dashes the legitimate expectations of the customers who come to the showroom but end up not buying the item because of the switch in price. Moreover, even those customers who buy the item at the higher price of $90 surely experience disappointment when they learn of the switch in price. With respect to those customers, the seller is guilty of the "bait and switch" tactic. Because the ploy dashes the legitimate expectations of all those who come to the showroom, the seller violates the interdict against causing someone needless mental anguish (*ona'at devarim*).[60]

Implicit in Preston's test for materiality is the notion that it is acceptable for an advertiser to make a false claim as long as the claim is not material. Jewish law clearly rejects this notion because its prohibition against lying applies, as discussed above, even when the lie is in a consequential sense harmless. Accordingly, discovery in the pilot-testing phase that a particular claim the ad makes is deceptive but not material requires the advertiser to revise the ad and eliminate the deceptive, non-material claim.

Let's now take up Craswell's proposition that the FTC should not ban a deceptive ad that conveys useful information if correcting the ad would obscure the useful information or generate new false impressions. Craswell's proposition is entirely consistent with Kaldor-Hicks, but it is unacceptable from the standpoint of Jewish law.

Consider Craswell's storm window case. If the manufacturer claims that installing storm windows will save consumers up to 85% of their heating bill, consumers have every right to rely on that claim. If, in fact, the actual savings is 40% to 50% at best, the seller is guilty of not delivering what he promised. While the disappointment the typical consumer experiences with respect to his actual savings may not make him regret the purchase and render the purchase a transaction entered into by mistake (*mekah ta'ut*), the disappointment does give rise to a claim of overcharge (price fraud). To be sure, the claim of "false bargain" does not lend itself to quantification and hence the consumer will have no legal recourse to get a rebate of any sort. Nonetheless, the seller has generated a false sense of bargain and hence violates the prohibition in Jewish law against creating a false impression (*geneivat da'at*).[61]

The same analysis would lead Jewish law to reject Professor Rubin's proposition that if a deceptive ad leads to a long-term benefit for consumers, the ad should be allowed.

There is, however, a more fundamental reason to object to Professor Rubin's proposition. Recall his example of a deceptive health claim consisting of a food producer letting the public know that its product is low in cholesterol, but at the same time failing to disclose that the product contains tropical oil. The circumstance that competition for the patronage of health-conscious consumers ultimately led other manufacturers to produce food that was low in both cholesterol and tropical oil in no way legitimizes an ad that was deceptive at the time it was released.[62]

Moral Test—Insider Trading

From the standpoint of Jewish law, considering whether insider trading should be prohibited based on the effect that the prohibition would have on the efficiency of the firm is misguided because it totally ignores the ethical dimensions of this issue.

Jewish law's approach to this issue is consistent with the "misappropriation theory" the Supreme Court applied in *United States v. O'Hagan*.[63] In that case, James O'Hagan, a partner in the law firm of Dorsey & Whitney, learned that a client of his firm, Grand Metropolitan PLC (Grand Met), planned to launch a tender offer for the Pillsbury Company. O'Hagan then began purchasing call options on Pillsbury's stock, as well as shares of the stock. Following Dorsey & Whitney's withdrawal from the representation, Grand Met publicly announced its tender offer. The price of Pillsbury's stock rose dramatically, and O'Hagan sold his Pillsbury call options and stock at a profit of more than $4.3 million.

An investigation by the Securities and Exchange Commission culminated in a 57-count indictment alleging that O'Hagan defrauded his law firm and his client, Grand Met, by misappropriating for his own trading purposes material, nonpublic information regarding the tender offer. A jury convicted O'Hagan on all counts, and he was sentenced to prison. On appeal, the Eighth Circuit reversed all the convictions.[64]

On further appeal, the Supreme Court reversed the Eighth Circuit on the basis of the misappropriation theory. In advancing that theory, the Court held that a company's confidential information qualifies as property to which the company has a right of exclusive use. Accordingly, misappropriation of that information in breach of a fiduciary duty owed to the source of the information constitutes fraud akin to embezzlement.

Jewish law's analogue for the "misappropriation theory" is R. Yose's dictum, recorded in the Mishnah at *Bava Metzia* 3:2:

> [If] one rents a cow from another and lends it to someone else, and it dies naturally, the renter must swear that it died naturally, and the borrower must pay the renter. Said R. Yose: "How does that person [i.e., the renter] do business with another's cow? Rather, the cow should be returned to the owner."

In the view of the first opinion expressed, when the animal dies, the renter becomes exempt from paying the owner, and acquires the animal. Since the renter is not liable for accidents, he takes the oath that the animal died naturally merely to placate the owner. Therefore, the borrower—who is responsible for accidents—must pay the renter.[65] R. Yose, however, regards the renter who lends out the cow as an agent of the owner.[66] Therefore, the payment for the cow should be given to the owner, not the renter.[67] Talmudic decisors follow R. Yose's dictum.[68]

Application of R. Yose's dictum to insider trading is clear-cut. Given that the insider information is the property of all the shareholders, no one may trade on this information. Doing so is akin to "doing business with someone else's cow." Disgorgement of the profits earned would therefore be called for.

Moral Test—Banning Cell Phone Use While Driving

Identifying a whole range of direct and external benefits that would ensue for society if cell phone use while driving is not banned does not in itself make the case against the ban. From the standpoint of Jewish law, we cannot ignore the statistic that under the present, mostly no-ban regime, several hundred people are killed in motor vehicle accidents each year because of cell phone use while driving.

In Jewish law, human life is assigned the highest value.[69] Accordingly, if someone's life is in danger, and the only way to save that person is by violating some prohibition, such as stealing, the sin should be committed to save the person's life. The only exceptions are the three cardinal sins, consisting of murder, idolatry, and forbidden sexual relations. These sins may not be violated even to save a life.[70]

Now, if Jewish law calls for transgressions to be violated, if necessary, to save human life, it follows that the law must prohibit cell phone use while driving to save lives, rather than to make the practice permissible in order to secure monetary benefits for society. The implication for public policy is that priority must be given to saving human life. Because the status quo results in several hundred deaths each year, the policymaker should ban cell phone use while driving. Moreover, the ban should be implemented even though it would reduce consumer surplus for drivers and eliminate certain external benefits that cell phone use generates.

Economic Morality and the Issues of this Volume

The above discussion of the normative positions of Jewish law and economic theory with respect to economic morality provides us with a frame of reference for introducing the chapters of this volume.

Chapter 1, "A Tale of Two Sermons (*Derashot*)," puts Jewish law's deontological ethical system within the context of a case study. The main objective of the case study is to show how well-meaning lies in a social context can easily lead to misguided economic decisions and cause much unnecessary disappointment and disillusionment. The unfolding of the scenarios presented will also illustrate the various rules of morality that Jewish law prescribes to provide guidance for modes of conduct.

Chapter 2, "The Sale of the Birthright and the Bilateral Monopoly Model," examines the Biblical account of Jacob's purchase of the birthright from his brother, Esau, in exchange for a stew of lentils. The transaction raises issues of economic morality concerning fairness of price and the apparent opportunistic nature of Jacob's conduct in negotiating the offer while Esau was famished.

Chapter 3, "The Coase Theorem as Treated in Jewish Law," compares Jewish law and the seminal theories of Ronald Coase on the issue of negative externalities. The comparison uses the cases that Coase analyzed to illustrate what he believed was the approach that economic theory would take to deal with the negative externality problem.

Chapter 4, "Price Controls in Jewish Law," presents the ancient Talmudic edict that required vendors of essential food to limit their profit to no more than 20% of their cost base to enable consumers to subsist without undue hardship. This edict is referred to as the *hayyei nefesh* (essential food) ordinance.

Despite the altruistic motive behind the ordinance, economic theory would be quick to note that price controls exert negative side effects, to the point of severely undermining their altruistic objective. The issue of economic morality explored in this chapter is whether Jewish law's version of price controls can be expected to generate the usual negative side effects of this type of intervention, and even render the ordinance self-defeating. Finally, we examine the relevance of the *hayyei nefesh* ordinance to current economic public policy.

In Chapter 5, "Reviving Yehoshua b. Gamla's Vision for Torah Education," our primary purpose is to propose a model for the Jewish community to achieve the goals of religious elementary education. Our model contemplates a system of private schools competing for community-raised funds based on their commitment to and success in achieving standards set by the community. Milton Friedman's classical paper on the role of government in education is used as the backdrop for this competitive model.[71]

Friedman first makes the case for government subsidization of elementary education. In making this case, Friedman preliminarily contends that the goals of primary school are to teach the youth basic reading, writing, and math skills, and most importantly, to inculcate the common core values of society. Success in achieving these goals generates significant external benefits for society in the form of fostering a stable democracy. Given the differences among families in their economic resources and number of children, we cannot rely on the private sector to devote the resources necessary to achieve universal education of the youth. To achieve optimal results here therefore requires government subsidization of elementary education.

Friedman's first point, albeit in modified form, is very pertinent for Jewish religious elementary education. Consider that the goals of Jewish religious elementary education extend considerably beyond the narrow goals Friedman specified for elementary education. For example, the goals of Jewish religious elementary education include establishing productivity standards for teachers, setting a maximum class size, and promoting parental involvement in the education of their children. Left to its own devices, an unregulated and unsubsidized marketplace will not achieve these goals. To be sure, taxation is not available to the Jewish community today, but setting standards for schools along with raising funds from the community to be distributed to schools based on their commitment to and success in achieving these goals is indicated.

Friedman's second point is that the government should use its tax revenue not to subsidize schools, but rather to provide parents of school-aged children with educational vouchers. Equipped with these vouchers, parents would be free to select the school of their choice for their children. This system promotes healthy competition among schools and hence produces optimal results for society.

Adopting the notion of a competitive system of private schools is particularly attractive for Jewish religious elementary education because with respect to religious education on all levels, Jewish law favors competition much more so than it does for commercial activity generally.

Chapter 6, "Aspects of the Lemons Problem as Treated in Jewish Law," begins with a presentation of the asymmetric information problem in commercial transactions. The problem arises when one side of the market, usually the seller, knows more about the quality of the product or service offered than the other side. In his seminal 1970 article, George Akerlof predicted that unless countervailing forces are in place, asymmetric information will cause the volume of transactions in this marketplace to shrink to the point where only the most inferior version of the product, called a lemon, will be traded.

The issue of economic morality in this chapter is the mechanisms that Jewish law establishes to protect the buyer from exploitation in a market characterized by asymmetric information. One such mechanism is warranty law. In that regard, we demonstrate how Jewish warranty law counteracts the lemons problem and compare its solutions to those of U.S. federal warranty law and state lemon laws.

Warranty law works best to counteract the lemons problem if it operates in an environment of trustworthiness. Jewish law assigns the task of moral education to parents and teachers, requiring them to cultivate the character trait of trustworthiness. Jewish warranty law hence operates together with societal efforts to foster an environment of trustworthiness.

We also argue that moral education takes on the characteristics of a pure public good and hence qualifies for government subsidization.

Chapter 7, "The Living Wage and Jewish Law," compares welfare economics and Jewish law with respect to the issue of the living wage.

From the standpoint of welfare economics, the only basis for government intervention in the economy is that the intervention will result in wealth maximization for society in the long run. Requiring firms to pay their workers a living wage does not promote wealth maximization. Moreover, welfare economics can show that not only are the goals of the living wage elusive, but pursuit of this agenda will hurt the very people the legislation is intended to help.

Aside from agreeing with the proposition that the objectives of the living wage are self-defeating, Jewish law, we will show, is opposed to this legislation because it does not satisfy Jewish ethical norms for industrial justice, charity law, or public policy for the working poor.

Chapter 8, "Short Selling and Jewish Law," addresses the ethics of short selling from the perspective of Jewish law. In short selling, an investor sells stock that he does not own. Typically, the investor borrows the stock from a brokerage firm's inventory or the margin accounts of the firm's clients. The investor executes the short sale because he believes that the price of the stock will decline. If that happens, the investor will buy back the stock at the lower price, return the stock to the lender, and thereby profit from the difference in price. If the price of the stock rises, however, the short seller will be required to buy back the stock at a higher price and incur a loss.

Short selling presents a number of issues for economic morality relating to the seller's motivation and the circumstances surrounding the short sale transaction. One type of short selling, called naked short selling, is illegal under U.S. law. That practice is also illegal under Jewish law because it constitutes doing business with someone else's property. Finally, we consider the issue of short selling from the standpoint of promoting efficiency and the role of government in the area of macroeconomic stabilization policy.

Notes

1. R. Moses Hayyim Luzzatto, *Mesilat Yesharim*, ch. 20.
2. Adam Smith, *An Inquiry into the Nature and Causes of the Wealth of Nations* (1776; repr., New York: Modern Library, 1937), 14.
3. Ibid., 717–734.
4. See Nicholas Kaldor, "Welfare Propositions of Economics and Interpersonal Comparisons of Utility," *Economic Journal* 49, no. 195 (1939): 549–552; J. R. Hicks, "The Foundations of Welfare Economics," *Economic Journal* 49, no. 196 (1939): 696–712.
5. See, e.g., Cass R. Sunstein, "Lives, Life-Years, and Willingness to Pay," *Columbia Law Review* 104 (2004): 205.
6. The exposition of the Pareto and Kaldor-Hicks criteria as they apply to social choice follows Richard A. Posner, *Economic Analysis of Law*, 7th ed. (New York: Aspen, 2007), 12–15. The explanation of why Kaldor-Hicks works to maximize society's wealth in the long run, even if the gainers do not compensate the losers, is the author's.
7. See Daniel M. Hausman and Michael S. McPherson, *Economic Analysis, Moral Philosophy and Public Policy*, 2nd ed. (Cambridge: Cambridge University Press, 2006), 12–23.
8. See Kaldor, "Welfare Propositions," 551; Hicks, "Foundations of Welfare Economics," 711–712.
9. Posner, *Economic Analysis of Law*, 24–26.
10. Federal Trade Commission, "FTC Policy Statement on Deception," (October 14, 1983), § IV.
11. Ibid.
12. Jef I. Richards and Ivan L. Preston, "Proving and Disproving Materiality of Deceptive Advertising Claims," *Journal of Public Policy and Marketing* 11, no. 2 (Fall 1992): 52–55.
13. Richard Craswell, "Interpreting Deceptive Advertising," *Boston University Law Review* 65, no. 4 (July 1985): 674.
14. Ibid., 678.
15. Ibid., 688.
16. Paul H. Rubin, "The Economics of Regulating Deception," *CATO Journal* 10, no. 3 (Winter 1991): 668–669.
17. Ibid., 682–683.
18. Henry G. Manne, *Insider Trading and the Stock Market* (New York: Free Press, 1966), 138–145.
19. Posner, *Economic Analysis of Law*, 449.
20. Henry G. Manne, "Insider Trading: Hayek, Virtual Markets, and the Dog that Did Not Bark," *Journal of Corporation Law* 31 (Fall 2005): 173–174.
21. See Laura Nyantung Beny, "Insider Trading Laws and Stock Markets Around the World: An Empirical Contribution to the Theoretical Law and Economics Debate," *Journal of Corporation Law* 32 (Winter 2007): 241–252.
22. Ibid.
23. Jonathan Macey, "Getting the Word out About Fraud: A Theoretical Analysis of Whistleblowing and Insider Trading," *Michigan Law Review* 105 (2007): 1933–1935.
24. Edgar K. Browning and Mark A. Zupan, *Microeconomics: Theory & Applications*, 10th ed. (Hoboken, NJ: John Wiley, 2009), 585. The authors promote their book, which is one of the most popular intermediate microeconomics textbooks, with the contention that they select only the best applications of economic theory. Ibid., vii.

25. Ibid., 585.
26. Robert W. Hahn and James E. Prieger, "The Impact of Driver Cell Phone Use on Accidents," *Advances in Economic Analysis and Policy* 6, no. 1 (2006): 29.
27. Browning and Zupan, *Microeconomics*, 585.
28. Kevin L. Brady, "The Value of Human Life: A Case for Altruism," *Natural Resources Journal* 48 (Summer 2008): 541–544.
29. Ibid., 550.
30. For a discussion of the differences between consequentialism and deontology, see Hausman and McPherson, *Economic Analysis*, 113–116, and Shelly Kagan, *Normative Ethics* (Boulder, CO: Westview Press, 1998), 70–78. The absolutist version of deontology maintains that the relevant rules may not be violated under any circumstances. Moderate deontology, by contrast, permits violation of the rules under certain limited circumstances. See Eyal Zamir and Barak Medina, *Law, Economics, and Morality* (New York: Oxford University Press, 2010), 46–48.
31. R. Jonah b. Abraham Gerondi (*Rabbeinu Yonah*, Spain, ca. 1200–1263), *Sha'arei Teshuvah* 3:181; R. Israel Meir ha-Kohen Kagan (*Hafetz Hayyim*, Radin, 1838–1933), *Sefat Tamim*, ch. 6; R. Abraham Isaiah Karelitz (*Hazon Ish*, Israel, 1878–1953), *Hazon Ish al Inyanei Emunah, Bitahon, ve-Od* 4:13 (Jerusalem: S. Greineman, 1954), pp. 53–55.
32. R. Dov Berish Gottlieb, *Yad ha-Ketanah, De'ot* 10:1.
33. R. Israel Meir ha-Kohen Kagan, *Sefer Hafetz Hayyim, Hilkhot Rekhilut* 1:8.
34. R. Nahum Yavruv, *Niv Sefatayyim*, 4th ed., *helek* 1, *kelal* 2:8 (Jerusalem, 2005), p. 30.
35. Ibid., *kelal* 2:25, p. 40.
36. R. Judah b. Samuel he-Hasid, *Sefer Hasidim* 426. R. Abraham Abele b. Hayyim ha-Levi Gombiner (Poland, ca. 1637–1683), *Magen Avraham* to R. Joseph Caro (Safed, 1488–1575), *Shulhan Arukh, Orah Hayyim* 156, and R. Moses Sofer (*Hatam Sofer*, Hungary, 1762–1839), *She'elot u-Teshuvot Hatam Sofer* 6:59, follow in R. Judah b. Samuel he-Hasid's line.
37. R. Yavruv, *Niv Sefatayyim, helek* 1, *kelal* 2:26, pp. 40–41.
38. Maimonides, *Mishneh Torah, Gezeilah va-Aveidah* 14:13. R. Hayyim Palaggi (Turkey, 1788–1869) follows Maimonides' line. See R. Hayyim Palaggi, *Lev Hayyim*, vol. 1, *Orah Hayyim, siman* 5.
39. R. Yavruv, *Niv Sefatayyim, helek* 1, *kelal* 2:7, p. 28.
40. R. Solomon b. Jehiel Luria, *Yam shel Shelomoh, Yevamot* 6:46.
41. R. Yavruv, *Niv Sefatayyim, helek* 1, *kelal* 2:14, p. 34.
42. R. Jonah b. Abraham Gerondi, *Sha'arei Teshuvah* 3:175–186.
43. Ibid., 3:181.
44. R. Yavruv, *Niv Sefatayyim, helek* 1, *kelal* 2:18, p. 38; *helek* 2, *siman* 12, p. 30.
45. The prohibition against making an insincere promise is derived by Abaye (4th cent.) at *Bava Metzia* 49a in the following manner:

> In connection with the Biblical prohibition against using false weights and measures, the Torah writes: "Just (*tzedek*) balances, just weights, a just *ephah* and a just *hin* you shall have" (Leviticus 19:36). Since the *hin* is a measure of smaller capacity than the *ephah*, its mention is apparently superfluous. If accuracy is required of a large capacity, it is certainly required in measures of small capacity. This apparent superfluity leads Abaye to connect *hin* with the Aramaic word for "yes" (i.e., *hen*), giving the phrase the following interpretation: Be certain that your "yes" is *tzedek* (sincere) and (by extension) be certain that your "no" is *tzedek* (sincere). If an individual makes a commitment or an offer, he should fully intend to carry it out.

The duty to ensure that a commitment is made in a sincere manner is referred to as the *hin tzedek* imperative.

46. See Maimonides, *Mishneh Torah, Mekhirah* 1:3–20.
47. R. Yaakov Yeshayahu Bloi, *Pit'hei Hoshen: Likkutim u-Ve'urim ba-Halakhah be-Dinei Kinyanim, Mekhirah u-Matanah* 7:1 and n. 3 (Jerusalem, 1994), pp. 170–171. *Kiddushin* 6b. The kerchief

is merely pulled by the acquirer and must then be returned to the owner. See R. Moses Isserles (*Rema*, Poland, 1525 or 1530–1572), *Rema* to *Shulhan Arukh, Hoshen Mishpat* 195:1, 4.

48. In some instances, verbal agreement alone creates a presumption of *gemirat da'at*, with the consequence that the courts will intervene, if necessary, to ensure specific performance. For a description of these cases, see Aaron Levine, *Free Enterprise and Jewish Law: Aspects of Jewish Business Ethics* (New York: Ktav, 1980), 34–35.

49. R. Abraham Isaiah Karelitz, *Hazon Ish, Hoshen Mishpat*, vol. 2, *Bava Kamma* 23:1 (Jerusalem: S. Greineman, 1950), p. 90. See, however, R. Shabbetai b. Meir ha-Kohen (*Siftei Kohen*, Poland, 1621–1662), *Siftei Kohen* to *Shulhan Arukh, Hoshen Mishpat* 333, n. 4.

50. For a description of these penalties and the scenarios where they apply, see Levine, *Free Enterprise and Jewish Law*, 44–49.

51. *Tosefta, Bava Metzia* 11:13; R. Solomon b. Simeon Duran (*Rashbash*, Algiers, ca. 1400–1467), *She'elot u-Teshuvot ha-Rashbash*, no. 112.

The specific case addressed by the *Tosefta* concerns the power of the community to restrain a publicly employed bath attendant, barber, baker, or money changer from leaving his post, even to join his family for the festival, if a replacement worker is not available.

R. Yehudah Gershuni (New York, 1908–2000) posits that the ruling of the *Tosefta* is not in accord with mainstream Jewish law. See R. Yehudah Gershuni, "*Ha-Shevitah le-Or ha-Halakhah*," in *Torah she-be-al Peh*, vol. 19, ed. Isaac Raphael (Jerusalem: Mossad HaRav Kook, 1977), 86. His theory is based on the fact that the *Tosefta* case is not recorded in the codes of Jewish law. Furthermore, its basic teaching appears to be contradicted by the Abtinas incident recorded at *Yoma* 38a. In that incident, the house of Abtinas was expert in preparing the Temple incense but would not teach the art to others. Consequently, the Sages sent for replacement workers from Alexandria. The replacement workers proved inadequate, however, because their incense produced smoke that scattered in all directions instead of rising straight up as a stick. Upon seeing that the Alexandrian replacement workers were not as skilled as the house of Abtinas, the Sages called back the workers from the house of Abtinas. The former workers refused to return to work until the Sages agreed to double their wages.

Now, if the community may restrain a public servant from leaving his post, why did the Sages not simply *force* the workers from the house of Abtinas to return to work without acceding to their wage demands?

R. Menahem b. Solomon Meiri (*Meiri*, Perpignan, 1249–1316) understands the action of the Sages in sending for replacement workers as imparting the message that the workers from the house of Abtinas were *formally* deposed from their position and, as punishment for refusing to teach their art, cut off from further installments of their yearly stipend drawn from the public treasury. Upon seeing that the replacement workers were not as skilled as the house of Abtinas, the Sages sought to restore the prior workers to their former position. See *Meiri, Beit ha-Behirah, Yoma* 38a.

Meiri's comments lead, in our view, to a ready reconciliation of the *Tosefta* case with the Abtinas incident. The *Tosefta* case demonstrates the power of the community to restrain a public employee *under contract* from leaving his post. In contrast, a *discharged* public employee, as in the Abtinas case, may not be forced to return to his job.

Tosafot Yeshanim and R. Joseph Caro comment that while it is certainly preferable that the smoke of the incense ascend straight up as a stick, this aspect of the incense service is not indispensable. Thus, if the smoke scatters in all directions, the service is nonetheless valid. See *Tosafot Yeshanim, Yoma* 38a, and R. Joseph Caro, *Beit Yosef* to R. Jacob b. Asher (*Tur*, Germany, 1270–1343), *Tur, Orah Hayyim* 133.

This comment of *Tosafot Yeshanim* and R. Joseph Caro leads, in our view, to another way of reconciling the *Tosefta* case with the Abtinas incident. Because the incense service of the Alexandrian compounders was fully valid, the Sages could not force the workers from the house of Abtinas to return to their jobs, for the community's power in this regard is inoperative when replacement workers are available.

In respect to R. Gershuni's first point, it should be noted that while the *Tosefta* case is not discussed in the codes, a derivative case is prominently mentioned. This case involves the financial obligations arising from the community's responsibility to maintain and not disrupt congregational worship during the High Holidays. *Shulhan Arukh, Orah Hayyim* 55:21. See also R. Elijah b. Solomon Zalman (*Gra*, Vilna, 1720–1797), *Be'ur ha-Gra* to *Shulhan Arukh*, ad loc. (mentioning *Tosefta* case).

52. R. Shalom Albeck, *Dinei ha-Mamonot ba-Talmud* (Tel Aviv: Dvir, 1976), 112–178.
53. R. Shneur Zalman of Liadi (Russia, 1745–1812), *Shulhan Arukh ha-Rav, Hoshen Mishpat, helek* 6, *Hilkhot Mekhirah u-Matanah, se'if* 1 (Brooklyn: Otzar ha-Hasidim, 2004), pp. 1728–1729.
54. R. Bloi, *Pit'hei Hoshen* 1:1–2, pp. 1–2.
55. *Rema* to *Shulhan Arukh, Hoshen Mishpat* 204:11 (first opinion); R. Moses Sofer, *Hatam Sofer, Hoshen Mishpat*, no. 102; R. Jehiel Michal Epstein (Belorus, 1829–1908), *Arukh ha-Shulhan, Hoshen Mishpat* 204:8.
56. This imprecation is known as "*Mi she-para*." See *Bava Metzia* 44a; *Mishneh Torah, Mekhirah* 7:1–6; R. Asher b. Jehiel (*Rosh*, Germany, 1250–1327), *Bava Metzia* 4:13.
57. *Rema* to *Shulhan Arukh, Yoreh De'ah* 258:13.
58. R. Yohanan, *Bava Metzia* 49a; R. Isaac b. Jacob Alfasi (*Rif*, Algeria, 1013–1103), *Rif*, ad loc.; *Mishneh Torah, Mekhirah* 7:8–9; *Rosh, Bava Metzia* 4:12; *Tur, Hoshen Mishpat* 204; *Shulhan Arukh, Hoshen Mishpat* 204:8; *Arukh ha-Shulhan, Hoshen Mishpat* 204:9. If the promise to confer a large gift is made by a group rather than an individual, the presumption of nonreliance is not valid, and thus it is morally objectionable for the group to renege on its promise. R. Mordekhai b. Hillel ha-Kohen (*Mordekhai*, Germany, ca. 1250–1298), *Mordekhai, Bava Metzia* 6:458 (quoted by *Beit Yosef* to *Tur, Hoshen Mishpat* 204, n. 9).
59. For an elaboration of and sources on this point, see Aaron Levine, *Case Studies in Jewish Business Ethics* (Hoboken, NJ: Ktav, 2000), 43–44.
60. For treatment of the *ona'at devarim* interdict as it pertains to the bait and switch tactic, see Levine, *Free Enterprise and Jewish Law*, 120–121.
61. For an explication of the prohibition of *geneivat da'at*, see Aaron Levine, *Moral Issues of the Marketplace in Jewish Law* (Brooklyn, NY: Yashar Books, 2005), 8–16.
62. For a halakhic basis for the assertion we make in the text, see *Bava Metzia* 60b.
63. 521 U.S. 642 (1997).
64. *United States v. O'Hagan*, 92 F.3d 612 (8th Cir. 1996).
65. *Bava Metzia* 35b; R. Solomon b. Isaac (*Rashi*, France, 1040–1105), ad loc.
66. *Rosh, Bava Metzia* 3:5.
67. Mishnah, *Bava Metzia* 3:2.
68. *Rif, Bava Metzia* 35b–36a; *Mishneh Torah, Sekhirut* 1:6; *Rosh, Bava Metzia* 3:5; *Tur, Hoshen Mishpat* 307; *Shulhan Arukh, Hoshen Mishpat* 307:5; *Arukh ha-Shulhan, Hoshen Mishpat* 307:5.
69. See J. David Bleich, "The Infinite Value of Human Life," in *The Value of Human Life: Contemporary Perspectives in Jewish Medical Ethics*, eds. Refoel Guggenheim et al. (New York: Feldheim, 2010), 24–27.
70. *Yoma* 82a.
71. Milton Friedman, "The Role of Government in Education," in *Economics and the Public Interest*, ed. Robert A. Solo (New Brunswick, NJ: Rutgers University Press, 1955), 123–144.

CHAPTER 1

A Tale of Two Sermons (*Derashot*)

JEWISH LAW'S DEONTOLOGICAL ETHICS AT WORK

In social interaction, truth-telling often clashes with other values. The conflict is not only with the demands of self-interest, but also with the apparent dictates of virtue, such as compromising truth to avoid embarrassing someone or to lift someone's spirits. Our purpose here will be to show how Jewish law reconciles these conflicts. We will do so through a case study involving the comments that people made to a rabbi on two *derashot* (sermons) he delivered. In the first scenario, no one actually listened to the *derashah*, but hardly anyone was prepared to admit that to the rabbi. In the second scenario, by contrast, everyone paid attention to the *derashah*, but hardly anyone who commented on it told the rabbi what he or she really thought.

Our main purpose in this chapter will be to show how a litany of well-meaning lies in a social context can lead to misguided economic decisions and cause much unnecessary disappointment and disillusionment. The chapter is designed to show Jewish law's deontological ethics at work.

Rabbi Elimelekh Pelt's Keynote Speech at the Rye Hilton

Rabbi Elimelekh Pelt took the applause that accompanied the conclusion of his keynote address at the Rye Hilton as affirmation that his remarks were a marvelous triumph in both creative thinking and oratorical brilliance. Pelt was also satisfied that he had successfully advanced the cause of the sponsoring organization, Mesos. Mesos is an international organization that promotes and finances settlement in the Land of Israel, especially among young and retired couples.

Seated at the dais right next to his wife, Abigail, Pelt used the brief spurt of laughter the next speaker elicited to steal a glance at her. Knowing that her husband was thinking about his *derashah*, Abigail took the cue to whisper her approval, "Eli, you were exemplary." "Abi," whispered back Pelt, "what about the jokes?" "Don't worry, Eli. The humor was good; couldn't you tell by the laughter?" responded Abigail.

In truth, Abigail almost totally tuned out when her husband got up to speak. For the past three months, Rabbi Pelt had used Abigail as a sounding board to rehearse different openings and closings for his *derashah*, not to mention the different possibilities he tried out on her for the content of the *derashah* itself. Abigail was already deep in negative marginal utility territory with the speech when she politely but firmly refused to listen to the final version. Instead, Abigail just exhorted her husband, "Remember, don't put your mouth too close to the microphone. Above all, don't get hyper or scream. If you get carried away, you'll spoil the whole effect, even if the content is superb."

As soon as the program was over, Dr. Shem Tov Lippman, Executive Director of Mesos, who was M.C. of the evening, enthusiastically approached Rabbi Pelt and said "Rav Elimelekh, your speech was a magnificent masterpiece. Mesos is in eternal debt to you. Your destiny is a growing national audience."

In truth, Dr. Lippman paid very little attention to Pelt's *derashah*. Thirty seconds into Pelt's 19-minute address, Lippman's mind began to wander. Much more important matters were on his mind. During the reception, Lippman had missed extending a few *mazel tovs* to some of the important patrons. Formulating remedies for these gaffes was foremost on his mind. Now, if Lippman didn't even pay attention to the *derashah*, why the lavish praise? Good question. You'll soon find out why.

Hungry for more compliments, Pelt began to amble along the narrow path behind the dais. Pelt's hope was that one or more of the dignitaries seated at the dais would spontaneously throw a compliment his way. No such luck. But before Pelt could return to his seat, he made eye contact with Rabbi Dr. Baruch Gerlenter, the charismatic president of Mesos and a fellow speaker at the Rye Hilton. Gerlenter had addressed the audience right after Pelt's speech. What better strategy to get a compliment, Pelt thought, than to praise Rabbi Gerlenter for his speech. Gerlenter would surely reciprocate in kind, reasoned Pelt.

Reflecting his high expectations for a satisfying trade, Pelt initiated his encounter with Gerlenter by saying, "Rabbi Gerlenter, I thoroughly enjoyed your very stimulating speech. The audience really warmed up to it. You could tell by the loud applause and the laughter that frequently interrupted your remarks." After absorbing Pelt's comments with obvious relish, Gerlenter responded, "Thanks. Your comments also elicited applause."

Because Gerlenter's remarks were terse and uttered without much feeling, Pelt was disappointed and felt that he got the raw end of the exchange. In truth, Gerlenter paid no attention to Pelt's speech. It was not because Gerlenter thought that Pelt's speech was not worth listening to. No. It was because Gerlenter felt a need to review his own speech again and again in his mind until the very last moment before he was called to speak. Accordingly, while Pelt was speaking, Gerlenter was not paying attention, but instead was preoccupied reviewing his own speech.

Between courses, Rabbi Pelt visited Table 6, where couples from his hometown in Dearborn Heights, Michigan, were seated. Before Pelt got a chance to mingle with his group, Mrs. Naomi Ziskind, who was not from this group, and was seated nearby at Table 8, got up and approached Rabbi Pelt. "Rabbi, what an inspiring talk you delivered," she gushed.

In truth, Naomi Ziskind did not pay attention to Rabbi Pelt's remarks. During the entire speech, she was busy admiring the flower arrangements at her own and nearby tables and figuring out which table would offer the least resistance when she would remove the flowers while saying, "I'm taking these flowers home." Just because Ziskind had no idea what Rabbi Pelt said in his keynote speech was no reason for her not to compliment him for his remarks. The rabbi, Ziskind reasoned, put a lot of effort into preparing his speech and even made a long trip from out of town. The *decent* thing to do therefore was to make Rabbi Pelt feel good about his speech.

Buoyed by Ziskind's compliment, Pelt made his way toward Marshall Grunder. "Marshall, do you have any comments, critical or otherwise, on the substance of my Torah remarks tonight?" Pelt asked. More often than not, Grunder, a member of the Dearborn Heights group, had something to say about the rabbi's *derashah*. Not so tonight. Grunder paid no attention to Pelt's speech. Instead of listening to the speech, Grunder spent the time figuring out the changes he wanted to make to his stock portfolio when the financial markets would open the next morning. If Grunder had wanted to hear the rabbi's speech, nothing would have prevented him from hearing every word. Embarrassed to tell the truth, Grunder replied: "Sorry, Rabbi. I was eager to hear your speech, but there was so much noise at my table that I could hardly make out what you said."

Pelt received some additional comment on his speech at the checkout line. As he stood in line with his wife, Pelt could not help but hear the gentleman directly behind him lavishly praise Gerlenter's speech. Feeling a bit jealous, Pelt introduced himself to the stranger, whose name turned out to be Mordechai Kushta. Pelt's hope was that engaging Kushta in conversation would lead Kushta to comment favorably on his own *derashah* as well. In short shrift, Pelt grasped that Kushta was a learned person. Pelt seized the moment and said, "Perhaps you have a critique or something to add to the Torah portion of the *derashah* I delivered tonight." With a pained look on his face, Kushta responded, "I must be absolutely honest; I did not pay attention to your remarks. I am therefore sorry to say that I can offer no comments."

Kushta's comments hurt Pelt deeply. But as Rabbi and Mrs. Pelt waited outside the hall for the valet service to retrieve their car, the comments of a colleague, Rabbi Shalom Friend, who was also waiting for his car, gave Pelt some consolation. As would be expected, Pelt asked Friend if he had any comment on the Torah portion of his *derashah*. You guessed it—Friend was among Pelt's non-listeners that night. To boot, Friend had no good excuse for not listening to the *derashah*. Thinking quickly on his feet, Rabbi Friend responded: "Please repeat it for me now. I'd love to hear it in all its fullness, including the fine points that the time constraints did not allow you to make in your address tonight."

Rabbi Pelt's Tryout Sermon (*Probeh*) at Eden Commons

On the flight back to Dearborn Heights, Pelt was in an ebullient mood and shared with Abigail his plan to apply for the position of Senior Rabbi at the prestigious Congregation Eden Commons in New York City. With a twinkle in his eye and an air of confidence, Pelt blurted out, "Abi, I'll call Shem Tov (Lippman). He'll arrange everything."

Pelt was right on the mark. If Pelt wanted something, Lippman was only too eager to accommodate him. Lippman looked upon Pelt as the key to getting access to Ralph Hartzman, the eccentric Dearborn Heights billionaire philanthropist. Pelt had influenced Hartzman and his family to become religiously observant. Because Hartzman felt eternally indebted to Pelt for this, Hartzman eagerly sought Pelt's advice on charity matters and blindly followed the rabbi's guideposts and recommendations. Because Lippman could secure larger donations from Hartzman through the good offices of Pelt, Lippman was constantly thinking of ways to curry favor with Pelt. You got it! It was Pelt's connection to Hartzman that made Lippman invite Pelt to be the keynote speaker at the Rye Hilton and to praise his speech, even though Lippman could have enlisted more prominent personalities for the assignment.

Predictably, Lippman arranged for Pelt to have a *probeh* for the position of Senior Rabbi at Eden Commons. To place himself in a strategic position to lobby for Pelt, Lippman even went to the trouble of getting himself invited for *Shabbat probeh* at the home of Mr. and Mrs. Mordechai Kushta, who were prominent members of Eden Commons

What an amazing contrast! At the Rye Hilton, Pelt could hardly muster a single serious listener. At *Shabbat probeh*, *everyone* paid close attention to Pelt's *derashah*; even the *shul*'s non-Jewish doorman moved away from his post to catch some snippets. Ironically, both talks elicited the same amount of truth-telling. Here are the comments.

As Rabbi and Mrs. Pelt made their way down the stairs to the social hall where the *shul* held their weekly *Shabbat kiddush*, a number of the *ba'alei batim* (householders) surrounded the candidate to hear him recite *kiddush*. At the first opportunity, Max Glass blurted out to Rabbi Pelt: "We had a pretty decent crowd today. We would have gotten an even bigger turnout, but some of the *ba'alei batim* went this *Shabbat* to the 'other side' to hear Baruch Gerlenter. In case you didn't hear, Gerlenter is your competition this *Shabbat*. He's the scholar in residence this week at Beit Eden. Rabbi, I'm sure you know Rabbi Gerlenter, at least by reputation. He's a real powerhouse, and what a sense of humor he has."

As matters turned out, some of the people who offered comments to Pelt on his *derashah* at the Rye Hilton were members of Eden Commons. These people were, of course, present at *Shabbat probeh* and eager to offer comments on this occasion again. One such person was Naomi Ziskind. Ziskind did not care for the rabbi's *derashah*, neither in style nor substance. But she dared not tell him the truth! Though she had no idea how anyone else felt about the *derashah*, she was sure that her opinion was shared by the overwhelming majority of the congregation. Because there was no chance, in her mind, that the congregation would select Rabbi Pelt as their rabbi, the gracious thing to do, she mused to herself, was to do her part to send the rabbi away with as pleasant a feeling as possible towards the *shul*. To this end, she used her encounter with the rabbi at the *cholent* station to say: "Rabbi, your *derashah* was food for thought and it was inspiring."

The next comment came from Lester Lefkowitz: "*Shabbat shalom*, Rabbi. I'm not going to go into the substance of your *derashah*, but let me comment on its length. It was 17½ minutes. Please know that if you become our Rabbi, we cannot tolerate *Shabbat* morning *derashot*, regardless of their content or merit, for more than 12 minutes. When you go past the 14-minute mark, some of the *ba'alei batim* will be wishing that a trap door opens under you."

Because Lefkowitz laughed at his own joke (or was it a joke?), Rabbi Pelt decided not to take the critical comment seriously. "I'll change their listening habits," Pelt murmured to himself. "If the *derashah* is really good, they *will* listen, even for 45 minutes."

The only substantive critique Pelt received came from Mordechai Kushta. When Kushta met up with Pelt, he was quick to remind Pelt of their encounter at the Rye Hilton. "Rabbi, I'm sure you recall that at the Rye Hilton, I was unable to comment on your *derashah* because I did not pay attention to it. Not to listen to your *probeh derashah* this morning would, however, be very irresponsible on my part. I *owe it to the shul* to listen to your *derashah*. Let me say that the basic idea of your *derashah* can be found in the *Meshekh Hokhmah*[1] on today's portion."

Seeing that Pelt was visibly shaken by Kushta's critique, Shalom Harmoni, who was listening in on the conversation, interjected: "Morty, I'm sure the rabbi's version is distinctive enough so that we can find some practical difference between the two approaches. Besides, 'No two prophets prophesize in the same style.'"[2]

Because Kushta hadn't seen the *Meshekh Hokhmah* he referred to for a number of years, he was not about to argue with Harmoni. Harmoni's comments noticeably lifted the rabbi's mood. Paradoxically, his success in deflecting Kushta's criticism of the rabbi left Harmoni with mixed emotions. On the one hand, Harmoni felt somewhat guilty that he made his remark without having any knowledge of what the *Meshekh Hokhmah* actually said on the topic. But because the comment assuaged the rabbi's hurt feelings, Harmoni was convinced that he did the right thing.

Just as Pelt was licking his wounds from his encounter with Kushta, Kalman Sunshine suddenly appeared in front of Pelt and weighed in with a nice compliment: "Rabbi, your sermon had a meaningful message for me. Thanks. You have my support. I hope you'll win the derby."

In truth, Sunshine got very little out of Pelt's *derashah*. Nonetheless, Sunshine believed that Pelt was the best candidate. Sunshine liked Pelt because he thought that he would do well with the youth of the *shul*, including his own teenage sons.

Pelt's skill as a *darshan* (one who delivers sermons) mattered very little to him. Much more important was the ability to teach the youth Torah and connect with them in other ways, such as in sports. From first-hand recommendations, Sunshine was confident the rabbi had these skills and would apply them well at Eden Commons.

Since the average age of the members of the *shul* was about 65, the high priority Sunshine placed on the rabbi's ability as a youth leader was not generally shared. For the great majority of the members, the rabbi's ability as a *darshan* was very important. Sunshine therefore assessed that to get the rabbi that he wanted, he would have to claim that his man was the best *darshan*. Accordingly, even though Sunshine got very little out of Pelt's *derashah*, he argued that Pelt was the best *darshan* among the candidates.

On the trip back to Dearborn Heights, the Pelts were very upbeat about the prospects of Elimelekh getting the nod for the rabbinical position at Eden Commons. Abigail attached much significance to the warm and friendly reception the *shul* gave the couple on Friday night. Not attaching much significance to the Friday night reception,[3] Elimelekh focused instead on the favorable comments he received from Kalman Sunshine and Naomi Ziskind, as well as the vigorous defense Harmoni had mounted to deflect Kushta's criticism.

Given the high expectations of the Pelts, you can well imagine their disappointment when Sheldon Sandman, the chairman of the search committee, called Rabbi Pelt to let him know that Eden Commons would not pursue his candidacy further. As the rejection sank in, the couple hardened in their conviction that "Eden Commons" wanted them, but the machinations of a few of the "difficult" *ba'alei batim* subverted the will of the great majority of the members, and it was not to be.

Rabbi Elimelekh Pelt's pursuit of a rabbinical position in New York City had a happy ending. You see, Ralph Hartzman's far-flung business enterprises made it necessary for him to spend more and more of his time in New York City. Because Hartzman understood from Rabbi Pelt's failed *probeh* at Eden Commons that his rabbi desperately wanted to relocate to New York City, Hartzman bought up some prime real estate parcels in the Upper East Side and built Pelt a magnificent synagogue. Hartzman handed over the *shul* lock, stock, and barrel to Pelt, with only one request: "Make sure there's a *minyan* (quorum of ten) on *Shabbat*." I don't think Pelt will have any trouble meeting that mandate. How could he miss when he plans a 45-minute *derashah* for every *Shabbat*?

Treatment of Falsehood in Jewish Law

The various scenarios described above all entail the challenge of how to reconcile conflicting moral duties. Specifically, the prohibition against falsehood ("Distance yourself from a false word" (Exodus 23:7)) must be reconciled with one's duty to achieve harmonious relations with one's fellow ("Seek peace and pursue it" (Psalms 34:15)). The following Talmudic text at *Ketubbot* 16b–17a, referred to as the "bad purchase" case, bears a striking resemblance to many of the scenarios described in our case study and can therefore serve as a springboard to analyze those scenarios:

> Our Rabbis taught: How does one dance [i.e., what does one sing or recite] before the bride? Beit Shammai says: "The bride as she is." And Beit Hillel says: "Beautiful and gracious bride!" But Beit Shammai said to Beit Hillel: "If she were lame or blind, does one say to her: 'Beautiful and gracious bride'? Whereas the Torah said: 'Keep thee far from a false matter (Exodus 23:7).'" Said Beit Hillel to Beit Shammai: "According to your words, if one has purchased a 'bad purchase' from the marketplace (*ha-shuk*), should one praise it in his eyes or deprecate it? Surely one should praise it in his eyes. Therefore, the Sages said: 'Always should the disposition of man be pleasant with *ha-briot* (lit., fellow man).'"

Talmudic decisors follow Beit Hillel's view.[4] Identifying the rationale behind the permissibility for the bystander to lie in the bad-purchase case is therefore critical before this case can be used as a model for analyzing the various scenarios of our case study.

Preliminarily, a number of basic issues must be clarified. In the bad-purchase case, does the buyer (*B*) have recourse to cancel or modify the sale? R. Samuel b. Joseph Strashun (*Rashash*, Lithuania, 1794–1872) rejects this possibility. If the bad purchase is reversible in some manner based on a defect or excessive price, it would be ethically wrong for one who comments on the purchase (*C*) to offer *B* "false praise" regarding the purchase. R. Strashun draws support for his thesis by pointing out that the Talmud refers to the bad purchase as having come not from any specific seller, but rather from the marketplace (*ha-shuk*). The indication is that *B* has no recollection of the identity of the seller. Because returning the item to get a refund or adjustment based on a defect or excessive price is not an option for *B*, it is permissible for *C* to lie and praise *B* for his selection.[5]

Understanding the bad-purchase case in the same manner as R. Strashun is R. Israel Meir ha-Kohen Kagan (*Hafetz Hayyim*, Radin, 1838–1933).[6]

What is the relationship between *B* and *C*? Perhaps the directive to praise the purchase applies only when *C* is a stranger. Given the reasonableness of the assumption that the parties will have no further contact, *C*'s goal should be to help *B* make the best of his situation. Praising the purchase is therefore the indicated course of action. But suppose *B* shows the item to a person he is close with, such as his parent, spouse, or good friend. Perhaps the response of such a person should take into account *B*'s long-term interest. To be sure, *B* has no recourse to fix his mistake, but the purchase manifests irresponsible marketplace conduct on his part. To set *B* straight, the closely connected person should tell the truth. By telling the truth, *B* will not *repeat* his mistake in the future.

Support for restricting the response of praise in the bad-purchase case to the instance where *C* is a stranger can be drawn from the nuance of expression the Talmud employs in connection with the aphorism it quotes, "Always should the disposition of man be pleasant with *ha-briot* (lit., fellow man)." Note that the Talmud describes the connection between *B* and *C* as *briot* (fellow human beings). Other expressions such as friends (*re'im*, *haverim*) or neighbors (*shekhenim*) could have just as easily been used. The use of the phrase *ha-briot* indicates that the prototypical case for the response of praise is when the parties are strangers.

Let us now proceed to the rationale behind the permissibility for *C* to lie in the bad-purchase case. Commentators have offered a number of approaches.[7] We take R. Yom Tov Ishbili's (*Ritva*, Spain, ca. 1250–1330) understanding as expressing the mainstream rationale here. In his view, Beit Hillel espouses the *darkhei shalom* (lit., ways of peace) principle.[8] According to this principle, falsehood is legitimate when its purpose is to end conflict or avert the outbreak of discord. But the ending of what type of conflict is referred to here? Recall the insight of R. Strashun and R. Kagan that the bad-purchase case refers to the instance where *B* has no recollection of the identity of the seller. *B*'s doubts about his purchase are thus producing ill feeling toward no particular seller. If the *darkhei shalom* principle is invoked, it must therefore refer to ending the purchaser's inner torment that he made a bad purchase and wasted his money. By telling the purchaser that he did well with his purchase, *C* helps the purchaser achieve inner peace.[9]

Once we understand that the *darkhei shalom* principle is the rationale for the bad-purchase case, the motivation of *C* in offering *B* false praise is all-important. Consider that false praise is an aspect of prohibited conduct called "one thing with the mouth (*ehad ba-peh*) and another thing with the heart (*ve-ehad ba-lev*)."[10] Hypocritical conduct of this sort is referred to in the rabbinic literature as *hanuppah* (false, prohibited praise).[11] What makes false praise permissible conduct in the bridegroom and bad-purchase cases therefore is the *darkhei shalom* motive of the speaker.

Authorities who explicitly invoke salutary motivation as the critical factor in permitting false praise in the bad-purchase and the bridegroom cases are R. Shlomo Zalman Auerbach (Israel, 1910–1995) and R. Shalom Yosef Elyashiv (Israel, contemp.). In the view of those authorities, *C*'s motive in the bad-purchase case is purely to make *B* feel good about his purchase. Similarly, the motive of the wedding guest in telling the groom that his bride is "beautiful and charming" is to make the groom feel good about his bride. Because the permissibility to utter false praise in those cases is predicated on the speaker's altruistic motive, both authorities aver that the false praise can be offered even if the speaker's opinion was unsolicited.[12]

What can be inferred from the above understanding is that if the speaker's motivation is to ingratiate himself with the purchaser or groom to extract some benefit from them in the future, offering false praise should constitute *hanuppah* and therefore be prohibited.

In considering the permissible bounds to offer false praise when the speaker has an altruistic motive, let's not lose sight of the fact that the license to engage in such conduct is rooted in *darkhei shalom*. But *darkhei shalom* is not a blanket dispensation for lying. Let's consider a number of caveats.

One caveat, enunciated by R. Kagan, is that lying for the purpose of preserving peace is permissible only when the objective cannot be achieved without lying.[13] R. Nahum Yavruv (Israel, contemp.), basing his opinion on R. Hayyim Kanievsky (Israel, contemp.), avers that even if considerable toil and effort must be exerted to achieve peace without lying, this route is preferable to lying.[14]

The *darkhei shalom* motive, in the opinion of R. Nahum Yavruv, legitimizes the telling of a lie, even if the one who tells the lie realizes that the lie will be exposed with time and the peace it achieves will dissipate. This is so because telling a lie to secure *temporary* peace is also legitimate. Nonetheless, if the peacemaker assesses that when his lie is exposed, the discord that it ended will re-emerge in an exacerbated form, *darkhei shalom* does not permit the telling of the lie.[15]

Lying to end discord, according to R. Solomon b. Jehiel Luria (*Maharshal*, Poland, 1510–1573), is legitimate only when the *darkhei shalom* setting requires a one-time lie. If peace is attainable only if the lie is repeated, the lie is not permitted.[16] The basis for this stringency is that repeated lies will accustom the peacemaker to lie.[17]

Once it is recognized that the *darkhei shalom* principle is the basis for permitting *C* to lie to *B* and tell him that he did well with his purchase, consideration of the impact of the lie on *B*'s long-term inner peace or welfare must be taken into account. Consider that *B*'s bad purchase might be just a fluke. On the other hand, it might manifest irresponsible marketplace conduct. If the latter is the case, *B* will repeat his mistake unless he is set straight.

What should *C* make of *B*'s mistake? If *C* is a stranger, why should he be concerned with the possible adverse long-term effect that his lie will have on *B*? Consider that the bad purchase may be nothing but a fluke that will not be repeated in the future. Assuming the worst, *C* should have the right to rely on those who are closely connected to *B* to correct *B*'s ways.

Consideration of possible adverse effects on *B* becomes decidedly relevant, however, if *C* is closely connected to *B*. If *C* is *B*'s parent or someone in charge of his guidance or education, responsibility devolves upon *C* to set *B* straight. "Wounds of a lover are faithful, whereas kisses of an enemy are burdensome" (Proverbs 27:6).

Several additional scenarios can be identified. Suppose *C* is a close friend of *B* but can reasonably assume that *B*'s parent or teacher will tell him the truth about the purchase. Here, *C*'s false compliment will harm relationships all around. Specifically, when *B* shows the item to, say, his parent (*P*), *P* will remonstrate with *B* on *B*'s poor judgment. Because *B*'s close friend, *C*, praised *B*'s purchase just a short while ago, *B* might be shocked by the scolding and resist *P*'s reproof. *C* is to blame for the extra, unnecessary tension between *B* and *P*. Moreover, when *B* is set straight, he will resent *C* for not offering an honest opinion. Had *C* only told the truth, he would have both softened the shock of reproof *B* encountered later and prevented *B* from resenting *C*.

One final scenario: Suppose *C* has reason to believe that no one will set *B* straight. Here, since *C* has a long-term close relationship with *B*, responsibility devolves upon *C* to do the job. Setting *B* straight involves much more than just criticizing *B* for his purchase. Pride may cause *B* to deflect the criticism and focus only on the hurt *C* inflicts. If *B* reacts in this way, *C* may very well violate the prohibition against causing someone needless mental anguish (*ona'at devarim*).[18] Rather, *C* should couple his criticism with a remark such as: "The candelabra is overpriced. Next time you're in the market for silver, be sure to check out Zlomowitz and Sander on Eden Commons Boulevard."

Hanuppah at the Rye Hilton

At the Rye Hilton, Rabbi Elimelekh Pelt received a number of compliments on his *derashah*, some of which were even lavish. But none of those who offered praise actually paid attention to his remarks. Let's analyze the ethics of this conduct. We begin with Pelt's wife, Abigail.

Abigail's spousal relationship to Pelt calls into question her *darkhei shalom* license to express false praise to her husband. Recall that the model for permissible *hanuppah* is the bad-purchase case. The application of this case, as discussed above, may well be limited to how a stranger should respond to a dejected purchaser who has no recourse to remedy his situation. In that case, the objective of the bystander should be to mollify the purchaser with false praise for his purchase. But if the bystander is closely connected to the purchaser, the bystander's objective should be to maximize the long-term welfare of the buyer. Since the purchase reflects poor judgment, the bystander is obligated to set the buyer straight so that the mistake will not be repeated.

Abigail apparently violates the above guideposts and hence engages in impermissible *hanuppah*. Consider that Abigail did not pay any attention to the *derashah*. For all she knew, the *derashah* might have had flaws, and if she would have only listened, she could have pointed them out to her husband. Getting an honest critique from his wife would motivate Pelt to correct his mistakes and save him from future embarrassment. By telling her husband that his speech was "exemplary" when she was in no position to comment on it, Abigail seems to have engaged in *hanuppah*.

Much mitigation can, however, be found in Abigail's conduct. In assessing whether she met the demands Halakhah imposes on a closely connected person in the bad-purchase case, it is wrong to focus exclusively on Abigail's conduct the night of the Rye Hilton affair. Recall that Elimelekh spent three months preparing his talk, and during that time Abigail provided an honest critique of his work.

Given that Abigail had satisfied her duty to foster her husband's continuing professional education, what would her duty have been at the Rye Hilton had she listened carefully to her husband's talk and found reason to criticize it? Criticism at that juncture would have served no useful purpose; it would have only demoralized her husband and been counterproductive. To be sure, Abigail did not listen to her husband's talk at the Rye Hilton. But since she had no duty to criticize his talk even if she had listened to it and found reason to criticize it, she was not remiss in meeting the demands that proceed from the bad-purchase case.

We are not out of the woods yet. The problem is that Abigail was not silent, but instead chose to tell her husband that his talk was "exemplary." Because she never paid attention to the talk, her comment is clearly *hanuppah*. Certainly Abigail's motive in giving her husband false praise is to preserve domestic harmony. But *darkhei shalom* does not legitimize *hanuppah* unless it is driven by a purely altruistic motive. This is not the case here. True, Abigail is driven to preserve domestic harmony, but it is her own domestic harmony, rather than the domestic harmony of third parties, she seeks to preserve.

A saving factor is that a number of exceptions apply to the prohibition against *hanuppah*. These exceptions, as enumerated in *Midrash Yelammedenu*, allow an individual to engage in *hanuppah* vis-à-vis his wife, creditor, or *rebbe* (religious teacher).[19] In each of those cases, according to R. David Ariav (Israel, contemp.), the speaker is motivated by a clearly meritorious goal (*mitzvah*). Accordingly, if false praise is the only expedient available for a husband to quiet a feud with his wife, the husband may resort to *hanuppah* to achieve his goal. Since *shalom bayit* (domestic peace) is a *mitzvah*, the use of *hanuppah* to achieve *shalom bayit* is legitimate, despite the husband's self-serving motive. Similarly, if a debtor has no means to pay his creditor, the debtor may resort to *hanuppah* with his creditor to forestall the creditor from pressing his claim. Because pressing for payment when the debtor has no means to pay constitutes oppressive behavior on the part of the creditor and violates for him "When you lend money to my people, to the poor person who is with you, do not act toward him *ke-noshei* (like a pressing creditor),"[20] *hanuppah* achieves a *mitzvah* goal for the debtor. Finally, using *hanuppah* to get one's *rebbe* to teach him Torah also amounts to the pursuit of a *mitzvah* goal and is permissible despite the student's self-serving motive.[21]

Let's take note that *Midrash Yelammedenu* mentions that *hanuppah* is permissible for a husband vis-à-vis his wife, but does not state whether a wife is permitted to engage in *hanuppah* towards her husband. If the rationale for the permissibility of *hanuppah* by a husband is the pursuit of domestic harmony (*darkhei shalom*), as R. Ariav has it, *hanuppah* by a wife towards her husband should also be permissible.[22]

The upshot of the above analysis is that Abigail should not be faulted for telling her husband that his talk was "exemplary" even though she paid no attention to it. This is so because she did everything Halakhah would expect of her leading up to the Rye Hilton affair to foster her husband's continuing professional education.

It would be terribly wrong to outrightly criticize his talk at the affair. Doing so would only demoralize her husband and be counterproductive. Moreover, given Abigail's *darkhei shalom* motive in telling her husband that his *derashah* was exemplary, her *hanuppah* was permissible notwithstanding her self-serving motive.

While Abigail's conduct can generally be defended, her comment that she thought "the humor was good" is very problematic. That comment was a deliberate, outright lie. The few "jokes" Pelt made during his address were the only thing Abigail picked up on from a *derashah* she otherwise did not listen to. In truth, Abigail felt that her husband's attempt at humor was pathetic and the polite laughter he elicited from the audience was more reflective of sympathy for a failed attempt at humor than an appreciation for its entertainment value.

Compounding the moral issue here is that over the next several months, Pelt will be asking Abigail many times to comment on his *derashah* at the Rye Hilton, including the quality of the humor in the speech. Pelt's hope, of course, is that Abigail will repeat and augment her initial compliments. To avoid a rift with her husband, Abigail will have to repeat her deliberate lie that the "humor was good," *many, many* times. Recall that *darkhei shalom* is not a carte blanche license to lie. Since repeating a lie over and over again will habituate the speaker to lie, the *darkhei shalom* motive does not legitimize the repeated lie. A saving factor here is that, as discussed earlier, a wife has an expanded license to engage in *hanuppah* vis-à-vis her husband. Perhaps included in this license is the right to repeat false praise. In any event, repeating a lie again and again should not be done when the dilemma at hand can be resolved in another manner.

Make no mistake—Abigail is a very clever woman. No sooner than she absorbed the poor humor in her husband's speech, she devised a plan to set her husband straight. The plan would generate, in her mind, little stress for the couple and entail minimum falsehood on her part. Notice that Abigail's comment about the humor was much less enthusiastic than her comment about the *derashah* in general. Instead of telling her husband that his humor was good because she got a hearty laugh out of it, she said that it was good because the audience laughed. The next time Elimelekh asks Abigail how his humor was at the Rye Hilton, she will simply say: "It must have been good; the audience laughed." Predictably, Pelt will shoot back, "Abi, that doesn't sound too enthusiastic." Abigail will then say: "Okay. You're asking for it. In truth, I didn't like the jokes. Get real! The audience gave you nothing more than polite laughter." Now, if Pelt still doesn't get it and insists that his humor was good because, for instance, Lippman laughed at the jokes, Abigail will come back with the killer and say: "Good morning, sunshine. Wake up from your dream world. Humor is not your stock in trade. Even if what you have to say is funny on paper, the tickle of the joke dissipates when it's released from your mouth. You're going to have to face up to it—*You're no Gerlenter*. Skip the humor and do the best you can with the talents and capabilities you do have."

Let's now move on to the next non-listener who lavished praise on Pelt, Dr. Shem Tov Lippman. Lippman's false compliment was entirely self-serving. His motive was to curry favor with Pelt to get better access to Ralph Hartzman. Lippman's *hanuppah* hence cannot be defended on the basis of the *darkhei shalom* principle.

But a saving factor can be identified here. Consider that Lippman is the Executive Director of Mesos and, to boot, the chairman of its fundraising event at the Rye Hilton. At the Rye Hilton, Lippman is, of course, an individual, but he is also a representative of an organization. As the representative of Mesos, Lippman has a duty to express a thank-you to Pelt for his speech. This duty should obtain even if Lippman did not care for Pelt's *derashah*. The fact that Lippman will benefit personally from thanking Pelt should not excuse him from his duty to thank Lippman as the representative of Mesos.

Support for the above proposition can be drawn from the prohibition against creating a false impression (*geneivat da'at*).[23] One aspect of this law is the prohibition for *A* to press *B* to accept his dinner invitation when *A* knows that *B* will not accept the invitation. Pressing *B* to accept the invitation will make *B* feel indebted to *A*. This indebtedness is undeserved, though, since *A* extends the invitation only because he is certain *B* will decline.[24] But this does not say that *A* should never invite *B* for a meal. No. If *A* assesses that ignoring *B* will cast *B* in a poor light, making people think that *B* is a lowly person who should be shunned, it is *A*'s duty to disabuse people of this notion by inviting *B* several times, even though *B* will become undeservedly indebted to him on account of the invitation.[25] Between the alternatives of reaping false goodwill from *B* or causing *B*'s stature to be diminished, the former outcome is preferred.

Lippman faces the selfsame alternatives at the Rye Hilton. As the representative of Mesos, Lippman is obligated to thank Pelt for his *derashah*. Because it is expected that an organization will thank its keynote speaker for his *derashah*, failure to do so will hurt Pelt's feelings. Accordingly, even though Lippman derives a personal benefit from the false praise he offers Pelt, his conduct should not be viewed as *hanuppah*.

One caveat, however, should be noted. Common courtesy requires Mesos to do no more than thank Pelt both for his *derashah* and for making the long trip to the Rye Hilton. While one may quibble about the nature of the thank-you that the protocol of an organization demands, Lippman went considerably beyond this by telling Pelt that his speech was a "magnificent masterpiece" and that Mesos was "eternally" indebted to him. Because those hyperboles extend beyond the expected protocol, they should render Lippman's false praise *hanuppah*.

Before we continue to analyze the comments Rabbi Pelt received about his *derashah* at the Rye Hilton, let's examine whether Pelt himself violated *hanuppah*. Recall that in his desperation to get a compliment, Pelt offered praise to Rabbi Gerlenter for his *derashah*. Pelt's hope was that Gerlenter would reciprocate and offer praise for Pelt's *derashah* as well. Now, if Pelt listened to Gerlenter's *derashah* and his complements were sincere, Pelt is not guilty of false praise in his interaction with Gerlenter. If Pelt is not guilty of *hanuppah*, his selfish motive in giving the compliments should not amount to any ethical breach. But it should come as no surprise that Pelt listened to not a single word of Gerlenter's address. Instead, as Gerlenter spoke, Pelt basked himself in the halo of glory he imagined had descended upon him when he concluded his address just a few minutes earlier in the program. The praise he offered Gerlenter was hence false praise. Since Pelt's praise was offered to induce Gerlenter to return a compliment, Pelt's self-serving conduct was impermissible *ḥanuppah*.

Let's now consider Gerlenter's comment. We take it as a given that Gerlenter should understand Pelt's compliment about his address to be an implicit request for him to reciprocate in kind. Now, if the bad-purchase case is the model for how *C* should respond to a request from *B* for an opinion on something regrettable *B* has done but that cannot be reversed, Gerlenter falls short of the standard the Talmud prescribes. Instead of making Pelt feel good about his speech by returning the compliment and saying simply "Your speech was also excellent," Gerlenter dashes Pelt's expectations and tells him that Pelt's speech "also received applause." Gerlenter's comment is nothing but a putdown. Protocol tells the audience to clap at the conclusion of a speech, whether they liked the speech or not. If that's all Gerlenter can manage to say about Pelt's speech, Pelt can reasonably interpret the remark as saying "Your speech was very pedestrian and is not worthy of any praise."

Let's however consider the possibility that Gerlenter did nothing wrong. The key here is that if Gerlenter has any duty to Pelt, it would be rooted in the *darkhei shalom* principle, with the bad-purchase case serving as the analogue. To determine whether Gerlenter owes any duty to Pelt, let's further refine the parameters of the bad-purchase case.

Several issues are relevant here. One basic point is that *darkhei shalom* is not a carte blanche license to lie. Recall that lying to end a conflict is not permitted when the lie used to achieve peace will be exposed with the passage of time and the conflict will resurface in an exacerbated form. Applying this principle to the bad-purchase case should therefore restrict the role of the bystander to highlighting the virtues of the purchase. Such a stratagem deflects the dejected buyer's attention from the defects of the purchased item and hence lifts his spirits. But lifting the spirits of the purchaser by making false statements regarding the defects of the item should be forbidden. Although the bystander's lies or misleading statements about the defects may temporarily cheer up the purchaser, the truth will undoubtedly come to light. When that happens, the purchaser will feel that the bystander mocked him, and his initial feelings of disappointment will return in an exacerbated form.

Relatedly, suppose an evaluation of the item cannot be made without expert assessment. For example, take a diamond ring. Specialized knowledge of the carat, cut, color, and clarity of the stone is necessary to assess whether the buyer received fair value for his money. If the bystander has no expertise in these matters, he should not pretend that he does and should not say something specific such as "The color of the ring is outstanding." Although the intention of the bystander is to cheer up the dejected buyer, reliable knowledge regarding the quality of the color of the ring will come to the buyer's attention in due time. This reliable knowledge may directly contradict the bystander's assessment and indicate that the color of the ring is, in fact, of poor quality. When the bystander's lie comes to light, the bystander will no longer be viewed by the buyer as someone who cheered him up, but instead as one who mocked him. All the more so if the bystander was himself an expert. Accordingly, when the bystander's lie comes to light, the buyer's initial misgivings will return in an exacerbated form.

For the ignorant bystander, the only way to cheer up the dejected buyer is to give a generic compliment that cannot later be contradicted by objective facts. In the case of the diamond ring, the non-expert bystander should say: "I have no expertise in diamond rings, but I think it's a beautiful ring." That comment momentarily cheers up the buyer. Regardless of what facts come to light later, the purchaser will not subsequently think that the bystander was mocking him.

What proceeds from the above caveat is that Gerlenter did not fall short of the standards the Sages set for the bystander in the bad-purchase case. Since Gerlenter did not listen to Pelt's speech, any comment he makes may entangle him in a lie that offends Pelt. This is so because Gerlenter has every right to believe that Pelt will react to anything he says and fully expect a more specific follow-up comment from him. If in the course of even a very short exchange it becomes evident to Pelt that Gerlenter never listened to his speech, Pelt will regard Gerlenter's initial praise as a patronizing lie. Because Pelt will probably be insulted by the time the conversation ends, the best course of action for Gerlenter is to either sidetrack the discussion of Pelt's *derashah* or make no comment on it at all.

To be sure, Pelt was offended that Gerlenter did not return a compliment. But Pelt brought this insult on himself. Pelt should not try to elicit a compliment from someone who probably did not pay attention to his speech. Gerlenter is such a person. Fully aware that Gerlenter followed him to the podium, Pelt should take into account the possibility that Gerlenter did not pay attention to his speech because Gerlenter was absorbed in thought reviewing his own speech during Pelt's presentation. If Pelt was disappointed with Gerlenter's blasé comment on his speech, he has no one to blame but himself.

Let's now move on to the comments of Naomi Ziskind. Recall that Ziskind was busy plotting about the floral arrangements while Rabbi Pelt was delivering his keynote address. Although she had no idea what Pelt said, she still complimented him on his speech. Does Ziskind violate *hanuppah*? Consider that her false praise was devoid of any self-serving motive and was motivated entirely by the purpose of generating a long-lasting, pleasant memory of the event for the rabbi. Moreover, she said nothing specific about the content, structure, or style of the *derashah*. She said only that the *derashah* was "inspiring." Nothing in the objective world of reality would render her comment a falsehood and end up offending Pelt. Ziskind therefore does not violate *hanuppah*.

Let's now examine Marshall Grunder's comment. Grunder fabricated an excuse for not listening to the rabbi's speech by claiming that he could not hear the speech because there was so much noise at his table. Grunder is guilty of a double lie. In truth, there was no impediment to hearing Pelt's speech. Instead, Grunder was just not interested in listening to the *derashah*. Grunder's lie about the conversations at his table is a very hurtful lie because it projects his tablemates, some of whom are members of Rabbi Pelt's congregation, as rude and inconsiderate. Grunder's lie about the non-existent noise defames his tablemates and hence makes him guilty of *motzi shem ra* (defaming a fellow).[26] Moreover, with his double lie, Grunder not only projects himself as well intentioned, but *magnifies* this virtue by contrasting himself with his purportedly rude tablemates. Accordingly, Grunder also violates the prohibition against elevating oneself at the expense of the degradation of a fellow.[27]

There is an irony here. Back home in Dearborn Heights, Grunder is one of Rabbi Pelt's most avid listeners. To motivate Pelt to exert his best efforts to teach him Torah and inspire him to be a God-fearing person, Grunder is permitted to offer false praise to his rabbi. Accordingly, instead of extricating himself from the embarrassing situation of having not paid attention to the *derashah* by resorting to a very hurtful lie, Grunder could have accomplished the same goal with permissible *hanuppah*. Grunder should have said: "Well done, Rabbi. This time, no comment. Can't wait until you repeat the *derashah* in *shul*."

Of all the non-listeners who interacted with Rabbi Pelt at the Rye Hilton, the only one who admitted openly and straightforwardly that he did not pay attention to the *derashah* was Mordechai Kushta. Admitting the truth is a virtue. It is counted among the 48 attributes one must have to acquire the Torah.[28] Kushta's response therefore appears to be praiseworthy.

But consider that the crowd came to the Rye Hilton specifically to reinforce their commitment to the goals of Mesos, and the keynote address is designed to promote that objective. Mesos placed its confidence in Rabbi Pelt to deliver the keynote address. Moreover, Rabbi Pelt put much toil and effort into his preparation, not to mention the burdensome airplane trip he took with his wife from Dearborn Heights, Michigan. Accordingly, telling the rabbi that you did not pay attention to his *derashah* will undoubtedly hurt him and dash his legitimate expectations. Certainly, it is not legitimate for the rabbi to expect every person present to listen to his *derashah*. For example, legitimate non-listeners, in the opinion of this writer, are the speakers at the event who follow Rabbi Pelt in the program. These people should be excused because they are preoccupied with their own speeches. There are surely other special situations as well. But it is reasonable for Rabbi Pelt to expect that the typical person present will be a listener. Kushta's revelation to the rabbi that he did not pay any attention to the *derashah* is thus an unethical response and violates the prohibition against causing someone needless mental anguish (*ona'at devarim*).

Reinforcing the case for Kushta not to disclose to Pelt that he did not listen to his *derashah* is the circumstance that Kushta had already blurted out to everyone in earshot that he, indeed, listened to Gerlenter's speech and thought very highly of it. If Kushta had no trouble listening to Gerlenter's speech, why did he block out Pelt's keynote address? Kushta certainly has no duty to lie to Rabbi Pelt and offer him false praise for a *derashah* he did not listen to. For a person of Kushta's caliber, who is dedicated to truth-telling, uttering false praise, even of the generic variety, for a *derashah* he never paid attention to is fraught with the danger of getting himself entangled in self-evident lies that will offend Pelt. But the situation at hand is a clear-cut case where one has a duty to lie to avoid generating bad feelings and disrupting a fellow's inner peace. To that end, Kushta had available to him any number of undetectable lies to avoid violating *ona'at devarim*. Kushta could have said, for example: "Sorry, Rabbi. I arrived late and caught only a few lines of your *derashah*. I am therefore in no position to comment."

Finally, let's get to Shalom Friend's comment. Friend's cleverness apparently avoids both the violation of falsehood and the prohibition against causing someone needless mental anguish. Friend lets on in only an oblique and obscure manner that he did not listen to the *derashah*. But there's no denying that Friend owns up to the truth that he did not listen to the *derashah*. Moreover, the eagerness and reverence Friend shows in his desire to get a second chance to hear the *derashah* apparently assuages Pelt's ruffled feelings for missing out on the *derashah* the first time around.

Friend's cleverness, however, comes at a price! Making an offer with no intention to follow through is unethical. Such conduct violates the Torah's "good faith" imperative.[29] Accordingly, if Friend wants to make Pelt feel good by offering to hear the "long version" of his *derashah*, he must be prepared to follow through. It will come as no surprise that Pelt immediately took up Friend's request to hear the long version. Pelt got in but a few sentences by the time Friend's car arrived. Now, if Friend is serious about hearing the long version, he should not part with Pelt without first saying, "I'll call you in Dearborn Heights to get the rest." Friend doesn't know what he's getting into. The short version was 19 minutes. The long version, how long? It's anyone's guess.

Hanuppah and *Ona'at Devarim* at *Shabbat Probeh*

Before analyzing the moral propriety of the various comments Pelt received at *Shabbat probeh*, let's take note that the backdrop Pelt faced at Eden Commons was vastly different from the one he faced at the Rye Hilton. At the Rye Hilton, Pelt was there only to make a speech. At *Shabbat probeh*, by sharp contrast, Pelt's *derashah* was an aspect of his profile on which his candidacy would be judged.

Two implications proceed from the difference in settings between Eden Commons and the Rye Hilton. One is that anyone who wants to make Pelt feel good about the *derashah* he delivered at Eden Commons must realize that the rabbi will interpret a favorable comment as support for his candidacy, unless the comment is properly hedged. Second, because Pelt's candidacy is on the line at *Shabbat probeh*, one who comments on his *derashah* must be sensitive that the rabbi might take any and all comments as relating to his candidacy.

Once we recognize the tension Rabbi Pelt is operating under at Eden Commons, Max Glass' comment must be regarded as insensitive and probably an infraction of the *ona'at devarim* interdict. Can there be any doubt that as Rabbi Pelt interacts with the congregants at the *kiddush*, he is groping to hear favorable comments about his *derashah*? If Max Glass did not like the rabbi's *derashah*, or otherwise does not favor Pelt's candidacy, he certainly should not comment favorably on the *derashah* just to make the rabbi feel good. If Pelt is disappointed because Glass had no compliment for him, the rabbi's dashed expectations are not Glass' responsibility. But why exacerbate this tension and generate a feeling of inferiority for Pelt by praising Gerlenter? Glass further exacerbates Pelt's disappointment by mentioning to him that some members of Eden Commons preferred to hear Gerlenter over him. Because Rabbi Pelt will relate all the information about Gerlenter to his own situation and naturally feel a sense of inferiority, mentioning this information manifests insensitivity and violates *ona'at devarim*.

At both the Rye Hilton and Eden Commons, Naomi Ziskind's motivation in offering Rabbi Pelt false praise for his *derashah* was purely altruistic, to give the rabbi a boost. While her conduct at the Rye Hilton was praiseworthy, the same cannot be said of her comment at *Shabbat probeh*. Ziskind does not support the candidacy of Elimelekh Pelt. By complimenting the rabbi on his *derashah*, she creates a false impression that she does support his candidacy. Offering the insincere praise, albeit with good intentions, violates for Ziskind the *geneivat da'at* interdict.

In evaluating Lester Lefkowitz's critical comment regarding the length of Rabbi Pelt's *derashah*, a most relevant consideration is the instruction the search committee gave the rabbi regarding the parameters for the length of his *derashah*. We assume that the committee expressly told the rabbi that his *derashah* should not exceed 12 minutes, and that this instruction strongly reflects the preferences of the membership. Accordingly, the rabbi will surely be told that his *derashah* exceeded the time limit when he gets the official feedback from the search committee. Lefkowitz should reasonably assume that the search committee will convey their disappointment to Rabbi Pelt that he exceeded the time limit, and that the rabbi himself knows this criticism is coming. Lefkowitz's comment on the excessive length of the *derashah* is therefore not only entirely superfluous but has the effect of rubbing in the rabbi's *faux pas*. Lefkowitz hence violates *ona'at devarim*.

Let's now consider Kushta's comments. Kushta's devotion to truth-telling is at the expense of unnecessarily hurting Pelt's feelings. By reminding Pelt that he did not listen to his *derashah* at the Rye Hilton, Kushta repeats the *ona'at devarim* infraction he committed then. Kushta is also guilty of hypocritical conduct. At once, he shows that he is devoted to truth-telling, even when it results in hurting someone's feelings. But if Kushta is so devoted to truth-telling, why does he tell Pelt that the basic idea of his *derashah* can be found in the *Meshekh Hokhmah* when he himself is not 100% sure of this assertion? The giveaway that Kushta is not sure of himself is that he backs down when Harmoni suggests that Pelt's approach is indeed different from the *Meshekh Hokhmah*'s. If Kushta is not 100% sure of what he is saying, he has no right to upset Pelt by essentially telling him that the law of proper attribution called for him to mention in his *derashah* his debt to the *Meshekh Hokhmah*.

Can Harmoni's interjection be defended on the basis of the *darkhei shalom* principle? Consider that Harmoni's comment is motivated by an altruistic purpose. He desires to assuage Pelt's hurt feelings and end the tense feelings between Kushta and Pelt. But Harmoni makes his comment without having any knowledge of what the *Meshekh Hokhmah* actually said. Making a statement without knowing whether it is correct is one aspect of the prohibition against lying.[30] Although lying is permitted to promote peace, there is no carte blanche license here to lie. Recall that lying to end a conflict is not permitted when the lie used to achieve peace will be exposed with the passage of time and the conflict will re-emerge in an exacerbated form. Harmoni must consider the possibility that at the first opportunity, Kushta will look up the *Meshekh Hokhmah* and find that his recollection of what the commentator said on the topic was accurate. When Kushta realizes that he was right after all, he will bear hard feelings towards Harmoni for pretending to be knowledgeable when he was not. Pelt will probably also look up the *Meshekh Hokhmah* and feel foolish and dishonest for appearing to go along with Harmoni's defense. In the long run, instead of promoting peace, Harmoni's lie may well have the opposite effect of aggravating relationships all around.

Finally, let's consider Kalman Sunshine's comments. Sunshine's approach is essentially a political one. He feels that Pelt is the best candidate and is willing to use any argument, whether he really believes in it or not, to get his man elected.

Does Sunshine's approach fit into the *darkhei shalom* framework? This issue must be analyzed from both a short-term and a long-term perspective. Consider that before the election was held at Eden Commons, each congregant pledged to support the winning candidate. Accordingly, no one can claim that only his or her candidate will bring unity to the *shul*. So much for the short run, which can be called the "honeymoon period" for a rabbi. But once the honeymoon period is over, the *darkhei shalom* framework becomes a live issue. This is so because Sunshine believes that Pelt is the best rabbi for the synagogue. If Pelt is the best choice, the synagogue will achieve a higher level of harmony and unity under him compared to other candidates. Sunshine's use of a lie to advance Pelt's candidacy should therefore apparently be permitted under the *darkhei shalom* principle.

Whether Sunshine's political approach meets the *darkhei shalom* criterion turns on the issue of defining the state of affairs that justifies the use of a lie. One view in this matter is advanced by R. Menahem b. Solomon Meiri (*Meiri*, Perpignan, 1249–1316). In *Meiri*'s view, a lie motivated by *darkhei shalom* is legitimate only when the objective of the peacemaker is to end an actual conflict or prevent the eruption of a new conflict. If the goal of the peacemaker is merely to spare someone from an unpleasant feeling, the use of a lie to achieve this end is not permitted.[31] Sunshine's conduct does not comport with *Meiri*'s conceptualization of *darkhei shalom* because his conduct is not directed at ending a conflict in Eden Commons.

Meiri's restrictive view of the *darkhei shalom* principle appears not to be followed by R. Shlomo Zalman Auerbach. In R. Auerbach's view, it is permissible for an individual to tell a father that he has a beautiful child even though the speaker does not believe what he says.[32] We assume that such conduct is permissible only if the speaker's motive is to strengthen the bond of love the father has for his child. If the motive of the speaker is to curry favor with the father, telling the father that his child is beautiful is *hanuppah* and therefore prohibited. What seems to proceed from R. Auerbach's ruling is that a *darkhei shalom* lie is permissible even if the motive of the speaker is not to end conflict, but instead only to lift someone's spirits.

The above understanding of R. Auerbach's ruling, however, is not accurate. R. Auerbach rationalizes his ruling on the basis that the father certainly agrees that his child is beautiful.[33] R. Auerbach hence follows the rationalization of *Maharal* et al. of the bad-purchase case. In *Maharal*'s view, falsehood applies only to mischaracterizing an objective reality. But with respect to an aesthetic judgment, it is a matter of individual taste. Proclaiming every bride beautiful and gracious hence does not violate the prohibition against falsehood. To be sure, in specific instances, the formula will run counter to popular sentiment. Nevertheless, the description presumably conforms to the bridegroom's feelings; if the bridegroom did not find his bride beautiful and charming, he presumably would not have married her. What constitutes beauty is a matter of judgment. Pronouncing the bride beautiful and gracious does not therefore constitute a mischaracterization of reality, notwithstanding majority opinion to the contrary. Similarly, approving the buyer's bad purchase does not amount to falsehood, because a sales transaction creates a presumption of buyer satisfaction.[34]

Once it is recognized that false praise in the bad-purchase case is rooted in the definition of falsehood from the perspective of the person who is offered the false praise, *Maharal*'s understanding of the bad-purchase case provides no basis for Sunshine to promote Pelt's candidacy based on arguments he himself does not believe in. Because Sunshine's arguments are directed at his fellow members of Eden Commons, truth must be defined by *objective* criteria, rather than in the realm of aesthetics.

Conclusion

Our glimpse into *Shabbat probeh* at Eden Commons shows that several of the favorable comments Pelt received were impermissible lies. These included comments by Ziskind, Harmoni, and Sunshine. Had those congregants not engaged in impermissible lies, perhaps the impression Pelt would have gathered about his chances of landing the position of Senior Rabbi at Eden Commons would have far better reflected reality, and the Pelts would not have been so disappointed when Rabbi Pelt was turned down for the job. For that matter, had there not been so much *hanuppah* at the Rye Hilton, Pelt would have never applied for the position in the first place.

Notes

1. At *Shabbat probeh*, Rabbi Pelt's theme was that although the Torah formally excludes any Jew who is not a descendant of Aaron from the position of *Kohen Gadol* (High Priest), the Torah gives each Jew an opportunity to fulfill his or her fantasy to become a *Kohen Gadol* by becoming a *nazir*. When a Jew becomes a *nazir*, he or she will experience first-hand that there is no reason to be jealous of the *Kohen Gadol*. What the *Kohen Gadol* is all about is not pomp and splendor, but rather the assumption of an awesome level of responsibility. Kushta felt that the basic idea for Pelt's theme can be found in the work of R. Meir Simhah ha-Kohen of Dvinsk (*Meshekh Hokhmah*, Latvia, 1843–1926) on Numbers 6:8. I suggest that you look up the *Meshekh Hokhmah* and decide for yourself.
2. *Sanhedrin* 89a.
3. Rabbi Pelt disagreed with his wife on this point. As Pelt put it, "What counts is not how they treat us *before* the *derashah*, but how they treat us *after* the *derashah*."
4. R. Jacob b. Asher (*Tur*, Spain, 1270–1343), *Tur, Even ha-Ezer* 65; R. Joseph Caro (Safed, 1488–1575), *Shulhan Arukh, Even ha-Ezer* 65:1; R. Jehiel Michal Epstein (Belorus, 1829–1908), *Arukh ha-Shulhan, Even ha-Ezer* 65:1.
5. *Rashash, Ketubbot* 17a.
6. R. Israel Meir ha-Kohen Kagan, *Sefer Hafetz Hayyim, Hilkhot Rekhilut* 9:12.
7. For two alternative explanations, see R. Judah Loew b. Bezalel (*Maharal*, Prague, ca. 1525–1609), *Hiddushei Aggadot Maharal mi-Prague*, vol. 1, *Ketubbot* 16b, and R. Nethanel b. Naftali Tzvi Weil (Germany, 1687–1769), *Korban Netanel* to R. Asher b. Jehiel (*Rosh*, Germany, ca. 1250–1327), *Rosh, Ketubbot* 2:2, n. 4.
8. *Ritva, Ketubbot* 16b.
9. For an explicit application of the notion that the *darkhei shalom* principle can refer to inner peace, see R. Jacob b. Joseph Reischer (Galicia, 1661–1733), *Iyyun Yaakov, Sanhedrin* 43a, to Jacob b. Solomon ibn Habib (Spain, ca. 1460–1516), *Ein Yaakov*.
10. *Pesahim* 113b; *Bava Metzia* 49b.
11. Let's take note that *hanuppah* (based on Numbers 35:33) comes in several forms. The most serious violation entails various nuances of praising or condoning an evildoer. In his treatment of *hanuppah*, R. Jonah b. Abraham Gerondi (*Rabbeinu Yonah*, Spain, ca. 1200–1263) identifies nine different levels of severity in the violation of this prohibition. *Sha'arei Teshuvah* 3:187. However, the prohibition also extends to offering "false praise" to someone who is not wicked. Cf. R. Eliezer Papo (Bulgaria, 1785–1828), *Pela Yoetz*, *helek* 1, *ot* 8, s.v. "*hanuppah*."
12. R. Shlomo Zalman Auerbach and R. Shalom Yosef Elyashiv, quoted in R. Yaakov Yehezkiyah Fisch, *Titen Emet le-Yaakov*, vol. 1 (Jerusalem, 1981), 5:46, pp. 90–91.
13. R. Kagan, *Sefer Hafetz Hayyim, Hilkhot Rekhilut* 1:8.
14. R. Nahum Yavruv, *Niv Sefatayyim, Hilkhot Issurei Sheker*, 4th ed. (Jerusalem, 2005), *helek* 1, *kelal* 2:8, p. 33.
15. Ibid., *kelal* 2:25, p. 40. R. Yavruv's thesis is apparently disputed by R. Jacob b. Joseph Reischer. R. Reischer's opposition emerges from his commentary on the following Talmudic story at *Yevamot* 63a:

> Rav was constantly tormented by his wife. If he told her "Prepare me lentils," she would prepare him small peas; [and if he asked for] small peas, she prepared him lentils. When his son, Hiyya, grew up, he gave her [his father's instructions] in reverse. "Your mother," Rav remarked to him, "has improved!" "It was I," the other replied, "who reversed [your orders] to her." "This is what people say," the first said to him, "'Your own offspring teaches you reason;' however, you must not continue to do so, for it is said, 'They have taught their tongue to speak lies, they weary themselves' [Jeremiah 9:4]."

Why Rav objected to Hiyya's conduct requires explanation. Insofar as Hiyya made use of lies to promote domestic harmony between his parents, his conduct should have been regarded as an application of the *darkhei shalom* principle and hence praiseworthy. Addressing himself to this issue, R. Reischer posits that Rav's objection is based on the assumption that his wife will eventually catch on to Hiyya's scheme. *Iyyun Yaakov*, *Yevamot* 63a.

R. Yavruv mentions R. Reischer's solution and disagrees with him. Since Hiyya's ploy will temporarily relieve his father from his mother's torment, the ploy should be legitimate even though it does not offer the prospect of permanent relief for his father.

In the opinion of this writer, R. Reischer's solution is consistent with R. Yavruv's approach. Consider Hiyya did not address the root cause of his parents' strife. His solution for putting an end to the torment his mother was causing his father was therefore merely a Band-Aid approach. Because Hiyya's ploy in no way addressed the root cause of the problem, when his mother would catch on to the clever ploy, she would feel that Hiyya took his father's side. Discovery of the ploy therefore may result in exacerbating the mother's anger and resentment.

In the text, we have adopted the position of R. Yavruv in this matter.

16. R. Solomon b. Jehiel Luria, *Yam shel Shelomoh*, *Yevamot* 6:46.
17. R. Yavruv, *Niv Sefatayyim*, *kelal* 2:26, p. 42.
18. Leviticus 25:17; Mishnah, *Bava Metzia* 4:10; R. Isaac b. Jacob Alfasi (*Rif*, Algeria, 1013–1103), *Rif*, *Bava Metzia* 58b; *Rosh*, *Bava Metzia* 4:22; *Tur*, *Hoshen Mishpat* 228; *Shulhan Arukh*, *Hoshen Mishpat* 228:1; *Arukh ha-Shulhan*, *Hoshen Mishpat* 228:1.
19. *Midrash Yelammedenu*, quoted in R. Simeon ha-Darshan (Frankfurt, 13th cent.), *Yalkut Shimoni*, *Kuntras Aharon*, reprinted in *Yalkut Shimoni ha-Shalem* (Jerusalem: Wagschal, 2003), p. 213, s.v. "*va-yigash elav Yehudah*" (Genesis 48:18). See also R. Elijah de Vidas (Hebron, 1518–1592), *Reishit Hokhmah*, *Sha'ar ha-Kedushah* 12.
20. Exodus 22:24.
21. R. David Ariav, *Le-Re'akha Kamokha*, vol. 1, *Halakhot u-Ve'urim be-Mitzvot*: *Lo Tahmod*, *Lo Tit'aveh*, *Lo Tahanifu*, *Issur Geneivat Da'at*, *Lo Tikallel*, *Lo Tikkom ve-Lo Tittor* (Jerusalem, 2000), 124, n. 83.
22. It should be noted that in *Midrash Yelammedenu*'s treatment of permissible *hanuppah*, another reverse case is omitted: Is a *rebbe* permitted to use *hanuppah* to motivate his student to learn Torah? Again, if the rationale behind the permissibility for a student to engage in *hanuppah* vis-à-vis his *rebbe* is the achievement of *talmud Torah* (learning of Torah), *hanuppah* should be permitted for the *rebbe* vis-à-vis his student for the same reason. See ibid., 130, ¶ 12. In his treatment of the latter case, R. Ariav finds a source at *Avot de-Rabbi Natan* that permits the conduct. See ibid., n. 91 (citing *Avot de-Rabbi Natan* 26:6).
23. *Hullin* 94a.
24. *Hullin* 94a; *Rif*, ad loc.; Maimonides (*Rambam*, Egypt, 1135–1204), *Mishneh Torah*, *De'ot* 2:6; *Rosh*, *Hullin* 7:18; *Tur*, *Hoshen Mishpat* 228; *Shulhan Arukh*, *Hoshen Mishpat* 228:6; *Arukh ha-Shulhan*, *Hoshen Mishpat* 228:3.
25. R. Joshua b. Alexander ha-Kohen Falk (*Sema*, Poland, 1555–1614), *Sema* to *Shulhan Arukh*, *Hoshen Mishpat* 228:6, n. 8.
26. The Biblical source for the prohibition against defamation is disputed at *Ketubbot* 46a. R. Elazar derives the warning from the verse: "You shall not go about as a talebearer among your people" (Leviticus 19:16). R. Natan derives the admonishment from the verse: "When you go out as a camp against your enemies, you must avoid everything evil" (Deuteronomy 23:10).

27. R. Yose b. Hanina, Palestinian Talmud, *Hagigah* 10a. The relevant Hebrew term is *mitkabbed be-kalon shel havero*. A person who acts in such a manner is said to lose his share in the World to Come.
28. *Avot* 6:6.
29. Abaye, *Bava Metzia* 49a. Abaye derives the "good faith" imperative from the following Biblical prohibition against false weights and measures: "Just (*tzedek*) balances, just weights, a just *ephah*, and a just *hin* you shall have" (Leviticus 19:36). Since the *hin* is a measure of smaller capacity than the *ephah*, its mention is apparently superfluous; if accuracy is required of a large capacity, it is certainly required in measures of small capacity. This apparent superfluity leads Abaye to connect *hin* with the Aramaic word for "yes" (i.e., *hen*). Abaye then interprets the use of the term *hin* to mean: Be certain that your "yes" is *tzedek* (sincere) and (by extension) be certain that your "no" is *tzedek* (sincere). If an individual makes a commitment or an offer, he should fully intend to carry it out.
30. R. Yavruv, *Niv Sefatayyim*, *kelal* 1:3, pp. 15–16.
31. *Meiri*, *Beit ha-Behirah*, *Yevamot* 63a.
32. R. Shlomo Zalman Auerbach, quoted in R. Fisch, *Titen Emet le-Yaakov*, 6:75, p. 130.
33. Ibid.
34. *Maharal*, *Hiddushei Aggadot Maharal mi-Prague*, vol. 1, *Ketubbot* 16b; R. Samuel Eliezer b. Judah ha-Levi Edels (*Maharsha*, Poland, 1555–1631), *Ketubbot* 16b.

CHAPTER 2

The Sale of the Birthright and the Bilateral Monopoly Model

Introduction

In the teaching of our Sages, Jacob personifies the character trait of *emet* (truth).[1] One of the challenges in understanding Jacob's character is that the Biblical accounts of a number of episodes of his life appear to be inconsistent with the attribute of *emet*. One such instance is the Biblical description of how Jacob acquired the birthright from his twin brother, Esau:

> Once when Jacob was making a stew, Esau came in from the fields famished. Whereupon Esau said to Jacob: "Let me swallow some of that red pottage, for I am exhausted[2] and famished!"[3] . . . Said Jacob: "First sell, as this day, your birthright to me." Said Esau: "Look, I am going to die; of what use is a birthright to me?" Said Jacob: "First give me your oath, as this day." So he gave him his oath, and sold his birthright to Jacob. Jacob then gave Esau bread and stewed lentils, and he ate and drank, got up and left; thus did Esau disdain the birthright. (Genesis 25:29–34).

Should we regard the sale of the birthright as a "fair deal" entailing a net gain for both Jacob and Esau? No. Mutual net gain can be presumed only in the context of a *voluntary* exchange. Specifically, if *A* and *B* enter into a transaction on a voluntary basis, *A* would not give up something to *B* unless *A* believed that he was receiving something more valuable in return from *B*. Similarly, *B* would not give up something to *A* unless *B* believed that he was receiving something more valuable in return from *A*. In the sale of the birthright, by contrast, mutual net gain cannot be presumed. Given Esau's exhausted and famished state when he sold the birthright, the sale should be regarded as *coercive* from the standpoint of Esau. How can conducting a coercive transaction be reconciled with the attribute of *emet*?

Consider that the birthright must inhere in the person of either Jacob or Esau, and cannot be transferred to anyone else.[4] Jacob's negotiation with Esau for the birthright therefore fits into the economic model of bilateral monopoly. The salient feature of this model is that only one seller and one prospective buyer exist for the item at hand. Accordingly, neither party can claim that a better opportunity was available at the time the transaction took place. The outcome of the negotiation will therefore depend on the relative leverage each party perceives he has over his opposite number.

From the perspective of economic theory, the birthright sale fits into the bilateral monopoly model. The distinctive feature of the birthright sale is that leverage was lopsidedly in the hands of Jacob.

Notwithstanding the ethically indifferent attitude economic theory would take with respect to the birthright sale, for Jewish law, the issue of fairness remains. In a commercial transaction, the price terms of an agreement are subject to the law of *ona'ah* (price fraud). Moreover, one may question the propriety of Jacob playing a waiting game and strategically making his bid for the birthright when Esau was exhausted and famished. Does this not constitute exploitative conduct on Jacob's part?

The Bilateral Monopoly Case in Jewish Law

Our purpose here will be to explore the sale of the birthright from the standpoint of fairness of price and the apparent use of strategic conduct on the part of Jacob. Let's begin with the issue of fairness of price within the context of the bilateral monopoly model. The relevant case here is the following *Baraita*:

> It has been taught, R. Judah b. Bathyra [mid-1st. cent.] said: The sale of a horse, sword and buckler on [the field of][5] battle are not subject to *ona'ah* (price fraud) because one's very life is dependent upon them.[6]

To see why the battlefield transaction falls within the ambit of the bilateral monopoly model, we need only note that under the life-threatening conditions of the battlefield, neither the buyer nor the seller will seek an alternative to the opportunity at hand. Consequently, the certainty that the seller's asking price exceeds the ordinary price for the item will not cause the buyer to withdraw. Likewise, certainty that the buyer's bid is below the price at which the item ordinarily trades will not cause the seller to withdraw. Since there is no alternative for either party other than the transaction at hand, the relative perceptions of leverage will determine the outcome of the negotiation.

Whether R. Judah's ruling represents mainstream Talmudic thought is a matter of dispute among the early decisors. R. Hai b. Sherira (*Hai Gaon*, Pumbedita, 939–1038)[7] and R. Isaac b. Jacob Alfasi (*Rif*, Algeria, 1013–1103)[8] rule that R. Judah's opinion represents a minority view and should therefore be rejected. R. Hananel b. Hushiel (*Rabbeinu Hananel*, North Africa, 11th cent.), however, rules in accordance with R. Judah.[9]

Note that the ethics of the battlefield case turn on whether the law of *ona'ah* applies in the setting of a battlefield.[10] Let's proceed to identify the ethical norm of *ona'ah* and the rationale behind it.

One of the Torah's central tenets for the marketplace is the prohibition against price fraud: "When you make a sale to your fellow or when you buy from the hand of your fellow, do not victimize one another" (Leviticus 25:14).

The law of *ona'ah* prohibits an individual from concluding a transaction at a price that is more favorable to himself than some reference price. Depending on how widely the price of the subject transaction departs from the reference price, the injured party may have recourse to void or adjust the transaction.

The Sages identified three degrees of *ona'ah*. Provided the price discrepancy is assessed to be within the margin of error,[11] the plaintiff's right to void the transaction is recognized when the difference between the sales price and the reference price is more than one-sixth.[12] We shall refer to this level of *ona'ah* violation as first-degree *ona'ah*. The plaintiff's rights here consist only of the right to cancel the transaction; the plaintiff does not have the right to keep the transaction intact and receive a price reduction for the *ona'ah* involved.[13]

Second-degree *ona'ah* occurs when the difference between the sales price and the reference price is exactly one-sixth. In that case, neither of the parties may void the transaction as a result of the price discrepancy. The plaintiff is, however, entitled to full restitution of the *ona'ah*.[14]

Finally, third-degree *ona'ah* occurs when the sales price differs from the reference price by less than one-sixth. Here, the transaction not only remains binding, but the plaintiff also has no legal claim to the price differential.[15]

Elsewhere we have demonstrated that the reference price for an *ona'ah* claim is nothing other than the competitive norm. Defining the reference price as the competitive norm makes the *ona'ah* complaint an opportunity cost claim. We demonstrated that the *ona'ah* claim is not just a claim of ignorance of the market norm at the time the transaction took pace. Instead, the law of *ona'ah* grants a market participant the right to transact on the basis of the competitive norm. This right is not lost unless the plaintiff signals that he waives the right.[16]

Once we recognize that *ona'ah* is an opportunity cost claim, the relevant marketplace for adjudicating the claim should be demarcated by the rule of *mekomo ve-sha'to* (lit., its place and its time). Pertaining to the liquidation procedure for property dedicated to the Sanctuary, the *mekomo ve-sha'to* rule provides that the sale of such property must be conducted both in the geographic area and the time period in which the dedication was made (*ein la-hekdesh ela mekomo ve-sha'to*).[17]

The *mekomo ve-sha'to* rule, according to Nahmanides (*Ramban*, Spain, 1194–1270)[18] and R. Yom Tov Ishbili (*Ritva*, Spain, ca. 1250–1330),[19] applies not only to the Sanctuary, but to monetary matters generally. Explicitly positing the *mekomo ve-sha'to* rule in connection with the law of *ona'ah* is R. Abraham David Wahrmann (Ukraine, ca. 1771–1841).[20] On a practical level, *mekomo* says that the reference marketplace for adjudicating an *ona'ah* claim is confined to the geographic area where the plaintiff would realistically engage in market search for alternatives. Similarly, *sha'to* says that the reference time period is confined to the window of time surrounding the transaction when supply and demand conditions are the same as when the transaction occurred.[21]

Proceeding from the above understanding of the underpinning of an *ona'ah* claim is the following explanation of the view that validates an *ona'ah* claim in the battlefield case: Crucial here is the notion that the market norm is always the reference point for judging the fairness of the price terms of a transaction. *Mekomo ve-sha'to* says only that if a market norm exists at the time the transaction takes place, we limit the reference price to the time frame and geographic area of the transaction. If, however, no market norm exists at the time of the transaction, the ordinary price that prevails under an organized marketplace is used as the reference price.

R. Judah, who throws out an *ona'ah* claim in the battlefield case, rejects the notion that the market norm is the exclusive determinant of fairness of price. To be sure, if a market norm exists at the time of the transaction, the market norm determines the fairness of the transaction. If, however, no market norm exists at the time of the transaction, the principle of *mekomo ve-sha'to* provides that the market norm is no longer the arbiter of fairness of price. Instead, according to R. Judah, the judgment of whether the plaintiff achieved subjective equivalence becomes the arbiter of fairness of price.

Bolstering the contention that subjective equivalence enters into the adjudication of an *ona'ah* claim can be seen from R. Asher b. Jehiel's (*Rosh*, Germany, 1250–1327) analysis of third-degree *ona'ah*. Noting the absence of any provision for legal redress in cases of third-degree *ona'ah*, R. Asher speculates whether it might be permissible, in the first instance, to contract into third-degree *ona'ah*. Pivotal to the resolution of this question, in R. Asher's view, is the definition of market price. Is market price to be understood as a single value, or instead as the range of prices that deviate less than one-sixth from the competitive norm?

R. Asher defends the range-of-prices view on the basis of both demand and supply considerations. Consider that if a buyer particularly likes the item at hand, he may be willing to pay a little more than what he believes the competitive norm is. Likewise, if a seller is in need of cash, he may deliberately agree to sell his merchandise at a price somewhat below what he believes the market norm is.[22] Adopting the range-of-prices view leads to the conclusion that third-degree *ona'ah* is not price fraud at all.

Subscription to the view that the reference price in an *ona'ah* claim is a single value rather than a range of values, however, leads to the conclusion that knowledge of the market norm prohibits either party from contracting into a price agreement that is even slightly more favorable to himself than the norm. The absence of legal redress for third-degree *ona'ah* would then be explained by the presumption that when the degree of *ona'ah* involved is of such a relatively small amount, the plaintiff waives his claim to restitution. This presumption follows from our inability to fix the value of the article sold—while some experts would insist that *ona'ah* occurred, others would just as vehemently deny it.[23] Because the experts are divided on whether *ona'ah* occurred and, if it did, by how much, we may safely presume that the victim of this possible price fraud waives his rights to restitution.[24]

In throwing out an *ona'ah* claim in the battlefield case on the basis of the judgment that the plaintiff achieved subjective equivalence, R. Judah finds precedent in the circumstance that third-degree *ona'ah* cases are thrown out, according to one approach in R. Asher, based on this self-same judgment that the plaintiff achieved subjective equivalence.

We should note that Halakhah adopts the view that it is prohibited to deliberately conduct a transaction that one knows entails third-degree *ona'ah*.[25] What follows from this rule is that the judgment that the plaintiff achieved subjective equivalence plays no role in adjudicating *ona'ah* cases. This leads to the proposition that mainstream Halakhah rejects R. Judah's view.

Based on the discussion above, the law of *ona'ah* would not invalidate the birthright sale. Unlike the battlefield case, where a market norm for the items traded under ordinary conditions can be identified, no such norm can be identified for the sale of the birthright. Since no market norm can be identified for the sale of the birthright under any conditions, the opinion that upholds an *ona'ah* claim in the battlefield case would deny an *ona'ah* claim in the birthright case. In addition, given Esau's exhausted and famished condition at the time he sold the birthright, he surely achieved subjective equivalence in the sale. Accordingly, R. Judah's view, which denies an *ona'ah* claim in the battlefield case on the basis that the plaintiff received subjective equivalence, would similarly deny an *ona'ah* claim in the birthright case.

The Ethics of Engaging in Strategic Behavior

The basic issue that Jacob's strategic conduct presents is the ethical propriety of springing an offer on Esau to buy the birthright when Esau was in an exhausted and famished state. Does this conduct not amount to maneuvering Esau into a situation where Esau would feel coerced to accept the offer to sell his birthright for a pittance? No. The economic concept of reservation price will clarify this point.

Reservation price is the minimum offer a party to a negotiation would accept. Characterizing Jacob's conduct as maneuvering Esau into a coercive situation would be valid only if *absent* his famished state, Esau would value the birthright at a price in excess of a stew of lentils. But let's not lose sight of what Esau said just after Jacob made his offer: "Look, I am going to die; of what use is a birthright to me?" (Genesis 25:32). R. Solomon b. Isaac (*Rashi*, France, 1040–1105) understands this to mean that Esau inquired about the nature of the sacrificial service.

In response, Jacob explained that several prohibitions and death penalties are associated with improper service, such as performing the Temple service after drinking wine. Esau then replied, "I am going to die through the birthright. If so, what is there in it that I would want?"[26]

R. Hezekiah b. Manoah (*Hizkuni*, France, mid-13th cent.) understands Esau's words "Look, I am going to die" as conveying the sentiment that the main benefit of the birthright is the right to inherit the Land of Israel. Since Esau was very familiar with the Divine promise that the descendants of Abraham would not inherit the Land of Israel until approximately 400 years later, and Esau did not expect to be alive then, Esau was content to accept a mere stew of lentils in exchange for the birthright. Alternatively, what Esau conveyed with his words "Look, I am going to die" was that the birthright had value to him only if he outlived his father. But given his dangerous preoccupation with hunting, Esau felt that he might not outlive his father and therefore was willing to sell his birthright for a pittance.[27]

These various interpretations of Esau's words signify that Esau's declaration "Look, I am going to die" conveyed that *absent* his exhausted and famished state, the birthright had a zero, or perhaps even negative, value for him.

Let's note that after the birthright sale, the Torah testifies: "Jacob gave Esau bread and stewed lentils, and he ate and drank, got up and left; thus did Esau despise the birthright" (Genesis 25:34). The clear message here, points out R. Hayyim b. Moses Attar (*Or ha-Hayyim*, Israel, 1696–1743), is that the zero or negative value Esau attached to the birthright reflected his attitude toward the birthright not only when he desperately needed the lentil stew to relieve his famished condition, but also when he was operating under normal and calm conditions.[28]

Now, if under normal conditions, Esau's reservation price for selling the birthright exceeded the value of a stew of lentils, Jacob's strategic conduct would be characterized as maneuvering Esau into a coercive situation to sell the birthright below the value that Esau would usually assign to the birthright absent his famished condition. But since Esau's reservation price for selling the birthright under normal conditions was zero or negative, Jacob's conduct should not be regarded as a maneuver to box Esau into a coercive situation. Instead, Jacob's conduct should be viewed only as a means of *distracting* Esau from focusing on Jacob's reservation price for the sale so that the sale could be concluded based on Esau's own reservation price.

Springing an Offer or Seizing an Opportunity?

Let's take note that Esau's reputation as a wicked person became public knowledge when Esau and Jacob reached the age of thirteen.[29] But Jacob's offer to buy the birthright from Esau took place in the aftermath of the death of their grandfather, Abraham, which occurred a full two years later. The stew of lentils that

Jacob gave Esau in exchange for the birthright was the traditional mourner's food Jacob had prepared for his father, Isaac.[30] The question then arises: Since Jacob was motivated to pursue the birthright only because he believed that Esau was unworthy to assume the responsibilities that accompany the privilege of the birthright,[31] why did Jacob not take the initiative and make his offer as soon as Esau's reputation as a wicked person became a public matter?

One possibility is to view Jacob's inaction as manifesting strategic conduct on his part to secure the birthright at the lowest possible price. To be sure, Jacob was certain that Esau placed no value on the birthright. But this circumstance in no way guaranteed that Jacob could buy the birthright for a pittance. Jacob's reputation as both a student of Torah and one not adept in deception[32] should have led Esau to believe that he could exact an exorbitant price for transferring the birthright to Jacob, who would prize its possession and, to boot, had no guile as a negotiator. Moreover, initiating negotiations for the birthright would place Jacob at a disadvantage because it would communicate to Esau an anxiousness and urgency to acquire the birthright. Based on these considerations, it might appear that Jacob deliberately played a waiting game. The right moment then presented itself when Jacob found Esau in an exhausted and famished state. As soon as this moment arrived, Jacob sprung his offer on Esau to sell him the birthright for a stew of lentils.[33]

We reject this approach because it does not flow naturally from the Sages' character portraits of Jacob and Esau. Let us see why:

Expounding on the Biblical description of Esau as an *ish tzayid* (a man who knows hunting) (Genesis 25:27), *Midrash Rabbah* explicates: "He knew how to ensnare and to deceive his father with his mouth. He would ask him: 'Father, how do we tithe salt and straw?'" His father would thus be under the impression that Esau was meticulous about the fulfillment of the commandments.[34]

In addition to being a deceiver, Esau was filled with self-righteousness. In this regard, *Yalkut Shimoni* depicts Esau in the World to Come as wrapping himself up in a prayer shawl and sitting himself down right next to Jacob. Esau's delusion that he is equal to Jacob is smashed when God Himself expels Esau from the exalted place he abrogated for himself and thrusts Esau into the pit of destruction.[35]

Jacob, on the other hand, is depicted by the Sages as the prototype of the person who has "no slander on his tongue" (Psalms 15:3).[36] This description indicates that Jacob meticulously adhered to the prohibition against *lashon ha-ra* (making an evil but true report).

Given the contrasting character traits of Jacob and Esau, it is understandable why Jacob did not report to Isaac the rumors of Esau's evil conduct. The prohibition against *lashon ha-ra* prevented Jacob from doing this. This is so because one aspect of these laws is that *A* is forbidden to report *B*'s evil conduct to *C* when *A* has no first-hand knowledge of *B*'s misconduct.[37] Accordingly, since Jacob's knowledge of Esau's misconduct was only second-hand, it would have been forbidden for him to report this misconduct to Isaac. Moreover, it would have been forbidden for Jacob to use the second-hand information in a manner that would cause harm to Esau.[38]

The practical import of the impermissibility for Jacob to use second-hand information against Esau is that Jacob was required to refrain from making an offer to buy the birthright. This is so because Esau, as Isaac's first-born son, was entitled to the birthright unless he proved himself unworthy to assume the responsibilities it entailed.[39] However, on the day Abraham died, Esau's declarations gave Jacob *first-hand* information that Esau was not worthy of the birthright. The *Midrash* underscores this point by connecting the words "And Jacob boiled a stew" (Genesis 25:29) with the words "Jacob said [to Esau], 'Sell, as this day, your birthright to me'" (Genesis 25:31). The connection is that Esau questioned why Jacob was preparing a stew of lentils. In reaction to Jacob's response that Abraham had died and the stew of lentils was the traditional mourner's food he had prepared for Isaac, Esau went into a tirade. He proclaimed that if the righteous Abraham died, there is no Divine reward for fulfilling God's commandments and there will be no resurrection of the dead.[40] Hearing *directly* from Esau that Esau was a non-believer, Jacob set out immediately to make an offer for the birthright.

Let's take note that as a proof text to support the notion that Jacob was the prototype of the person who has "no slander on his tongue," the Talmud cites the verse: "Perhaps my father will feel me and I shall seem to him as a deceiver" (Genesis 27:12). Consider that this verse relates to the episode where Rebecca instructed Jacob to masquerade as Esau and thereby secure for himself the blessings meant for Esau. Commenting on this dictum, R. Samuel Eliezer b. Judah ha-Levi Edels (*Maharsha*, Poland, 1555–1631) understands Jacob's objection to his mother's scheme to be based on the fear that if Isaac discovered the masquerade, Jacob would be forced to justify his actions by repeating the evil talk he had heard about Esau.[41]

We take both the proof text and R. Edels' comments as indicating that Jacob's encounter with the temptation to speak *lashon ha-ra* was not limited to the masquerade incident. No. Jacob showed his mettle earlier when he refused to take the initiative to buy the birthright based on the second-hand information he had heard about Esau. Jacob's most difficult test in resisting the temptation of *lashon ha-ra* came, however, when he had first-hand information about Esau but did not want to use the information as the justification for the masquerade.

We need not venture far to theorize why Jacob did not want to use first-hand information to condemn Esau. Isaac considered Esau a righteous person. Accordingly, it stands to reason that Isaac would make no judgment against Esau that he was unworthy of the birthright until he would hear Esau's reaction. Given Esau's self-righteousness, can there be any doubt that Esau would vehemently deny any accusations against him and even turn the tables by relating that Jacob played a "waiting game" and timed his offer to buy the birthright for a stew of lentils only after he found Esau in a famished state?

The upshot of the above analysis is that Jacob's inaction for two years in not pursuing the acquisition of the birthright was not motivated by the hope that the framework for the negotiations with Esau might become more favorable and allow him to strike a better deal. To be sure, Jacob heard rumors that Esau was a wicked person. But as an exemplar of adherence to the laws of *lashon ha-ra*, Jacob would not act on rumors alone to launch an initiative to buy the birthright from Esau. It was not until Esau made statements directly to Jacob demonstrating that Esau was not worthy of the birthright that Jacob pursued the birthright. This moment of truth about Esau happened to coincide with the circumstance that Esau was famished. Jacob's purchase of the birthright hence did not manifest the execution of a plan to make an offer to Esau for the birthright when Esau was famished. Instead, the timing of the purchase reflected only Jacob's desire to buy the birthright as soon as he was certain that Esau was not worthy of holding it.

Conclusion

We have analyzed the sale of the birthright from the standpoint of its price terms, consisting of a stew of lentils, and what appears to be strategic conduct on the part of Jacob in acquiring the birthright. From the perspective of fairness of price, the law of *ona'ah* would not modify or overturn the transaction because no objective market value is available to serve as a reference price for the transaction. Moreover, there should be no ethical objection to Jacob's strategic conduct because Esau's reservation price for the birthright *absent* his famished state was either zero or negative. Accordingly, Jacob's strategic behavior of springing his offer on Esau to buy the birthright when he found Esau in a famished state should not be viewed as timing his offer to exploit Esau's weak condition. Instead, Jacob's conduct can be viewed as a means of distracting Esau to induce him to focus on the zero or negative value that he assigned to the birthright rather than on the value that Jacob assigned to the birthright.

More fundamentally, given that Jacob is cited as the prototype of the person who has "no slander on his tongue," it stands to reason that Jacob did not engage in strategic conduct to obtain the birthright for a pittance. Quite to the contrary, Jacob had no interest in acquiring the birthright until he became aware through Esau's own declarations that Esau was unqualified to carry out the responsibilities of the birthright. Because Esau's famished state spurred him on to make declarations indicating that he was unworthy of the birthright, the motivational force to acquire the birthright and the opportunity to buy it for a pittance came together for Jacob at the same moment. Accordingly, Jacob seized the opportunity that was thrust upon him. Jacob's conduct was therefore not opportunistic, but was instead driven by a desire to remove the birthright privilege from unworthy hands as soon as possible.

Notes

1. Nahmanides (*Ramban*, Spain, 1194–1270), *Ha-Emunah ve-ha-Bitahon*, ch. 15; R. Bahya b. Asher (*Rabbeinu Behaye*, Saragossa, d. 1340) to Genesis 25:27, s.v. "*ve-Yaakov ish tam.*"
2. According to R. Solomon b. Isaac (*Rashi*, France, 1040–1105), Esau was exhausted from committing murder. *Rashi* to Genesis 25:29 s.v. "*ve-hu ayef.*" Cf. R. Hezekiah b. Manoah (*Hizkuni*, France, mid-13th cent.), *Hizkuni* to Genesis 25:29 (attributing the exhaustion to Esau's hunting activities).
3. *Hizkuni* to Genesis 25:29; R. Hayyim b. Moses Attar (*Or ha-Hayyim*, Israel, 1696–1743), *Or ha-Hayyim* to Genesis 25:31.
4. *Or ha-Hayyim* to Genesis 25:33.
5. *Rashi* to *Bava Metzia* 58b, s.v. "*ba-milhamah.*"
6. *Baraita*, *Bava Metzia* 58b.
7. R. Hai b. Sherira, cited in *Rif*, *Bava Metzia* 58b.
8. *Rif*, *Bava Metzia* 58b.
9. *Rabbeinu Hananel*, quoted by R. Joseph ibn Habiba (*Nimmukei Yosef*, Spain, early 15th cent.), *Nimmukei Yosef* to *Rif*, *Bava Metzia* 58b.
10. In the opinion of R. Moses ha-Kohen of Lunel (*Ramach*, Provence, 12th cent.), the disposition of the battlefield case hinges on whether it can be compared to a similar case recorded at *Bava Kamma* 115a. See R. Bezalel Ashkenazi (Egypt, 1520–ca. 1594), *Shitah Mekubbetzet*, *Bava Metzia* 58b. In the *Bava Kamma* case, an absconding criminal agrees to pay a ferryman an above-market price for providing him with conveyance across a river. Given the coercive circumstances, the criminal is entitled to recoup the differential. For an analysis of the two cases, see Aaron Levine, *Case Studies in Jewish Business Ethics* (Hoboken, NJ: Ktav, 2000), 159.
11. *Bava Batra* 78a and *Rashi*, ad loc., s.v. "*be-khedei she-ha-da'at to'ah.*"
12. R. Joseph Caro (Safed, 1488–1575), *Shulhan Arukh*, *Hoshen Mishpat* 227:4.
13. Ibid.; R. Joshua b. Alexander ha-Kohen Falk (*Sema*, Poland, 1565–1614), *Sema* to *Shulhan Arukh*, *Hoshen Mishpat* 227, n. 6. Nullification rights in this case, according to Maimonides and R. Joseph Caro, rest exclusively with the plaintiff. *Mishneh Torah*, *Mekhirah* 12:4; *Shulhan Arukh*, *Hoshen Mishpat* 227:4. Expressing a minority opinion in this matter is R. Jonah b. Abraham Gerondi (*Rabbeinu Yonah*, Spain, ca. 1200–1263), quoted in R. Jacob b. Asher (*Tur*, Spain, 1270–1343), *Tur*, *Hoshen Mishpat* 227.
14. *Shulhan Arukh*, op. cit., 227:2.
15. *Shulhan Arukh*, op. cit., 227:3.
16. Aaron Levine, "*Onaa* and the Operation of the Modern Marketplace," *Jewish Law Annual* 14 (2003): 225–258.
17. Mishnah, *Arakhin* 6:5.
18. Nahmanides, *Hiddushei ha-Ramban*, *Kiddushin* 12a.
19. R. Yom Tov Ishbili, *Hiddushei ha-Ritva*, *Kiddushin* 12a, ed. R. Avraham Dinin (Jerusalem: Mossad HaRav Kook, 2008), *turim* 131–132, s.v. "*kan le-keddushei vaddai, kan le-keddushei safek.*"
20. R. Abraham David Wahrmann, *Kesef ha-Kadashim* to *Shulhan Arukh*, op. cit., 227:9.
21. While the *mekomo ve-sha'to* rule applies to the liquidation procedure for property dedicated to the Sanctuary and to the reference price for the purpose of adjudicating *ona'ah* claims, the relevant marketplace for these two issues is not the same. For a development of this theory, see Levine, "*Onaa* and the Operation of the Modern Marketplace," 243–248.
22. In defending the range-of-values approach to third-degree *ona'ah*, R. Asher anticipates by at least 500 years the modern economic concepts of consumer surplus and inventory cycle. For a detailed presentation of this contention, see ibid., 236–238.
23. Implicit in R. Asher's analysis is the presumption that the product is differentiated. It is for this reason that experts would likely not be in agreement whether price fraud took place when the degree of the *ona'ah* under dispute is third-degree *ona'ah*. If the product market is homogeneous, however, there would be no dispute among experts; everyone would agree that price fraud took place. For an elaboration of and sources for this point, see ibid., 239.

24. *Rosh, Bava Metzia* 4:20.
25. Maimonides, as understood by R. Isser Zalman Meltzer (Lithuania, 1870–1953), *Even ha-Ezel* to *Mishneh Torah, Mekhirah* 12:2; Nahmanides to Leviticus 25:14; *Rosh, Bava Metzia* 4:20; R. Jehiel Michal Epstein (Belorus, 1829–1908), *Arukh ha-Shulhan, Hoshen Mishpat* 227:6–7. For the minority view on this matter, see R. Aaron b. Joseph ha-Levi (*Ra'ah*, Barcelona, 1235–ca. 1290), *Sefer ha-Hinnukh, mitzvah* 337 (Jerusalem: Machon Yerushalayim, 1992), p. 502.
26. *Rashi* to Genesis 25:32.
27. *Hizkuni* to Genesis 25:32. Nahmanides' understanding of Esau's words is consistent with *Hizkuni*'s second rationale. See Nahmanides to Genesis 25:34.
28. *Or ha-Hayyim* to Genesis 25:34.
29. *Bereishit Rabbah* 63:10.
30. R. Jacob Culi (Constantinople, ca. 1685–1732), *Me-Am Lo'ez*, Genesis 25:29, trans. R. Shemuel Yerushalmi, *Yalkut Me-Am Lo'ez* (Jerusalem: Mossad Yad Ezra, 1968), 521.
31. *Bereishit Rabbah* 63:13.
32. *Rashi* to Genesis 25:27.
33. R. Ephraim Solomon b. Aaron Lunshits (*Keli Yakar*, Leczyca, 1550–1619) apparently takes an approach along these lines. See *Keli Yakar* to Genesis 25:32.
34. *Bereishit Rabbah* 63:10.
35. See full text of *Yalkut Shimoni* based on the verse "If you go up high like an eagle, and if you place your nest among the stars (interpreted to mean Jacob), from there I (God) will bring you down" (Obadiah 1:4), reprinted in *Yalkut Shimoni al Nevi'im le-Rabbeinu Shimon ha-Darshan: Nevi'im Aharonim*, ed. Dov Hyman (Jerusalem: Mossad HaRav Kook, 2009), p. 715, s.v. "*im tagbihah ka-nesher.*"
36. *Makkot* 24a.
37. R. Israel Meir ha-Kohen Kagan (*Hafetz Hayyim*, Radin, 1838–1933), *Sefer Hafetz Hayyim, Hilkhot Issurei Lashon ha-Ra* 10:2.
38. Ibid., 6:11.
39. Jacob's motivation in pursuing the birthright was only to rescue the birthright from unworthy hands. See *Bereishit Rabbah* 63:13.
40. *Bereishit Rabbah* 63:11.
41. *Maharsha* to *Makkot* 24a, s.v. "*lo ragal al leshono.*"

CHAPTER 3

The Coase Theorem as Treated in Jewish Law

Introduction

In the most widely read article ever written in economics, Ronald Coase sets out an efficiency approach for dealing with an economic activity that generates harm to unrelated third parties.[1] Referred to in the economic literature as the "negative externality problem," the typical case entails the emission of smoke pollution by a factory.

The traditional approach to the negative externality problem, as typified in the work of Arthur Pigou, is to cast the problem as a case of a perpetrator and a victim in which one party is causally and legally liable.[2]

In the smoke pollution case, the desirability of holding the owner of the factory liable for the damage caused by the smoke is taken as a given. The only issue is to determine the most efficient means of accomplishing this objective. Alternative approaches include: (1) requiring the factory owner to compensate those injured by the smoke; (2) imposing a tax on the factory owner that varies in accordance with the amount of the smoke produced and the damage caused by the smoke;[3] and (3) excluding the factory from residential areas.

Coase rejects the Pigovian formulation of the negative externality problem. What is fundamentally missing in the Pigovian approach is the recognition that the negative externality problem is reciprocal. The smoke pollution case easily illustrates this point. Holding the industrial polluter responsible for the smoke damage increases the cost of doing business for the factory owner, regardless of the form the responsibility takes. Forcing the factory owner to internalize the smoke damage inflicted by his enterprise thus results in some combination of lower profits, higher prices, and reduced employment.

In contradistinction to the Pigovian approach, Coase casts the negative externality problem in terms of the goal of maximizing social value. The key here is to compare the total product yielded under alternative social arrangements. An important aspect of this comparison is the economic value the market ascribes to the alternative outputs. But as Coase points out, the comparison should be made in broader terms. Citing Frank H. Knight, Coase notes that "the problems of welfare economics must ultimately dissolve into a study of aesthetics and morals."[4] Accordingly, the comparison of the outputs of alternative social arrangements should take into account the total effect of those arrangements in all spheres of life.

The Pigovian approach to the negative externality problem conceptualizes the factors of production as merely physical entities that the businessman acquires and uses. In Coase's conceptualization, by contrast, factors of production are viewed as rights to carry out a circumscribed list of actions. To be sure, the rights of a resource owner are never absolute.

To illustrate the difference between Coase's theorem and the traditional approach to the negative externality problem, let's briefly return to the smoke pollution case. Assume that smoke pollution causes $100 of damage per annum. Two methods of eliminating the damage are available. One method is to tax the polluter $100 for the damage. A second method is to install a smoke-prevention device in the factory. The cost of running the device is $90 per annum. Because the smoke-prevention device is the least-cost method of restraining the polluter, the Pigovian approach would call for the installation of the device.

Instead of determining the least-cost method of restraining the industrial polluter, Coase compares what the alternative productions would be with and without a liability rule against the polluter. Within that framework, the relevant question is: What cost would those who suffer the smoke damage be willing to incur to avoid the damage? Suppose the damage could be avoided by relocating the factory to a different district, and the cost of that alternative is only $40 per annum. Under those conditions, not taxing the polluter and thus forcing the adjustment on those who face injury allows society to achieve a *gain* of $50 compared to the result that would obtain if we required the polluter to install a smoke-prevention device.[5]

In examining various judicial decisions, Coase shows that the courts do not follow the approach of maximizing society's output.[6] A far better approach, in Coase's view, would be for the courts to adopt a *laissez-faire* attitude in these cases and allow the affected parties to negotiate a deal. Negotiation between the parties would enable the economic activity with the higher economic value to prevail.

Following as a corollary is that, regardless of the decision of a court, if transaction costs are zero or very minimal, the losing party will be driven to negotiate with the winning party to modify the court decision. Even if a court has rendered a decision, negotiation between the parties can produce an optimal allocation of resources between their conflicting economic activities.

Our purpose in this chapter will be to extrapolate how Jewish law deals with the negative externality problem. To that end, we will compare Jewish law's approach to this issue with the approach Coase took in the major cases he analyzed in his article. Let's begin with the case of the straying cattle.

The Straying Cattle Case

In the straying cattle case, a farmer and a cattleman occupy neighboring properties. When the cattleman's steers stray onto the farmer's property, the farmer's crops are damaged. Without any fencing between the neighboring properties, an increase in the size of the cattleman's herd increases the anticipated damage to the farmer's crop in the relationship set forth in Table 3.1.

Assume that the annual cost of fencing the farmer's property is $9 and that the market price of the crop is $1 per ton. Assume further that before the arrival of the cattleman, the farmer earned a total revenue of $12 and incurred a total cost of $10 in producing and selling his crop each year, resulting in a net annual profit of $2.

Coase uses this example to demonstrate that if the price system works without cost, negotiations between the farmer and the cattleman will result in society maximizing its output. Let's show this under alternative arrangements.

Suppose that the legal system holds the cattleman liable for any crop destruction caused by his herd. Under that liability rule, in deciding whether to expand his herd, the cattleman would be required to take into account the additional penalty he would incur for crop destruction. To illustrate, if the cattleman expands his herd from two to three steers, he will have to factor in as part of his marginal cost the additional penalty of $3 for the additional three-ton crop loss. To be sure, the cattleman might be able to avoid the crop loss by incurring an expenditure of less than $3, such as by hiring additional herdsmen. Whatever the minimum marginal cost is to avoid the crop loss, the cattleman will balance it against the anticipated additional revenue he can earn by expanding his herd from two to three steers. Accordingly, if meat production would yield a higher value compared to crop production, meat production will supplant crop production.

Suppose the legal system does not hold the cattleman liable for the crop damage. The same result as under the liability rule described above should obtain. Specifically, if the law does not protect the farmer, self-interest should drive the farmer to take action to minimize his loss. Recall that before the arrival of the cattleman, the farmer was earning an annual profit of $2. To stay in business in

Table 3.1 **The Straying Cattle Case: Anticipated Crop Damage**

Number in Herd *(Steers)*	***Annual Crop Loss*** *(Tons)*	***Crop Loss per Additional Steer*** *(Tons)*
1	1	1
2	3	2
3	6	3
4	10	4

the long run, the farmer must earn at least a "normal profit." Normal profit obtains when total revenue equals total cost.[7] If avoiding the loss causes the farmer to earn less than a normal profit, the farmer will go out of business. Given the incompatibility of the farming and cattle-raising enterprises, driving the farmer out of business is efficient and therefore optimal from a societal perspective because the activity yielding the higher economic value (i.e., cattle-raising) prevails.[8]

In the real world, conducting market transactions is not costless. To make use of the price mechanism, transaction costs must be incurred. Transaction costs include amounts expended for items such as drafting and negotiating a contract, and monitoring the activities of the parties to ensure compliance with the terms of the contract. If transaction costs are significant, the price mechanism might not lead to negotiation between the parties.

As a result of transaction costs, there is no guarantee that the economic activity with the higher economic value will displace the economic activity with the lower value. The court system will therefore have to deal with the dispute. To achieve an economically efficient result, the courts should understand the economic consequences of their decisions and take those consequences into account when rendering their decisions.[9]

The Straying Cattle Case and Jewish Law

In extrapolating Jewish law's approach to the straying cattle case, the most fundamental point to note is that the cattleman is obligated to compensate the farmer for the crop damage caused by the cattleman's herd.

Before addressing Coase's specific case, let's consider a few points of Jewish law regarding damage inflicted by an animal. In Jewish law, damage inflicted by an animal is characterized as *keren* (lit., horn), *shen* (lit., tooth), or *regel* (lit., foot). Each of those categories signifies damage caused by a different behavioral mode of the animal. *Keren* is damage inflicted through an aberration in the animal's normal behavior, such as when the animal bites, kicks, or attacks with its horns.[10] *Shen* is damage precipitated by an animal's pleasure-seeking activities, such as eating or scratching itself against a wall.[11] *Regel* is damage caused by an animal's natural movement, such as when the animal steps on and breaks an article in its path.[12] In the shorthand notation of the Talmud, damage inflicted by an animal is referred to as *shor ha-mazik* (lit., an ox that inflicts damage).

An important consideration in assessing liability in cases of *shor ha-mazik* is the geographic location where the damage is inflicted. *Shen* and *regel* incur liability only if the damage is inflicted in the private domain of the victim; if the damage is inflicted in the public domain (*reshut ha-rabbim*), no liability is incurred for the damage.[13] Nonetheless, if the damage is caused by the animal's consumption of food, the owner of the animal is considered to have derived a benefit from the damage in the form of being spared the expense of feeding his animal that day. The amount of the expense is assumed to be equal to two-thirds of the price of barley, which is the usual fodder for animals. Because that amount is considered a bargain price, a claim by the owner of the animal that he did not benefit from the damage caused by his animal because he would not have fed his animal that day has no credibility.[14]

Keren incurs liability regardless of whether the damage is inflicted in the public domain or the private domain of the victim. For the first three episodes of *keren*, the owner of the animal is liable for only half the amount of the damage, up to a maximum amount equal to the value of the animal that inflicted the damage. If the owner was properly warned after each of these three incidents, the fourth episode of *keren* incurs liability for the full amount of damage,[15] without limiting liability to the value of the animal.[16]

With respect to an animal that has not inflicted damage three times (i.e., a *tam*, lit., innocent), the payment for half the amount of the damage in the case of *keren* is in the nature of a fine, and this type of damage is not at all common.[17] Moreover, a *shor ha-mazik* is not considered a habitual attacker (i.e., a *mu'ad*, lit., forewarned) unless a court whose judges have a special accreditation, called *semikhah*, makes this determination.[18] This credential consists of an ordination that goes back in a link all the way to Moses. The institution of *semikhah* became moribund in the latter part of the 4th century.[19] Taken together, these factors effectively remove cases of *keren* from the jurisdiction of the Jewish court in contemporary society.[20] Because *keren* is very uncommon, we will assume that the type of damage Coase refers to in the straying cattle case is *shen* or *regel*.

In the straying cattle case, a clear-cut difference emerges between Coase's and Jewish law's treatment of the case. For Coase, the law should not hold the cattleman liable for the damage his herd causes to the farmer's crop. Self-interest, however, tells the farmer that he should not be passive, but instead should try to save his enterprise by implementing the least-cost method of avoiding damage to his crop. If taking that action would drive his enterprise into a loss, the cattle-raising enterprise will prevail and the farmer will go out of business. In sharp contrast, Jewish law entitles the farmer to be compensated for the crop destruction.

Further clarification is, however, in order. Consider that Coase addresses the case where the farmer's fields are not fenced in. Perhaps liability for *shen* and *regel* obtains only when the farmer fences in his field and sustains damage despite taking this precaution. Relevant here is the following Talmudic passage:

> The Tarbu family had goats that would cause damage to the property of R. Joseph. So he said to Abaye: "Go tell their owners that they should keep them inside their property." Abaye said [to him]: "For what purpose shall I go? What will I accomplish? For if I go and tell them what you, the master, have, they will tell me that the master should rather build a fence

> around his own land. But if he [every landowner] would be required to fence his property, how would you find a case where the Merciful One in His Torah obligates a person for damages done through the *shen* of his animal—You find it where [the animal] burrows under the fence into the property. Or also, you find it where the fence fell down during the night and the animal entered the property before the property owner became aware that his fence was down."[21]

Codifiers generally follow R. Joseph's position. These authorities include R. Isaac b. Jacob Alfasi (*Rif*, Algeria, 1013–1103),[22] Maimonides,[23] R. Solomon b. Jehiel Luria (*Maharshal*, Poland, 1510–1573),[24] R. Joseph Caro,[25] and R. Jehiel Michal Epstein.[26]

A significant minority of authorities, however, exempts the cattleman from liability unless the farmer fences in his fields and despite this measure the steers break through and damage the crop. These authorities include R. Hananel b. Hushiel (*Rabbeinu Hananel*, North Africa, 11th cent.),[27] R. Asher b. Jehiel (*Rosh*, Germany, ca. 1250–1327),[28] and R. Shabbetai b. Meir ha-Kohen (*Siftei Kohen*, Poland, 1621–1662).[29] These authorities limit the exemption, however, to the case where the relevant terrain is farmland or grazing land. The exemption does not apply in the context of an urban setting because it is unreasonable to expect a householder in a populated area to keep his courtyard under constant lock.[30]

What follows from the majority view is that the farmer is not expected to fence in his land to avoid crop damage from straying cattle. To the contrary, the onus is on the cattleman to guard his herd against straying onto the farmer's field and eating or destroying his crops.

Let's take note that liability for the cattleman holds only if he did not guard his herd in the prescribed manner. But if the cattleman did what the law required of him, he bears no liability for the damage his herd causes the farmer.

In determining the preventative measures that should be prescribed for the cattleman, the Sages took their cue from the language the Torah employs in describing *regel* and *shen*: "If a man leads an animal to a field or vineyard, and he sends forth (*ve-shillah*) his animal and it consumes (*u-vi'er*) in the field of another. . . ." (Exodus 22:4). The phrase "he sends forth" refers to *regel*. This language indicates that the owner was negligent, akin to personally sending forth his animal. The phrase "and it consumes" refers to *shen*. The use of the masculine form for consume (i.e., "*u-vi'er*," which refers to the owner) instead of the feminine form (i.e., *u-vi'arah*, which would signify the animal) indicates that the owner was negligent, as if he personally fed the animal from the victim's field.[31] Consequently, in the case of *shen* and *regel*, the owner escapes liability only if he was not guilty of negligence in guarding his animal.[32]

While the Sages did not specify the preventative measures that they expected the cattleman to take to avoid harm to a neighboring farmer's crop, they did mandate specific conduct for a householder who is a neighbor of a farmer. The rule is that a householder should keep his livestock locked up in a barn, and the door of the barn should be strong enough to withstand an ordinary wind. If the householder took these precautions but an extraordinary wind lodged open the door of the barn and the animal inflicted *shen* or *regel* damage to the farmer's crop, the householder is not responsible for the damage.[33]

Using the preventative measures the law requires for the householder as the model for what the law would require of the cattleman tells us that leaving the herd unsupervised in the pasture is negligent behavior. What seems to be indicated is a level of supervision that, under ordinary conditions, would ensure that the cattle will not stray onto the property of the farmer and destroy his crops. The number of herdsmen required to accomplish this would, of course, depend on the size of the herd.

The preceding analysis has demonstrated that Jewish law's treatment of the straying cattle case is incompatible with Coase's notion that the negative externality problem is reciprocal and the farmer should therefore have no right to be protected against the damage the cattleman causes his crop. Rather than granting both the cattleman and the farmer equal rights to conduct their incompatible enterprises and allowing the price system to determine which enterprise prevails, Jewish law holds the cattleman responsible for the crop damage caused by his herd. The farmer's protection against that damage is not limited to the instance where he constructs an adequate fence. Instead, the farmer is entitled to compensation for damages even if he does not fence in his fields.

Recall Coase's notion that if the price system works without cost, the initial delineation of rights established by the legal system is not a barrier to allowing society to maximize the value of its output. But once we take into account the reality of transaction costs, the only hope for an efficient solution is for the legal rule to be based on the goal of maximizing society's output. Given that Jewish law's approach to the straying cattle case is not designed to maximize society's output, that approach is not compatible with Coase's approach to this case.[34]

Breeding Small Cattle in the Land of Israel

The gap between Jewish law and Coase in their approaches to the straying cattle case widens when we consider the ordinance the Talmudic Sages instituted that prohibited raising *behemah dakkah* (lit., small cattle; i.e., sheep and goats) in the Land of Israel. Out of fear that small cattle would wander into neighboring fields and destroy crops, the Sages prohibited the breeding of small cattle in the Land of Israel except in the desert. Importation of small cattle for consumption purposes was permitted under controlled conditions. The ordinance thus did not merely hold the cattleman responsible for crop damage inflicted by his herd, but outlawed the breeding of small cattle altogether.[35] In contrast to Coase's approach, which forces internalization of the negative externality but allows bargaining between the cattleman and the farmer to determine the land-use pattern, Jewish law *dictates* a land-use pattern of farming, regardless of the implications for economic efficiency.

Why the Sages did not find it sufficient to adopt a liability rule against the cattleman is explained by Maimonides on the basis of the inevitability of the crop damage that would result from the cattle-breeding enterprise. Dealing with the negative externality by merely imposing a liability rule would be tantamount to licensing the cattleman to destroy the farmer's crop, but calling for the cattleman to compensate the farmer as damage occurs.[36]

Standing at the basis of the ordinance, according to R. Solomon b. Isaac (*Rashi*, France, 1040–1105), is a desire to promote Jewish settlements and population growth in the Land of Israel.[37] *Rashi*'s rationale explains why the Sages were not satisfied with merely establishing a liability rule against the cattleman. A liability rule would allow subsequent bargaining between the parties to determine the land-use pattern, regardless of the effect on population growth. To ensure that the narrow interests of the parties would not produce a bargaining result that would subvert the goal of promoting population growth, the Sages prohibited outright the breeding of small cattle in the Land of Israel.

Sturges v. Bridgman

The 1879 British court case of *Sturges v. Bridgman* involved a successful suit by a doctor to enjoin a confectioner from operating his business on adjacent premises.[38] In that case, Dr. Sturges had been living next door to the confectioner, Bridgman, for eight years without objecting to the confectioner's business. Sturges then built a consulting room at the end of his garden, right next to Bridgman's kitchen. After building the consulting room, Sturges sought an injunction to prevent Bridgman from conducting his business on the grounds that the operation of Bridgman's mortars and pestles produced noise and vibrations that made it impossible for Sturges to conduct his medical practice in his consulting room. Specifically, the noise interfered with the use of the doctor's stethoscope and prevented him from performing any work that required continuous thought. Sturges also claimed that the noise was a nuisance and interfered with his domestic comfort. To bolster that claim, Sturges produced affidavits from neighbors who testified that the noise was such that it interfered with one's domestic comfort.

In *Sturges v. Bridgman*, the court formulated the issue as whether Bridgman's longstanding use of his machinery without protest from Sturges entitled Bridgman to continue the operation even after Sturges protested. In legal parlance, such an entitlement is called an easement. Noting that Sturges had no right to prevent Bridgman from operating his machinery while the noise it produced was not a nuisance to Sturges, Sturges' silence during this period could in no way be interpreted as consent to Bridgman's pounding even after he built the consulting room.[39]

By ruling in favor of Sturges, the court failed to take into account that the negative externality problem is reciprocal. The economic activities of the doctor and confectioner interfered with each other—more doctoring was only at the expense of less candy production, and more candy production was only at the expense of less doctoring. Recognition of the reciprocal nature of the negative externality problem should have led the court to reject Sturges' claim that Bridgman's pounding activity interfered with Sturges' domestic comfort.

In Coase's view, the court should not have taken sides in this case. A *laissez-faire* attitude would have allowed bargaining between the parties to ensure that the activity with the highest social value would prevail.[40]

In his presentation of *Sturges v. Bridgman*, Coase omitted one of the details of the case: Sturges used Bridgman's kitchen door as one of the walls in constructing his consulting room.[41] The confectioner's kitchen door thus served as a party wall[42] between the doctor's consulting room and the place where the confectioner operated his machinery. Indeed, one of the defenses Bridgman offered was that, had Sturges built his consulting room with a separate wall, and not against the wall of Bridgman's kitchen, the doctor would not have suffered any serious annoyance.[43]

In all probability, Coase omitted this detail because it would not have changed his analysis. For Jewish law, however, the fact that one of the walls of the consulting room was the party wall between the confectioner's kitchen and the doctor's consulting room is a critical factor in deciding the case. Accordingly, our analysis of *Sturges v. Bridgman* will be divided into two parts. In the first part, we will analyze *Sturges v. Bridgman* from the standpoint of Jewish law based on the actual facts of the case. We will call this part *Sturges v. Bridgman (1)*. In the second part, we will consider a variant of the actual case, one in which Sturges did not make use of Bridgman's kitchen door in constructing his consulting room. The second scenario will be called *Sturges v. Bridgman (2)*.

Sturges v. Bridgman (1) and Jewish Law

In analyzing *Sturges v. Bridgman (1)* from the standpoint of Jewish law, the critical factor in the case is that Sturges used Bridgman's property to construct his consulting room.

The relevant model here, discussed in the Talmud, is the case where *A*'s courtyard adjoins *B*'s wall. In that case, *A* has no right to make use of *B*'s wall.[44] To show how strict the application of this rule is, consider the following dispute between the decisors, R. Judah (Barcelona, late 12th cent.) and R. Jacob b. Asher (*Tur*, Spain, 1270–1343). In R. Judah's view, the prohibition does not apply when *A* seeks to build only a small projection into *B*'s wall that is less than a *tefah* (lit., a handsbreadth), a measure of length equal to the width of four thumbs. The principle here is that if *A* seeks a benefit from *B*, and *B* sustains no harm as a result of letting *A* have his benefit, the Jewish court will coerce *B* to allow *A* the benefit. Referred to in short as the *kofin* (coercion) principle, the dictum says *kofin oto al middat Sedom* (i.e., we coerce him not to act like a Sodomite).[45]

R. Judah sees no disadvantage for *B*. Given the limited use *A* can make of the small structure he builds into the wall, *A*'s use of the wall will perforce be ad hoc rather than routine. Consequently, *B* need not worry that if he subsequently desires to take down the wall, *A* will object on the basis that *A* already acquired a *hazakah* (prescriptive right) to make use of the wall. Moreover, given that the small structure that *A* wants to build into the wall cannot support anything heavy, there should be no concern that *A*'s use will damage or undermine the wall. Because R. Judah sees no possible disadvantage for *B*, the Jewish court will force *B* to allow *A* the use of the wall.[46]

R. Jacob b. Asher disputes R. Judah's conclusion. In objecting to R. Judah's conclusion, R. Jacob b. Asher apparently follows the view that the *kofin* principle applies only when the issue is denying someone a benefit when it entails no cost to the one who wants to deny it. However, the *kofin* principle cannot coerce *B* to allow *A* to affirmatively make use of his property, even though by doing so *B* would suffer no discernable loss.[47] Because the essence of a property right is the *control* the owner has over his property, forcing the owner to relinquish control over his property is an emasculation of the property right, which is not unreasonable to object to.[48]

Although R. Joel Sirkes (*Bah*, Poland, 1561–1640) finds R. Judah's analysis and conclusion compelling,[49] the major codifiers, R. Moses Isserles (*Rema*, Poland, 1525 or 1530–1572)[50] and R. Jehiel Michal Epstein (Belarus, 1829–1908),[51] follow R. Jacob b. Asher.

Denying *A* the right to make affirmative use of *B*'s property even when that use causes no discernable loss for *B* has direct application for *Sturges v. Bridgman (1)*. Most fundamentally, the rule allows Bridgman to obtain injunctive relief from the courts to ensure that Sturges does not use Bridgman's kitchen door as a party wall for Sturges' consulting room. Moreover, absent any protest during the construction, Bridgman does not lose his right to continue the operation of his machinery. Legitimacy would be given to Bridgman's argument that had he only known that Sturges' intended use for the construction was incompatible with the operation of his confectionary business next door, he would have secured a court order to nip the project in the bud.

The upshot of the above analysis is that in *Sturges v. Bridgman (1)*, the Jewish court would not grant an injunction to force Bridgman to stop using his machinery during Sturges' office hours.

Sturges v. Bridgman (2) and Jewish Law

We will now proceed to analyze a variant of *Sturges v. Bridgman*. In our variant case, we assume the following facts: First, in his construction project, Sturges did not make use of Bridgman's kitchen door as a party wall for his consulting room.

Instead, Sturges built four new walls. As a result, the noise and vibrations emitted by Bridgman were muted by the presence of two walls that separated Bridgman's kitchen from the consulting room. Second, despite the double wall between the pounding machinery and the doctor's consulting room, the operation of the mortars and pestles made it impossible for Sturges to concentrate.

From the perspective of Jewish law, two arguments in support of Sturges' complaint should be analyzed. One argument is that the operation of Bridgman's mortars and pestles prevents Sturges from pursuing his livelihood as a medical practitioner. The second is that the pounding is a nuisance that interferes with Sturges' domestic comfort.

NEGATIVE EXTERNALITIES AND LIVELIHOOD ACTIVITIES

Let's first take up the argument that Bridgman prevented Sturges from earning a livelihood. The model case here for the treatment of *Sturges v. Bridgman (2)* in Jewish law is the following Talmudic discussion:

> One may not open a bakery or a dye shop under the storeroom of his fellow, nor may he open a cattle barn under a storeroom.[52]
>
> A *Tanna* taught the following *Baraita*: If the establishment of the cattle barn preceded that of the storeroom, it is permitted to maintain the cattle barn.[53]

What can be extrapolated from this Talmudic discussion is a rule regarding how the economic activities of neighboring property owners are regulated when one has a destructive effect on the other. The rule is that if *A* initiated an economic activity on his property, *B* can be restrained from conducting an economic activity on *B*'s own property that would exert a destructive effect on *A*'s enterprise. But if *B* had already set up an economic activity on his own premises, *A* has no right to demand that *B* remove the enterprise because it will destroy an enterprise that *A* is planning.

Application of the above rule to *Sturges v. Bridgman (2)* is very straightforward. To be sure, Bridgman's pounding machinery makes it impossible for Sturges to conduct his medical practice in the adjacent consulting room. But consider that Bridgman operated his confectionary business next door to Sturges for many years before Sturges built his consulting room. Accordingly, Sturges has no right to force Bridgman to make the necessary adjustments so that he can practice medicine in his newly constructed, adjacent consulting room.

Further analysis of the Talmudic model case referred to earlier will show that there is even a more fundamental reason to reject Sturges' complaint. Consider that the operation of a dye shop or cattle barn in the lower level of a building is not only incompatible with the operation of a storeroom in an upper level of the building, but the joint operation of these enterprises will result in the *spoilage* of the produce in the storeroom. This model does not describe Sturges' complaint. Bridgman's confectionary operation does not result in the destruction or spoilage of Sturges' assets. Instead, the pounding renders Sturges' stethoscope inoperative, making it impossible for him to pick up the heartbeat of his patients. The distinction we draw is between an enterprise that destroys the assets of a neighboring enterprise and one that merely makes it impossible for a neighbor to conduct certain activities on his own premises. That distinction finds expression in the work of a number of Jewish law authorities.

Let's begin with the work of R. Yehezkel Abramsky (London, 1886–1976). R. Abramsky's analysis of an aspect of Jewish privacy law, called *hezek re'iyah* (visual penetration of someone's privacy), shows that a negative externality is actionable only when it destroys the assets of the neighboring property owner, but not when it merely makes it impossible for the neighbor to conduct certain activities on his premises. Preliminarily, let's take note of the following examples of duties the law of *hezek re'iyah* imposes on a property owner.

1. *A* and *B* are partners in a courtyard. They agree to break up their partnership and divide the courtyard between them. To protect the privacy rights of both parties, Jewish law demands that *A* and *B* share in the construction of a party wall.[54]
2. If *A*'s home faces *B*'s courtyard, *A* has no right to install a window in his home that faces *B*'s courtyard. The basis of the prohibition is that the installation of the window invades *B*'s privacy.[55]

What is the basis of the *hezek re'iyah* duties of property owners? R. Abramsky proposes two competing theories. One possibility is that, absent the duties described above, invasion of privacy between neighbors would be inevitable. The purpose of *hezek re'iyah* law is therefore to *restore* privacy that is otherwise lost. Alternatively, out of fear that his privacy would be invaded, a neighbor would refrain from engaging in private activities. Under that approach, the purpose of *hezek re'iyah* law is to impose rules to *prevent* the loss of privacy.

R. Abramsky rejects the notion that *hezek re'iyah* law is based on the entitlement of a property owner not to be forced to desist from conducting private activities on his premises out of concern that he will be observed by his neighbor. What is fascinating here is that R. Abramsky invokes the reciprocity principle as the basis for rejecting this approach. Imposing restrictions on how *A* may make use of his property to afford the neighboring property owner, *B*, free exercise of his property cannot be defended if it can just as easily be argued that it is *B* who should be restricted to afford *A* free exercise of his property right. If the negative externality does not damage or destroy a neighbor's property, but instead makes the neighbor desist from certain uses of his property, Jewish law would take a *laissez-faire* approach. Unless *A* can demonstrate *hazakah*, Jewish law would not stop the neighboring property owner from a use of his property that would effectively make it impossible for *A* to continue his enterprise.[56]

Demonstrating the limited ability to stop a negative externality when it does not exert a destructive effect in the form of either bodily injury or property damage is the law of *davshah* (lit., treading). This law says that if a wall is standing on *A*'s property and a neighboring property owner, *B*, wants to build a wall on his own property, *B* must distance his wall at least four *ammot*[57] from *A*'s wall.[58] The rationale here is that if the distance between the walls is at least four *ammot*, pedestrians will not hesitate to walk between the walls and this pedestrian traffic will harden the earth and thereby strengthen the foundations of the walls. If the gap between the walls is narrower, by contrast, pedestrians will not walk between the walls and the foundations of the walls will be undermined.[59]

Commenting on the law of *davshah*, *Tosafot* and R. Solomon b. Abraham Adret (*Rashba*, Spain, 1235–1310) posit that this law does not restrict *A* from constructing a wall on the very edge of his own property. To be sure, *A*'s construction precludes his neighbor, *B*, from constructing a wall on his own property within four *ammot* of *A*'s wall. Nevertheless, there is no legal objection to *A*'s wall-building. *A*'s wall-building merely prevents treading from occurring, but does not generate any destructive effect on *B*.[60]

Commenting on the above *Tosafot*, R. Aaron Kotler (New York, 1892–1962) derives the general principle that a negative externality is not actionable when the adverse effect consists only of preventing the plaintiff from conducting income-producing activities on his premises.[61]

NEGATIVE EXTERNALITIES IN THE FORM OF A NUISANCE

Let's now consider the argument that the noise from Bridgman's activities constituted a nuisance. The analogue in Jewish law is the case where a resident of a courtyard decides to conduct a commercial activity either in his own residence or in his courtyard. Suppose the commercial activity generates neither bodily harm nor property damage, but constitutes a nuisance to one or more of the fellow residents. Do the residents have a right to object to the commercial activity based on the nuisance alone?

Relevant here is the issue of whether residents of a courtyard have the right to prevent a fellow resident from conducting a noise-generating enterprise on his own premises, such as a mill that generates noise from grinding, or a blacksmith operation that generates noise from hammering. In the opinion of Maimonides and R. Joseph Caro, fellow residents do have a right to block the enterprise based on the nuisance the grinding or hammering entails.[62] Once it can be established, however, that the grinding or hammering occurred and none of the residents protested, the business whose operation involves a nuisance in the form of noise acquires a prescriptive right (*hazakah*) to continue the enterprise.[63]

Disputing R. Caro, R. Moses Isserles is of the view that, in general, fellow residents of the courtyard have no right to block the operation of the noise-generating business. If, however, the noise is not only a nuisance but would cause one of the residents to become ill, that resident can stop the operation of the enterprise.[64]

On the facts of *Sturges v. Bridgman (2)*, all authorities should agree that Bridgman's confectionary business cannot be stopped, provided that Bridgman's grinding activity does not cause actual sickness to any of his neighbors.

Contemporary Society and the Nuisance Externality

In contemporary society, local governments adopt zoning codes. Those codes designate permitted uses of land based on mapped zones. Urban zones are generally categorized as single-family residential, multiple-family residential, commercial, or industrial. Within each category, most zoning systems have a procedure for granting variances, usually because of some perceived hardship caused by the nature of the property in question.[65]

Within the framework of modern zoning codes, the treatment of the nuisance externality would have to take into account applicable secular laws. The relevant principle is *dina de-malkhuta dina* (lit., the law of the kingdom is the law).[66] To be sure, Jewish law requires disputes between Jews to be adjudicated in a Jewish court. But with respect to monetary matters, the Jewish court generally should decide the matter on the basis of *dina de-malkhuta*.

While authorities dispute the ambit of *dina de-malkhuta dina*,[67] contemporary decisors follow R. Isserles' formulation.[68] In his view, *dina de-malkhuta dina* applies to civil law generally and is recognized only when the law either benefits the government or was enacted for the benefit of the people of the land.[69] Conflict between Halakhah and *dina de-malkhuta*, in his view, is generally decided in favor of *dina de-malkhuta*.[70]

Exceptions to this rule, however, apply. *Dina de-malkhuta dina* does not hold in relation to the law of inheritance.[71] In addition, this rule does not allow Jews to take their disputes to secular courts[72] or be bound by a secular court's evidentiary procedures.[73]

In his analysis of *dina de-malkhuta dina*, R. Yosef Eliyahu Henkin (New York, 1881–1973) argues that the disappearance of the self-governing Jewish community makes for a compelling case to follow R. Isserles' view in contemporary society. In the Middle Ages, secular governments granted Jews autonomy in matters of civil law. Under that license, Jews established a communal organization, called *kehillah*, and enacted legislation (*takkanot ha-kahal*, lit., ordinances of the community) and imposed penalties for violations of law. In former times, the legal import of *dina de-malkhuta dina* was no more than to establish a duty to conduct oneself as a good citizen vis-à-vis civil laws and regulations of the government.

In more recent times, however, in the absence of the *kehillah* organization, *dina de-malkhuta* may assume the legal character of *takkanot ha-kahal* themselves. Specifically, in democracies where various governmental entities either legislate or have regulatory authority, Jews, who have a say in these matters, effectively cede their *takkanot ha-kahal* function to those governmental bodies. When civil law assumes the status of *takkanot ha-kahal*, civil law prevails, according to R. Henkin, even when the statute involved varies from Jewish law's position on the matter at hand. Accordingly, as the venue of initial jurisdiction for disputes between Jews, the Jewish court (*Beit Din*) must consider the relevant civil law before rendering its decisions.[74]

Adopting R. Isserles' guidepost for the parameters of *dina de-malkhuta dina* entitles a resident of a neighborhood zoned as a residential area to protest the operation of a manufacturing enterprise in that area. Absent a successful application for a variance, the objection should be valid even when the manufacturing enterprise does not generate noise or additional traffic. Thus, in contemporary society, the halakhic rights of a manufacturer to conduct a noise-generating enterprise in his home would give way to the zoning codes.

The Railroad Sparks Case

Another instance mentioned by Pigou that illustrates the divergence between private and social cost is the railroad sparks case. Suppose a locomotive emits sparks from its engine as it passes over adjoining woods and the sparks cause fire damage to the woods. If the law does not hold the railroad company liable for the damage, the company would have no incentive to install spark-prevention equipment on its locomotives. Closing the gap between private and social costs requires the government to hold the railroad liable for the damage.

In his critique of Pigou, Coase points out that the railroad sparks case is by no means a hypothetical matter. Since 1858, the British court system has dealt with this issue. Specifically, in *Vaughan v. The Taff Vale Railway Company*, the owner of a wooded area that adjoined the banks of a railroad sued the railroad for damage caused by sparks emitted from a locomotive's engine as the locomotive passed over the wooded area. While the lower court ruled in favor of the plaintiff,[75] the decision was reversed on appeal.[76]

The basis of the appellate court's ruling was that the legislature authorized the railroad to operate.[77] In granting that license, the legislature must have anticipated that the operation of the railroad would cause damage to nearby woods. The legislature therefore had the right to expect the railroad to take every practical precaution to prevent its locomotives from causing damage to the woods. All evidence pointed to the conclusion that the railroad did everything practicable to make its locomotive safe. Specifically, a cap had been placed on the chimney of the locomotive, the ash pan had been secured, and the locomotive had traveled at the slowest pace consistent with practical utility.[78]

The Railway (Fires) Act, enacted in 1905 and amended in 1923, established a rule that departed from the holding in *Taff Vale*. Under that legislation, the railroad is generally held liable for up to £200 (£100 in the 1905 Act) of damage to agricultural land or crops caused by sparks emitted from a locomotive.[79]

For Coase, the desirability of establishing a liability rule against the railroad turns on the aggregate social outputs that would obtain under alternative legal rules. He illustrates his point with the following arithmetic example: Let's initially assume that a no-liability rule applies to the railroad. Suppose the total revenue the railroad realizes by running one train is $150, while running two trains increases its total revenue to $250. The cost of running each train is $50. In addition, running one train causes $60 of crop damage and running two trains causes $120 of crop damage.

In calculating the social values obtainable under alternative legal rules, we must also take into account the losses and gains in output that would result from the reaction of farmers to the no-liability rule. Because the law does not protect the farmer against crop loss caused by the sparks emitted from a passing train, it would be rational for the farmer to withdraw some land from cultivation.[80] Instead of cultivating the land, the farmer would divert his efforts to his next best marketplace opportunity. In this regard, Coase assumes that the loss in output from withdrawing some land from cultivation is $160, and the gain in output of the farmers in pursuing their next best opportunity is $150.

We are now in position to calculate the net value to society that would be produced under a no-liability rule. Total revenue is equal to the combined value of railroad services from running two trains (i.e., $250) and the output the farmers would produce instead of cultivating the abandoned land (i.e., $150). Total revenue is thus $400 (i.e., $250 + $150). Total cost is the cost of running the two trains (i.e., $50 × 2 = $100), the crop loss the farmers would sustain as a result of the no-liability rule (i.e., $120), and the lost output from the abandonment of some land from cultivation (i.e., $160). The total cost is thus $380 (i.e., $100 + $120 + $160). Because total revenue of $400 exceeds total cost of $380, the railroad would run both trains under the no-liability rule.

Let's now switch to a liability rule. Several of the figures given for the previous model will change. For one, since the law holds the railroad liable for the damage to the farmer's crops, the farmer does not have a strong incentive to cut production. Specifically, if the crop survives, the farmer can sell his crop in the market, and if the crop is damaged, the farmer can recover the damage from the railroad because the law is on his side. Between those two outcomes, the farmer, according to Coase, is indifferent.[81] Accordingly, Coase assumes that the crop damage under a liability rule would be double the figure that it would be under a no-liability rule. Thus, the crop damage would be $120 when one train is run and $240 when two trains are run. This same reasoning leads Coase to assume that under a liability rule, the farmer would not be motivated to abandon cultivation.

Let's now proceed to calculate revenues and losses under a liability-rule regime. The total revenue the railroad earns from running one train is $150. Running the train entails a cost of $50. Add to this the crop loss damage of $120, for which the railroad is required to pay compensation to the farmer. The total cost under a liability rule is thus $170 (i.e., $50 + $120). Since the total cost of $170 of running the train is $20 greater than the total revenue earned of $150, the railroad will not run the first train. Running two trains would only increase the railroad's losses to $90, as the loss of $340 (i.e., double the loss of $170) exceeds the revenue of $250 from running two trains. Because costs are greater than revenue regardless of whether the railroad operates two trains or only one train, the liability rule results in the railroad shutting down.

Working with the above figures of revenues and costs under alternative legal rules leads Coase to the conclusion that society would maximize its social product by adopting a legal regime of no liability for the railroad. Under the no-liability rule, the railroad would find it to its own advantage to run two trains, which would result in a net social product of $20.

Of course, by altering the figures, it could be shown that under different assumptions, the railroad should be held liable. Nonetheless, Coase's point is that his illustration, rooted in reasonable assumptions, shows that it is not necessarily undesirable that the law should exempt the railroad from liability in the railroad sparks case.[82]

The Railroad Sparks Case and Jewish Law

In this section, we will show that the railroad sparks case is analyzed in Jewish law from the perspective of tort law and the authority of the community to adopt legislation governing matters with respect to which the rights of the individual must be balanced against the rights of society.

Let's begin with tort law. In extrapolating how Jewish law would treat the railroad sparks case, two issues must be decided. The first is the determination of the precautionary measures that an individual should be required to take when conducting a fire on his premises to prevent the fire from blazing out of control and damaging a neighbor's property. Once the standard of precaution is established, the next step is to decide whether one who conducts a fire in accordance with this standard should nevertheless be held responsible for any damage the fire inflicts. What follows are two competing models that address both issues.

One model is the set of precautions the Sages prescribed for occupants of upper-floor and lower-floor apartments when operating an oven on their premises and the allocation of liability in the event of fire damage from the oven. In this regard, Jewish law requires the occupant of the lower-floor apartment to ensure that his oven is distanced from his ceiling by at least four *ammot*.[83] Similarly, to prevent a fire from catching onto the floor pillars, the occupant of the upper story must install plaster below his oven with a height of at least three *tefahim*. In any event, if an oven causes damage to a neighbor's property despite adoption of these precautionary measures, the operator of the oven is still liable for the damage.[84]

Another model in the Talmud that addresses precautionary measures and liability for fire is the rules the Sages established for neighboring field owners, *A* and *B*. If *A* wants to conduct a fire in his field, he must ensure that, under ordinary circumstances,[85] his fire is incapable of reaching *B*'s field. Rather than prescribing a uniform distancing requirement, decisors follow R. Shimon's approach, under which the distancing requirement depends on the nature of the fire. Factors such as the height of the fire, whether the fire is bent by the wind, the amount of fuel, and the combustible materials on site are taken into account. Finally, if *A* complied with the distancing requirement and a fire nevertheless broke out and caused damage to a neighbor, *A* bears no responsibility for the damage.[86]

In extrapolating the standard the Sages would impose in the railroad sparks case, three options present themselves: a minimum standard, a stringent standard, and a standard somewhere in between those two extremes. The key to which standard is appropriate for the railroad sparks case is the rationale behind the different treatment of the tortfeasors in the oven and field cases. Specifically, why is the field owner exempt from liability for damage that his fire causes by spreading to his neighbor's field if he took the proper precautions, whereas the apartment occupant is always responsible for fire damage even when he installed his oven in compliance with the prescribed precautions?

R. Isaac b. Jacob Alfasi addresses this issue.[87] Because his presentation includes many points, commentators differ on what R. Alfasi regards as the critical difference between the cases. Several interpretations are described below.

According to *Siftei Kohen*'s understanding of R. Alfasi, the key is the amount of supervision required in the two cases. When *A* conducts a fire on his field, the law can require of him no more than to take proper precautions to prevent the fire from spreading beyond the boundaries of his property. If a fire blazes out of control despite the adoption of those precautions, *A* can do nothing to prevent its further spread. Consequently, if the fire spreads further and causes damage, *A* should bear no responsibility for the damage. In sharp contrast, the fire of an oven burns constantly. In addition to requiring *A* to take proper precautions at the time the fire is ignited, the law expects *A* to be in a constant state of vigilance while the fire is lit so that if the fire escapes the oven, *A* will be in position to stop its spread.[88]

R. Jacob Moses Lorberbaum (*Netivot*, Lissa, 1760–1832) understands R. Alfasi to say that the law established different standards of care for the two cases. Given the recurring and routine use the householder makes of his oven, it would be too onerous to require him to install the oven in such a manner that it would never cause damage to his neighbors' property. Instead, the law established a standard that, if adopted, would ordinarily be safe, but only in conjunction with the watchful eye of the householder. In the case of the field owner, by contrast, since the setting of a fire in his field is only an ad hoc activity, the law does burden him to ensure that his fire does not spread to a neighboring field. Because the standard of precaution the law imposes on the field owner is the most stringent necessary to make the surrounding fields safe, any fire damage that results despite the adoption of these precautions is not regarded as the fault of the one who made the fire, but rather simply an act of God.[89]

R. Abraham Isaiah Karelitz (*Hazon Ish*, Israel, 1878–1953) understands R. Alfasi to say that the precautionary standards the Sages set for both the field and oven cases were not set with the expectation that the fires would as a matter of certainty not spread if those standards were adopted. The Sages recognized, however, that a householder who operates an oven is capable of immediately ascertaining that the applicable standard prescribed by the Sages is not sufficient in his case. The oven owner can then make an immediate adjustment to prevent his fire from spreading out of control. The field owner, by contrast, is not capable of immediately ascertaining that the standard of precaution prescribed for conducting a fire in a field would not prevent his particular fire from spreading out of control. Accordingly, as long as the field owner complies with the required standard, the law does not hold the field owner liable for the damage his fire causes.[90]

Finally, let's take note of the insight R. Aryeh Leib b. Joseph ha-Kohen Heller (*Ketzot*, Poland, ca. 1745–1813) offers in explaining the different treatment of the two cases. Preliminarily, let's note that R. Heller offers his insight not as his understanding of R. Alfasi, but rather as an independent idea.

R. Heller proposes that the standards the Sages set for the oven owner were only minimum standards. Those standards were designed only to ensure that if damages occurred, the law would not regard *A* as having operated his oven in a manner that would deliberately cause damage to *B*. Given that the safety standards prescribed for the oven case are only minimum standards, if the operation of *A*'s oven causes damage to *B*, *A* bears responsibility. The standard the Sages prescribed for the field owner, by contrast, extended beyond minimum precautions, as those distancing requirements were designed to prevent *A*'s fire from spreading out of control. Accordingly, if *A*'s fire spreads out of control and damages *B*'s property despite the adoption of those precautions, the damage is regarded as an act of God and *A* bears no responsibility.[91]

Analysis of the four opinions described above points to how Jewish tort law would handle the railroad sparks case. Preliminarily, let's note that in the thinking of both R. Lorberbaum and R. Heller, the standard of care the Sages set for *A* when he makes use of his oven in his apartment is decidedly a lower standard of care compared to the standard of care the Sages set for the case when *A* conducts a fire in his field. Nothing in the other opinions contradicts this. We take it that the lower standard of care the Sages set for the operation of an oven is based on the fact that an oven is used on a daily basis. Consequently, the Sages believed that it would be too onerous to impose the highest standard of care for use of an oven.

Another point that emerges from R. Lorberbaum is that when the Sages impose the highest standard of care as a prerequisite for conducting a fire, one who sets a fire in conformity with this standard is exempt from liability if the fire spreads out of control and damages a neighbor's property. Here too, nothing in the other opinions contradicts this conclusion.

What emerges from the above analysis is that the appropriate standard for the railroad sparks case is certainly not a standard that is so stringent that it would make it impossible for the locomotive's engine to emit sparks as the locomotive travels along its route. Because the operation of a railroad is a recurring day-to-day routine, imposing the highest standard of care would be too onerous. Instead, a lower standard would be imposed.

Recall the thinking of R. Heller that the standard of care the Sages imposed in the oven case was just a minimum standard. Perhaps only a minimum standard of care should be imposed on the railroad too? No. A minimum standard of precaution is sufficient in the oven case because the operator of the oven is expected to be in proximity of the oven while it is in operation and be in a state of readiness to prevent the fire from causing damage if it spreads out of control. By contrast, once the locomotive's engine emits a spark, there is nothing the motorman can do to ensure that the spark does not cause damage. Imposing more than a minimum standard of care is therefore indicated. At the other extreme, imposing a standard of care that is intended to make it impossible for the locomotive's engine to emit sparks as the locomotive moves along its route would be so onerous as to make the railroad enterprise unprofitable. Accordingly, the setting of a standard consistent with allowing the railroad to be a profitable enterprise is indicated.

We have discussed the three possible standards of care for the railroad sparks case in abstract terms. Examination of the details of the *Taff Vale* case transforms the abstract notion of various levels of standards of care into concrete terms.

In the litigation, all evidence supported the conclusion that the railroad did everything practicable to make its locomotive safe. Specifically, a cap was placed on the locomotive's chimney, its ash pan was secured, and the locomotive traveled at the slowest pace consistent with practical utility.[92]

Considering that once the locomotive's engine emits sparks, the motorman can do nothing to prevent the sparks from causing damage to the adjoining woods, the Sages would not be satisfied with setting only a minimum standard of care for the railroad. Did the precautions the railroad adopted in *Taff Vale* satisfy more than a minimum standard of care? No. One of the factors Jewish law considers in deciding whether the defendant adopted the appropriate distancing requirement is the presence of combustible material along the path to the neighboring property.[93] Accordingly, suppose combustible material in the form of long grass is present along the railroad's embankment. Unless the railroad removes the combustible material by cutting the long grass along its embankment with appropriate regularity, the railroad will not be doing all it can to prevent flying sparks from burning the adjoining woods. In *Taff Vale*, the railroad had not cut the grass along its embankment for three or four months. In addition, it was clear that the sparks emitted from the engine of the train initially burnt the railroad embankment and from there proceeded to burn the adjoining woods.[94]

The upshot of the above analysis is that for the railroad sparks case, the Sages would insist that the railroad operate its locomotives with all the precautions against the emission of sparks mentioned in *Taff Vale*. The Sages would also insist that the railroad cut the grass that grows along its embankment with appropriate regularity. To be sure, all those measures will not guarantee that sparks will never be emitted by a locomotive as it travels along its path. To accomplish that, the rate of speed of the railroad would also have to be regulated. Because insistence on the most stringent standard of care would drive the railroad out of business, we take it as a given that the Sages would not impose a standard that would ensure no sparks, but only a standard that, under ordinary conditions, would rarely cause damage. However, since exemption from liability applies only if the defendant implemented the most stringent precautions and, despite those precautions, the fire caused damage, the railroad would be liable for all damage the sparks cause.

The Railroad Sparks Case and Communal Legislation

The treatment of the railroad sparks case under Jewish tort law is not the end of the discussion of this matter. In contrast to the oven case and the adjoining property owner case where the competing rights of neighbors must be balanced, the issue in the railroad sparks case is the balancing of the rights of the individual against the rights of society. Society as a whole is implicated here on several levels. Most basically, the operation of the railroad expands the marketplace and spurs economic development and growth by reducing the cost of freight. Because the railroad promotes much greater efficiency in the distribution of society's goods and services, everyone benefits in the long run, including the neighboring farmers who suffer destruction of their crops. Another consideration for society is that the railroad's route covers many hundreds of miles. Inevitably, the railroad tracks will either expropriate private property or infringe upon its use. Society as a collective must therefore set rules for the rights of private property owners.

In matters affecting society as a whole, Jewish law assigns the community legislative authority to craft policies that maximize social welfare. Certain functions are mandated for the Jewish community, while other functions, particularly with respect to monetary matters, require majority approval.[95]

In the railroad sparks case, the task for the Jewish community would be to require the railroad to get a government-issued charter before beginning operations. The charter would balance the property rights of private property owners against the rights of the railroad to expropriate or infringe upon those rights, provided the railroad pays proper compensation to the owners. The charter would specify the conditions under which the property owners may refuse to sell their rights. In addition, when compensation is deemed appropriate, the charter would specify whether the price of relinquishing property rights to the railroad should be determined by negotiation or instead by a formula for determining a fair price.

The charter would also spell out the precautionary measures the railroad is expected to take to prevent fire damage to surrounding woods and the liability the railroad would bear if damage occurs despite the adoption of those measures.

Let's now move to the issue of safety rules and compensation. Since the very essence of the benefit the railroad provides to society is speed of transportation, this benefit will never be achieved unless the government allows the railroad to operate at a speed consistent with making the railroad a viable business. We assume that the speed needed to accomplish this would not be attainable if the railroad were required to adhere to the highest standards of safety. If so, requiring the railroad to operate in accordance with the highest level of safety that is compatible with keeping the railroad in business should be considered tantamount to imposing the highest level of safety on the railroad.

Using *Taff Vale* as our model, the government would insist that the railroad operate its locomotives with all the precautions against the emission of sparks that the railroad in *Taff Vale* adopted. The government would also insist that the railroad regularly cut the grass that grows along its embankment. Since adopting all those measures amounts to imposing the highest standard of care as far as a social project is concerned, once the railroad adopts these measures, it should not be held responsible for damage that flying sparks cause to neighboring fields.

Consider the effect these safety rules will have on farmers. Because the standard of safety that Jewish law sets for the railroad is higher than the standard the railroad adhered to in *Taff Vale*, we should not expect the neighboring farmers to abandon cultivation on a widespread basis. The higher standard of safety might be just enough to induce the farmers to take a chance and continue their enterprise, but with an adjustment. This would consist of managing their properties more carefully to ensure that combustible material does not lie close to the railroad embankment.

Professor Yehoshua Liebermann on Coase

In his paper "The Coase Theorem in Jewish Law," Professor Yehoshua Liebermann disaggregates the Coase theorem into three components: (1) the reciprocity principle; (2) the trading principle; and (3) the independence principle. Liebermann then proceeds to show that authorities in Jewish law throughout the centuries adopted these three principles.[96]

I am in agreement with Professor Liebermann with respect to two of these components, but disagree with respect to the third.

Turning first to my areas of agreement, let's begin with what Professor Liebermann calls the trading principle. This principle says that harmful effects of business activities can be traded in the marketplace by the concerned parties.

What Professor Liebermann calls the trading principle can be restated in familiar terminology under Jewish law as simply saying that an individual can always waive his rights in monetary matters. To find authority for this principle, there is no need to examine the Responsa literature, as Professor Liebermann does, since this principle was first enunciated by the *Tanna*, R. Judah.

> [If a man] says to a woman, "Behold, you are betrothed to me, on condition that you shall have no claim upon me for food, clothing or marital relations," she is betrothed, but his stipulation is void, since the Torah obligates a husband to provide these things. These are the words of R. Meir. However, R. Judah says, "Regarding monetary matters, such as his obligation to provide food and clothing, his stipulation stands in effect."[97] Decisors follow R. Judah's view.[98]

Another aspect of Coase's theorem is what Professor Lieberman calls the independence principle. This principle states that if negotiation costs are relatively low, it is possible for the losing party to take the initiative and offer the winning party a payment that would make it worthwhile for the winner to waive his rights and thereby achieve an economically efficient result.

Professor Liebermann's independence principle, as it appears to this writer, is very much intertwined with the trading principle. Once it is recognized that an individual may waive his rights in monetary matters, there should be no objection for one of the concerned parties to take the initiative and offer his opposite number a payment to induce him to waive his rights. This right should apply both before and after a judicial decision is rendered in the matter.

My point of disagreement relates to what Professor Liebermann calls the reciprocity principle. This principle, which is the methodology Coase uses in all the cases we have dealt with in this chapter, states that the most important factor in addressing the negative externality problem is that we should not view the circumstances as a case of a perpetrator and a victim. Instead, we should recognize that the negative externality problem is reciprocal and the goal in solving the problem should be to maximize social value.

In Professor Liebermann's assessment, mainstream Jewish law embraces the reciprocity principle as the way to deal with the negative externality problem. In making this judgment, Professor Liebermann relies solely on a ruling of R. Moses Sofer (*Hatam Sofer*, Hungary, 1762–1839).[99]

In the case presented to R. Sofer, three brothers inherited a two-story house. Two of the brothers received the upper story, while the third received the lower story. A dispute arose when one of the occupants of the upper story wanted to open a business on his premises that included the operation of a bar. Because the operation of the bar could be expected to generate significant new traffic in the courtyard, which was jointly owned by the three brothers, the occupant of the lower story felt he had the right to object on the grounds that the operation of the bar would generate a nuisance in the form of traffic congestion in the courtyard.

The rabbi who submitted the question to R. Sofer was certain that Jewish law would side with the plaintiff, but was reluctant to render such a ruling because the public would find it odd that a neighbor could actually stop someone else's livelihood based on the anticipated nuisance of increased traffic. Moreover, the actual practice of neighbors at the time the case arose was not to complain in this type of case.

Why did neighbors not exert their rights here? In the opinion of R. Sofer's interlocutor, the practice of not protesting developed in response to the obstacles Jews faced in earning a livelihood during the long and protracted Diaspora. At the time the question was posed to R. Sofer, Jews had great difficulty finding rental property for their businesses. If neighbors would protest and exert their rights, a Jew who conducted a retail outlet in his home would be driven out of business and would have nowhere to go. Out of compassion for their brethren, neighbors did not exert their rights and did not protest the operation of a retail trade in one of the dwellings facing their courtyard.

In his response, R. Sofer agreed with his interlocutor that the occupant of the upper story should not be enjoined from conducting a bar on his premises. Moreover, R. Sofer averred that refusing to issue an injunction against the bar is consistent with mainstream thought in defining when it is legitimate to enjoin the economic activity a resident of a courtyard conducts on his premises.

R. Sofer understands the mainstream criterion to be whether the nuisance consists of noise or an increase in traffic congestion in the courtyard. When the nuisance consists only of noise, such as a noise from the hammering activity of a blacksmith, neighbors have no right to object. When the nuisance consists of an increase in traffic congestion in the courtyard, however, fellow residents may object. Establishing a retail store either in one's apartment or in the courtyard assuredly increases traffic in the courtyard. Residents, therefore, have a right to object.

This distinction between noise and traffic, R. Sofer contends, is not the end of the analysis. As far as noise is concerned, a hammering sound is much more annoying than the noise generated by an increase in traffic congestion. Addressing this issue, R. Levi ibn Habib (*Ralbach*, Jerusalem, ca. 1480–1545) proposed that the difference between a manufacturing activity and a retail activity conducted in a residential area is essentially the cost of transferring the enterprise from the residential area to the public domain, where marketplace activities are usually situated. Since relocating a manufacturing activity ordinarily can be accomplished only at great cost, a plaintiff's request for a court to order a manufacturing activity to move from one of the houses or from the courtyard to the marketplace would be denied because honoring the request would ruin the livelihood of the manufacturer. When the objectionable commercial enterprise is a store, however, the injunction would be granted because in most cases, a store can easily move to the marketplace without ruining its business.[100]

The case at hand hence hinges on whether moving the bar from the upper story of the house to the marketplace can be accomplished only at a prohibitive cost.

R. Sofer answers in the affirmative. Liquor is by its very nature not just a beverage but rather a "social drink." People do not drink in the street. Instead, they prefer to consume liquor in a setting conducive to socializing. Because forcing the brother to sell the liquor in the street would ruin his business, R. Sofer ruled that an injunction should not be issued against him.

Liebermann points to R. Sofer's ruling as representative of how Jewish law deals with the negative externality problem. He then uses this ruling to demonstrate that Jewish law adopts the reciprocity principle and concludes that the ruling's approach to the negative externality case is hence consistent with Coase's approach.

Liebermann's conclusion is unwarranted. Recall that R. Sofer's interlocutor makes prominent mention that Jewish businessmen at the time had great difficulty in finding outlets to operate their businesses. Consequently, they were forced to operate their businesses in their residences. Against this backdrop, the Jewish court would not issue an injunction because an injunction would ruin the defendant's business.

Suppose, however, it is common practice not to conduct a business in one's residence or in the courtyard of the building where one lives. Under those conditions, the court's refusal to grant the injunction confers on the defendant a significant competitive cost advantage. Accordingly, the cost of moving the enterprise should not be a factor in deciding the case. Instead, the criterion should be whether the objectionable activity causes only an increase in noise, or rather an increase in traffic.

Now, if the differential cost involved in moving the business enterprise cannot be invoked in explaining why hammering activity is treated differently from the operation of a store, what is the essential difference between these two kinds of nuisances?

Addressing this issue, R. Meir b. Todros ha-Levi Abulafia (*Ramah*, Spain, ca. 1180–1244) posits that the basis for allowing a fellow resident to object to the operation of a store in either a jointly owned courtyard or a house facing the courtyard is the right of a fellow resident to object to the operation of an enterprise that radically changes the character of the common property of the residents. Accordingly, manufacturing activity per se cannot be stopped, even if it is a nuisance to the fellow residents in the form of, say, hammering, because the private nature of the courtyard is preserved. When the objectionable activity consists of a store, by contrast, an injunction would be issued because the increase in traffic that the enterprise attracts changes the character of the courtyard from a private area into a marketplace.[101]

Since R. Abulafia's explanation of the different treatment of the defendants in the two cases is consistent with mainstream thought, the explanation should be applicable to the contemporary scene where the conduct of noise-generating or traffic-generating enterprises in private residences is unusual. In addition, zoning laws make it illegal to conduct business activities in residential buildings.

The upshot of the above analysis is that R. Sofer's ruling in the bar case is unique to the facts of that case and should not be understood as demonstrating that mainstream Jewish law embraces the reciprocity principle in dealing with negative externality cases.

Conclusion

This chapter compared Jewish law's treatment of the negative externality problem with economic theory's approach to the issue. As the backdrop for the comparison, we made use of the cases that Ronald Coase analyzed to illustrate what he felt was the approach economic theory would take to address the negative externality problem.

For Coase, the key is to recognize that the negative externality problem is reciprocal. Illustrating Coase's approach is how the emission of smoke pollution by a factory is treated. Forcing the industrial polluter to be responsible for the smoke damage raises the cost of doing business for the factory owner by causing some combination of lower profits, higher prices, and reduced employment.

Instead of viewing the industrial polluter as a perpetrator and society as the victim of the smoke pollution, society should deal with the negative externality problem with the goal of maximizing social value. An important aspect of this analysis is ascertaining the alternative productions as measured by the marketplace.

To extrapolate Jewish law's approach to the negative externality problem, this chapter examined the major cases Coase analyzed in his seminal paper. In each instance, the reciprocity principle was never utilized in Jewish law as an analytical device for arriving at a ruling in these cases. Instead, the ruling for each case was based on determining the rights of each party in the matter at hand.

No better illustration of the gap between Jewish law and Coase in their approaches to the negative externality problem can be found than the cattleman–farmer case in the context of the Land of Israel. Here, to promote population growth, the Sages prohibited the raising of small cattle except in the desert. That approach precludes the possibility for the cattleman to offer a payment to the farmer as an incentive to allow him to graze his herd on land adjacent to the farmer's land.

Another instance of a wide gap in the two approaches is *Sturges v. Bridgman*. In analyzing this case, Coase omits the detail that Sturges made use of Bridgman's kitchen door as a party wall in the construction of his consulting room. In all probability, Coase omitted this detail because it was not relevant to his reciprocity principle. In sharp contrast, under Jewish law, making use of Bridgman's kitchen door without permission forfeits for Sturges any right to protest the noise emitted by Bridgman's equipment.

This chapter also investigated Professor Yehoshua Liebermann's contention that mainstream Jewish law embraces the reciprocity principle. Liebermann bases his contention on the approach R. Moses Sofer adopted in the bar case. At the time that the case arose, it was not uncommon for Jews to conduct both manufacturing and retail businesses in a residential building. The change in socioeconomic conditions since that time, however, renders the application of R. Sofer's approach irrelevant for the contemporary scene. What has changed is that it is now uncommon and usually forbidden by zoning laws to conduct a commercial enterprise in a residential area. Since refusal to dislodge a commercial enterprise from a residential area confers an unfair cost advantage on the owner of the business relative to his competitors, the Jewish court would enjoin the operation of the business in the residential area.

Notes

1. Ronald H. Coase, "The Problem of Social Cost," *Journal of Law and Economics* 3 (October 1960): 1–44.
2. Arthur C. Pigou, *The Economics of Welfare*, 4th ed. (London: Macmillan, 1932), 183.
3. This is referred to as a "Pigovian tax" (or "Pigouvian tax"). See William J. Baumol, "On Taxation and the Control of Externalities," *American Economic Review* 62, no. 3 (1972): 307.
4. Coase, "Problem of Social Cost," 43.
5. Ibid., 1–2, 41–43. See also Richard R. Butler and Robert P. Garnett, "Teaching the Coase Theorem: Are We Getting it Right?," *Atlantic Economic Journal* 31, no. 2 (June 2003): 137–138. The numbers used in the text are for illustrative purposes only.
6. See, for example, Coase's treatment of *Sturges v. Bridgman* at Coase, "Problem of Social Cost," 8–10.
7. The key to understanding why the situation where total revenue equals total cost is not simply a breakeven point is the concept of opportunity cost. Opportunity cost is defined as the price or income a resource owner can command in his next best market opportunity. Thus, the owner of the enterprise may decide to take a salary out of the business that is considerably less than he could command working for someone else. Economic theory would record the cost of owner-provided labor and managerial skill not on the basis of what the owner sets as his own salary, but rather based on opportunity cost. Now, if the revenue the enterprise earns covers all the explicit costs of the inputs of the business and all the opportunity costs of the owner, this position is not breakeven. Instead, it is a position of contentment for the owner, as he has no incentive to abandon his present business for another venture.
8. Coase, "Problem of Social Cost," 2–8.
9. Ibid., 16–19.
10. Maimonides (*Rambam*, Egypt, 1135–1204), *Mishneh Torah, Nizkei Mamon* 1:2; R. Jacob b. Asher (*Tur*, Spain, 1270–1343), *Tur, Hoshen Mishpat* 389, 390; R. Joseph Caro (Safed, 1488–1575), *Shulhan Arukh, Hoshen Mishpat* 389:2.
11. *Mishneh Torah*, op. cit., 1:2, 10; *Tur*, op. cit., 389, 391; *Shulhan Arukh*, op. cit., 389:2, 391:1–3.
12. *Mishneh Torah*, op. cit., 1:2, 10; *Tur*, op. cit., 389, 390; *Shulhan Arukh*, op. cit., 389:2, 390:1–9.
13. *Mishneh Torah*, op. cit., 1:8; *Tur*, op. cit., 389; *Shulhan Arukh*, op. cit., 389:11, 15.

14. *Mishneh Torah*, op. cit., 3:1–2; *Tur*, op. cit., 391; *Shulhan Arukh*, op. cit., 391:8; R. Moses Isserles (*Rema*, Poland, 1525 or 1530–1572), *Rema* to *Shulhan Arukh, Hoshen Mishpat* 391:8.
15. R. Jehiel Michal Epstein (Belarus, 1829–1908), *Arukh ha-Shulhan, Hoshen Mishpat* 389:13.
16. *Mishneh Torah, Nizkei Mamon* 7:3; *Tur*, op. cit., 389; *Shulhan Arukh*, op. cit., 389:9.
17. *Arukh ha-Shulhan*, op. cit., 1:1–4, 389:5–6.
18. *Arukh ha-Shulhan*, op. cit., 389:12.
19. *Sanhedrin* 14a; Nahmanides (*Ramban*, Spain, 1194–1270) to Maimonides, *Sefer ha-Mitzvot*, Positive Commandment no. 153; Isaac Levitats, Aaron Rothkoff and Pamela S. Nadell, "*Semikhah*," in *Encyclopedia Judaica*, 2nd ed., vol. 18, eds. Michael Berenbaum and Fred Skolnik (Detroit: Macmillan Reference, 2007), 274–279.
20. *Arukh ha-Shulhan*, op. cit., 1:1–4.
21. *Bava Kamma* 23b.
22. *Rif*, *Bava Kamma* 23b.
23. *Mishneh Torah, Nizkei Mamon* 5:1, as understood by R. Jehiel Michal Epstein, *Arukh ha-Shulhan*, op. cit., 397:2.
24. R. Solomon b. Jehiel Luria *Yam shel Shelomoh, Bava Kamma* 2:25.
25. *Shulhan Arukh, Hoshen Mishpat* 397:1.
26. *Arukh ha-Shulhan, Hoshen Mishpat* 397:1.
27. R. Hananel b. Hushiel, cited in *Tur, Hoshen Mishpat* 397.
28. *Rosh, Bava Kamma* 2:10, as understood by R. Shabbetai b. Meir ha-Kohen, *Siftei Kohen* to *Shulhan Arukh, Hoshen Mishpat* 397, n. 1.
29. *Siftei Kohen* to *Shulhan Arukh, Hoshen Mishpat* 397, n. 1.
30. R. Asher b. Jehiel, explaining the opinions that agree with Abaye (*Rosh, Bava Kamma* 2:10).
31. *Bava Kamma* 55b; *Tosafot*, ad loc.; *Tosafot Rabbeinu Peretz* (Corbeil, second half of 13th cent.), quoted in R. Bezalel Ashkenazi (Egypt, 1520–ca. 1594), *Shitah Mekubbetzet, Bava Kamma* 55b.
32. *Arukh ha-Shulhan*, op. cit., 396:1–3.
33. *Mishneh Torah, Nizkei Mamon* 4:1; *Shulhan Arukh*, op. cit., 396:1; *Arukh ha-Shulhan*, op. cit., 396:1–3.
34. Final judgment in this matter should apparently be reserved in light of Jewish law's judicial rule called *kim li* (lit., I am certain). This rule allows a defendant in a civil judicial proceeding to insist that the judges consider the merits of his case based on the opinion of a particular substantial minority legal opinion.

    The *kim li* plea is recognized only if the authority invoked is a very substantial one. In the opinion of R. Jonathan Eybeschuetz (Poland, 1690–1764), *Urim ve-Tummim, Hoshen Mishpat* 25, validity is given to the *kim li* plea only if the dissenting opinion that rules against the *Shulhan Arukh* is either R. Shabbetai b. Meir ha-Kohen or R. Joshua b. Alexander ha-Kohen Falk (*Sema*, Poland, 1555–1614). Recall that R. Shabbetai b. Meir ha-Kohen is among the authorities who exempt the cattleman from liability unless the farmer fenced in his fields and, despite the fencing, the steers broke through and damaged the crop. Accordingly, if the farmer did not fence in his fields, the cattleman's *kim li* plea to dismiss the complaint based on the legal opinion of R. Shabbetai b. Meir ha-Kohen et al. will prevail.

    The *kim li* plea is largely irrelevant today because the organized Jewish courts routinely require the litigants to sign an agreement as a prerequisite for adjudicating the case that they will abide by the rules and decision of the court. Signing this agreement amounts to forfeiting any right to require the court to decide the case on the basis of a minority opinion.
35. *Bava Kamma* 79b, 80a; *Rif*, *Bava Kamma* 79b; *Mishneh Torah, Nizkei Mamon* 5:2; *Rosh, Bava Kamma* 7:13; *Tur*, op. cit., 409; *Shulhan Arukh*, op. cit., 409:1; *Arukh ha-Shulhan*, op. cit., 409:1–2.
36. *Mishneh Torah, Nizkei Mamon* 5:1.
37. *Rashi* to *Bava Kamma* 79b
38. (1879) L.R. 11 Ch. D. 852
39. Ibid. at 863–865.
40. Coase, "Problem of Social Cost," 8–10.

41. *Sturges*, L.R. 11 Ch. D., at 854.
42. A "party wall" is a wall that divides two adjoining, separately owned properties and is shared by the neighboring property owners. Four possible theories of the shared ownership of the wall are: (1) the neighbors own the wall as tenants-in-common; (2) the wall is divided longitudinally into two strips, one belonging to each of the two neighbors; (3) the wall is divided longitudinally into two strips, but each half is subject to an easement in favor of the owner of the other half; and (4) the wall belongs entirely to one of the adjoining owners, but is subject to an easement in favor of the other to have the wall maintained as a dividing wall. See Bryan A. Garner, ed., *Black's Law Dictionary*, 9th ed. (St. Paul, MN: West Publishing, 2009), s.v. "party wall."
43. *Sturges*, L.R. 11 Ch. D., at 854.
44. *Shulhan Arukh*, op. cit., 153:15.
45. R. Judah of Barcelona, quoted by *Tur*, op. cit., 153. For an extensive taxonomy of cases drawn from the *Rishonic* and Responsa literature where *Beit Din* applies *kofin*, see Aaron Kirschenbaum, *Equity in Jewish Law: Halakhic Perspectives in Jewish Law* (Hoboken, NJ: Ktav, 1991), 185–236. See also Shmuel Shilo, "*Kofin al Midat S'dom*: Jewish Law's Concept of Abuse of Rights," *Israel Law Review* 15, no. 1 (1980): 49–78.
46. R. Judah of Barcelona, quoted by *Tur*, op. cit., 153. See also R. Shalom Mordekhai Segal (Israel, contemp.), *Mishkan Shalom* (Jerusalem: Zihron Aharon, 2002), 322, *ot* 85.
47. R. Aaron b. Joseph ha-Levi (*Ra'ah*, Barcelona, 1235–ca. 1290), quoted by R. Joseph ibn Habiba (*Nimmukei Yosef*, Spain, early 15th cent.), *Nimmukei Yosef* to *Rif*, *Bava Kamma* 20b; see also R. Abraham Hirsch b. Jacob Eisenstadt (Byelostok, 1812–1868), *Pit'hei Teshuvah* to *Shulhan Arukh*, *Hoshen Mishpat* 363, n. 3.
48. R. Shimon Yehudah ha-Kohen Shkop (Poland, 1860–1939), *Hiddushei Rabbi Shimon Yehudah ha-Kohen*, vol. 3, *Bava Kamma*, *siman* 19:3.
49. *Bah* to *Tur*, op. cit., 153, n. 10.
50. *Rema* to *Shulhan Arukh*, *Hoshen Mishpat* 153:4.
51. *Arukh ha-Shulhan*, op. cit., 153:7.
52. Mishnah, *Bava Batra* 2:2.
53. *Baraita*, *Bava Batra* 20b; *Rif*, ad loc.; *Mishneh Torah*, *Shekhenim* 9:12; *Rosh*, *Bava Batra* 2:6; *Shulhan Arukh*, op. cit., 155:2; *Arukh ha-Shulhan*, op. cit., 155:3–4.
54. *Shulhan Arukh*, op. cit., 157:1; *Arukh ha-Shulhan*, op. cit., 157:1.
55. *Bava Batra* 59b; *Mishneh Torah*, *Shekhenim* 7:5; *Shulhan Arukh*, op. cit., 154:3; *Arukh ha-Shulhan*, op. cit., 154:7.
56. R. Yehezkel Abramsky, *Tosefta im Perush Hazon Yehezkel*, *Seder Nezikin*, vol. 2, *Bava Batra* 1:5 (Jerusalem, 1986).
57. *Ammot*, the plural of *amma*, is a common measure used in the Torah and the Talmud. It is equivalent to 18 inches according to some scholars, and 22.9 inches according to others.
58. Mishnah, *Bava Batra* 2:4 and Rava's understanding of the Mishnah at *Bava Batra* 22b.
59. *Rashi* to *Bava Batra* 22b. In various ways, the Talmud ad locum limits the practical application of *davshah*. More fundamentally, R. Vidal Yom Tov of Tolosa (*Maggid Mishneh*, Spain, ca. 1300–1370) posits that the law of *davshah* applies only when *A* acquired his parcel of land from the king. Here, we say that implicit in *A*'s purchase is a right to prohibit a neighboring property owner, *B*, from using *B*'s property in a manner that would undermine the foundation of *A*'s wall. See *Maggid Mishneh* to *Mishneh Torah*, *Shekhenim* 9:9. See also *Arukh ha-Shulhan*, op. cit., 155:14.
60. *Tosafot* to *Bava Batra* 22a, s.v. "*ve-kamma heikhi samikh*"; R. Solomon b. Abraham Adret, *Hiddushei ha-Rashba*, *Bava Batra* 22a.
61. R. Aaron Kotler, *Mishnat Rabbi Aharon*, *Hilkhot Shekhenim* (Jerusalem: Machon Mishnas Rabbi Aaron, 2003), 68.
62. *Mishneh Torah*, *Shekhenim* 6:12; *Shulhan Arukh*, op. cit., 156:2.
63. Maimonides and R. Joseph Caro, as interpreted by R. Joshua b. Alexander ha-Kohen Falk, *Sema* to *Shulhan Arukh*, op. cit., 156, n. 11.
64. *Rema*, op. cit., 156:2.

65. See Edward H. Ziegler, Arden H. Rathkopf, and Daren A. Rathkopf, *Rathkopf's The Law of Zoning and Planning*, 4th ed., vol. 1, § 10.1, vol. 3, § 58.1 (St. Paul, MN: Thomson Reuters, 2011).
66. Samuel, *Gittin* 10b.
67. Four views on this issue can be identified:

    1. Taking the narrowest view of the scope of *dina de-malkhuta dina* is R. Joseph Caro. In his view, Halakhah recognizes *dina de-malkhuta* only with respect to matters in which the government has a financial stake, such as taxes and currency regulation. *Shulhan Arukh, Hoshen Mishpat* 369:6–11.
    2. Adopting a much wider scope for *dina de-malkhuta* is R. Isserles. Representing the mainstream opinion, R. Isserles' view is explicated in the text.
    3. R. Shabbetai b. Meir ha-Kohen posits that in litigation between Jews, the law of the land finds its validity only when the secular law does not contradict Halakhah or the practical application of Halakhah is not clear. *Siftei Kohen* to *Shulhan Arukh, Hoshen Mishpat* 73, n. 39. In litigation between Jew and non-Jew, *dina de-malkhuta* is operative. *Siftei Kohen* ad loc.
    4. Following R. Shabbetai b. Meir ha-Kohen's line, R. Abraham Isaiah Karelitz (*Hazon Ish*, Israel, 1878–1953) sharply disputes the notion that lacunae exist in Halakhah. A halakhic position can be extrapolated for any issue. If *dina de-malkhuta* contradicts Halakhah, the law of the land must be set aside, even if the Halakhah was derived by means of extrapolation. *Hazon Ish, Hoshen Mishpat, Likkutim* 16:1 (Bnei Brak: S. Greineman, 1994), p. 464.

68. R. Mosheh Feinstein (New York, 1895–1986), *Iggerot Mosheh, Hoshen Mishpat* 2:62; R. Yosef Eliyahu Henkin (New York, 1881–1973), *Kitvei ha-Gri'a Henkin*, vol. 2, *Teshuvot Ivra*, ed. R. Abraham Hillel Henkin (New York: Ezras Torah, 1989), no. 96, pp. 174–176. See also the list of authorities cited by Professor Shmuel Shilo, *Dina de-Malkhuta Dina* (Jerusalem: Hebrew University Press, 1974), 157, n. 26.
69. *Rema* to *Shulhan Arukh, Hoshen Mishpat* 369:11.
70. Ibid.
71. Ibid.
72. *Rema*, op. cit., 26:1.
73. *Rema*, as understood by R. Mordecai b. Abraham Jaffe (Prague, ca. 1535–1612), *Levush Malkhut, Levush Ir Shushan, Hoshen Mishpat* 369, n. 11.
74. R. Yosef Eliyahu Henkin, *Kitvei ha-Gri'a Henkin*, vol. 2, *Teshuvot Ivra*, no. 96, ¶ 1(4), pp. 174–176.
75. *Vaughan v. Taff Vale Ry. Co.*, (1858) 157 E.R. 667, *rev'd*, (1860) 157 E.R. 1351.
76. *Vaughan v. Taff Vale Ry. Co.*, (1860) 157 E.R. 1351, *rev'g* (1858) 157 E.R. 667.
77. *Taff Vale*, (1860) 157 E.R., at 1354–1356.
78. Ibid. at 1353.
79. Coase, "Problem of Social Cost," 30. The Railway (Fires) Act also requires that certain procedural requirements must be satisfied before the railroad is held liable, such as the provision of notice to the railroad within seven days of the fire. Ibid.
80. In *Taff Vale*, the fire started on the railroad bank, which was the property of the railroad, and contained long grass that was highly combustible. *Taff Vale*, (1858) 157 E.R., at 669. Considering the possibility that just cutting the grass of the railroad embankment would remove the danger of flying sparks to the surrounding woods, the least-cost reaction of the farmers to the introduction of a no-liability rule might very well be not to abandon their land, but rather simply to cut the grass and make sure other flammable material is not situated near the railroad tracks. Indeed, in *Taff Vale*, the railroad company argued that the plaintiff brought the fire damage on himself by not cutting the grass near the railway bank. See id. at 671 (reviewing argument that "the plaintiff himself, in allowing the long grass to remain till it was dry and highly combustible close to the bank of the railway, by his own negligence contributed to the injury he suffered").

81. Coase, "Problem of Social Cost," 32. As it appears to this writer, a farmer would much prefer to sell his crop in the marketplace rather than sue the railroad for crop damage caused by flying sparks. Suing the railroad by no means ensures recovery and will entail litigation costs and other opportunity costs.
82. Ibid., 32–34.
83. For the definition of *ammot*, see endnote 57.
84. *Tanna Kamma*, Mishnah, *Bava Batra* 2:2; *Rif, Bava Batra* 20b; *Mishneh Torah, Shekhenim* 9:11; *Rosh, Bava Batra* 2:5; *Tur*, op. cit., 155; *Shulhan Arukh*, op. cit., 155:1; *Arukh ha-Shulhan*, op. cit., 155:1–2.
85. *Arukh ha-Shulhan*, op. cit., 418:2.
86. R. Shimon, Mishnah, *Bava Kamma* 6:4; *Rif, Bava Kamma* 61b; *Mishneh Torah, Nizkei Mamon* 14:1–3; *Rosh, Bava Kamma* 6:13; *Tur*, op. cit., 418; *Shulhan Arukh*, op. cit., 418:1–5; *Arukh ha-Shulhan*, op. cit., 418:22–25.
87. *Rif, Bava Kamma* 60a.
88. *Siftei Kohen* to *Shulhan Arukh, Hoshen Mishpat* 155, n. 2.
89. R. Jacob Moses Lorberbaum, *Netivot ha-Mishpat* to *Shulhan Arukh, Hoshen Mishpat* 155, n. 1.
90. R. Abraham Isaiah Karelitz, *Hazon Ish, Hoshen Mishpat*, vol. 3, *Bava Batra* 14:14 (Jerusalem: S. Greineman, 1954), p. 42.
91. R. Aryeh Leib b. Joseph ha-Kohen Heller, *Ketzot ha-Hoshen* to *Shulhan Arukh, Hoshen Mishpat* 155, n. 1.
92. *Vaughan v. Taff Vale Ry. Co.*, (1860) 157 E.R. 1351, 1353.
93. *Bava Kamma* 61a; *Rosh, Bava Kamma* 6:13; *Mishneh Torah, Nizkei Mamon* 14:3; *Tur*, op. cit., 418; *Shulhan Arukh*, op. cit., 418:4; *Arukh ha-Shulhan*, op. cit., 418:24.
94. *Taff Vale*, 157 E.R., at 1353.
95. For a description of the communal legislative process and the role Jewish law assigns government, see Aaron Levine, *Free Enterprise and Jewish Law: Aspects of Jewish Business Ethics* (New York: Ktav, 1980), 131–160.
96. Yehoshua Liebermann, "The Coase Theorem in Jewish Law," *Journal of Legal Studies* 10, no. 2 (June 1981): 293–303.
97. *Baraita, Kiddushin* 19b.
98. *Mishneh Torah, Ishut* 6:9–10; *Tur, Even ha-Ezer* 38; *Shulhan Arukh, Even ha-Ezer* 38:5; *Arukh ha-Shulhan, Even ha-Ezer* 38:9.
99. R. Moses Sofer, *She'elot u-Teshuvot Hatam Sofer, Hoshen Mishpat*, no. 92.
100. R. Levi ibn Habib, *She'elot u-Teshuvot Ma-ha-Ralbach*, no. 97.
101. *Ramah, Yad Ramah, Bava Batra* 2:56.

CHAPTER 4

Price Controls in Jewish Law

Introduction

Undoubtedly, Jewish's law most intrusive intervention in the marketplace takes the form of the ancient *hayyei nefesh* (essential food) ordinance. Enacted in approximately 240–250 C.E.,[1] the ordinance called for vendors of essential food to restrict their profit margin to no more than 20% of their cost base.[2] To ensure its enforcement, the *hayyei nefesh* edict required the Jewish court to appoint price commissioners to supervise the marketplace.[3] The prohibition was meant to be operative in the Land of Israel and in other places where Jews constituted a majority of the population.[4]

The motivational force behind the *hayyei nefesh* ordinance, according to R. Joshua b. Alexander ha-Kohen Falk (*Sema*, Poland, 1565–1614), was rooted in the Biblical injunction: "And let your brother live with you" (Leviticus 25:36).[5] R. Falk's comment makes the edict a mandate to sellers of essential foodstuff to forgo a portion of their potential profit to allow consumers to achieve subsistence without undue hardship.

Notwithstanding the altruistic motive behind the *hayyei nefesh* ordinance, economic theory would be quick to point out that price controls exert negative side effects, even to the point of undermining the goal of the ordinance.

Our purpose here will be to make the economic case against price controls. We will then evaluate the *hayyei nefesh* ordinance in light of the economic arguments against price controls. Finally, we will analyze the relevance of the *hayyei nefesh* ordinance to economic public policy today.

Price Controls in Economic Theory

The economic case against price controls begins with the demonstration that an unregulated marketplace provides an effective device for rationing goods in the short run as well as an effective means to signal resource owners where they can most profitably offer their services in the long run. Price controls deprive society of these benefits. Let's briefly demonstrate this proposition.

Within the framework of an unregulated free market, the price of a good will gravitate toward the price that will clear the market. This price is called the equilibrium price. The equilibrium price is the price at which the number of units suppliers want to offer is equal to the number of units consumers want to buy. Any other price is inherently unstable. Accordingly, if demand exceeds supply at the current price, competition among those who want to acquire the good will drive up price. Under this disequilibrium condition, price will continue to rise until supply equals demand. On the other hand, if at the prevailing price, supply exceeds demand, competition among sellers to liquidate their inventory will cause price to drop. Under this disequilibrium condition, price will continue to drop until supply equals demand. This pricing mechanism thus rations the available supply of the good to those who want to acquire it on the basis of competitive bidding.

Let's now turn to the allocation function of price. Under the assumption that unregulated markets will tend toward equilibrium in the long run, price provides a signal to resource owners regarding where they can most profitably offer their services and inputs. Self-interest will ensure that resources flow to those markets that earn the highest profits.

Given the altruistic motive behind the *hayyei nefesh* ordinance, it is reasonable to assume that the regulated price for essential goods would not be adjusted upward even if market forces made it clear that demand exceeded supply at the regulated price. In that case, the available supply of essential goods would have to be rationed based on a mechanism other than competitive bidding. Assuming the price ceiling would be vigorously enforced, distribution based on the seller's discretion or a "first come, first served" system would take over. Many would find both of those mechanisms very distasteful. The first puts the consumer at the mercy of the biases of the sellers, and the second involves a huge time investment on the part of the buyer. Ironically, neither of these mechanisms guarantees that the neediest will be among those who acquire essential goods. To ensure a fair distribution of essential goods, price controls for these goods have historically been accompanied by the issuance of rationing coupons.

Historical experience has shown that price controls are often not effective. Instead of a product being sold at the regulated price, black markets develop and the product is sold on the basis of whatever price the market will bear.

By imposing a limit on profits for essential food, price controls also discourage new entry into the necessity sector, as resource owners are naturally attracted to the unregulated sectors of the economy where no restraints on profits are imposed.

The economic case against price controls pertains only when a good is sold in a competitive marketplace. If an unregulated good is sold in a monopoly marketplace, by contrast, setting a price ceiling will in all likelihood not exert the unfavorable consequences outlined above. Consider that under a monopoly, price is typically higher and output is typically lower than under competitive conditions.

In addition, a monopoly typically earns profits above opportunity cost earnings. Accordingly, under a monopoly, regulators can set price at the level it would have been had the marketplace been a competitive one. Here, the price ceiling corrects the misallocation effects of the monopoly and hence does not generate the negative side effects described above.

The *Hayyei Nefesh* Ordinance

In this section, we will identify the category of items included in the *hayyei nefesh* ordinance and address the issue of whether the prices at which producers sold their output were also regulated under the ordinance.

SCOPE OF THE *HAYYEI NEFESH* ORDINANCE

The ambit of the *hayyei nefesh* ordinance is a matter of dispute. Three schools of thought can be identified.

The most expansive view of the coverage of the ordinance is taken by R. Joseph Caro (Safed, 1488–1575). In his view, all food, even spices, fell within the category of essential items.[6]

At the other end of the continuum stands R. Vidal Yom Tov of Tolosa (*Maggid Mishneh*, Spain, ca. 1300–1370). In his view, only foods that are dietary staples, such as wine, oil, and flour, were included in the ordinance. Eggs, in his view, are not regarded as an essential item and were not included in the ordinance.[7]

An intermediate position is taken by R. Falk. In his view, the 20% profit rate applied only to dietary staples, such as wine, flour, and oil. The allowable profit margin expanded to 100% for less essential food items. An example of such an item, specifically mentioned in the Talmud, is eggs. Included also in this category were food additives (*makhsherei okhel nefesh*), such as cumin, spices, and pepper. Finally, for all other items, such as frankincense, no profit limitation was set.[8]

PRODUCER PRICES

A critical issue regarding the scope of the *hayyei nefesh* ordinance is whether the profit constraint applied even at the level of producer prices. Noting that the Talmud lists flour but not grain in its enumeration of essential food items, R. Abraham David Wahrmann (Ukraine, ca. 1771–1841) posits that perhaps the Sages did not regulate the price of grain and instead left the price to the determination of the free market. R. Wahrmann does not, however, take a firm position on this matter.[9]

As it appears to this writer, a much earlier authority, R. Samuel b. Aaron of Joinville (France, ca. 1190–1233), dealt directly with the issue of whether producer prices were regulated under the *hayyei nefesh* ordinance. R. Samuel's position on this matter emerges from his analysis of the following *Baraita* at *Bava Batra* 91a:

> Our Rabbis taught: It is not permitted to make a profit on eggs twice. [As to the meaning of "twice"] Mari b. Mari said: Rav and Samuel are in dispute. One says: two for one [100% profit margin], and the other says: by a dealer to a dealer.

Commenting on the opinion that limits the profit rate in the egg industry to 100%, *Tosafot* query why the egg industry is not subject to the same 20% profit rate limitation applicable to other sectors of the essential food industry. Addressing himself to this dilemma, R. Samuel of Joinville posits that the initial market transaction in the *hayyei nefesh* sector is usually not regulated. The egg farmer, by contrast, is limited to a 100% markup.[10]

Let's take note that in their treatment of the *hayyei nefesh* ordinance, the codifiers of Jewish law do not record R. Samuel of Joinville's ruling that producer prices in the *hayyei nefesh* sector are ordinarily not subject to a profit constraint. If R. Samuel's ruling is normative, it should, however, appear as an underlying premise for other laws. Indeed, this is the case.

We begin with the prohibition against emigrating from the Land of Israel. Under certain strenuous economic conditions, the Sages allowed an exception to this prohibition:

> The rabbis taught in a *Baraita*: One may not leave the Land of Israel to live outside the Land unless grain prices have risen so sharply that two *se'ah* of grain cost a *sela*. R. Shimon said: "When is this permitted? When one cannot find grain to purchase (*she-eino motzei likah*). But when one is able to find grain to purchase (*motzei likah*), even if grain is so expensive that a *se'ah* costs a *sela*, one may not leave."[11]

Preliminarily, let's note that commentators understand the ordinary price of grain to be four *se'ah* per *sela*.[12] This makes the rise in the price of grain to two *se'ah* per *sela* an increase of 100%.

The *Baraita* clearly describes the grain market as a freely fluctuating market. This can be explained with the proposition that the *hayyei nefesh* ordinance was enacted after the Mishnah was redacted.[13] However, the prohibition against emigrating from the Land of Israel is codified in the works of R. Isaac b. Jacob Alfasi (*Rif*, Algeria, 1013–1103) and Maimonides (*Rambam*, Egypt, 1135–1204).[14] We would expect these decisors to discuss how the prohibition against emigrating from the Land of Israel operated under the *hayyei nefesh* ordinance. In their treatment of the prohibition against emigrating from the Land of Israel, however, these decisors do not relate the prohibition to the *hayyei nefesh* ordinance. The omission indicates that the *hayyei nefesh* ordinance was never intended to regulate producer prices.

Another source for extrapolating whether producer prices were regulated under the *hayyei nefesh* ordinance is an examination of the details of the law pertaining to forward contracts. A forward contract may violate one of the rabbinical extensions of the Biblical prohibition against charging interest (*ribbit*), called *avak ribbit* (lit., the dust of *ribbit*).

In a forward contract for the sale of agricultural produce, a buyer pays a farmer for goods to be delivered at a later date but at a price fixed at the time the parties enter into the contract.[15] Let's note that to acquire legal title to a product, a buyer must perform an appropriate symbolic act (*kinyan*).[16] By dint of a special enactment, the rabbis decreed that payment for a good in the class of moveable property does not suffice to accomplish a transfer of legal title.[17] In a forward contract, the combined circumstances that the buyer's payment does not accomplish a transfer of legal title and that the payment is in advance of receipt of the goods create a problem for *ribbit* law. These circumstances make the rabbis view the forward contract not as a sale, but as a disguised loan. Mechanically, the buyer advances money to the farmer and the farmer pays back the advance with the delivery of produce over a period of time. Out of concern that the price of the produce will increase over the delivery period, and the increase will be viewed as interest, the Sages prohibited the forward contract.[18]

The prohibition against entering into a forward contract is not absolute. The Talmudic Sages provided a number of exemptions.

One exemption obtains when the price of the produce involved is well established at the time the parties enter into the forward contract. This is called *yatza ha-sha'ar* (lit., the price went out).[19]

Illustrating *yatza ha-sha'ar* is the operation of the grain market in Talmudic times. In the beginning of the harvest season, only a few producers put their grain on the market. At this very early stage, the preponderance of the current crop of grain was not yet on the market, and the price obtained by these few producers had no stability. The market price for grain was not established until the entire supply was on the market.[20] This occurred sometime later and was identified with *dormus*, the price of the central market located in a big city where large quantities of grain were sold.[21] In this vein, R. Josiah b. Joseph Pinto (Damascus, 1565–1648) posits that the salient feature of *yatza ha-sha'ar* is stability. An established price, according to R. Pinto, is a price that holds for two or three months.[22]

Yatza ha-sha'ar removes the appearance of a disguised loan. This is so because the existence of a price that holds for a significant amount of time gives credence to the buyer's claim that had he not entered into the forward contract, he could have procured grain in the amount of his entire order from the marketplace at the current market price before the market price rose.[23] Accordingly, any subsequent appreciation of the price of the commodity over the term of the contract is considered an appreciation of something that was already in the domain of the buyer since the forward contract was entered into.[24]

A second exculpating circumstance for the forward contract obtains when the farmer has produce in stock (*yesh lo*) to cover the entire order at the time he enters into the contact.[25] Since the seller can sell his entire supply for immediate delivery at the low price of the forward contract, we can regard the entire order as already in the possession of the forward contact buyer at the time the parties entered into the contract.[26]

When the *yesh lo* condition is satisfied, the forward contract does not violate *avak ribbit* law, even if the price of the produce has not yet been established (*lo yatza ha-sha'ar*). Accordingly, even if the wheat farmer is the "first of the reapers" and the price of wheat is not yet established, the forward contract of the wheat farmer is, nonetheless, valid if the *yesh lo* condition is satisfied.[27] When the *yesh lo* condition has been satisfied, the wheat farmer, according to R. Solomon b. Isaac (*Rashi*, France, 1040–1105) and R. Joseph ibn Habiba (*Nimmukei Yosef*, Spain, early 15th cent.), is permitted to charge whatever price he desires for the forward contract.[28]

Underlying the various details of the law of the forward contract is the premise that producer prices were not regulated under the *hayyei nefesh* ordinance.

First, consider that the earliest time it is permissible to enter into a forward contract through the *yatza ha-sha'ar* mechanism is when the *dormus* price emerges. But why must the farmer wait so long? If producer prices are regulated under the *hayyei nefesh* ordinance, *Beit Din* (the Jewish court) must set up an administrative apparatus on farms to survey costs. As soon as the crop is produced, all the cost information is available and the rabbis can set the producer price for grain for the season based on that information. Since the price of the commodity over the entire delivery period cannot rise above the preset level, a forward contract that uses the regulated price as the guaranteed delivery price should be permissible.

If, on the other hand, producer prices are not regulated under the *hayyei nefesh* ordinance, the prohibition against entering into a forward contract until the *dormus* price arrives is understandable. This is so because under a free market, the price of grain can fluctuate widely even over a short period of time. Accordingly, it is not until such time that the free market price becomes predictably stable that a forward contract based on that price is valid.

Analysis of the underlying premise of the *yesh lo* exemption will also show that producer prices were generally not regulated under the *hayyei nefesh* ordinance. Recall *Rashi*'s and *Nimmukei Yosef*'s proposition that under the *yesh lo* exemption, the first reaper may charge any price he likes for the forward contract. Why does the "first reaper" have the liberty to charge any price he likes? To be sure, the first reaper enjoys temporary monopoly power, as he is now the only farmer who is offering the new crop for sale. But grain is a *hayyei nefesh* item, and the farmer who produces grain for sale should be under a 20% profit rate constraint. Giving carte blanche to the grain producer to set the price of his forward contract tells us that producer prices were not regulated under the *hayyei nefesh* ordinance.

R. Asher b. Jehiel advances a different opinion regarding the type of forward contract the first reaper is allowed to enter into. In R. Asher's opinion, the guaranteed price may not be lower than the gleaners' price (*sha'ar ha-lakotot*).[29] The gleaners are paupers who camp about in the fields at harvest time and collect their mandatory agricultural gifts.[30] Part of what the gleaners collect, they sell in the open market. Representing the first market transactions for the new crop, the price at which the gleanings trade is called *sha'ar ha-lakotot*. Setting the guaranteed price of the forward contract below *sha'ar ha-lakotot* would make it certain that the price of the commodity at delivery time would be higher than the prevailing price at the time the forward contract is entered into. The forward contract would therefore have the appearance of a disguised loan that calls for a *ribbit* premium. R. Asher, however, imposes no ceiling price in this case. The same issue we raised above can be raised here: If producer prices in the *hayyei nefesh* sector are subject to the 20% profit constraint, why is the guaranteed price of the first reaper's forward contract not subject to an upper limit? The absence of an upper limit indicates that producer prices in the *hayyei nefesh* sector were not regulated.

As noted earlier, the codifiers of Jewish law do not record R. Samuel of Joinville's ruling that producer prices in the *hayyei nefesh* sector are ordinarily not subject to a profit constraint. This lacuna should not be taken as an indication that these authorities hold that producer prices in the *hayyei nefesh* sector were regulated. To the contrary, the underlying premise of the law governing the forward contract, as discussed by these authorities, is that producer prices in the *hayyei nefesh* sector were not regulated.

In light of the above discussion, we will take it as a given that all opinions are in agreement that producer prices in the *hayyei nefesh* sector were not regulated.

The proposition that producer prices in the *hayyei nefesh* sector were not regulated makes the *hayyei nefesh* price ceiling a moving price ceiling rather than a fixed one. To illustrate, suppose the free market producer's price of wine is $10 a barrel and retailers incur an additional cost of $2 per barrel for transportation, rental, and selling expenses. The total cost base is thus $12 per barrel. Implementing the *hayyei nefesh* ordinance requires *Beit Din* to set the markup for retailers at 20%, and the price ceiling at $14.40 per barrel. If the manufacturer's free market price rises to $15, the price ceiling rises to a retail price of $20.40 (i.e., [$15 + $2] × 120%).

Three Interpretations of the *Hayyei Nefesh* Ordinance

We now turn to a description of how the *hayyei nefesh* ordinance actually worked. The *Rishonim* offer three different models of the ordinance.

1. RASHBAM

In his explication of the *hayyei nefesh* ordinance, R. Samuel b. Meir (*Rashbam*, France, ca. 1080–1174) understands the 20% profit rate constraint as a maximum markup set for a retailer who buys from a wholesaler and sells to individual customers. The examples that *Rashbam* gives for the application of the *hayyei nefesh* ordinance are the retail grain dealer and the retail wine merchant. *Rashbam* then states that the 20% limit applies only if the market price has not increased. But if a retailer bought his commodity at harvest time and the price of the commodity subsequently increased, the retailer is not bound by the 20% limit. Instead, he may sell at the current market norm, even if his profit rate will be 100%.[31] Thus, in *Rashbam*'s conceptualization, the *hayyei nefesh* ordinance did not operate as a price ceiling in a competitive marketplace. Within the framework of the *hayyei nefesh* ordinance, sellers were generally not prevented from transacting at the unregulated market norm.

If so, according to *Rashbam*, the 20% profit rate constraint is relevant only for situations where the seller is not a price taker, but rather a price setter. One situation of this sort is the monopolist seller. In that case, the Talmudic Sages tell the monopolist seller not to set his price above a 20% markup from cost.

A similar application is the dominant firm leadership model. Under that model, the marketplace features many sellers. All the sellers are, however, small firms, with the exception of one large dominant firm. Because the little firms fear head-on competition with the dominant firm, they are quite content to follow the pricing lead of the dominant firm. Accordingly, whatever price the dominant firm adopts, the little firms follow suit.[32] In recognition of the price leadership role of the dominant firm, the *hayyei nefesh* ordinance requires the firm to limit its markup to 20%.

Yet another application of the *hayyei nefesh* ordinance in *Rashbam*'s conceptualization of this edict is the prohibition against collusion among sellers to raise the market price to a level that affords participating sellers a profit margin above the intended 20% level. To achieve this result, participating sellers would have to agree to quotas to ensure that supply does not exceed demand at the price level they set. Because cartelization artificially raises market price to a level where individual participants earn above the 20% level, the conduct violates the *hayyei nefesh* ordinance.

Let's take note that in an imperfectly competitive marketplace, collusion among firms to fix price can occur in an implicit form too. The relevant construct here is the Sweezy model for oligopoly.[33] In this model, the marketplace features a few sellers and all the competitors charge the same price. Price rigidity is the norm here, as each firm is afraid to budge from the status quo. Each firm shares the perception that if it raises price, its rival firms will not follow suit and it will lose a significant amount of business to the other firms. Under the assumption that aggregate demand will increase very little if all firms reduce price, a particular firm will also find it too risky to initiate a price reduction. The mindset of the individual firm is that if it lowers price, its rivals will have no choice but to follow suit. The crux of the Sweezy model hence is that each rival firm perceives the demand it faces as elastic if it raises price and inelastic if it reduces price. This set of expectations makes the demand curve faced by the oligopoly a kinked demand curve.[34]

Notwithstanding the uniformity in price that prevails in the Sweezy model, this price should in no way be confused with the notion of a competitive price. This is so because all firms in the Sweezy model are earning above opportunity cost earnings. Since it is the duty of *Beit Din* to institute a 20% profit rate constraint in the *hayyei nefesh* sector, it becomes the mandate of *Beit Din* to impose a 20% markup limitation on all the firms in the oligopolistic industry.

Within the framework of *Rashbam*'s conceptualization of the *hayyei nefesh* ordinance, the price ceiling operated only within an imperfectly competitive marketplace. Recall the proposition that producer prices in the *hayyei nefesh* sector were not regulated. This makes the operation of the price ceiling in the imperfectly competitive marketplace a moving price ceiling, as opposed to a fixed one.

2. R. JACOB B. ASHER ET AL.

Another version of the *hayyei nefesh* ordinance emerges from the work of R. Jacob b. Asher (*Tur*, Spain, 1270–1343), R. Joseph Caro (Safed, 1488–1575) and R. Jehiel Michal Epstein (Belarus, 1829–1908).

In their treatment of the retailer in connection with the *hayyei nefesh* ordinance, all three of these authorities give license to these vendors to sell at the current market norm, notwithstanding any windfall above the 20% return they may realize as a result of an increase in market prices.[35]

The above formulation appears to follow *Rashbam*'s line of reasoning that the *hayyei nefesh* ordinance was not enacted for a competitive marketplace. Instead, in a competitive marketplace, the prices of *hayyei nefesh* items are free to change in accordance with the vagaries of supply and demand.

These same authorities, however, codify a ruling of R. Meir b. Todros ha-Levi Abulafia (*Ramah*, Spain, ca. 1180–1244) that in the event that the *hayyei nefesh* sector does not generally submit to *Beit Din*'s authority, *Beit Din* should not urge an individual vendor who is submissive to its authority to restrict his profit margin to 20%.[36] The rationale behind R. Abulafia's ruling is that *Beit Din* should not impose a profit rate restriction on an individual *hayyei nefesh* operator when little benefit will result for consumers. Given that the compliant vendor caters to only a small portion of the market, when his supplies run out, consumers will have to make their purchases from vendors who charge whatever the market will bear.[37]

It is understood from R. Abulafia's dictum that when the authority of *Beit Din* is recognized, *Beit Din* will not allow even the competitive marketplace to be left to its own devices. R. Abulafia's conceptualization of the *hayyei nefesh* ordinance is apparently not consistent with the notion that prices are free to fluctuate without restraint in this sector. How then can R. Jacob b. Asher, R. Caro, and R. Epstein rule that if the market price increases, vendors are free to sell at the higher market price, even if they realize a windfall above the 20% benchmark?

Resolution of the above difficulty is readily achieved under the assumption that producer prices in the *hayyei nefesh* sector were not regulated. Recall that the implication of an unregulated producer price is to make the *hayyei nefesh* price ceiling a moving price ceiling rather than a fixed one. Within the framework of a moving price ceiling, it is meaningful to talk about selling at the market norm. What this refers to is the liberty given to an individual *hayyei nefesh* vendor to sell at the new higher price ceiling, even if he is selling out inventory and hence is experiencing no increase in his own cost base at this juncture. The legitimacy of this practice tells us that for the purpose of the price ceiling, Halakhah values inventories at their replacement cost rather than historical cost.

3. MAIMONIDES

A third version of the *hayyei nefesh* ordinance is derived by Maimonides:

> We have already explained that he who does business on trust (*nosei be-emunah*) and says "I make so much and so much profit" is not subject to the law of overreaching (*ona'ah*), and even if he says "I bought this article for a *sela* and am selling it to you for ten," it is legitimate. Nevertheless, the court is obligated to regulate prices and appoint officers of the law, so that people at large will not be able to reap whatever profit they desire, but should earn a profit of only one-sixth [i.e., 20%].[38] A seller should not profit more than a sixth [of his cost base]. When does the above apply? With regard to articles on which our lives depend—wine, oil and fine flour. But with regard to herbs, such as costus, frankincense, and the like, a set limit is not established [by the court] and [the seller] may [take any measure of] profit he desires. Profit may not be taken twice [when selling] eggs. The first merchant who sells them may take a profit, and the person who buys them from him must sell them at cost.[39]

Commenting on Maimonides' formulation of the *hayyei nefesh* ordinance, R. Isser Zalman Meltzer (Lithuania, 1870–1953) avers that the ordinance is not directed at individual vendors, but rather consists of the enactment of a price ceiling.[40]

Does Maimonides hold that the *hayyei nefesh* ordinance applies even to a competitive marketplace? Yes. Let's demonstrate this proposition by drawing out the implications of the connection Maimonides makes between the *hayyei nefesh* ordinance and the *nosei be-emunah* case.

Preliminarily, let's note that the Talmud discusses the *nosei be-emunah* case in the context of the law of *ona'ah*.[41] The law of *ona'ah* makes the competitive norm the arbiter of whether the price of a transaction was "fair" and if an adjustment or cancellation is in order: "When you make a sale to your fellow or when you buy from the hand of your fellow, do not victimize one another" (Leviticus 25:14).

The law of *ona'ah* requires market participants to transact at the market norm.[42] The market norm is defined as either the price most firms charge or the price that is reflected in the greatest volume of sales.[43] A transaction concluded at a price at variance with the market norm is regarded as a form of theft.[44]

The Sages identified three degrees of *ona'ah*. Depending on how widely the price of the subject transaction departs from the market price, the injured party may have recourse to void or adjust the transaction. No recourse for cancellation or adjustment is provided, however, when the price discrepancy is not within the margin of error.[45]

The plaintiff's right to void the transaction is recognized when the difference between the sales price and the reference price is more than one-sixth.[46] We'll call this case first-degree *ona'ah*. Second-degree *ona'ah* occurs when the differential is exactly one-sixth. In such a case, neither of the parties may subsequently void the transaction on account of the price discrepancy. The plaintiff is, however, entitled to full restitution of the *ona'ah* involved.[47] Finally, third-degree *ona'ah* occurs when the sales price differs from the reference price by less than one-sixth. Here, the transaction not only remains binding, but the complainant also has no legal claim to the price differential.[48]

The law of *ona'ah* applies only to a competitive marketplace. Accordingly, by presenting the *nosei be-emunah* case against the backdrop of the law of *ona'ah*, it will become clear that Maimonides holds that the *hayyei nefesh* ordinance applies to a competitive marketplace.

The *nosei be-emunah* case represents an instance where the law of *ona'ah* does not govern the ethics of a commercial transaction. The prototypical case involves the following elements: *S* informs *B* that his cost base involved *ona'ah* and the competitive price of the article at hand is only half the price he actually paid for the item. *S* then proposes that *B* should agree to buy the article for a certain percentage markup above *S*'s cost. If *B* agrees to these terms, he forfeits any right to cancel or modify the transaction on the ground that *S*'s cost base involved *ona'ah*. This is so because the validity of the transaction is based on the circumstance that the parties agreed that the market would not be the arbiter of what constituted a fair price for the article. Instead, the agreement called for a certain markup for *S* above his cost base. Accordingly, notwithstanding that *S*'s cost base entailed *ona'ah*, *B* forfeited any *ona'ah* claim.[49]

Let's now apply the same elements of the above case to the *hayyei nefesh* sector. Suppose the item at hand is flour. *S* informs *B* that his cost base for the flour is $2 per pound. As matters turned out, however, *S* was victimized by *ona'ah* and could have bought the same flour for $1.50 per pound. *S* then proposes that *B* allow him a 30% markup above the price he actually paid, asking for $2.60 per pound. *B* agrees to this price, and the transaction is concluded. Later, it is discovered that the official price ceiling of flour is $1.40 per pound. Even though *S* and *B* agreed to ignore the price ceiling and instead concluded their deal at a price that is at a 30% markup above the cost figure *S* disclosed, the ceiling price of $1.40 prevails. An official price ceiling is hence controlling in an absolute sense, regardless of whether it is an equilibrium price.

Two scenarios present themselves. In one scenario, the marketplace is an imperfectly competitive one and the price ceiling *Beit Din* sets eliminates the economic rent that vendors were previously enjoying. In this instance, the price ceiling is an equilibrium price. But it is also possible that the price ceiling *Beit Din* sets is a disequilibrium price. In that case, the price that would equate supply with demand is a higher price than the one *Beit Din* sets for the *hayyei nefesh* item.

Maimonides' intention to make the official price ceiling controlling regardless of whether it turns out to be a market clearing price is seen from the repetition he employs in presenting the *hayyei nefesh* ordinance: "so that people at large will not be able to reap whatever profit they desire, but should earn a profit of only one-sixth [i.e., 20%]. A seller should not profit more than a sixth [of his cost base]." The repetition of phrases indicates that Maimonides speaks of two different market structures. The first clause, "so that people at large will not be able to reap whatever profit they desire," refers to a competitive marketplace. In that context, sellers have the ability to exploit the ignorance of a naïve and trusting consumer who erroneously imagines that whatever deal a particular seller offers him is the same deal another seller would offer him. The second phrase, "A seller should not profit more than a sixth [of his cost base]," refers to an imperfectly competitive marketplace, where there are few sellers and each seller enjoys a degree of leverage over his customers because of the market power he wields. Here, *B* does not operate in the marketplace with ignorance. To the contrary, *B* is fully aware of the available alternatives. But because those alternatives are limited and entail disadvantages of all sorts, *S* has some degree of leverage over *B*. Hence, *B* submits to *S*'s price terms.

By drawing a contrast between the *nosei be-emunah* case and the *hayyei nefesh* ordinance, Maimonides conveys the notion that the price ceiling for *hayyei nefesh* items is absolute and precludes the possibility for *S* and *B* to strike a deal that effectively allows *S* to earn a profit in excess of 20%. Implicit in the sweeping application Maimonides proposes for the 20% profit rate constraint is the view that the price ceiling was legislated even for a competitive marketplace.

The *Hayyei Nefesh* Ordinance and Economic Efficiency

In this section, we will address the issue of whether the *hayyei nefesh* ordinance can be expected to exert the usual negative side effects associated with price controls, as described in the beginning of this chapter. The issue is particularly germane because, as we have seen, *Rashbam* stands alone in proposing that the *hayyei nefesh* ordinance was not enacted for a competitive marketplace.

Given that the negative side effects of price controls occur because the price ceiling diverges from the equilibrium price, any factor that reduces this gap would be viewed favorably from the standpoint of economic efficiency. Pivotal in narrowing this gap for the *hayyei nefesh* ordinance is how the cost base for essential food items is calculated. If the cost base is defined very broadly, the gap between the equilibrium price and the price ceiling is narrowed.

Arguing that the *hayyei nefesh* ordinance defined cost very broadly is the circumstance that the cost base included the value of owner-provided labor services.[50] Including owner-provided labor services in the cost base makes the 20% profit rate a return on *all* costs.

Once it is recognized that the determination of the value of the owner's own labor services is within the jurisdiction of *Beit Din*, it also becomes the purview of *Beit Din* to determine the proper premium for the risk component of the owner's labor services. This problem becomes particularly knotty when the risk factor suddenly becomes more important. To illustrate, suppose war breaks out and the marketplace becomes a war zone. Suppose further that *hayyei nefesh* purveyors expose themselves to a greater risk in running their businesses than the risk customers incur in continuing to purchase these essential products. How should the cost base change to reflect the extra risk the sellers are now incurring to provide their customers with the staples they need?

In addressing this issue, it becomes relevant to observe that in the context of an unregulated marketplace, a sharp negative supply shock affords sellers the opportunity to earn much higher profits than they had been earning previously. But if increased danger for sellers accompanies the negative supply shock, a portion of the increased profit is illusionary. What sellers report as increased returns over outlays is not entirely an increase in profit, but instead partially reflects an increase in the opportunity cost sellers incur in expending toil and effort under dangerous conditions. Including the risk premium of owner-provided labor services in arriving at the cost base of *hayyei nefesh* items is hence a potential significant loophole in the 20% profit rate constraint.

Another factor that contributes to a broadening of the cost base is the distinct possibility that operating costs differed among the various sellers. For example, suppose a survey among local retail wine dealers shows that some keep store hours for a six-hour day while others keep a seven-hour day. What is the appropriate amount of labor time that should be included in the cost base? Another complication arises when some vendors incur a particular cost while other do not incur that cost altogether. An illustration of this type of cost in Talmudic times is the cost of the *barzanyata* (announcer). The role of this individual was to take barrels of wine into the street and announce to the public that they were for sale.[51] The cost of the *barzanyata* is explicitly mentioned in the Talmud as a legitimate cost to include in the cost base in determining the 20% profit rate for a *hayyei nefesh* item.[52]

Now, if some retail wine merchants in the local area use a *barzanyata* and others do not, should *Beit Din* include the cost of the *barzanyata* in the cost base? We take it as a given that *Beit Din* does not want to get involved in making a judgment about whether a particular expense constitutes a necessary cost. Instead, *Beit Din* would be content to leave it to the competitive pressures of the marketplace to decide this. Specifically, if a particular cost is an unnecessary cost, vendors generally would not incur it. In addition, if most vendors do not incur the cost, vendors who do incur the cost would be forced to drop it or face lower profit margins or even elimination from the marketplace. Because *Beit Din* has no choice other than to be nonjudgmental with respect to what constitutes a necessary cost, it must arrive at the price ceiling by assessing the weighted average cost base of the industry. The cost base that *Beit Din* determines would undoubtedly have an upward bias.

Another factor contributing to the narrowing of the gap between the price ceiling and the equilibrium price is that producer prices in the *hayyei nefesh* sector were not regulated. Letting producer prices go unregulated makes the regulated good responsive to the demand side of the marketplace. The concept of derived demand explains why. Consider that the demand for an input arises from and varies with the demand for the consumer good that the input helps to produce. Accordingly, an increase in the price of grain is not the cause of an increase in the price of bread. Rather, it is the reverse; the price of grain rises when the demand for bread is brisk because grain is the main ingredient in the production of bread.

While the phenomenon of derived demand, other things being equal, narrows the gap between the price ceiling and the equilibrium price, it is for the most part an insignificant factor in narrowing the gap. This is so because a negative supply shock can also cause the equilibrium price to rise. Accordingly, the phenomenon of derived demand in no way guarantees that the price ceiling is also an equilibrium price. Moreover, let's assume for argument's sake that the price ceiling is set at the equilibrium price and supply conditions are stable throughout the relevant time period. Will an increase in demand manifest itself in a proportional increase in the cost base? Ordinarily not. If the *hayyei nefesh* sector is experiencing unemployment and excess capacity, the responsiveness of the cost base will ordinarily be less than proportionate to the percentage increase in demand. Moreover, even at full employment, the supply of the key input (i.e., labor) may be very elastic in relation to the prevailing wage rate. In the real world, we should therefore expect the cost base of the *hayyei nefesh* index to lag behind the percentage increase in the demand for the final product. The derived demand phenomenon will hence not make the price ceiling an equilibrium price.

The *Hayyei Nefesh* Ordinance and the Law of *Ona'ah*

Once it is recognized that the cost base for the *hayyei nefesh* ordinance was defined in very robust terms, it becomes reasonable to theorize that the rabbis set the price ceiling above the equilibrium price. An important aspect for evaluating the above proposition is the law of *ona'ah*.

The law of *ona'ah* apparently argues against the proposition that the rabbis deliberately set the *hayyei nefesh* price ceiling above equilibrium. Consider that setting a price above the competitive norm subverts the entire purpose of the *hayyei nefesh* ordinance, which is to reduce the price of staple commodities from the price that would otherwise prevail in an unregulated marketplace. If the entire goal of the ordinance is missed by the price that is set, the price ceiling should be in violation of the law of *ona'ah*. This is so because if supply exceeds demand at the price ceiling, vigorous price competition among vendors to liquidate their inventories would make vendors accept a price for their commodity below the ceiling price. Mandating buyers to pay a higher price for a commodity than vendors would freely request amounts to legalizing the vendors to engage in theft.

Ready reconciliation of the duty to set a price ceiling with the law of *ona'ah* is achieved under the proposition that the price ceiling was never meant to supplant the competitive norm. To the contrary, when the price ceiling is initially set, it is deliberately set above the competitive norm. However, the operative price for the marketplace is not the price ceiling but rather the competitive norm. Because the price ceiling is a matter of public knowledge, some may, however, erroneously regard it as a mandated price. Within this confusion, vendors may get away with charging at the price ceiling even though the competitive price is below the price ceiling. Herein lies the role of the price commissioners. It is the role of these supervisors to survey the marketplace and make sure that no one sells above the competitive norm.

The role of the price commissioners to ensure that no one sells above the competitive norm assumes heightened importance when the competitive norm rises to the level of the official price ceiling. Within the framework of the economically stagnant economy the Sages lived in, the rise of the competitive norm to the level of the price ceiling undoubtedly reflected a negative supply shock. Because panic-buying based on the deliberate spread of misinformation is likely to occur under conditions of economic dislocation, the rise of the competitive norm to the level of the price ceiling puts the price commissioners on guard to ensure that the information channels function with a minimum of distortion and market participants make informed decisions based on the most accurate information available.

If we are correct in assuming that the rise of the competitive norm to the price ceiling is accompanied by economic dislocation, the usefulness of setting a price ceiling is that it signals the rabbis when remedial measures should be put in place. Once the price ceiling becomes the competitive norm, the rabbis should implement a plan that allocates the necessities of life in a manner that ensures that no one suffers deprivation as a result of cascading market prices for these necessities. These actions may include moral exhortations that a rationing system should be adopted.

Price Controls and Communal Legislative Authority

Price controls operate under the greatest inefficiency when a sharp negative supply shock suddenly impinges on the marketplace. A case in point is the sudden outbreak of war. The new environment of danger and risk causes the minimum price demand of all resource owners, called the supply price, to increase sharply. If the price ceiling was previously operating as an equilibrium price, it will no longer be a market-clearing price.

For the *hayyei nefesh* price ceiling to avoid the inevitable severe inefficiencies resulting from a negative supply shock, a mechanism must be in place to modify and even override the ordinance. This mechanism must be in place before the adverse event actually happens. We propose that the community's authority to fix prices and wages is such a mechanism. Maimonides, R. Jacob b. Asher, R. Joseph Caro, and R. Jehiel Michal Epstein all record this authority.[53] Analysis of the nature of this authority will point to a mechanism to avoid certain aspects of inefficiency associated with price controls.

We begin with Maimonides' treatment of the legislative authority of the community to fix prices and wages. Maimonides' treatment of this topic is typical of how the other authorities mentioned above treat this subject matter:

> The residents of a city may agree among themselves to fix a price for any article they desire, even for meat and bread, and to stipulate that they will inflict such-and-such penalty upon one who violates the agreement.[54]

Preliminarily, let's note that communal legislative authority must be linked to religious law. In this regard, communal legislation enjoys no halakhic sanction when it conflicts with ritual prohibitions. In matters of civil and criminal law, however, communal enactments are generally recognized even if they conflict with a particular rule of Halakhah.[55]

Communal price-fixing legislation in the *hayyei nefesh* sector may conflict with the 20% profit rate the *Beit Din* of the town sets for this sector. Maimonides' failure to qualify communal legislative authority in this regard clearly indicates that, in his view, communal price-fixing authority is absolute and may, if necessary, supersede the 20% profit constraint the Talmudic ordinance prescribed for the *hayyei nefesh* sector. Accordingly, if it becomes evident that the price regulation called for under the *hayyei nefesh* ordinance is causing shortages or other inefficiencies, the community can always legislate that the price ceiling should be increased to an appropriate level.

From the standpoint of economic efficiency, the best arrangement is for the legislative body and *Beit Din* to have a cooperative relationship rather than operate independently and in competition with each other. Having a cooperative relationship with the body in charge of the *hayyei nefesh* ordinance (i.e., *Beit Din*) makes it likely that the communal legislative body would assume a proactive rather than a reactive role in ensuring that the *hayyei nefesh* ordinance does not work to society's detriment. Facilitating this cooperative working relationship is the requirement that communal enactments must be approved by the locally recognized religious authority and communal leader (*adam hashuv*). Given the community-wide prestige the *adam hashuv* enjoys, this individual can serve as an integrative force between *Beit Din* and the legislative body. To be sure, if the town has no *adam hashuv*, communal legislation is fully valid without any outside approval.[56] Nonetheless communal social welfare cries out for a cooperative relationship between these two bodies.

If communal legislative authority may override the existing *hayyei nefesh* ordinance, the community should also have the authority to decide that the ordinance should not be imposed in the first place. Similarly, the community should have the authority to legislate in advance any necessary modifications or contingency plans for the price ceiling in the event of war or another type of supply shock.

Price Regulation of Staples and the Modern State

In extrapolating the significance of the Talmudic *hayyei nefesh* ordinance for the modern state, we begin with the comment of R. Falk, referred to earlier, that the 20% profit rate constraint was rooted in the Biblical injunction: "And let your brother live with you" (Leviticus 25:36). R. Falk's comment makes the edict a mandate to sellers of essential foodstuff to forgo a portion of their potential profit to enable consumers to achieve subsistence without undue hardship.

The lofty goal behind the *hayyei nefesh* ordinance leads us to expect that the Sages would give the ordinance wide application beyond food items to other necessities of life, including clothing, shelter, and *mitzvah* objects. Yet the only category of necessity the ordinance applies to is food, and even here, as we have seen earlier, authorities dispute the extent of its application.

Why did the rabbis craft the 20% profit rate constraint in such narrow terms? Perhaps the answer is that the rabbis had an intuitive understanding that interference with market forces to implement a notion of fairness in economic return may bring in its wake unwanted side effects. If implementing a notion of equity carries with it unwanted baggage, the practicality of implementing the idea in the first place must be revisited. This is so because when everything is considered, we may be worse off than before.

The analysis above leads to the proposition that the price control element of the *hayyei nefesh* ordinance survives today as a notion of fairness in the pricing of essential goods. What survives is not the 20% figure per se. This figure made sense only for the marketplace and economic conditions that existed at the time the ordinance was enacted. The general objection to "excessive profits" for those who deal in essential products should, however, remain. What should be substituted for the 20% figure today is the notion that the ideal is to craft government tax and regulatory policy to eliminate economic rent in the *hayyei nefesh* sector. In other words, the goal should be to prevent profits in the *hayyei nefesh* sector from exceeding opportunity cost earnings. One application of this principle is that the price of kosher poultry and Passover products should be regulated to limit profits to opportunity cost earnings. Another industry ripe for regulation on the basis of the opportunity cost concept is the pharmaceutical industry. We have dealt with the latter issue elsewhere.[57]

Conclusion

In this chapter, we examined the *hayyei nefesh* ordinance enacted by the rabbis in ancient times. This ordinance called for sellers of essential food items to limit their profit margin to no more than 20% of their cost base. The ordinance reflected the economic morality that sellers of essential foodstuff should forgo a portion of their potential profit to allow consumers to achieve subsistence without undue hardship.

Despite the altruistic motive behind the *hayyei nefesh* ordinance, economic theory would be very critical of the ordinance by pointing out that price controls exert negative side effects, even to the point of making the measure self-defeating.

Was the enactment of the *hayyei nefesh* ordinance bad economics? Pivotal in making this judgment is an analysis of whether the *hayyei nefesh* ordinance legislated a disequilibrium price for essential food items.

One factor to consider is the type of market structure in which the edict was meant to operate. Given that the unfavorable side effects of price controls occur when a regulated item is sold in a competitive marketplace, the *hayyei nefesh* ordinance would be mostly free of criticism of inefficiency if it was not meant for a competitive marketplace. But market structure is not an exculpating factor here, as mainstream opinion applies the ordinance even to a competitive marketplace.

One redeeming factor, however, is that producer prices were not regulated under the *hayyei nefesh* ordinance. Because the demand for producer goods is a derived demand, letting producer prices go unregulated makes the regulated good responsive to the demand side of the marketplace.

While the phenomenon of derived demand, other things being equal, narrows the gap between the price ceiling and the equilibrium price, it is for the most part an insignificant factor in narrowing the gap. This is so because a negative supply shock can also cause the equilibrium price to rise.

There is, however, one aspect of the *hayyei nefesh* ordinance that makes it reasonable to propose that in implementing the edict, the rabbis deliberately set the price ceiling above equilibrium. This factor is the manner in which the cost base was calculated. Consider that the value of owner-provided labor services was included in the cost base. Relatedly, we theorized that a premium for the risk component of the owner's labor services was also included in the cost base.

Another factor that contributes to a broadening of the cost base is the distinct possibility that operating costs differed among the various sellers. We take it as a given that *Beit Din* does not want to get involved in making a judgment about what constitutes a necessary cost. Instead, *Beit Din* would be content to leave it to the competitive pressures of the marketplace to decide this. Because *Beit Din* has no choice other than to be nonjudgmental with respect to what constitutes a necessary cost, it must arrive at the price ceiling by assessing the weighted average cost base of the industry.

Consider that in calculating the price ceiling, 20% was added to whatever the cost base turned out to be. Consider also that producer prices were not regulated. Based on these factors, we theorized that the rabbis deliberately set the price ceiling above the equilibrium level.

Our proposition that the rabbis deliberately set the price ceiling of *hayyei nefesh* items above equilibrium makes the operative price for these items the competitive price. Because the price ceiling is a matter of public knowledge, some may, however, erroneously regard it as a mandated price. Within this confusion, vendors may get away with charging at the price ceiling even though the competitive price is below the price ceiling. Herein lies the role of the price commissioners. These supervisors must survey the marketplace and make sure that no one sells above the competitive norm

The role of the price commissioners to ensure that no one sells above the competitive norm assumes heightened importance when the competitive norm rises to the level of the official price ceiling. Within the framework of the economically stagnant economy the Sages lived in, the rise of the competitive norm to the price ceiling level undoubtedly reflected a negative supply shock. Because panic-buying based on the deliberate spread of misinformation is likely to occur under conditions of economic dislocation, the rise in the competitive norm to the level of the price ceiling puts the price commissioners on guard to ensure that the information channels function with a minimum of distortion and market participants make informed decisions based on the most accurate information available.

If we are correct in assuming that the rise of the competitive norm to the level of the price ceiling is accompanied by economic dislocation, the usefulness of setting a price ceiling is that it signals the rabbis when remedial measures should be put in place. Once the price ceiling becomes the competitive norm, the rabbis should implement a plan that allocates the necessities of life in a manner that ensures that no one suffers deprivation as a result of cascading market prices for these necessities. These actions may include moral exhortations that a rationing system should be adopted.

Another factor that acts as a check to ensure that the *hayyei nefesh* ordinance does not work to society's detriment is the legislative authority of the community to abrogate or adjust this edict. From the standpoint of economic efficiency, the best arrangement is for the legislative body and *Beit Din* to have a cooperative relationship rather than operate independently and in competition with each other. Having a cooperative relationship with the body that is in charge of the *hayyei nefesh* ordinance makes it likely that the communal legislative body would assume a proactive rather than a reactive role in ensuring that the *hayyei nefesh* ordinance does not work to society's detriment.

Finally, we addressed the significance of the *hayyei nefesh* ordinance for the modern state. We proposed that the *hayyei nefesh* ordinance survives today as a notion of fairness in the pricing of essential goods. What survives is not the 20% figure per se. This figure made sense only for the marketplace and economic conditions that existed at the time of the enactment of the ordinance. The general objection to "excessive profits" for those who deal in essential products should, however, remain. What should be substituted for the 20% figure today is the notion that the ideal is to craft government tax and regulatory policy to eliminate economic rent in the *hayyei nefesh* sector. In other words, the goal should be to prevent profits in this sector from exceeding opportunity cost earnings. One application of this principle is that price in the kosher poultry and Passover food product industries should be regulated to limit profits to opportunity cost earnings. Another industry ripe for regulation based on the opportunity cost concept is the pharmaceutical industry.

Notes

1. We arrive at this date based on the consideration that the first mention of the enactment is recorded in the *Tosefta*. See *Tosefta*, *Bava Batra* 5:4. The consensus among scholars is that the *Tosefta* was redacted 40 to 50 years after the Mishnah (i.e., ca. 240–250 C.E.). See Stephen G. Wald, "*Tosefta*," in *Encyclopedia Judaica*, 2nd ed., vol. 20, eds. Michael Berenbaum and Fred Skolnik (Detroit: Macmillan Reference, 2007), 70. Hence, the *hayyei nefesh* ordinance was enacted sometime before 240–250 C.E. Peculiarly, the Mishnah itself makes no mention of the *hayyei nefesh* ordinance. It is therefore tempting to theorize that the *hayyei nefesh* ordinance was enacted sometime between 240 and 250 C.E.
2. The *Amora*, Samuel of Nehardea, reports the essential food ordinance at *Bava Metzia* 40b in the following manner: "One who profits [from selling staple commodities] should not profit by more than a sixth." Though Samuel reports the maximum profit as a sixth, it is widely understood to mean 20% of the cost base. The sixth Samuel speaks of is an "outside sixth," which is the same as an "inside fifth." A numerical illustration will clarify this matter. Suppose the cost base is $10. To calculate an outside sixth, we ask the question: What sum put alongside five equal parts will make six equal parts? The answer is $2. This calculation allows the vendor to sell the item at $12. To calculate the "inside fifth," we begin by taking a fifth of the cost base of $10. This amounts to $2. Adding $2 to the cost base of $10 allows the vendor to sell the item at $12. Cf. R. Shneur Zalman of Liadi (Russia, 1745–1812), *Shulhan Arukh ha-Rav*, *Hoshen Mishpat*, *helek* 6, *Hilkhot Middot u-Mishkalot va-Hafka'at She'arim*, *se'if* 17 (Brooklyn: Otzar ha-Hasidim, 2006), p. 58.
3. Maimonides (*Rambam*, Egypt, 1135–1204), *Mishneh Torah*, *Mekhirah* 14:1–2; R. Jacob b. Asher (*Tur*, Spain, 1270–1343), *Tur*, *Hoshen Mishpat* 231; R. Joseph Caro (Safed, 1488–1575), *Shulhan Arukh*, *Hoshen Mishpat* 231:20; R. Jehiel Michal Epstein (Belarus, 1829–1908), *Arukh ha-Shulhan*, *Hoshen Mishpat* 231:20.
4. R. Joshua b. Alexander ha-Kohen Falk (*Sema*, Poland, 1555–1614), *Sema* to *Shulhan Arukh*, *Hoshen Mishpat* 231, n. 42.
5. Ibid., n. 43.
6. R. Joseph Caro, *Kesef Mishneh* to *Mishneh Torah*, *Mekhirah* 14:2.

7. R. Vidal Yom Tov of Tolosa, *Maggid Mishneh* to *Mishneh Torah*, ad loc.
8. *Sema* to *Shulhan Arukh, Hoshen Mishpat* 231, n. 36.
9. R. Abraham David Wahrmann, *Kesef ha-Kadashim* to *Shulhan Arukh*, op. cit., 231:20.
10. R. Samuel b. Aaron of Joinville, *Tosafot* to *Bava Batra* 91a.
11. *Baraita, Bava Batra* 91a.
12. See R. Samuel b. Joseph Strashun (*Rashash*, Vilna, 1794–1872), *Haggahot ve-Hiddushei ha-Rashash, Bava Batra* 91a.
13. See note 1 above.
14. *Rif, Bava Batra* 91a; *Mishneh Torah, Melakhim* 5:9.
15. Mishnah, *Bava Metzia* 5:7; *Rif, Bava Metzia* 72b; *Mishneh Torah, Malveh ve-Loveh* 9:1; *Rosh, Bava Metzia* 5:60; *Tur, Yoreh De'ah* 175; *Shulhan Arukh, Yoreh De'ah* 175:1.
16. Cf. *Mishneh Torah, Mekhirah* 1:3.
17. *Bava Metzia* 47a.
18. R. Isaac b. Sheshet Perfet (*Ribash*, Spain, 1325–1408), quoted by R. Joseph Caro, *Beit Yosef* to *Tur, Yoreh De'ah* 173.
19. Mishnah, *Bava Metzia* 5:7; *Rif, Bava Metzia* 72b; *Mishneh Torah, Malveh ve-Loveh* 9:1; *Rosh, Bava Metzia* 5:60; *Tur, Yoreh De'ah* 175; *Shulhan Arukh, Yoreh De'ah* 175:1.
20. R. Solomon b. Isaac (*Rashi*, France, 1040–1105), *Rashi* to *Bava Metzia* 62b, s.v. "*ein poskin al ha-peirot.*"
21. R. Assi, *Bava Metzia* 72b; *Rif*, ad loc.; *Mishneh Torah, Malveh ve-Loveh* 9:4; *Shulhan Arukh, Yoreh De'ah* 175:1. Another view in this matter is that a farmer may enter into a forward contract as soon as a market price becomes established in the local town. This price appears earlier than the *dormus* price, but is less stable. The latter view is taken by R. Jacob b. Asher and R. Moses Isserles (*Rema*, Poland, 1525 or 1530–1572). *Tur, Yoreh De'ah* 175; *Rema* to *Shulhan Arukh, Yoreh De'ah* 175:1.
22. R. Josiah b. Joseph Pinto, quoted in R. Bezalel Ashkenazi (Egypt, 1520–ca. 1594), *Shitah Mekubbetzet, Bava Metzia* 72b.
23. Rabbah and R. Joseph, *Bava Metzia* 63b; *Rosh, Bava Metzia* 5:60; *Beit Yosef* to *Tur, Yoreh De'ah* 175. *Tosafot* at *Bava Metzia* 62b, however, understand the rationale of *yatza ha-sha'ar* to relate to the conduct of the seller rather than the buyer. In this understanding, the entire order should be viewed as if it was procured by the seller before any rise in price could occur because once the seller takes money from the buyer, the seller is obligated to procure the order for the buyer to avoid being subject to the judicial curse of "He who exacted punishment from the generation of the Flood and the generation of the Dispersion will exact punishment from one who does not stand by his word" (Mishnah, *Bava Metzia* 4:2). This imprecation is know as "*Mi she-para.*" See *Bava Metzia* 44a; *Mishneh Torah, Mekhirah* 7:1–6; *Rosh, Bava Metzia* 4:13. For an explanation of why the rationales from both the perspective of the buyer and the seller are necessary, see R. Isaac Blaser (Russia, 1837–1907), *She'elot u-Teshuvot Peri Yitzhak* 2:46. See also R. Yom Tov Ishbili (*Ritva*, Spain, ca. 1250–1330), *Hiddushei ha-Ritva, Bava Metzia* 72b.
24. R. Shabbetai b. Meir ha-Kohen (*Siftei Kohen*, Poland, 1621–1662), *Siftei Kohen* to *Shulhan Arukh, Yoreh De'ah* 175, n. 1.
25. *Shulhan Arukh, Yoreh De'ah* 162:2.
26. R. Abraham Danzig (Prague, 1748–1820), *Hokhmat Adam* 141:3.
27. Mishnah, *Bava Metzia* 5:7; *Rif, Bava Metzia* 72b; *Mishneh Torah, Malveh ve-Loveh* 9:1; *Rosh, Bava Metzia* 5:60; *Tur, Yoreh De'ah* 175; *Shulhan Arukh, Yoreh De'ah* 175:4.
28. *Rashi* to *Bava Metzia* 72b; *Nimmukei Yosef* to *Rif, Bava Metzia* 72b. See, however, *Rosh, Bava Metzia* 5:60.
29. *Rosh, Bava Metzia* 5:60.
30. The mandatory gifts to the poor are fallen stalks (*leket*), forgotten stalks or sheaves (*shikhehah*), and stalks left at the edge of the field (*pe'ah*). See Leviticus 19:9, Leviticus 23:22, and Deuteronomy 24:19.
31. R. Samuel b. Meir (*Rashbam*, France, ca. 1080–1174), *Bava Batra* 90a, s.v. "*ein mosifin al ha-middot.*"

32. For a discussion of the dominant firm leadership model, see Edgar K. Browning and Mark A. Zupan, *Microeconomics: Theory & Applications*, 10th ed. (Hoboken, NJ: John Wiley, 2009), 387–390.
33. Paul M. Sweezy, "Demand under Conditions of Oligopoly," *Journal of Political Economy* 47, no. 4 (August 1939): 568–573.
34. See William J. Baumol and Alan S. Blinder, *Economics: Principles and Policy*, 11th ed. (Mason, OH: South-Western, 2009), 247–250.
35. *Tur, Hoshen Mishpat* 231; *Shulhan Arukh, Hoshen Mishpat* 231:20; *Arukh ha-Shulhan, Hoshen Mishpat* 231:20.
36. *Tur*, op. cit.; *Shulhan Arukh*, op. cit.; *Arukh ha-Shulhan*, op. cit.
37. *Tur*, op. cit. R. Abulafia's ruling presents a difficulty. To be sure, we should not expect the God-fearing vendor to limit himself to only a 20% profit when prevailing practice is to charge whatever the market will bear and this seller represents only a tiny portion of the market supply. But there is another issue here. Should not *Beit Din* instruct the God-fearing seller that he has no right to exploit the ignorance of consumers and charge them whatever price he can get away with as the other sellers do? Instead, he should use his best efforts to determine the prevailing market price and charge customers that price. Provided he uses his best efforts to determine the market norm, there would be no objection if he ended up earning a profit in excess of 20% on a *hayyei nefesh* item.

    The issue the above difficulty raises is one of *ona'ah* (price fraud). Does the law of *ona'ah* apply even in a marketplace where each seller charges a different price for the same item? In the rabbinical literature, this case is referred to as "*sha'ar she-eino yadu'a*" (indeterminate price).

    We note parenthetically that from the perspective of economic theory, *sha'ar she-eino yadu'a* is an anomaly. Self-interest would be expected to drive consumers to engage in comparative shopping. Aggressive market search of this sort would quickly bring about convergence of price in this market.

    Examples of *sha'ar she-eino yadu'a* in ancient times were the wool and milk markets. The salient feature of these ancient markets was that each seller sold different quantities to individual customers at different prices. Since the market price here is not readily ascertainable, an *ona'ah* claim, according to R. Caro, is not honored in these markets. *Beit Yosef* to *Tur, Hoshen Mishpat* 209, n. 1. Disputing this ruling, R. Moses Isserles et al. aver that even though each seller charges a different price, the market price is nevertheless ascertainable through estimation, and hence the *ona'ah* claim should remain intact. See R. Moses Isserles, *Darkhei Mosheh* to *Tur, Hoshen Mishpat* 209, n. 1.

    The dispute between R. Caro and R. Isserles apparently turns on how the reference price for the purpose of adjudicating an *ona'ah* dispute is determined. Should the reference price be defined as the *best estimate* of the market value of the item at hand? Or should the reference price be defined as the price that was *reasonably accessible* to the plaintiff at the time he entered into the disputed transaction? R. Caro apparently subscribes to the latter view. Accordingly, if each seller charges a different price, the *ona'ah* claim is dismissed. This is so because no particular price can be said to be more accessible to the plaintiff than any other price. The plaintiff therefore cannot prove that a better marketplace opportunity was available to him at the time he entered into the disputed transaction. If we define the reference price as the *best estimate* of the market value of the item at hand, however, the plaintiff's *ona'ah* claim remains intact because we can be sure that the price he paid exceeded the market value of the item.

    Under the assumption that the law of *ona'ah* is not operative in the *sha'ar she'eino yadu'a* case, R. Abulafia's ruling is readily understandable. Because limiting the seller in this case to only a 20% profit will confer little benefit on the vast number of remaining consumers when his supplies run out, we do not insist that the God-fearing seller abide by the 20% profit margin for *hayyei nefesh* items. In addition, the law of *ona'ah* is not operative here because it cannot be said that the buyer has ready access in the marketplace to any one price more than another.

38. See note 2 above.
39. *Mishneh Torah, Mekhirah* 14 1–3.
40. R. Isser Zalman Meltzer, *Even ha-Ezel, Hilkhot Mekhirah* 14:2–3.
41. *Bava Metzia* 51b.
42. The law of *ona'ah* prohibits an individual from concluding a transaction at a price that is more favorable to himself than some reference price. *Baraita, Bava Metzia* 51a. For the development of the thesis that the reference price is the prevailing competitive norm, see Aaron Levine, *Case Studies in Jewish Business Ethics* (Hoboken, NJ: Ktav, 2000), 127–135.
43. See R. Yehudah Itach (Israel, contemp.), *Netiv Yosher: Hilkhot va-Halikhot Mekah u-Memkar* (Jerusalem, 1992), 86, n. 14.
44. *Bava Metzia* 61a; *Tur, Hoshen Mishpat* 227; *Sema* to *Shulhan Arukh, Hoshen Mishpat* 227, n. 1.
45. *Bava Batra* 78a; *Rashbam*, ad loc.; *Rif, Bava Batra* 78a; *Mishneh Torah, Mekhirah* 27:5; *Rosh, Bava Batra* 5:7; *Tur, Hoshen Mishpat* 220; *Shulhan Arukh, Hoshen Mishpat* 220:8; *Arukh ha-Shulhan, Hoshen Mishpat* 220:7.
46. *Bava Metzia* 50b; *Rif*, ad loc.; *Mishneh Torah, Mekhirah* 12:4; *Rosh, Bava Metzia* 4:15; *Tur*, op. cit., 227; *Shulhan Arukh*, op. cit., 227:4; *Arukh ha-Shulhan*, op. cit., 227:3. Nullification rights in this case, according to Maimonides and R. Joseph Caro, rest exclusively with the plaintiff. *Mishneh Torah*, op. cit.; *Shulhan Arukh*, op. cit. Expressing a minority opinion in this matter, however, is R. Jonah b. Abraham Gerondi (*Rabbeinu Yonah*, Spain, ca. 1200–1263). In his view, as long as the plaintiff does not uphold the transaction, the offender too is given the prerogative of voiding it. The offender's rights in this matter proceed from the magnitude of the price discrimination involved. Since the price at which the transaction was concluded diverged more than one-sixth from the market norm, the offender may insist the original transaction be treated as an agreement consummated in error (*mekah ta'ut*). Once, however, the transaction is upheld by the plaintiff, the offender loses his right to void the sale. Denying the offender full nullification rights here follows from the fact that the offender enjoys no such rights when his offense consists of the less severe violation of contracting for a sales price involving second-degree *ona'ah*. Granting him full nullification rights when his offense is graver than second-degree *ona'ah* seems to run counter to all canons of equity. R. Jonah b. Abraham Gerondi, quoted in *Tur*, op. cit., 227, *Rema* to *Shulhan Arukh*, op. cit., 227:4, and *Arukh ha-Shulhan*, op. cit., 227:3. Ruling in accordance with R. Jonah is R. Asher b. Jehiel. See *Rosh, Bava Batra* 5:14.
47. *Bava Metzia* 50b, *Rif*, ad loc.; *Mishneh Torah, Mekhirah* 12:2; *Rosh, Bava Metzia* 4:15; *Tur, Hoshen Mishpat* 227; *Shulhan Arukh, Hoshen Mishpat* 227:2; *Arukh ha-Shulhan, Hoshen Mishpat* 227:3.
48. *Bava Metzia* 50b; *Rif*, ad loc.; *Mishneh Torah, Mekhirah* 12:3; *Rosh, Bava Metzia* 4:15; *Tur*, op. cit., 227; *Shulhan Arukh*, op. cit., 227:3; *Arukh ha-Shulhan*, op. cit.
49. *Bava Metzia* 51b; *Rif*, ad loc.; *Mishneh Torah, Mekhirah* 13:5; *Rosh, Bava Metzia* 4:17; *Tur*, op. cit., 227; *Shulhan Arukh*, op. cit., 227:27; *Arukh ha-Shulhan*, op. cit., 227:28. A variation of this case occurs when *S*'s upfront disclosure acknowledged only that the article was worth less than what he paid for it, but failed to disclose by what amount. Here, some authorities regard the transaction price as subject to adjustment or cancellation if the *ona'ah* turned out to be very significant. Given that the amount of the *ona'ah* was not disclosed upfront to *B*, credibility is given to *B*'s claim that had he only known at the time of the transaction that *S*'s cost price entailed such a significant amount of *ona'ah*, he would have never entered into the transaction. See *Shulhan Arukh*, op. cit., 227:21; *Arukh ha-Shulhan*, op. cit., 227:22.

    One more variation: If it can be established that *S* knew at the time of the transaction that his cost price entailed *ona'ah*, but failed to disclose this, *B* will have a right to adjust or overturn the transaction based on the *ona'ah*, notwithstanding that *B* agreed to *S*'s stipulated markup. *Arukh ha-Shulhan*, op. cit., 227:28.
50. R. Menahem b. Solomon Meiri (*Meiri*, Perpignan, 1249–1316), *Beit ha-Behirah, Bava Metzia* 40b; *Rosh, Bava Metzia* 3:16; *Tur*, op. cit., 231; R. Joshua b. Alexander ha-Kohen Falk, *Perishah* to *Tur*, op. cit., 231, n. 26; *Shulhan Arukh*, op. cit., 231:20; *Arukh ha-Shulhan*, op. cit., 231:20.

In his treatment of cost base, Maimonides makes no mention of an allowance for a return for the labor services of the owner. R. Joel Sirkes (*Bah* to *Tur*, op. cit., 231, n. 26) takes this lacuna to imply that, according to Maimonides, the value of the owner's labor services does not enter into the cost base and the 20% markup is allowed only for out-of-pocket expenditures. The 20% markup on out-of-pocket expenditures is what serves as the return for the owner's labor services.

R. Sirkes draws this conclusion based on Maimonides' treatment of the regulation of the egg industry. Recall the *Amoraic* dispute. One opinion understands the regulation to restrict the egg trader's profit to 100%, while the second opinion understands the regulation to consist of allowing only the trader who deals with the egg farmer to earn a profit, but subsequent traders in the chain must all sell at cost. Why does the first opinion allow egg traders a 100% markup, while other *hayyei nefesh* traders are restricted to a 20% markup? The higher maximum markup for egg traders, posits R. Sirkes, is in recognition of the extraordinary efforts an egg trader may expend by going from one farmer to another collecting eggs. See *Rashbam, Bava Batra* 91a. Note that Maimonides rules according to the opinion that understands the regulation in the egg industry to consist of allowing profits only to the trader who buys directly from the egg farmer. What can be inferred from Maimonides' rejection of the first *Amoraic* opinion, according to R. Sirkes, is that no matter the amount of toil and effort the *hayyei nefesh* vendor expends, the maximum markup allowed is 20% of out-of-pocket expenditures.

R. Sirkes' interpretation of Maimonides' position is, however, not compelling. Consider that R. Caro, who understands the cost base to include the value of the owner's labor services, presents both *Amoraic* opinions regarding the treatment of egg traders. R. Caro records the opinion that allows only the first trader in the egg industry to profit as a primary opinion and refers to the opinion that sets the profit for egg traders at a limit of 100% as "some say" ("*ve-yesh mi she-omer*"). See *Shulhan Arukh, Hoshen Mishpat* 231:22. What follows is that R. Caro's broad conceptualization of the cost base of *hayyei nefesh* to include the value of the owner's own labor services is entirely consistent with the notion that the profit rate for *hayyei nefesh* never exceeds 20%, regardless of the amount of the owner's labor services. The two points are consistent because the value of the owner's labor services is included in the cost base against which the 20% profit rate is calculated.

51. *Rashi* to *Bava Metzia* 40b.
52. *Bava Metzia* 40b.
53. *Mishneh Torah, Mekhirah* 14:9; *Tur, Hoshen Mishpat* 231; *Shulhan Arukh, Hoshen Mishpat* 231:27; *Arukh ha-Shulhan, Hoshen Mishpat* 231:27.
54. *Mishneh Torah, Mekhirah* 14:9.
55. For sources, see Menachem Elon, Isaac Levitats, and Aviad Hacohen, "*Takkanot ha-Kahal*" in *Encyclopedia Judaica*, 2nd ed., vol. 19, eds. Michael Berenbaum and Fred Skolnik (Detroit: Macmillan Reference, 2007), 453–460.
56. R. Meir b. Todros ha-Levi Abulafia, *Yad Ramah, Bava Batra* 1:103; R. Vidal Yom Tov of Tolosa, *Maggid Mishneh* to *Mishneh Torah, Mekhirah* 14:11.
57. Aaron Levine, "Aspects of the Firm's Responsibility to Its Customers: Pharmaceutical Pricing and Consumer Privacy," in *Jewish Business Ethics: The Firm and Its Stakeholders*, eds. Aaron Levine and Moses Pava (Northvale, NJ: Jason Aronson, 1999), 79–83.

CHAPTER 5

Reviving Yehoshua b. Gamla's Vision for Torah Education

Introduction

In this chapter, we will describe a model that economic theory proposes for the provision of elementary education. We will then show that the goals of Jewish religious elementary education can be optimally achieved by adopting the basic elements of this model.

ECONOMIC THEORY AND THE MODEL FOR ELEMENTARY EDUCATION

In his seminal paper on the role of government in the area of elementary education, Milton Friedman expresses a view that is consistent with the prescriptions of welfare economics. Preliminarily, Friedman notes that a stable and democratic society is impossible without widespread acceptance of a common set of values and a minimum degree of literacy and knowledge on the part of most citizens. Education contributes to the inculcation of values and the development of a literate populace, and hence generates external benefits in the form of promoting a stable and democratic society.

Given the differences among families in their economic resources and number of children, we cannot rely on the private sector to devote the resources necessary to achieve universal education of the youth. Friedman therefore would assign government the role of subsidizing the education of the youth and setting minimum standards for schools.

Because Friedman considers the goals of elementary education to be to teach the youth basic reading, writing, and math skills, and to inculcate the core values of society, he does not see much controversy with the government setting standards for this sector of the educational marketplace. Friedman finds no economic justification, however, for the government to run the schools. Instead, the government should give vouchers to parents who, in turn, would give them to the schools of their choice to cover the cost of their children's education.[1]

Proponents of educational vouchers contend that implementing a voucher system would increase the quality of both private and public education. Supporting this assertion is the experience of higher education, where the quality of education generally improves when both private and publicly funded institutions of higher learning are available to students.[2] Relatedly, Caroline Minter Hoxby has found that public schools in Milwaukee that faced competition as a result of a voucher system, and public schools in Arizona and Michigan that faced competition from charter schools, experienced higher rates of student achievement than public schools that did not face such competition.[3]

JEWISH LAW AND RELIGIOUS ELEMENTARY EDUCATION

Milton Friedman finds a role for government in the financing of elementary education because successful schooling produces significant external benefits to society in the form of a literate populace and a stable democracy. In Friedman's thinking, the goal of government in a free and open society is to foster an environment that maximizes economic freedom.

Judaism's vision is for a society that maximizes the study of the Torah[4] and lives every aspect of the life experience in accordance with the moral and ethical teachings of the Torah.[5] Successful schooling should therefore be designed to foster this outcome.

Our overriding thesis in this chapter is that the goals of Jewish religious elementary education can be best achieved by adopting elements of Milton Friedman's model. With the aim of directing our proposal toward those who would be most receptive to its adoption, we direct our proposal to Orthodox Jewish communities, particularly in the United States. Given that this proposal is not directed to the Jewish State, but rather the Jewish community, taxation is not an aspect of this proposal. What survives for adaptation, however, is Friedman's notion that the government should set standards for schools and subsidize the financing of schooling.

With respect to the setting of standards, the standards we propose for Jewish religious education, as we shall see, are either rooted in the ancient ordinance of Yehoshua b. Gamla or consistent with the objectives of his edict.

Milton Friedman's proposal calls for the government subsidy to take the form of an educational voucher for individual families. Our proposal, by contrast, calls for the Jewish community to raise funds to finance the religious education of poor families in the community. Participating schools would initially be eligible for these funds based on their overall enrollment. In subsequent years, a school's entitlement to funds would be adjusted based on changes in its overall enrollment from one year to the next.

We formulate our proposal in these terms out of practical considerations. For one, our proposal is designed, as we shall see, to build on existing successful precedents. Second, since the subsidy is not a universal one but is meant to subsidize the education of only poor families, it is desirable to avoid the creation of a communal bureaucracy to determine which families are eligible for the subsidy. Instead, participating schools would be left to determine their own policies in this matter.

Yehoshua b. Gamla and Jewish Religious Elementary Education

Investigation into the goals of Jewish religious elementary education begins with an analysis of the edict that Yehoshua b. Gamla, a High Priest in the time of the Second Temple, enacted in approximately 64 C.E. His edict transferred responsibility for both the operation and the financing of religious elementary schools for boys from the household to the community. Yehoshua b. Gamla's vision was therefore for the community to set standards for Torah elementary schools and enforce those standards.

Jewish communities today generally do not have a formal structure, let alone coercive power.[6] Consequently, we are now far removed from Yehoshua b. Gamla's vision for Torah education of the youth. To be sure, *yeshivot* (religious boys' schools) espouse ideologies that manifest themselves in programs of distinctive character and specific emphasis, but this is a far cry from the adoption of uniform standards.

We assume that it is desirable that the Torah educational enterprise should move closer toward Yehoshua b. Gamla's ideal. To this end, our concern in this chapter will be to propose a set of standards for Torah elementary schools. These standards, as we will show, are either inherent in or consistent with Yehoshua b. Gamla's ordinance. In addition, if the standards are to have any impact on the school system, incentives must be created for the schools to adopt them and compete with each other on the basis of these standards. Accordingly, in the second part of this chapter, we will briefly outline a Religious Education Subsidy Program (RESP) that is designed to incentivize schools to compete on this basis. Throughout this chapter, schools that participate in the RESP are referred to as "participating schools."[7]

Yehoshua b. Gamla's Ordinance

The backdrop against which Yehoshua b. Gamla's ordinance was enacted was the widespread neglect of the Torah education of orphans. This neglect stemmed from the general attitude that the duty to teach a boy Torah was primarily the responsibility of his father. The Torah education of orphans therefore suffered. After a few unsuccessful attempts to remedy the situation, Yehoshua b. Gamla enacted his ordinance:

> [Local authorities] should install (*moshivin*) teachers of children in every district (*medinah*) and town (*ir*) and they should bring in [children] of age six or seven to be taught by these teachers.[8]

The Sages regarded Yehoshua b. Gamla's ordinance as a significant milestone in Jewish history:

> For R. Judah said in the name of Rav: Indeed, remember that man—namely, Yehoshua b. Gamla—in a favorable way, for were it not for him, the Torah would have been forgotten by Israel.[9]

Let's now proceed to show that the essential feature of Yehoshua b. Gamla's ordinance was to transfer the supervision of teachers from private hands to the community.

Proving this thesis begins with an examination of how the classical codifiers, R. Isaac b. Jacob Alfasi (*Rif*, Algeria, 1013–1103), Maimonides (*Rambam*, Egypt, 1135–1204), R. Asher b. Jehiel (*Rosh*, Germany, 1250–1327), R. Jacob b. Asher (*Tur*, Spain, 1270–1343), and R. Joseph Caro (Safed, 1488–1575), record Yehoshua b. Gamla's ordinance. Because the impetus for the ordinance was the neglect of the Torah education of orphans, we would have expected these codifiers to describe the ordinance as requiring the establishment of Torah schools for orphans and the poor. Under such a formulation, private educational arrangements would continue for households of means. None of these codifiers, however, suggest that Yehoshua b. Gamla's ordinance was concerned only with the Torah education of orphans. Quite to the contrary, they say that each town must install (*moshivin*) a school for its youth.[10] Since the schools were established for everyone, it follows that both the financing and the operation of the schools were matters for the community.

What is implicit in the codifiers' description of Yehoshua b. Gamla's ordinance finds explicit expression in the commentary of R. Meir b. Todros ha-Levi Abulafia (*Ramah*, Spain, ca. 1180–1244). In analyzing Yehoshua b. Gamla's ordinance, R. Abulafia finds the word "*moshivin*" in the above Talmudic passage critical to understanding the implications of the ordinance. The term "*moshivin*" signifies that Yehoshua b. Gamla required the community to establish elementary schools and pay teachers from communal funds. These schools were for both the rich and the poor.[11]

R. Abulafia's basic notion that Yehoshua b. Gamla's ordinance required the community to establish elementary Torah schools and hire teachers for these schools with communal funds is consistent with the formulations of later authorities.

Let's begin with the formulation of R. Simeon b. Tzemach Duran (*Tashbetz*, Algiers, 1361–1444). In *Tashbetz*'s understanding, Yehoshua b. Gamla's ordinance called for the Jewish community to hire an individual to perform the specific task of teaching Torah to the youth of the town. Citing the Talmudic dictum that "Any town in which there are no school children studying Torah is eventually destroyed,"[12] *Tashbetz* posits that the responsibility for the community to appoint a *melammed tinokot* (Torah teacher for children) is more fundamental than the responsibility to appoint a cantor to help the townspeople fulfill their duty in communal prayer. The specific issue *Tashbetz* addressed was whether the *melammed tinokot* is exempt from paying taxes. In his ruling, *Tashbetz* exempts the *melammed tinokot* from taxes. Just as the cantor is exempt from paying taxes, *a fortiori* a *melammed tinokot* is exempt because he is a public employee.[13]

Following closely the basic contours of R. Abulafia's understanding of Yehoshua b. Gamla's ordinance, R. Shneur Zalman of Liadi (Russia, 1745–1812) posits that the ordinance required the community to set up elementary-level Torah schools for all the youth of the town, both rich and poor. The tax that supported the school was proportional to wealth. All the townspeople were required to participate in the school tax levy, even families with no children in the school system. Moreover, since the tax supported the Torah education of the poor, it assumed the character of a charity levy. Accordingly, Torah scholars, who are usually exempt from communal levies, were required to pay the school tax levy, as they too must support the Torah education of the poor.[14]

Another authority who follows R. Abulafia's line of reasoning is R. Meir Simhah ha-Kohen of Dvinsk (Latvia, 1843–1926). Noting that in the first Scriptural passage of the *Shema*, the duty to teach Torah is written in the singular: "You shall teach them to your sons,"[15] R. Meir Simhah posits that in this passage, the Torah speaks of the obligation of the community to teach its members Torah. This verse indicates that the community must establish and finance the operation of Torah schools for its young and pay these teachers out of communal funds. The harsh Talmudic dictum that "Any town in which there are no school children studying Torah is eventually destroyed"[16] is based on the verse "You shall teach them to your sons." The duty for the community to set up schools for its young, concludes R. Meir Simhah, hence is not based solely on Yehoshua b. Gamla's ordinance.[17]

Finally, let's take note of the view of R. Joel Teitelbaum (New York, 1887–1979). Preliminarily, R. Teitelbaum points out that a father's duty to teach his son Torah requires the father to hire a tutor for this purpose if necessary. The innovation of Yehoshua b. Gamla was to mandate for the community the establishment of Torah schools for everyone. The objective of the ordinance was that Torah education for the youth should reach the rich child, the poor child, and especially the child who had no father to worry about his spiritual needs.[18]

The formulations described above indicate that Yehoshua b. Gamla's focus was not just on the Torah education of orphans.[19] Rather, his ordinance ended the system of private educational arrangements and required each town to set up a school for its children.

Given that Yehoshua b. Gamla's ordinance essentially ended private educational arrangements by parents in favor of a community school, it would stand to reason that in addition to establishing and maintaining schools, the community undertook to supervise teachers. Indeed, the position of *sofer mata* mentioned in the Talmud is understood by R. Solomon b. Isaac (*Rashi*, France, 1040–1105) to mean "a head teacher who appoints *melammedim* and supervises their work."[20] If the *sofer mata* was in charge of hiring and supervising teachers, the standards Halakhah sets for the work routine and performance of *melammedim* and its rules to ensure that the educational process is working well were in the hands of this functionary to enforce.

Religious Educational Standards

In this section, we will delineate a set of standards for the Torah educational enterprise. These standards are either inherent in or consistent with Yehoshua b. Gamla's ordinance.

PERFORMANCE APPRAISAL FOR TEACHERS

Participating schools should be required to implement a performance appraisal system for their teachers.

In the modern scene, the workplace is often established with a performance appraisal system. In this system, an employer sets performance goals for his employees in advance and provides employees with feedback so that corrective action can be taken before an adverse personnel decision is rendered. Without such a system in place, legitimate expectations would be dashed and personnel decisions would be perceived as arbitrary. Elsewhere we have detailed the halakhic sources that require such a system.[21]

For the Torah educational sector, a performance appraisal system would ensure that the productivity standards Halakhah sets for the *melammed* are achieved. To get an idea of what these standards are like, we need only look at the routine Halakhah prescribes for the *melammed*. This routine requires the *melammed* to hold classes for his students the entire day and part of the night.[22] This schedule applies to *Shabbat* as well, except that on *Shabbat*, the *melammed* does not teach new material but instead reviews prior lessons.[23] The only exceptions to the full schedule are that the pupils are dismissed early on Friday, and no classes are held on the holidays.[24] Nothing is better evidence of the requirement that the pupils should not be idle than the law that the *melammed* must remain on his post if no one is available to replace him, even during the week that he is in mourning for a relative.[25]

In addition to this rigorous work schedule is a demanding productivity expectation for the teacher. Preliminarily, let's note that causing an employer a *peseida de-lo hadra* (irretrievable loss) is grounds for discharging a worker.[26] For a teacher of Torah, idling on the job is considered to cause a *peseida de-lo hadra*, as time lost for the pupils can never be retrieved.[27] Teaching inaccurately[28] is also considered to cause a *peseida de-lo hadra* and subjects the teacher to dismissal.[29] Abusing a pupil, physically or sexually, should also fit into the category of conduct that causes a *peseida de-lo hadra*.[30]

Temperament is no less important than getting quick results. In this regard, Maimonides cautions the teacher not to get angry if his students do not immediately absorb his lesson. Instead, the teacher should have patience and review the material many times so that his students obtain full comprehension.[31]

Once it is recognized that Halakhah has definite standards for the *melammed*, the case for setting up a performance appraisal system is reinforced. This is so because Halakhah does not allow a teacher to be fired on the basis of anecdotal evidence or hearsay.[32] Instead, a teacher may be fired only based on first-hand observation of his misconduct by a reliable witness. Enforcing Halakhah's productivity standards hence requires a school to have in place a formal system of observing its teachers.

Given that labor relations require the implementation of a performance appraisal system, a school should adopt this system for its secular teachers as well.[33]

TESTING REQUIREMENT FOR PUPILS

Another aspect of ensuring that the educational process is working effectively is to monitor how well pupils are absorbing their lessons. Participating schools should therefore be required to ensure that their pupils are tested on the curriculum.

Testing pupils has a basis in Halakhah. It follows from a duty the *melammed* acquires vis-à-vis his pupils when they are placed under his tutelage. This duty is set out in the Talmudic passage at *Kiddushin* 30a:

> "*Ve-shinnantam* (you shall thoroughly teach them) to your sons and you shall speak of them while you sit in your home and while you walk on your way, when you lie down and when you rise" [Deuteronomy 6:7]. This conveys that the words of the Torah should be sharply honed in your mouth, such that if a man asks you something concerning a point of Torah knowledge, you will not stammer before answering him; rather, you will be able to answer him immediately. This idea emerges from other verses too, as it is written: "Say to Wisdom: 'You are my sister'" [Proverbs 7:4].

In the description of the *ve-shinnantam* duty at Deuteronomy 6:7, the Sages take the word "sons" to refer not to biological sons, but instead to students. In addition, they understand the word "father" to mean a spiritual father, which is how a teacher of Torah is often designated.

One could argue that the *ve-shinnantam* duty for an elementary school teacher is limited. Consider that the Mishnah at *Avot* 5:21 sets the curriculum for an elementary school pupil as consisting mainly of *Mikra* (Scripture): "A 5-year old begins *Mikra*; a 10-year old begins Mishnah . . . a 15-year old begins *Gemara* (Talmud)." The issue then becomes whether *ve-shinnantam* applies to the teaching of *Mikra* to children in the age range of 5 to 10 years old. In the opinion of R. Naftali Tzvi Yehudah Berlin (*Netziv*, Russia, 1817–1893) and R. Jehiel Michal Epstein (Belarus, 1829–1908), the *ve-shinnantam* duty makes sense and has pedagogical application only when the subject matter is Mishnah or Talmud.[34]

Let's note, however, that *yeshivot* and day schools today do not generally follow the rigid sequence prescribed at *Avot* 5:21. Instead, pupils are exposed to Talmud as early as age eight.[35] Since in current practice pupils are taught Mishnah and Talmud at a very early age, the *melammed*'s *ve-shinnantam* duty sets in at the same time he begins to instruct his pupils in Mishnah.

What proceeds from the *ve-shinnantam* duty is that in order for a school to qualify as a participating school, it must have a testing requirement for its pupils. But testing is not an end in and of itself. Rather, it is a means of ascertaining if students have absorbed their lessons on the level of *ve-shinnantam*. Accordingly, if students perform below par on these tests, they must repeat their lessons until retesting shows that *ve-shinnantam* has been achieved.

If we accept the notion that *ve-shinnantam* does not apply to *Mikra*, it appears that participating schools that teach only *Mikra* to their youngest grades should not be subject to any testing requirement for those grades. Recall, however, that Halakhah requires employers to implement a performance appraisal system. Requiring pupils to be tested is just another component of a performance appraisal system designed to ensure that the learning process is working well. Moreover, given that under RESP, the community solicits funds to support the education of the poor that will take place in schools committed to ensuring that the learning process is working well, the standards the community sets must promote excellence as much as possible. Consequently, participating schools should be subject to the testing requirement for all their grades, even grades that learn only *Mikra*.

Should the testing requirement extend to the secular part of the curriculum? Yes. While Torah authorities debate the permissible parameters of the study of secular subjects,[36] there should be little or no debate that the secular curriculum of elementary schools consists predominantly of subjects that are preparatory for or an aspect of Torah learning itself. Basic reading and writing skills in the English language are tools for the comprehension, articulation, and communication of the Torah portion of the curriculum. In this regard, R. Yosef Eliyahu Henkin (New York, 1881–1973) believed that it is educationally optimal to teach students Torah in their native language.[37] Similarly, basic knowledge of mathematics and science is essential for the understanding of Torah. In addition, an understanding of history and the acquisition of basic knowledge of the sciences and mathematics gives us an inkling of God's wisdom and governance of His world. Study of these disciplines hence is a path to fulfilling our duty to fear and love God.[38]

Since the secular subjects taught in elementary school are preparatory for or an aspect of Torah study itself, the testing requirement should apply to the secular part of the curriculum.

MAXIMUM CLASS SIZE

Torah education law sets rules regarding maximum class size:

> And Rava also said: The number of students that teachers have in their classes is 25 children. If there are 50 students, we install two teachers. If there are 40 students, we appoint a *reish dukhna* [i.e., an assistant to the teacher], and the teacher is given some financial support from the town to defray the cost of hiring the assistant.[39]

Insofar as this rule is designed to ensure effectiveness in the education process, its enforcement in Talmudic times was undoubtedly in the hands of the *sofer mata*. What follows is that maximum class size should be one of the standards the community sets for participating schools. In formulating that standard, there is room for flexibility because the exact meaning of Rava's dictum is a matter of dispute.

Maimonides understands Rava to say that one *melammed* suffices for a class of 25 students. If the class numbers anywhere between 26 and 40 students, the *melammed* must be given an assistant. If the class reaches more than 40 students, the class is divided into two classes and two teachers must be hired.[40]

R. Asher b. Jehiel, however, interprets Rava to say that if a class size is below 40, one *melammed* suffices. For a class size between 40 and 49, an assistant must be provided for the *melammed*. Once the class size reaches 50, the class must be split and two *melammedim* appointed.[41]

Decisors take opposing views in the matter of class size. R. Joseph Caro follows Maimonides,[42] while R. Jacob b. Asher rules in accordance with his father, R. Asher b. Jehiel.[43]

Commenting on the controversy over maximum class size, R. Shabbetai b. Meir ha-Kohen (*Siftei Kohen*, Poland, 1621–1662) offers the opinion that the appropriate standard for class size depends on the nature of the *melammed* and the particular pupils under his tutelage.[44] *Siftei Kohen*'s comments argue for the adoption of a flexible standard for class size for participating schools.

Reinforcing the case for a flexible standard is *Tashbetz*'s proposition that the rules regarding maximum class size and the provision of assistants were designed specifically to equip the *melammed* with the right to demand help in handling his duties as a teacher. The analogy here, according to *Tashbetz*, is that if an employee is hired to perform a specific task entailing light physical work, his employer may not give him a different assignment requiring heavier physical labor.[45] This analogy implies that *Tashbetz* views the rules regarding maximum class size as intended for the benefit of the *melammed* rather than to promote optimal learning conditions for the pupils. Under that view, a *melammed* should be allowed to accept a class size larger than the parameters Rava's dictum sets. Maintaining that *Tashbetz*'s view here is normative, R. Moshe Bleich (New York, contemp.) finds support for *Tashbetz*'s position in R. Jonah b. Abraham Gerondi's (*Rabbeinu Yonah*, Spain ca. 1200–1263) analysis of the law of *reish dukhna*.[46]

Notwithstanding the view that maximum class size is intended only for the benefit of the *melammed*, in setting the standard for maximum class size, rabbinical authorities might want to consider the evidence in the secular literature regarding the relationship between class size and pupil performance.[47]

MINIMUM ENROLLMENT AND COMPULSORY ATTENDANCE RECORDS

To qualify as a participating school, a school would be required to meet a minimum enrollment standard. We will show that a corollary of this standard is the requirement for a school to keep attendance records to ensure that its students are not just enrolled, but receive their education in the setting of a school.

The requirements regarding minimum enrollment and compulsory attendance can be derived from further analysis of Yehoshua b. Gamla's ordinance. What needs to be clarified is the extent to which the ordinance required school-aged children of a town to combine into a single school.

R. Solomon b. Abraham Adret's (*Rashba*, Spain, 1235–1310) commentary in connection with the following Talmudic passages, which deal with the rights of a father in a town to send his son to a school in a neighboring town, is relevant to the issue at hand:

> Rava said: From the time Yehoshua b. Gamla's ordinance was enacted, one may not take a child from his town to attend classes in another town. However, one may take a child from the vicinity of one synagogue to the vicinity of another synagogue within the same town. But if a river separates the two districts, a child should not be taken from one to the other. If a bridge spans the river, one may take a child across it. But if there is a bridge that consists of only a narrow plank, one may not take a child across it.[48]

R. Adret finds it very puzzling that Rava derives a prohibition against "busing" children from Yehoshua b. Gamla's ordinance. Since in R. Adret's view, it was Yehoshua b. Gamla's primary objective (*ikkar takkanato*) to make it an absolute requirement for a town to have its own local school if its pupil population numbered 24,[49] what does

Rava tell us that we don't already know? This leads R. Adret to conclude that Rava's prohibition refers to the instance where the local pupil population is less than 24. In disagreement with other opinions, R. Adret states that even if the local pupil population is less than 24, and some parents insist that the entire group hire one teacher for all the children while others want to hire in smaller groups, the group must hire one teacher for all the children. At the conclusion of his exposition, R. Adret informs us that his *rebbe*, Nahmanides (*Ramban*, Spain, 1194–1270), concurs with his understanding of Yehoshua b. Gamla's ordinance.[50]

Proceeding from the opinions of Nahmanides and R. Adret is that Yehoshua b. Gamla's edict mandated not only compulsory education for elementary school children, but also required cooperative efforts on the part of parents to set up one school for all their children.[51]

A different view here is taken by *Tosafot* and R. Asher b. Jehiel. According to this school of thought, communal coercion to establish a local school applies only if the pupil population of the town is at least 25. Consequently, if the pupil population of the town is less than 25, the parents are not denied the right to satisfy their duty to provide their children with a Torah education by sending their children to a school in a neighboring town.[52]

The discussion above has demonstrated that Yehoshua b. Gamla's ordinance extended beyond mandating compulsory education for the youth and decreed that parents in a town should join together in establishing a school. The only point of disagreement among the authorities is whether this requirement applies only if the town has a certain minimum number of pupils.

Given the expected cooperative efforts of parents in a town, does Jewish education law approve of home schooling? R. Jehiel Michal Epstein addresses this issue. Suppose some of the fathers in a town are willing to undertake to teach their sons Torah themselves, while other fathers who cannot undertake this task demand that all the parents join together to hire one teacher for their children. For this case, R. Epstein rules that a father who wants to home school his child cannot be coerced to join in the hiring of a Torah teacher for all the children. The right to home school his own child exempts the father from sharing the expense of the other parents in hiring a teacher for their children, provided, of course, that the father of the home-schooled child pays his fair share in the Torah education of the poor.[53]

The legitimacy R. Epstein accords home schooling should apply only if the father undertakes to be the *melammed* of his own child without requesting public assistance for this task. Home schooling should not qualify for a public subsidy. This is so because a one-pupil school was not the vision of Yehoshua b. Gamla. Instead, his vision was for parents of school-aged children to join together and establish a Torah school for their children. To be sure, if a father's desire to home school his child does not disrupt the viability of the local school, we cannot stand in the way of the father who wants to be the *melammed* of his own child. But subsidizing a one-pupil school undermines Yehoshua b. Gamla's ordinance.

A number of implications for participating schools proceed from the notion that the ideal for Jewish education is for a child to attend a school together with the other children of his town. One implication is a responsibility for a school to maintain attendance records to ensure that its pupils are not just enrolled, but are in actual attendance. In addition to the requirement that the school maintain attendance records, excessive absences by a student without a medical excuse should forfeit for the school the subsidy it would otherwise be entitled to receive on account of the student. The community should therefore implement a truancy policy in tandem with its compulsory attendance requirement.

Another implication is that to qualify as a participating school, a school would need to have enough pupils so that it could be minimally regarded as a school rather than a private tutoring service. It would be up to the Torah authorities to decide what the minimum school size should be for a school to qualify as a participating school.

The minimum enrollment requirement may well result in conferring temporary monopoly status on some participating schools. Consider that almost 40% of Jewish day schools today enroll fewer than 100 students.[54] These schools are too small to have realized the advantages of economies of scale. If the pupil population in a particular neighborhood is too small to support two schools, the existing school should be conferred temporary monopoly status, provided that the established school accepts the community's standards. Economists call this type of situation a natural monopoly. A regulated monopolist is far better than an unregulated one. Commitment to standards and submission to an audit to ensure that those standards are met make the school responsive to criticism and receptive to new ideas that promise to enhance its ability to meet those standards. The school's future now becomes tied to how well it meets the community's standards.

PARENTAL INVOLVEMENT IN THE TORAH EDUCATION OF THEIR CHILDREN

In this section, we will show that to qualify as a participating school, a school must require its parent body to be involved in the Torah education of their children.

The case for parental involvement in the Torah education of their children begins with the Biblical verse "And you shall teach them to your children."[55] Talmudic explication of this verse makes it a Biblical duty for a father to teach his son *Mikra*.[56] Several considerations, however, point to a much broader *talmud Torah* (teaching Torah) duty for the father. For one, R. Joseph Caro understands the Talmudic passage to refer to the obligation of a father to hire a tutor for his son. It is here with respect to a hiring duty that the obligation extends only to *Mikra*. With respect to the duty to spend time with his son, by contrast, the father's duty applies also to Mishnah and Talmud.[57] Second, R. Abulafia posits that when the Talmud limits the father's responsibility to *Mikra*, it refers to the instance where "circumstances press him" (*de-dehika leih sha'ata*). Otherwise, the father must teach his child Mishnah, *halakhot*, and *aggadot*, in addition to *Mikra*.[58]

The extensive *talmud Torah* duty of the father vis-à-vis his son tells us that Yehoshua b. Gamla's ordinance to establish communal schools was never meant to supplant the father's *talmud Torah* duty. To be sure, Torah education law calls for a very long school day. But whenever a child is not under the tutelage of a *melammed*, the father's *talmud Torah* duty should apply to fill the gap. Reinforcing the father's duty to fill gaps is the dictum that it takes no less than constant study of Torah to prevent the forgetting of the Torah one has already learned.[59] Unless the father minimizes the time his child spends away from Torah study, the father bears some responsibility for the Torah the child forgets as a result of the child's idleness outside of school.

Let's now apply the father's *talmud Torah* duty to the modern scene. Children currently spend much more time outside the formal setting of school compared with the school schedule prescribed by the codes of Jewish law. As a result, a father's *talmud Torah* duty vis-à-vis his son is operative today much more so than in former times. How this duty translates in practical terms will depend on the father's educational background, financial status, and time constraints. But at a minimum, this duty speaks of a responsibility for the father both when school is in session and when it is not. When school is in session, a father must ensure that his child does his homework and reviews his lessons. When school is out, such as on *Shabbat*, holidays, and summer vacations, a father must make sure that learning Torah is an important part of his child's routine.

Let's consider the possibility that from a halakhic perspective, a mother too has a *talmud Torah* duty toward her children. For one, according to a number of authorities, the duty to train and educate a child in the performance of *mitzvot*, called the duty of *hinnukh*, devolves on the mother as well as the father.[60] Accordingly, the *hinnukh* duty tells the mother that she is responsible to ensure that her child does his homework. Reinforcing this duty is that on a typical day, the child spends much more time with his mother than with his father. This circumstance, according to R. Isaiah ha-Levi Horowitz (*Shelah*, Poland, ca. 1565–1630), makes it the duty of the mother much more so than the father to correct the child's misconduct.[61] Ensuring that homework is done certainly falls under this duty. Since the *hinnukh* duty devolves on the mother too, she must lend a hand in the continuing Torah education of her children.

Recall R. Abulafia's dictum that unless "circumstances press him," a father must go beyond *Mikra* and theoretically teach his son the entire Torah. Commenting on that dictum, R. Abraham Isaiah Karelitz (*Hazon Ish*, Israel, 1878–1953) understands R. Abulafia to say that a father's duty to go beyond *Mikra* is not a *talmud Torah* duty emanating from "And you shall teach them to your children." Instead, it is an aspect of the rabbinical duty of *hinnukh* incumbent upon a father to educate his child in the performance of all his obligations as a Jew, which include the obligation to study Torah.[62]

Recall the contention that much of the secular curriculum in elementary school should be regarded as either preparatory for or an aspect of Torah study. Involvement of parents in the Torah education of their children should therefore apply to the secular part of the curriculum as well.

Is parental involvement in the education of their children consistent with Yehoshua b. Gamla's ordinance? Yes. Consider that the driving force behind Yehoshua b. Gamla's ordinance was the neglect of the Torah education of orphans. It stands to reason therefore that the ordinance was not intended to plug a gap in one area and at the same time create a void elsewhere. The call to establish a school in each town was thus not meant to signal a complete transfer of responsibility for the Torah education of the youth from parents to the schools.

The responsibility of parents for the education of their children is relevant more so today than in the time of Yehoshua b. Gamla because the amount of time children currently spend in school is much less than the amount of time prescribed by the codes of Jewish law. The gap parents need to fill is therefore much wider than in the time of Yehoshua b. Gamla. To prevent Yehoshua b. Gamla's vision for the Torah education of children from becoming distorted, it is essential that the requirement for parents to participate in the Torah education of their children not be left to self-enforcement. Instead, this requirement should be a standard the community demands of participating schools. By making this requirement a standard for its schools, the community at once shows fealty to Yehoshua b. Gamla's vision and also takes action to eradicate the notion that the establishment of schools relieves parents of any responsibility for the education of their children.

NEIGHBORHOOD SCHOOLS

In this section, we address several issues relating to geography.

Consider that Yehoshua b. Gamla's ordinance called for each *ir* (town) to set up its own school and that local children should not be made to travel back and forth to a school in another town. If Yehoshua b. Gamla's ordinance is taken as the vision for Torah elementary school education today, a subsidy program set up by the community should not undermine the ideal of the local school. Accordingly, to qualify as a participating school, a school would have to be located in the *ir* of the community group that establishes the RESP fund. What becomes critical therefore is how *ir* is defined in the modern setting. For this purpose, we turn to the work of R. Mosheh Feinstein (New York, 1895–1986), who addressed the issue of the definition of *ir* in a different context.

The specific issue R. Feinstein considered was whether Monsey, New York, should be regarded as a separate city and therefore be required to have its own *mikveh* (ritual bath house). Preliminarily, R. Feinstein noted that the definition of *ir* has profound practical ramifications. For example, Halakhah gives residents of a city the power to coerce each other to set up the basic needs of the city, such as a synagogue. In these matters, the minority can coerce the majority. In addition, in the Land of Israel, Halakhah calls for each *ir* to appoint its own judges. R. Feinstein then asserted that in deciding whether a particular geographic area should be called an *ir*, the name of the area is not determinative. Instead, an area is considered an *ir* if people generally regard the residents of the area as being much more connected to each other than to some other town. On the basis of this criterion, R. Feinstein ruled that Monsey, New York, in 1959 had the halakhic status of an *ir* and should therefore have its own *mikveh*.[63]

Another issue for RESP is whether pupils who attend a participating school in one neighborhood but reside in a different neighborhood should be counted as part of the enrollment base of the participating school. The issue turns on the application to the modern setting of Rava's dictum, recorded earlier, that pupils should not be made to travel back and forth to a school outside their local area. To make this judgment, let's take note of the diverse comments of the early authorities on Rava's dictum.

A key consideration here is *Rashi*'s contention that Rava's dictum is rooted in the concern that school children should not be subjected to the dangers of travel on a daily basis.[64]

While no competing rationale for Rava's dictum appears in the writings of the *Rishonim*, *Tosafot*'s analysis of the dictum articulates the view that the prohibition against sending children to a school in another town is not absolute, and that the prohibition is motivated by another consideration in addition to the desire to protect children from the dangers of travel. Preliminarily, recall that Rava makes his dictum a consequence of Yehoshua b. Gamla's ordinance. Recall also *Tosafot*'s position that Yehoshua b. Gamla's ordinance becomes operative only if the pupil population of the town reaches 25. Noting the link between Rava's dictum and Yehoshua b. Gamla's ordinance, *Tosafot* posit that Rava's dictum applies only when the pupil population of the town reaches 25. *Tosafot* then proceed to identify the case where the prohibition applies: Town *A*'s 25 pupils are currently instructed by a single *melammed*. Town *B* has two *melammedim*, each instructing a class of 25 pupils. By sending their children to the neighboring town, the parents in town *A* avoid hiring a teacher locally for 25 pupils. Instead, they can divide up the 25 between the two classes in town *B*, putting, say, 13 in one class and 12 in the other class. Rava's dictum prohibits this cost-saving arrangement.[65]

One could argue that the cost-saving arrangement is prohibited because making the children travel back and forth to town *B* causes the school in town *A* to close down, leaving town *A* without a school. By extension, transporting children to another town that results in driving the local school population below 25 decidedly undermines Yehoshua b. Gamla's ordinance and should also be prohibited.

Suppose, however, that the school in town *A* has 28 pupils and the parents of three of the pupils want to arrange for their children to be transported back and forth to town *B* for their education. In that case, because the transfer of the pupils does not reduce the school population in town *A* below 25, Yehoshua b. Gamla's ordinance is not undermined. No objection should therefore be raised.

Taken together, *Rashi*'s and *Tosafot*'s commentary on Rava's dictum results in a leniency for the modern scene. This leniency is that if the transfer of children to a school outside their neighborhood does not disrupt the local school, and the pupils who are transferred neither travel significantly longer nor are subject to greater dangers in travel than their local counterparts, Rava's dictum is not violated. If the transfer of children to a school outside their neighborhood does not violate Rava's dictum, the school that enrolls these children should qualify for a subsidy for these pupils.

Also relevant to the issue at hand is a query put to R. Mosheh Feinstein whether boys attending a day school in Sunderland, England, could be taken out of the local school and bused to a day school in Gateshead. The underlying motive of their parents was both to give their children a better Torah education and place them in a more religious milieu. The downside, however, was that withdrawal of the children would leave the Sunderland school with so few pupils that it might be forced to close. If the school closed, Yehoshua b. Gamla's ordinance that each town should have its own school would be undermined.

In his ruling, R. Feinstein drew a distinction between boys aged seven and those below this age. For boys below age seven, the anticipated gains in their Torah education from switching schools were not very significant. This factor combined with the recognition that long daily travel is very burdensome for children below age seven led R. Feinstein to recommend that these children remain in the local school. For boys aged seven and older, the anticipated gains from the switch were much more significant and the children could handle long daily travel better. Accordingly, for this age group, R. Feinstein ruled that the switch should be made, even at the expense of causing the local Sunderland school to close.[66]

What appears to emerge from R. Feinstein's analysis is that the long daily travel today for children to and from school may not in all instances entail subjecting the children to danger, but rather only to something burdensome. If danger is not a concern, other considerations may support allowing children to be bused to a school in a different neighborhood.

The upshot of the above analysis is that a case can be made that a participating school's per capita entitlement under RESP should not be reduced if some of its pupils reside in a different neighborhood.

COMPLIANCE WITH THE LAW OF THE LAND (*DINA DE-MALKHUTA DINA*)

Finally, Halakhah insists on compliance with the law of the land with respect to the rules the government adopts as a condition to granting a school a charter and providing financial aid.[67] This operational requirement, although not derived from Yehoshua b. Gamla's ordinance, should not be left to self-regulation. Consider that *yeshivot* and day schools receive government aid. Dishonest dealings with the government would therefore make a *yeshivah* guilty not only of theft but also of profaning the name of God (*hillul ha-Shem*).[68] The *dina de-malkhuta* standard has a positive message too. It makes a public statement to society at large that honesty is the bedrock of our dealings with everyone, not just with our co-religionists.

Religious Education Subsidy Program (RESP)

In this section, we will briefly describe a subsidy program that is designed to encourage *yeshivot* to adopt and compete on the basis of the standards outlined above.

The first step of the proposal is for each local community to convene a conference of its rabbinical leaders to establish minimum halakhic standards for the religious elementary schools in their neighborhood. Neighborhood schools would then be asked to accept these standards and submit to an audit to ensure compliance with the standards. Acceptance of the standards would earn for the school the designation of a participating school.

The next step is the establishment of a RESP for participating schools. Solicitations for this fund would be made from the community at large on a continuous basis. The RESP would distribute funds each month to participating schools. Initially, the distribution would be made based on enrollment figures alone. Subsequent allotments would adjust the subsidy based on changes in enrollment figures. This adjustment would be designed to provide special rewards for schools that experienced very significant growth in enrollment and downward adjustments per capita for schools that experienced a decline in enrollment. Changes in enrollment could be attributable to demographic factors. In structuring the incentive system, demographic factors should therefore be considered.

RESP—A CHARITY APPEAL OF THE HIGHEST PRIORITY

By establishing a Torah education fund for the entire community, RESP enables the community to solicit funds for the highest priority of charitable giving. This is so because the RESP fund can appeal to the public to contribute for the Torah education of all the needy elements of the community.

Both the individual and the community are often faced with competing claims for assistance. When all demands cannot be satisfied, Halakhah sets priorities. One of the highest priorities is the support of the Torah study of children.[69] This duty stands lower in priority only to the duty to respond to a request that relieves a life-threatening situation.[70] Support for the Torah study of young children takes precedence over the support for Torah study of mature rabbinical scholars.[71] This priority holds even if the children are not desperately poor and the funds support enabling them to study under comfortable conditions.[72]

Given the priorities Halakhah sets, we take it as a given that donors want an opportunity to practice charity on the highest level without the solicitation for this need being intertwined with a solicitation for items of lower priority.

In the hierarchy of charitable priorities described above, supporting the Torah education of young and poor children occupies the highest position.

Under present arrangements, the existence of a number of alternative *yeshivot* and day schools in a community almost guarantees that none of the schools will get the priority it deserves in the hierarchy of charitable giving. Out of fear of charges of favoritism, no synagogue is willing to respond to the request by one of the institutions that it be given an appeal. To be sure, all the *yeshivot* in the community could obtain a joint appeal from each synagogue. But to pull this off, much cooperation and goodwill among the *yeshivot* is necessary. Infighting over the formula for allocating donations would alone present a formidable sticking point. The void created by this bottleneck allows other organizations standing lower in the hierarchy of charitable causes to step in and become part of the quota of appeals. Complicating matters further is that often one of the prominent members of a synagogue will be prevailed upon to run a parlor or mock parlor meeting for the benefit of a particular *yeshivah*. Once his friends have been corralled for the cause of this particular *yeshivah*, they will be much less receptive to support the other *yeshivot* in the neighborhood.

RESP offers the prospect of catapulting the support of the Torah education of the youth to the priority it deserves. Once neighborhood schools become participating schools and the RESP fund is established, each synagogue can be approached to run an appeal for the RESP fund. The lure of such an appeal is that the money raised supports the Torah education of *all* the needy pupils in the neighborhood and hence fits within the category of the highest priority of charitable giving. Moreover, because the participating schools have all adopted the community's standards, the contributions will foster competition among the schools to achieve increasingly higher standards.

PRECEDENT FOR RESP

My proposal finds precedent in the subsidy program that the Kehillah Jewish Education Fund established in Chicago. Founded by Dr. Yosef Walder in 2004, the Kehillah fund makes monthly allocations to Chicago's religious elementary schools. Allocations are based on enrollments of the schools. The fund solicits the Chicago Jewish community at large to make monthly contributions to the fund. In 2004, 214 families contributed to the fund, and the program distributed a total monthly allotment of $36,000, divided up among eight Chicago elementary schools. George D. Hanus' Superfund for Jewish Education and Continuity, which also operates in the Chicago area with its own program, boosts the Kehillah fund with a matching grant.[73]

Since the inception of the Kehillah Jewish Education Fund, the trend has been for both the number of contributors and the monthly allocation figures to rise. Specifically, in 2007, 640 families contributed and the monthly allocation figure was approximately $47,000, divided up among nine schools. In 2009, the fund raised $600,000 from 1,153 contributors, and the funds were distributed among 12 religious elementary schools in Chicago. The Kehillah Jewish Education fund sets no requirements or standards for religious elementary schools as a condition to receiving these funds.[74]

The manner in which my proposal differs significantly from existing programs is that it ties the subsidy to the acceptance and enforcement of standards. Succeeding in increasing enrollment therefore is a school's way of demonstrating the superiority of its programs over those of competing schools. An increasing RESP allocation is a trophy a participating school can display to potential donors as an indication of the worthiness of its programs.

For a financially strapped school, attracting an increasing RESP allocation therefore carries financial weight considerably beyond the value of the subsidy it receives. Within RESP, a school should be driven to stretch its resources to achieve a higher level of performance and satisfaction among its clientele.

The united appeal of a RESP creates new avenues of receptivity to the message that support for the Torah elementary school education of the needy youth is the highest priority in charitable giving. Once the system is established, competition among participating schools fosters the channeling of tuition payments and charity dollars to the schools that can best achieve Torah educational goals.

Competition Based on Standards

REDUCING CONFLICT BETWEEN SCHOOL AND PARENTS

In his critique of the contemporary religious education scene, Rabbi Dr. Aharon Hersh Fried finds the major problem to be that schools and parents are in conflict.

Let's first examine this tension from the perspective of parents. One issue is that by virtue of a teacher's expertise and professionalism, the teacher feels that his teaching should not be put to question by parents. If a teacher receives criticism for his interpretation of sources, for example, he may decide not to double-check his sources, but instead either to ignore the criticism or, worse, hurl some form of denigration at his students or their parents.

Another source of conflict is that at times, a teacher or administrator takes the initiative to offer a student advice on an important matter without involving the child's parents or even taking into account the interests or perspective of the child's parents.

Yet another source of conflict is that schools do not always openly and honestly inform parents of a significant academic problem their child is experiencing. By the time a child's parents realize that their child indeed has a problem, it may be too late to take remedial action. For example, the child may no longer be able to gain admission into a high school.

From the school's perspective, parental conduct may be a source of much frustration. This occurs when parents flout school rules or place their child in the care of a professional without informing the school of the specific problem their child is experiencing and how they are addressing it.

Conflicts can be reduced if schools would only clearly articulate their educational vision, goals, rules, boundaries of responsibility for the children entrusted to their care, and grievance procedures. Under current arrangements, schools feel little or no pressure to formulate policies for these matters, let alone promulgate rules and procedures upfront. If each Jewish community would set standards and raise money to help in the finances of their local schools, the community would have leverage to mandate policies that would reduce conflict between parents and schools.[75]

By setting into motion competitive pressure, RESP encourages schools to both formulate policies and promulgate rules and procedures upfront to reduce conflict between parents and schools.

MERIT PAY

Requiring participating schools to implement a performance appraisal system for their teachers encourages experimentation in rewarding teachers based on the achievement of specified performance goals for their students. In this regard, the work of education economists, particularly Eric A. Hanushek, in the public educational sector is very relevant. The major finding is that school resources are not closely related to student performance. Thus, mandating smaller classes, increasing the requirements to become a teacher, or increasing teacher salaries does not produce better pupil performance. What does work in producing better pupil performance is rewarding teachers based on the achievement of specific pupil performance goals.[76]

PARENTAL INVOLVEMENT

With respect to the requirement that parents participate in the education of their children, suppose the community requires parents to certify that their children did their homework. School *A* decides to comply only minimally with this standard by requiring parents to send regular notes to their children's teachers certifying that their children did their homework. School *B* decides to go further and promises to arrange for parents to spend, on a rotation basis, an hour each evening during the school week with a group of children to help them do their homework and review the day's lessons. School *C* adopts *B*'s program but goes further and implements this rotational system for *Shabbat* learning as well. Now, if parents find the programs of schools *B* and *C* superior to the program of school *A*, the competitive process will force all schools to adopt a higher standard for parental involvement in the education of their children.

NON-GRADED SCHOOLS

The typical structure for elementary schools today is that students are divided into a series of grade levels based on chronological age. For the United States, the system of grouping students according to their age is relatively new, finding its beginnings in the innovation Horace Mann, the Secretary of the Massachusetts Board of Education, introduced in 1843. Graded education is based on the assumption that students of the same chronological age generally are at the same level of development and will progress at basically the same rate. It is now widely recognized that children of the same age vary in abilities, readiness to learn, and learning styles.[77] John I. Goodlad and Robert H. Anderson, for example, found that children entering the first grade differ in mental age by approximately four years.[78]

In an oral history project, conducted in 1992, Robert L. Leight and Alice D. Rinehart interviewed over 40 people who were former students or teachers in one-room schools in southeastern Pennsylvania. This report provides us with a glimpse into the routine and advantages of a school where all the pupils from grade one to eight were under the supervision and instruction of just one teacher in a single room.[79]

The most salient feature of the one-room school was that the pedagogical technique called for the pupils to take turns in making as many as 25 recitations over a typical school day. When one grade performed recitations, the other grades were involved in "seat work." The serial nature of recitations had two distinct advantages over a school that was age-graded. One advantage was that the student who was alert heard the recitations of the other grades and learned from them. The other advantage was that the bright students could accelerate by getting assigned a recitation according to their teacher's assessment of their abilities, rather than the same assignment as their age group.[80]

Andrea M. Hallion describes a multi-age program she successfully conducted in Hopedale, Massachusetts, in 1994. Her program emulated a successful multi-age program she observed in a school in Maine. Both programs combined a span of three age groups: K–2, 3–5, and 6–8.[81]

From the standpoint of Halakhah, the one-room school is not an innovation but rather a return to the structure of Torah elementary education as it existed in the time of Yehoshua b. Gamla. Recall that according to Yehoshua b. Gamla's ordinance, one *melammed* sufficed for a pupil population of 25, and no exception was made based on the age composition of the school children. This indicates that the one-room school was the norm in the time of Yehoshua b. Gamla.

Another advantage of the one-room school from the perspective of Halakhah is that it solves the ability-grouping problem. In the opinion of R. Judah b. Samuel he-Hasid (Regensburg, d. 1217), the *tinok harif* (perspicacious child) should not be instructed together with the average child, but rather should have the benefit of his own *melammed*.[82] Multi-age groupings solve the problem of *tinok harif* without the need to hire separate *melammedim* for the pupils of significantly different abilities. If the *tinok harif* is at the younger end of the combined age groups, he can be given the advanced lesson he needs by including him in the lesson of older children. If the *tinok harif* is at the higher end of the age spectrum, the *melammed* can assign him an advanced recitation or promote him to the next multi-age grouping.

THE VOLUNTARY *REISH DUKHNA*

One of the major problems *yeshivot* and day schools face today is overcrowding. Many schools have up to 35 children in a class. In addition, principals report that generally one out of five pupils in each class requires special attention.[83]

Recall that one aspect of the maximum class size recorded in the codes of Jewish law is the requirement that a *reish dukhna* (teacher's assistant) be hired when the class size exceeds 25. While the *reish dukhna* need only be competent in the role of assisting the teacher and need not himself have the credentials of a qualified teacher,[84] filling this position entails an expense. Within the framework of RESP, schools would naturally be driven to reduce this expense. An exciting possibility here is to fill the position by enlisting the voluntary services of retired laymen. Since a grandfather has a *talmud Torah* duty vis-à-vis his grandson,[85] appealing to a grandfather to serve as *reish dukhna* of his grandson's class would appear to be the most promising and therefore the primary target for the campaign.

INTEGRATING THE SECULAR CURRICULUM WITH THE TORAH PROGRAM

RESP could prove a boon for innovation in achieving greater integration of the secular portion of the curriculum with both Torah materials and ideology. Since achieving this goal is not predicated on the establishment of a new school but only on the selling of an idea, plan, or textbook to an existing school, RESP offers every good prospect of promoting innovation of this type.

Competition and New Entry

The contention that RESP will result in greater efficiency in the provision of Torah education is predicated on the assumption that there are no legal barriers for new entrants. To the extent these barriers exist, the pressure on established providers of Torah education to become more efficient is diminished. Examination of the degree to which Halakhah protects established firms from new entrants is therefore critical in reaching any judgment regarding the efficiency claims of our proposal. This examination will show that Halakhah adopts a much more *laissez-faire* attitude toward new entry in the Torah educational sector than it does for commercial enterprises generally.[86]

Elsewhere we have taken up the issue of "fair competition" as it pertains to commercial activity in general. With respect to commercial activity in general, we take the mainstream view to favor competition, with the caveat that an established firm is entitled to protection against ruinous competition.[87]

Competition in the Torah educational sphere is, however, treated differently. This can be seen from the following comment the Talmud makes with respect to R. Huna, who expressly espouses the view that an established firm is entitled to protection against ruinous competition:

> R. Joseph said: And R. Huna himself concedes that with regard to those who teach Torah to children, he [a teacher who is established in a particular alley] cannot prevent another from teaching in that alley. For master said "*kinat soferim tarbeh hokhmah*" (jealousy between scholars increases wisdom). Each teacher, fearful of his rival, will perform his role with extra care.[88]

Given that R. Huna ordinarily protects a competitor from ruinous competition, the import of the above Talmudic passage is that all disputants agree that when it comes to the Torah educational enterprise, freedom of entry reigns supreme, even when the impact is to ruin an established firm.

Support for this contention can be seen from an analysis of Rava's dictum, referred to earlier, that from the time of Yehoshua b. Gamla's ordinance, children may not be transported to a school in a different town. In *Tosafot*'s opinion, as will be recalled, Rava's dictum applies only if the local pupil population numbers at least 25. It is here that Rava prohibits transporting the pupils from a school in town *A* to a school in town *B*. But is not the inference Rava draws from Yehoshua b. Gamla's ordinance self-evident? Consider that if a town has at least 25 pupils, a teacher must be hired for them. Educating the pupils locally will therefore require the parents to hire a teacher, but sending the children off will require them to hire a teacher just the same. Since the parents gain nothing by sending their children to another town, it should be obvious that such action is prohibited and violates Yehoshua b. Gamla's ordinance. An advantage obtains, *Tosafot* answer, when the neighboring town has two separate classes, each with 25 pupils. By sending their children to the neighboring town, the parents avoid hiring a teacher locally for 25 pupils. Instead, they can divide up the 25, putting, say, 13 in one group and 12 in the other group.[89]

Consider that absent safety concerns, such as the need to traverse a shaky bridge to reach the second school, Rava does not prohibit the shifting of students from one school to another school *within* the local area. Accordingly, suppose the local area has three schools, *A*, *B*, and *C*, and each has a pupil population of 25. To save money, the parents of the pupils in school *A* should be allowed to split up their children into two groups and have one group enroll in school *B* and the other enroll in school *C*. What follows is that in a given Torah educational marketplace, there is no interference with legitimate market forces, even when the result is ruination for an established firm.

Another aspect of the issue of ruinous competition as it pertains to the Torah educational enterprise is whether non-taxpaying outsiders are permitted entry to teach Torah. Ordinarily, non-taxpaying outsiders are denied entry into a local town.[90] Does this rule apply to teachers of Torah as well? In a responsum, R. Joseph Saul ha-Levi Nathansohn (Ukraine, 1810–1875) addresses this issue. In the case presented to R. Nathansohn, local *melammedim* used the secular governmental authorities to expel *melammedim* who came from outside the town to offer their services to the local population. Vigorously objecting to the practice, R. Nathansohn invoked the Talmudic dictum of *kinat soferim tarbeh hokhmah*. This dictum, argues R. Nathansohn, guarantees *melammedim* unencumbered freedom of entry. With respect to the freedom of entry *melammedim* enjoy, there is no difference, avers R. Nathansohn, between teachers of *Mikra* and teachers of Mishnah and Talmud. Among the various factors R. Nathansohn invoked was that the outsiders, who were not burdened with significant financial obligations, were willing to offer their services at a low fee.[91] Considering that the underlying reason for the price differential between the outsiders and the local teachers was the difference in financial need, it would be reasonable to conclude that the price competition caused a ruinous impact on some of the local *melammedim*.

Quoting the particulars of R. Nathansohn's case, R. Abraham Isaiah Karelitz cites R. Nathansohn's ruling approvingly.[92]

The above analysis indicates that for the Torah educational sector, even outsiders are conferred freedom of entry. This freedom of entry is conferred even if it results in ruinous competition.

One more area of special treatment for the teacher of Torah is the zoning code prescribed for a residential area. In Mishnaic times, houses were grouped around courtyards. In recognition that the residents shared rights in the courtyard, the residents were restricted in their use of the courtyard. In this regard, the general rule was that a resident of a courtyard had the right to prevent a fellow resident from setting up a commercial enterprise in the courtyard.[93]

Authorities are in dispute regarding the basis of this zoning law. *Rashi* understands the basis of the objection to be that residents of a courtyard have a right to protest noise generated by outsiders who come in and out to buy merchandise.[94] Nahmanides et al., however, understand the basis of the objection to be the increase in traffic occasioned by the comings and goings of the customers, rather than the noise per se.[95] The right of residents to object to the traffic congestion caused by outsiders is not recognized, however, if one of the residents wants to set up a Torah school in his apartment.[96]

The suspension of the zoning code, according to the Talmud, is rooted in Yehoshua b. Gamla's ordinance. R. Joseph ibn Habiba (*Nimmukei Yosef*, Spain, early 15th cent.) explains the connection here. By accommodating the *melammed*'s preferences and not insisting that he set up his school in the town synagogue or study hall, which are more suitable for this purpose, implementation of Yehoshua b. Gamla's ordinance is facilitated. We should therefore not look upon the *melammed* as an individual bent on setting up a private enterprise in the courtyard. Rather, it is the Jewish court, acting to implement Yehoshua b. Gamla's ordinance, that is installing him in the courtyard.[97]

Kinat Soferim and Teacher Productivity

From the perspective of Halakhah, *kinat soferim* is a mechanism that improves teacher productivity in the Torah educational enterprise. Analysis of the following Talmudic passage sheds light on the nature of this link:

> And Rava also said: If the current teacher (*A*) of a class of children teaches at a certain pace, and there is another teacher (*B*) available who teaches at a faster pace, we do not remove *A* and appoint *B* in his stead. For if *B* were to be appointed, he might become lax in his work, arrogantly believing that his teaching abilities are beyond compare and he will never be dismissed.
>
> R. Dimi from Nahardea said: If *B* is given the position, all the more so will he teach at a fast pace, for *kinat soferim tarbeh hokhmah*.[98]

Talmudic decisors rule in accordance with R. Dimi, who takes the position that the current teacher should be replaced with the superior one.[99] In his explanation of R. Dimi's view, *Rashi* understands the phrase "*kinat soferim*" as having a very narrow purpose. It is invoked only to deflect Rava's concern that *B* will be overtaken with a feeling of superiority and become lax. *Kinat soferim* says this will not happen. Out of fear that *A*, the person whom he replaced, is always in a state of readiness to "embarrass him publicly" for any misstep, *B* will perform at his best.[100]

In contradistinction to *Rashi*, *Nimmukei Yosef* understands the phrase "*kinat soferim*" to explain why a legal environment in which an incumbent can be replaced if someone better is found motivates both the incumbent (*A*) and the one who takes over (*B*) to perform at a higher level of productivity. Out of fear of being fired, *A* performs at his best. Likewise, if *B* takes over, the prospect that *A* will be restored to his position motivates *B* to perform at his best.[101] Another difference between *Rashi* and *Nimmukei Yosef* is the nature of the force that motivates *B* to perform at his best. *Nimmukei Yosef* identifies it as the fear that he also will be fired and *A* will be restored to his original position. *Rashi*, however, understands that what motivates *B* is the fear that *A* will embarrass him publicly for any misstep.

What seems to proceed from *Rashi*'s commentary is that *kinat soferim* comes into play only when a *melammed* is replaced with someone who is deemed better suited for the job. But this understanding of *Rashi* must be rejected. Recall that R. Huna concedes that freedom of entry is the reigning principle for the Torah educational enterprise. Freedom of entry here is defended on the principle of *kinat soferim*. This demonstrates that *kinat soferim* is the *sine qua non* of a competitive environment and does not first set in when *melammed B* replaces *melammed A*. *Rashi*'s comments on R. Dimi's view should therefore not be taken to say that *kinat soferim* first comes into play when *B* replaces *A*. Instead, what *Rashi* is saying is that *kinat soferim* works even to overcome the sense of superiority that *B* naturally feels when he replaces *A*. To be sure, dislodging *A* may convince *B* that his job is secure, but *kinat soferim* makes *B* worry that *A* will be right there to embarrass him publicly for any misstep *B* commits. *B*'s fear of embarrassment therefore motivates him to perform at his best.

Before we show how the concept of *kinat soferim* fits into RESP, let's take note of the following comment of R. Yitzhak Yaakov Weiss (Israel, 1902–1989) on R. Dimi's dictum. In R. Weiss's view, R. Dimi's dictum applies only when *melammedim* are hired on a per diem basis. If a *melammed* is hired for a term and his employment agreement is entered into by contract, however, the employment of the *melammed* is secure for the term unless he is guilty of *peseida de-lo hadra* conduct.[102]

R. Weiss's ruling gives *kinat soferim* wide application to the modern scene where term contracts are the norm. It says that for the Torah educational enterprise, long-term security is all a matter of contract law. By injecting competitive pressures into Torah educational enterprises, RESP will undoubtedly undermine long-term security for weaker teachers, but at the same time will strengthen the long-term security of the best performers. This shakeup in long-term security arrangements should, however, be acceptable because *kinat soferim* says that greater competition in the Torah educational enterprise elevates the quality of Torah education and hence works for the good of society.

Consider also that one of the principles of RESP is that schools must implement a performance appraisal system for its teachers. Now, if parents are entitled to see the performance appraisal of their child's teacher, the teacher faces the prospect of public embarrassment for a poor or mediocre performance, regardless of the term of the teacher's contract. Recall that according to *Rashi*, fear of embarrassment for a misstep is what motivates a replacement teacher to perform at his best. Likewise, this same motivational force can be artificially inserted in a job-secure environment to motivate teachers to perform at higher levels of productivity.

Conclusion

In this chapter, we demonstrated that Jewish law's goals for religious elementary education can best be achieved by adapting Milton Friedman's model for the provision of elementary education. Since our proposal is directed to the Jewish community rather than to the Jewish State, Friedman's call for the government to tax society for the purpose of achieving optimal provision of elementary education is not incorporated in our model. What survives for adaptation for our purposes is Friedman's notion that the government should set standards for schools and ensure vigorous competition among qualifying schools by equipping parents with educational vouchers to pay tuition at qualifying schools.

Adapting the above two elements of the Friedman model translates into the proposition that the Jewish community should set standards for religious elementary education and establish a fund for poor families who send their children to qualifying schools.

With respect to the setting of standards, the standards we propose for Jewish religious education are either rooted in the ancient ordinance of Yehoshua b. Gamla or consistent with the objectives of that ordinance. These standards are performance appraisal for teachers; a testing requirement for pupils; minimum enrollment; compulsory attendance; neighborhood schools; maximum class size; and parental involvement in the education of their children.

One final standard is that participating schools must agree to run their schools in compliance with the law of the land (*dina de-malkhuta*). This requirement, although not derived from Yehoshua b. Gamla's ordinance, should not be left to self-regulation. By tying its subsidy to the enforcement of this standard, the community communicates to society at large that honesty is the bedrock of our dealings with everyone, not just with our co-religionists.

Milton Friedman's proposal calls for the government subsidy to take the form of an educational voucher for individual families. Our proposal, by contrast, calls for the Jewish community to raise funds to finance the religious education of poor families in the community. Participating schools would initially be eligible for these funds based on their overall enrollment. In subsequent years, a school's entitlement to funds would be adjusted based on changes in its overall enrollment from one year to the next.

We formulated our proposal in these terms out of practical considerations. For one, our proposal is designed to build on existing successful precedents. Second, since the subsidy is not a universal one but is meant to subsidize the education of only poor families, it is desirable to avoid the creation of a communal bureaucracy to determine which families are eligible for the subsidy. Instead, participating schools would be left to determine their own policies in this matter.

By tying the subsidy to acceptance of standards, RESP motivates schools to compete based on standards. A school earns larger allocations by achieving higher enrollments. It secures higher enrollments, in turn, by acquiring a reputation that it outperforms other schools with respect to the common standards adopted by participating schools. Given the financial straits schools find themselves in today, obtaining increasing allocations from the RESP would have economic significance considerably beyond the money received from the program. It would be a school's way of convincing potential donors of the worthiness of its programs.

The united appeal creates new avenues of receptivity to the message that support for the Torah education of the youth is the highest priority in charitable giving. Once the system is implemented, competition among participating schools fosters the channeling of tuition payments and charity dollars to the schools that can best achieve Torah educational goals.

Creating incentives for schools to compete on the basis of the standards that the community establishes will not in and of itself promote vigorous competition among participating schools based on these standards unless barriers for the entry of new schools are removed. In this regard, we demonstrated that Jewish law embraces free entry in the religious educational enterprise much more so than it does for commercial activity generally.

Notes

1. Milton Friedman, "The Role of Government in Education," in *Economics and the Public Interest*, ed. Robert A. Solo (New Brunswick, NJ: Rutgers University Press, 1955), 123–144.
2. See David D. Dill, "Allowing the Market to Rule: The Case of the United States," *Higher Education Quarterly* 57, no. 2 (April 2003): 140–143.
3. Caroline Minter Hoxby, "Rising Tide," *Education Next* (Winter 2001): 72–74.
4. See Mishnah, *Avot* 1:15 and R. Obadiah b. Abraham of Bertinoro (Italy, ca. 1456–ca. 1516), *Bartenura*, ad loc., s.v. "*aseh toratekha keva*"; Mishnah, *Avot* 4:10.
5. Palestinian Talmud, *Berakhot* 1:2; Palestinian Talmud, *Shabbat* 1:2.
6. Despite the lack of a formal structure in Jewish communities, ample precedent exists for a community to unite when vital concerns for all Jews of the community are at stake. A case in point is the screening of charity collectors and the rating of the worthiness of the causes they represent. Going by various names, communal organizations for this purpose have sprung up in Baltimore, Bergen County, Toronto, Chicago, Los Angeles, Lakewood, Miami, and the Five Towns. These organizations typically issue letters of approval to qualified collectors. The letters are written on high-security paper with a raised seal. Another feature is that the community produces and sells script to the householders of the community. When the collectors solicit funds, householders use the script to make their donations. The collectors then submit the script to the community organization for redemption at face value. One of the clear-cut successes of these organizations has been to ferret out fraud (interview with Dr. Avrum Pollack, President, Star-K Kosher Certification). The author thanks Rabbi Shmuel Heinemann, Rabbinic Administrator of Star-K Kosher Certification, for making available a number of documents that describe the work of these communal organizations.
7. While it is evident from the discussion in this chapter that our proposal relates to boys' schools, the proposal has application to girls' schools as well. Consider that R. Israel Meir ha-Kohen Kagan (*Hafetz Hayyim*, Radin, 1838–1933) approved formal education for girls in the early 1920s and defended the innovation as no less than vital to the transmission of the Jewish heritage to future generations. R. Israel Meir ha-Kohen Kagan, *Likkutei Halakhot*,

Sotah 20b (Warsaw, 1922). Since our proposal relates to the form that a communal subsidy for education should take, the proposal is relevant for girls' schools even though the specific arguments presented cannot be applied literally to girls' schools.

The focus of this chapter is on religious education. As will be discussed, however, many of the points made regarding standards for religious education apply equally to secular education on the elementary school level.

8. *Bava Batra* 21a.
9. Ibid.
10. *Rif, Bava Batra* 21a; *Mishneh Torah, Talmud Torah* 1:1–7; *Rosh, Bava Batra* 2:6; *Tur, Yoreh De'ah* 245; *Shulhan Arukh, Yoreh De'ah* 245:7.
11. R. Meir b. Todros ha-Levi Abulafia, *Yad Ramah, Bava Batra* 21a.
12. *Shabbat* 119b.
13. R. Simeon b. Tzemach Duran, *Sefer ha-Tashbetz: Teshuvot*, vol. 3, eds. Yoel Katan, Shimon Shmuel Goldschmidt, and Abraham Yaakov Goldmintz (Jerusalem: Machon Yerushalayim, 2007), no. 153.
14. R. Shneur Zalman of Liadi, *Shulhan Arukh ha-Rav, Yoreh De'ah, helek* 5, *Hilkhot Talmud Torah* 1:3 (Brooklyn: Otzar ha-Hasidim, 2004), p. 444.
15. Deuteronomy 6:7.
16. *Shabbat* 119b.
17. R. Meir Simhah ha-Kohen of Dvinsk, *Or Sameah* on *Mishneh Torah, Talmud Torah* 1:2.
18. R. Joel Teitelbaum, *Va-Yoel Mosheh, Ma'amar Lashon ha-Kodesh* (Brooklyn: Sender Deutsch: 1961), *ot* 7.
19. Contrary to the views cited in the text, R. Moses Sofer (*Hatam Sofer*, Hungary, 1762–1839) on *Bava Batra* 21a apparently understood that Yehoshua b. Gamla's entire focus was on the Torah education of orphans. R. Sofer begins his thesis by positing that a father's Biblical duty to teach his son Torah is not fulfilled by merely offering his son lessons. Rather, the father must ensure that his child actually receives and absorbs the instruction. Accordingly, if the father is not up to the task of teaching his son Torah, he must hire a tutor to accomplish this. Since it is forbidden to take money for teaching someone Torah, the fee the tutor takes is to make sure that the child will stay put and not run away from the lesson. This fee is called *sekhar shimmur* (compensation for "watching" the child).

    For a father, discharging his duty to teach Torah to his son always takes precedence over his duty to teach Torah to others. This holds even if teaching one's own son Torah entails an expense while teaching someone else Torah involves no expense. Within these parameters, a void naturally existed in the Torah education of orphans. Since no individual is obligated or has the authority to coerce an orphan to study Torah, the Torah education of orphans went neglected. To fill this void, Yehoshua b. Gamla promulgated a decree that required the community to assume the responsibility for the Torah education of orphans. It consisted of hiring a teacher for the orphan children and ensuring their attendance. See R. Moses Sofer, *Hiddushei Hatam Sofer, Seder Nezikin, Bava Batra* 21a.
20. *Rashi* to *Bava Batra* 21a. *Tosafot* to *Bava Batra* 21a, however, understand the term "*sofer mata*" to refer to the person who drafts the legal documents of the town. R. Israel Schepansky (Israel, contemp.) notes that a *melammed tinokot* in the Mishnah (*Shabbat* 11:1) is also called a *hazan*. See R. Israel Schepansky, *Ha-Takkanot bi-Yisrael*, vol. 4 (Jerusalem: Mossad HaRav Kook, 2004), 267. Putting together *Rashi*'s understanding of the role of the *sofer mata* and the functionary called *hazan* leads R. Schepansky to posit that the Torah educational system had a hierarchal organizational structure. The one who actually taught the children of the town was the *hazan*, and the one who supervised him was the *sofer mata*.
21. Aaron Levine, *Case Studies in Jewish Business Ethics* (Hoboken, NJ: Ktav, 2000), 304–320.
22. *Mishneh Torah, Talmud Torah* 2:2; *Tur, Yoreh De'ah* 245; *Shulhan Arukh, Yoreh De'ah* 245:11; R. Jehiel Michal Epstein (Belarus, 1829–1908), *Arukh ha-Shulhan, Yoreh De'ah* 245:12.
23. *Mishneh Torah*, op. cit.; *Tur*, op. cit.; *Shulhan Arukh*, op. cit., 245:14; *Arukh ha-Shulhan*, op. cit.
24. *Mishneh Torah*, op. cit.; *Tur*, op. cit.; R. Joseph Caro, *Beit Yosef* to *Tur*, ad loc.; *Shulhan Arukh*, op. cit., 245:12; R. Shabbetai b. Meir ha-Kohen (*Siftei Kohen*, Poland, 1621–1662), *Siftei Kohen* to *Shulhan Arukh*, ad loc., n. 9; *Arukh ha-Shulhan*, op. cit.

25. *Arukh ha-Shulhan*, op. cit., 384:6.
26. *Bava Metzia* 109b; *Rif*, ad loc.; *Mishneh Torah*, *Sekhirut* 10:7; *Rosh*, *Bava Metzia* 9:38; *Tur*, *Hoshen Mishpat* 306; *Shulhan Arukh*, *Hoshen Mishpat* 306:8; *Arukh ha-Shulhan*, *Hoshen Mishpat* 306:16.
27. *Mishneh Torah*, op. cit.; *Tur*, op. cit.; *Shulhan Arukh*, op. cit.; *Arukh ha-Shulhan*, op. cit.
28. According to R. Vidal Yom Tov of Tolosa (*Maggid Mishneh*, Spain, ca. 1300–1370), teaching correctly but failing to catch the mistakes of a pupil does not constitute *peseida de-lo hadra* conduct and hence does not rise to the level of an offense that warrants dismissal. See *Maggid Mishneh* to *Mishneh Torah*, *Sekhirut* 10:7, s.v. "*u-melammed tinokot*."
29. *Mishneh Torah*, op. cit.; *Tur*, op. cit.; *Shulhan Arukh*, op. cit.; *Arukh ha-Shulhan*, op. cit. In the opinion of R. Jehiel Michal Epstein, a single isolated incident of *peseida de-lo hadra* conduct does not warrant immediate dismissal. What is needed is three incidents of such conduct or a forewarning against this conduct. See *Arukh ha-Shulhan*, op. cit.
30. For a description of the nature of the damage sexual abuse does to a child, see Judith Herman, *Trauma and Recovery: The Aftermath of Violence—From Domestic Abuse to Political Terror* (New York: Basic Books, 1997), 96–114. For a discussion of how Halakhah deals with the issue of child abuse, see Steven Oppenheimer, "Confronting Child Abuse," *Journal of Halacha and Contemporary Society* 44 (Fall 2002): 31–50.
31. *Mishneh Torah*, *Talmud Torah* 4:4.
32. See *Arukh ha-Shulhan*, *Orah Hayyim* 53:26. The case specifically deals with the prohibition against firing a cantor based on rumor. Firing someone based on rumor violates the prohibition against accepting an evil report, recorded at Leviticus 19:16. See *Arakhin* 15b; *Mishneh Torah*, *De'ot* 7:3.
33. Although much of the curriculum of elementary school education can be viewed as necessary preparation for Torah study, there can be no doubt that *peseida de-lo hadra* would not be defined in the same terms for a teacher of secular subjects as it is for the Torah educator. Specifically, Torah study and Torah study alone is designated by our Sages as *hayyei olam* (everlasting life). In this regard, an act of prayer rises only to the level of *hayyei sha'ah* (temporal life) compared to the *hayyei olam* status of Torah study (*Shabbat* 10a). The *hayyei olam* status of Torah study makes every *lost* moment of Torah study an irreplaceable loss. In the imagery of the Sages, the Torah proclaims: "If you forsake me for one day, I will forsake you for two days" (*Midrash Shemuel Rabbati*, *parashah* 1). The irreplaceable nature of lost time in Torah study makes the *melammed tinokot* subject to immediate dismissal if he idles on the job. Secular studies, by contrast, do not fall within the category of *hayyei olam*. Consequently, lost time in secular studies as a result of idleness can be made up and should therefore not be classified as *peseida de-lo hadra*. What the above argues is only that idleness per se on the part of a secular teacher should not be equated with idleness per se by a teacher of Torah. If the idleness of the secular teacher is, however, frequent or continues despite repeated warnings, the conduct could very well warrant firing.
34. R. Naftali Tzvi Yehudah Berlin, *Ha'amek She'elah* on R. Ahai Gaon (Palestine, 8th cent.), *Sefer She'iltot*, *Parshat va-Et'hannan* 142; *Arukh ha-Shulhan*, *Yoreh De'ah* 245:4.
35. R. Yaakov Kamenetsky (New York, 1891–1986), *Emet le-Yaakov*, *Avot* 5:21 (New York, 1989). The present practice is apparently rooted in *Siftei Kohen* to *Shulhan Arukh*, *Yoreh De'ah* 245, n. 5.

    For an alternative theory of why the sequence of study prescribed at *Avot* 5:21 changed over time, see R. Jacob Culi (Constantinople, ca. 1685–1732), *Yalkut Me-Am Lo'ez* on *Massekhet Avot*, *Avot* 5:21, trans. R. Samuel Yerushalmi (Jerusalem: Or Hadash, Mossad Yad Ezra, 1972), p. 263.
36. For an excellent article on this debate, see R. Moshe Weinberger, "On Studying Secular Subjects," *Journal of Halacha and Contemporary Society* 11 (Spring 1986): 88–128.
37. R. Yosef Eliyahu Henkin, *Kitvei ha-Gri'a Henkin*, vol. 1, part 2, *Edut le-Yisrael* (New York: Ezras Torah, 1981), *ot* 62, p. 158.
38. For sources that support my contention that the secular curriculum of *yeshivot* and day schools should be regarded predominately as preparatory for Torah study, an enhancement

of the understanding of Torah, or a vehicle to acquire love and fear of God, see Maimonides, *Mishneh Torah, Yesodei ha-Torah* 2:2–3; Maimonides, *Moreh Nevukhim* 1:34; R. Jonathan Eybeschuetz (Poland, 1690–1764), *Ya'arot Devash* 2:7 (Jerusalem: Machon Or ha-Sefer, 2nd ed. 1988), pp. 122–124; and R. Abraham Isaiah Karelitz, *Hazon Ish al Inyanei Emunah, Bitahon, ve-Od* 1:8 (Jerusalem: S. Greineman, 1954), p. 11. Many of these sources are quoted in R. Moshe Weinberger's article, cited in note 36 above.

39. *Bava Batra* 21a.
40. *Mishneh Torah, Talmud Torah* 2:5.
41. *Rosh, Bava Batra* 2:7.
42. *Shulhan Arukh, Yoreh De'ah* 245:15.
43. *Tur, Yoreh De'ah* 245.
44. *Siftei Kohen* to *Shulhan Arukh, Yoreh De'ah* 245, n. 10. In contradistinction to *Siftei Kohen*, the 17th-century decisor, R. Aaron Samuel b. Israel Kaidanover (Poland, 1614–1676), *She'elot u-Teshuvot Emunat Shemuel* no. 26, averred that the maximum class size benchmark prescribed in the Talmud was no longer operative in his time. To give pupils proper individual attention, R. Kaidanover felt that, for his time, maximum class size should be no more than 10 or 12 students.
45. R. Simeon b. Tzemach Duran, *Sefer ha-Tashbetz* 2:64, 3:153.
46. See Moshe Bleich, "Class Size—A Halakhic Perspective," *Tradition* 38, no. 4 (Winter 2004): 32–33 (citing *Sefer ha-Tashbetz* 2:64, which mentions *Rabbeinu Yonah*'s view). *Rabbeinu Yonah*'s analysis can be found at *Aliyot de-Rabbeinu Yonah, Bava Batra* 21a, s.v. "*ve-amar Rava*," reprinted in R. Moses Herschler, ed., *Aliyot de-Rabbeinu Yonah ha-Shalem* (Jerusalem: Machon ha-Talmud, 1990), 82.
47. See, e.g., American Educational Research Association, "Class Size: Counting Students Can Count," *Research Points: Essential Information for Research Policy* 1, no. 2 (Fall 2003).
48. *Bava Batra* 21a.
49. R. Adret's text on Rava's dictum departs from the standard texts and records the benchmark to be 24 rather than 25. See *Hiddushei ha-Rashba, Bava Batra* 21a, ed. R. Mordecai Leib Katzenelenbogen, vol. 1 (Jerusalem: Mossad HaRav Kook, 2008), 358, n. 14.
50. Ibid., 358.
51. Nahmanides' and R. Adret's thesis that Yehoshua b. Gamla's ordinance applies even if the local pupil population is less than 25 finds support in the work of other authorities. In their presentation of Yehoshua b. Gamla's ordinance, R. Isaac b. Jacob Alfasi, Maimonides, R. Jacob b. Asher, and R. Joseph Caro make no mention that the ordinance does not apply if the pupil population numbers less than 25. The silence of the codifiers regarding a minimum pupil population indicates that there is no minimum. Silence on the matter of the minimum pupil population does not, however, firmly establish the position of these authorities on the specific case of less than 25 pupils that Nahmanides and R. Adret address. That case is where some of the parents want to go it alone and others want a single teacher to be hired for all the children.

The key here, in the opinion of this writer, is Nahmanides' comment that Yehoshua b. Gamla's ordinance applies "even when the pupil population is only two or three" (Nahmanides, *Hiddushei ha-Ramban, Bava Batra* 21a). What can be inferred from Nahmanides' comment is that Yehoshua b. Gamla's ordinance does not apply when there is only *one* pupil in the town. The notion here is that it takes at least two pupils studying together under a teacher to be called a school. This implies that one aspect of a school is the interactive process between the pupils with each other and the teacher. We'll assume that the benefit of the interactive force keeps increasing until the number of pupils reaches 25, but further increases in the class size exert a diminishing effect.

Let's now relate the interactive effect to Yehoshua b. Gamla's ordinance. Given that Yehoshua b. Gamla did not merely require each town to educate its youth, but instead required each town to set up a school, parents may not execute their duty to educate their children in a manner that undermines the viability of the local school. Since "going their own way" both increases the cost per child for the remaining households and also reduces the potential benefit of the interactive force that would have obtained had all the children been combined into a single class, parents would be denied the option to "go it alone" when the pupil population of the town is less than 25.

52. *Tosafot, Bava Batra* 21a; *Rosh, Bava Batra* 2:7.

    In his work *Jewish Education and Society in the High Middle Ages* (Detroit: Wayne State University Press, 1992), Rabbi Dr. Ephraim Kanarfogel offers the thesis that no communally funded and administered elementary Torah education existed in Ashkenaz (i.e., Germany and northern France) during the 11th, 12th, and 13th centuries. Instead, private arrangements were made between fathers and tutors. "In many cases the tutor was hired for just one student, but sometimes he taught several." Ibid., 19.

    Among the various pieces of evidence R. Kanarfogel draws upon to support his thesis is a survey of 40 responsa emanating from Ashkenaz that deal with the hiring and terminating of *melammedim*. In all instances, it is the parents rather than the community who hired or supervised the *melammed*. One example is a ruling by R. Meir b. Barukh of Rothenburg (*Maharam me-Rotenburg*, Germany, ca. 1215–1293) that a father should be forced to hire a *melammed* for his son or teach the boy himself. Ibid. (citing *Haggahot Maimuniyyot* to *Mishneh Torah*, *Talmud Torah* 1:1 and *Teshuvot*, *Pesakim u-Minhagim*, ed. Isaac Z. Kahana [Jerusalem: Mossad HaRav Kook, 1960], vol. 2, p. 255, *ot* 193). Now, if organized schools existed at the time, R. Meir would have certainly directed the recalcitrant father to enroll his child in the local school. Kanarfogel, *Jewish Education*, 19. R. Kanarfogel's thesis is in opposition to the earlier works of the historians Robert Chazzan and Moritz Güdemann, who maintained that an organized system of elementary education existed at that time. Ibid., 17.

    The discussion in the text regarding the parameters of Yehoshua b. Gamla's ordinance can put R. Kanarfogel's theory into a halakhic framework. Recall the position of *Tosafot* and R. Asher b. Jehiel that Yehoshua b. Gamla's ordinance required parents to join together and hire a single teacher for all their children only if the school-aged population is at least 25. If the number is less than 25, however, the parents are free to make their own private arrangements for the education of their children and cannot be coerced into making a joint arrangement. Consider that the main Ashkenazic authority R. Kanarfogel cites in support of his thesis is R. Meir b. Barukh of Rothenburg, who was R. Asher b. Jehiel's main teacher. Now, if we take *Tosafot* and R. Asher b. Jehiel as representative of the rabbinical authorities in Ashkenaz, we need only postulate that the towns where Jews lived were small and the pupil population did not reach the critical mass of 25 in each town. Moreover, even if we assume that some towns had at least 25 elementary school children, other factors might have exempted parents from the requirement to combine their children into one class. For example, the age differences of children in a town might have been so wide as to make it pedagogically impossible to join the children into a single class under the instruction and supervision of one *melammed*.

53. *Arukh ha-Shulhan*, *Yoreh De'ah* 245:27.
54. Marvin Schick, "A Census of Jewish Day Schools in the United States, 2008–2009," AVI CHAI Foundation (October 2009): 19.
55. Deuteronomy 11:19.
56. *Kiddushin* 30a.
57. *Shulhan Arukh*, *Yoreh De'ah* 245:6. R. Pinhas ha-Levi Horowitz (Frankfort, 1730–1805), *Sefer ha-Makneh*, *Kiddushin* 30b, interprets Maimonides (*Mishneh Torah*, *Talmud Torah* 1:7) to concur with *Shulhan Arukh*. See, however, R. Joseph Caro, *Kesef Mishneh*, ad loc.
58. *Ramah*, quoted in *Tur*, *Yoreh De'ah* 245.
59. *Mishneh Torah*, *Talmud Torah* 1:10. For sources and implications for specific conduct emanating from the prohibition not to forget the Torah one has studied as well as from the affirmative duty to remember what one has studied, see R. David Pollack, *Be-Torato Yehgeh*, vol. 1, ch. 10 (Jerusalem: Mahon Minhat Israel, 1997), 183–198.
60. See R. Samuel b. Nathan ha-Levi Kolin (Bohemia, 1720–1806), *Mahatzit ha-Shekel* to *Shulhan Arukh*, *Orah Hayyim* 343, n. 1.

61. R. Isaiah ha-Levi Horowitz, *Shenei Luhot ha-Brit, Sha'ar ha-Otiot, ot* 4, s.v. "*derekh eretz*."
62. R. Abraham Isaiah Karelitz, *Hazon Ish, Yoreh De'ah, Hilkhot Melammedim ve-Hilkhot Talmud Torah* 152 (Bnei Brak: S. Greineman, 1973), pp. 182–183.
63. R. Mosheh Feinstein, *Iggerot Mosheh, Hoshen Mishpat* 1:40.
64. *Rashi* to *Bava Batra* 21a. R. Joseph ibn Habiba (*Nimmukei Yosef*, Spain, early 15th cent.), *Nimmukei Yosef* to *Rif*, *Bava Batra* 21a, also follows *Rashi*'s line of reasoning.
65. *Tosafot*, *Bava Batra* 21a.
66. R. Mosheh Feinstein, *Iggerot Mosheh, Yoreh De'ah* 3:75.
67. For a summary of the various views on the halakhic principle of "the law of the kingdom is the law" (*dina de-malkhuta dina*), see Aaron Levine, *Moral Issues of the Marketplace in Jewish Law* (Brooklyn, NY: Yashar Books, 2005), 144–145.
68. R. Tzvi Hirsch Ashkenazi (*Hakham Tzvi*, Germany, 1660–1718) shows that the Torah prohibits theft not in consideration of the victim, but rather because dishonest conduct debilitates the character of the perpetrator and sullies his soul. Hence, dishonest conduct directed at any human being is equally prohibited (*Hakham Tzvi*, no. 26). When the victim is a Jew, discovery that the perpetrator is a fellow Jew presumably does not incite the offended party to rail against his own religion and call it a false belief system. In contrast, when the victim is a gentile, the discovery that the perpetrator is a Jew could very well incite the non-Jewish victim to disgrace the Jewish religion and call it a false belief system. Accordingly, in the latter instance, the offender compounds the sin of theft with the additional sin of *hillul ha-Shem*. R. Bahya b. Asher (*Rabbeinu Behaye*, Saragossa, d. 1340), *Rabbeinu Behaye al ha-Torah*, Leviticus 25:50, s.v. "*ve-hishav im konehu*."
69. *Shulhan Arukh, Yoreh De'ah* 249:16.
70. R. Abraham Danzig (Prague, 1748–1820), *Hokhmat Adam* 145:7. Included in the case entailing a threat to life, according to R. Danzig, ad locum, is the duty to respond to the call for support of a poor man who is very ill, or who is healthy but lacks "bread in a time of famine." In his treatment of the parameters of a life-threatening situation as it relates to responding to a charitable solicitation, R. Yaakov Yeshayahu Bloi (Israel, b. 1920) quotes *Hokhmat Adam* as his source, but formulates the desperately poor healthy man a bit differently than *Hokhmat Adam*. In R. Bloi's formulation, the desperately poor healthy person is the man who lacks "bread." R. Yaakov Yeshayahu Bloi, *Tzedakah u-Mishpat*, 2nd ed., ch. 3, *ot* 26 (Jerusalem: 2000), p. 78 & n. 82.
71. R. Bloi, *Tzedakah u-Mishpat*, ch. 3, *ot* 25, p. 77, n. 77 (quoting R. Samuel b. Moses di Medina [*Rashdam*, Solonica, 1505–1589], *She'elot u-Teshuvot Ma-ha-Rashdam, Yoreh De'ah* 167); R. Yitzhak Yaakov Weiss (Israel, 1902–1989), *She'elot u-Teshuvot Minhat Yitzhak* 2:39 (Jerusalem, 1993). But see R. Judah Assad (*Mahari Assad*, Hungary, 1796–1866), *Teshuvot Mahari* (a.k.a. *Yehudah Ya'aleh*), *Yoreh De'ah* 315 & 3:243.
72. R. Bloi, *Tzedakah u-Mishpat*, ch. 3, *ot* 25, p. 78, n. 78.
73. Micah Greenland, "Who Should Pay for Jewish Education?" *Jewish Action* (Fall 5766/2005): 28.
74. Telephone interview and e-mail correspondence with Nesanel Siegal, Executive Director of the program.
75. Aharon Hersh Fried, "The Respect We Owe Each Other—For the Sake of Our Children," *Hakirah: Flatbush Journal of Jewish Law and Thought* 9 (Winter 2010): 139–171.
76. Eric A. Hanushek, "The Failure of Input-Based Schooling Policies," *Economic Journal* 113 (February 2003): F64–F98.
77. Joan Gaustad, "Nongraded Education: Mixed-Age, Integrated, and Developmentally Appropriate Education for Primary Children," *Oregon School Study Council* 35, no. 7 (March 1992): 5, 14.
78. John I. Goodlad and Robert H. Anderson, *The Nongraded Elementary School*, rev. ed. (New York: Teachers College Press, Columbia University, 1987), 3.
79. Robert L. Leight and Alice D. Rinehart, "Revisiting Americana: One-Room School in Retrospect," *Educational Forum* 56, no. 2 (Winter 1992): 134.
80. Ibid., 142–143.

81. Andrea M. Hallion, "Strategies for Developing Multi-Age Classrooms" (paper presented at the annual convention of the National Association of Elementary School Principals Association, Orlando, FL, March 4–9, 1994).
82. R. Judah b. Samuel he-Hasid, *Sefer Hasidim* 308.
83. Aaron Twerski, "Our Burgeoning Yeshivos: Triumphant Growth? Or Compounding Critical Shortfall?," *Jewish Observer* 38, no. 1 (January 2005): 17.
84. Compare R. Joseph ibn Habiba, *Nimmukei Yosef* and *Rif*, *Bava Batra* 21a; R. Menahem b. Solomon Meiri (*Meiri*, Perpignan, 1249–1316), *Beit ha-Behirah*, *Bava Batra* 21a.
85. This duty is based on the Biblical verse "and you shall teach them to your sons and grandsons" (Deuteronomy 4:9). See *Kiddushin* 30a; *Mishneh Torah*, *Talmud Torah* 1:2; *Tur*, *Yoreh De'ah* 245; *Shulhan Arukh*, *Yoreh De'ah* 245:3; *Arukh ha-Shulhan*, *Yoreh De'ah* 245:8.
86. The following discussion regarding the general parameters in Halakhah for fair competition draws from my work *Moral Issues of the Marketplace in Jewish Law* (Brooklyn, NY: Yashar Books, 2005), 95–138.
87. Ibid., 95–106.
88. *Bava Batra* 21b–22a.
89. *Tosafot*, *Bava Batra* 21a.
90. R. Moses Isserles (*Rema*, Poland, 1525 or 1530–1572), *Rema* to *Shulhan Arukh*, *Hoshen Mishpat* 156:7.
91. R. Joseph Saul ha-Levi Nathansohn, *Yad Shaul*, *Yoreh De'ah* 245.
92. R. Abraham Isaiah Karelitz, *Hazon Ish al Inyanei Emunah*, *Bitahon*, *ve-Od* 3:14 (Jerusalem: S. Greineman, 1954), pp. 28–29.
93. *Mishnah*, *Bava Batra* 2:3; *Rif*, *Bava Batra* 21a; *Mishneh Torah*, *Shekhenim* 6:12; *Rosh*, *Bava Batra* 2:6; *Tur*, *Hoshen Mishpat* 156; *Shulhan Arukh*, *Hoshen Mishpat* 156:2; *Arukh ha-Shulhan*, *Hoshen Mishpat* 156:2.
94. *Rashi* to *Bava Batra* 21a, s.v. "*me'akkevin alav*."
95. Nahmanides, *Hiddushei ha-Ramban*, *Bava Batra* 21a; *Rashba*, *Hiddushei ha-Rashba*, *Bava Batra* 20b; R. Nissim b. Reuben Gerondi (*Ran*, Spain, 1320–1376), *Hiddushei ha-Ran*, *Bava Batra* 20b; *Nimmukei Yosef* to *Rif*, *Bava Batra* 21a.
96. *Bava Batra* 21a; *Rif*, ad loc.; *Mishneh Torah*, op. cit.; *Rosh*, *Bava Batra* 2:6; *Tur*, op. cit., 156; *Shulhan Arukh*, op. cit., 156:3; *Arukh ha-Shulhan*, op. cit., 156:3. R. Joseph Caro (*Shulhan Arukh*, loc. cit.) extends the exemptions to other *mitzvah* activities. Nahmanides (*Bava Batra* 21a), however, avers that the exemption applies only for the establishment of a Torah school.
97. *Nimmukei Yosef* to *Rif*, *Bava Batra* 21a, s.v. "*benei hatzer me'akkevin alav*."
98. *Bava Batra* 21a.
99. *Rosh*, *Bava Batra* 2:8; *Tur*, *Yoreh De'ah* 245; *Shulhan Arukh*, *Yoreh De'ah* 245:18; *Arukh ha-Shulhan*, *Yoreh De'ah* 245:18.
100. *Rashi* to *Bava Batra* 21a, s.vv. "*dilema asei le-israshulei*" and "*kol she-ken*."
101. *Nimmukei Yosef* to *Rif*, *Bava Batra* 21a, s.v. "*kinat soferim*."
102. R. Yitzhak Yaakov Weiss, *Minhat Yitzhak* 4:75.

CHAPTER 6

Aspects of the Lemons Problem as Treated in Jewish Law

Introduction

Commercial transactions are often characterized by asymmetric information between the buyer and seller—one side of the market, usually the seller, knows more about the quality of the product or service offered than the other side. In his seminal 1970 article, George Akerlof predicted that unless countervailing forces are in place, the asymmetric information phenomenon will cause the volume of transactions in this marketplace to shrink to the point where only the most inferior version of the product, called a lemon, will be traded.[1]

As a practical matter, numerous institutions mitigate the asymmetric information problem so that the marketplace does not deteriorate into a lemons market. These countervailing forces include seller guarantees, brand names, product liability laws, consumer screening, third-party comparisons, and the institution of standards and certification by the government or consumer and industry groups.[2]

Our purpose here will be to analyze one aspect of the lemons problem from the perspective of Jewish law. Specifically, we will show how Jewish warranty law counteracts the lemons problem. We will also compare Jewish law's solutions to the lemons problem to those of American warranty law and state lemon laws.

Warranty law works best to counteract the lemons problem if it operates in an environment of trustworthiness. We will show that Jewish law assigns the task of moral education to parents and teachers with the goal of producing the character trait of trustworthiness. Jewish warranty law hence operates in tandem with societal efforts to foster an environment of trustworthiness. We will also show that all the mechanisms that counteract the lemons problem require the operation of a commercial environment of trustworthiness to be effective.

Finally, we will explain that the creation of an environment of trustworthiness takes on aspects of a pure public good and should be viewed as an expenditure on basic, rather than applied, research. Fostering trustworthiness is hence a form of social capital, and government investment to foster this environment is consistent with economic efficiency.

We begin our analysis with an elucidation of the lemons problem in economic theory.

George Akerlof's Lemons Model

George Akerlof captured the essence of the asymmetric information problem with the used car marketplace.[3] Akerlof asks us to consider the implications of the fact that the seller's first-hand experience with his car places him in a much better position than a prospective buyer to know the defects of the car.[4]

To demonstrate Akerlof's point that the asymmetric information phenomenon may cause the marketplace to deteriorate to the point where only lemons are traded, assume that all participants in the used car market are fully informed. Assume further that only two types of used cars are traded: good cars and bad cars. Finally, assume that a good car sells for $12,000, a bad car sells for $6,000, and a total of 50,000 cars are sold in each market.

Once we assume asymmetry of information, the two separate markets will merge into a single market, and a single price will prevail for both good and bad cars. The price for a used car in this market will depend on the typical buyer's assessment of the probability of a buying a lemon. If the typical buyer assesses the probability of buying a lemon to be 50%, the price the marketplace will charge will be the average value of a used car when half turn out to be good, or $9,000:[5]

$$\tfrac{1}{2}(\$12,000) + \tfrac{1}{2}(\$6,000) = \$9,000$$

But the $9,000 price is not an equilibrium price. If sellers can fetch no more than $9,000 for a good car, they will offer fewer cars for sale than they would have when the expected price was $12,000. Similarly, we should expect that the number of bad cars offered at the $9,000 price will increase substantially.

What will the next price move be? To answer that question, we'll need to make a few assumptions. First, let's assume that when the two markets merge, the $9,000 price will cause the same total number of cars to be offered for sale as before, but the mix between good and bad cars offered for sale will change. Let's assume that the mix between good and bad cars offered for sale will now be 25,000 good cars and 75,000 bad cars. This new distribution alters the buyer's assessment of the probability of buying a lemon. If the typical buyer now assesses the probability of buying a lemon to be 75%, the market will not clear at the $9,000 price. Instead, the price will decline to $7,500. This amount reflects the weighted average when 25% of the cars are valued at $12,000 and 75% of the cars are valued at $6,000:

$$\tfrac{1}{4}(12,000) + \tfrac{3}{4}(6,000) = \$7,500$$

Exactly where this process ends depends on how responsive the supply of good and bad cars is to the market price as it keeps dropping. While the equilibrium price cannot be identified with any precision, what is certain is that the proportion of used cars sold that are of high quality will be lower than when consumers know the quality of all cars before making their purchases.[6]

Countervailing Mechanisms and Jewish Law

In extrapolating Jewish law's approach to the asymmetric information problem, we should note that the existence of a lemons market is decidedly against the economic interests of both the buyer and seller. We take it therefore as a given that any countervailing mechanism that is rooted in economic self-interest would emerge in a Torah society no less frequently than it has in American society. Seller guarantees, brand names, consumer screening, and third-party for-profit certification are all countervailing forces that preserve economic self-interest. To the extent that these mechanisms emerge through self-help and voluntary exchange and do not impose unlawful external costs on third parties, Jewish law would unqualifiedly embrace these developments in the marketplace. The same judgment, however, cannot necessarily be made about countervailing forces in the form of government intervention in the marketplace because these interventions, particularly product liability laws and licensure requirements, redistribute property rights.

In this chapter, we will limit our discussion to the effect of Jewish warranty law on the lemons market and describe the backdrop of moral education under which it operates. In drawing out the details of Jewish warranty law, we will compare Jewish law's approach to this issue with American law, particularly the Uniform Commercial Code (UCC) adopted by the states beginning in 1953,[7] and the federally enacted Magnuson-Moss Warranty Act of 1975.[8]

Jewish Warranty Law

Since the appearance of Akerlof's article, warranty law has developed significantly and has been successful in bringing an otherwise frightened-off buyer back into the marketplace. Most fundamentally, warranty laws say that the government will enforce any express promise a seller (*S*) makes to a buyer (*B*) regarding the performance of a product. If the competitive pressures of the relevant market are weak, and dishonesty is widespread, warranty law will make possible many transactions that would not otherwise take place. Warranty laws, however, go further. As a result of the common law principle of "fair value for money spent," warranty laws provide that *S*, by virtue of being a merchant, makes certain unspoken and unwritten promises to *B* regarding the performance of the product. These promises are known as "implied warranties." Indeed, the law often provides that these implied warranties cannot be negated even through an advance disclaimer by *S*.

As we will see, Jewish law extends to *B* far greater rights than those granted by American law. The comparatively greater advantage that Jewish law confers on *B* will be seen in the scope of the implied warranties and in the way Jewish law restricts *S* from limiting implied warranties.

IMPLIED WARRANTIES

Under the UCC, if *S* is a merchant and offers a written warranty for a good, he automatically guarantees that the good would pass without objection in the trade and is fit for the ordinary purposes for which such a good is used.[9] This guarantee is referred to as the implied warranty of merchantability. For example, if *S* sells an oven to *B*, *S* implicitly warrants that the oven will bake food at controlled temperatures that *B* selects.[10] If the oven fails to heat, or heats at the wrong temperature, *S* has breached the implied warranty of merchantability.[11] Similarly, if *S* sells a water glass to *B*, *S* implicitly warrants that the water glass will hold water. If *B* discovers that water leaks from the glass, *B* has a right to return the glass based on a breach of the implied warranty of merchantability.[12]

In addition, if *S* is a merchant, *S* offers an implied warranty of fitness for a particular purpose when *B* relies on *S*'s advice that a product can be used for a particular purpose.[13] For example, if *B* specifically requests from *S*, an appliance retailer, a washing machine that can handle 15 pounds of laundry in one load and *B* buys that model on the strength of *S*'s express recommendation that it can handle the load, the law says that *S* has made a warranty of fitness for a particular purpose. If the model that *S* recommended proves unable to handle 15-pound loads, *S* has breached the implied warranty of fitness for a particular purpose, even if the machine washes 10-pound loads well.[14]

Jewish warranty law subscribes to both the implied warranty of merchantability and the implied warranty of fitness for a particular purpose, which find wide expression in the rabbinic literature. Let's first take up the implied warranty of merchantability.

MERCHANTABILITY

Under Jewish law, *S* provides an implied warranty of merchantability in a commercial transaction based on the presumption that *B*'s intention is to acquire the item of sale free of any defect.[15] To protect himself against product defects, *B* therefore need not extract from *S* an explicit guarantee of the quality of the product.[16]

Given the prevailing presumption that a product offered for sale will be free of defects, it becomes *S*'s duty under Jewish law to disclose to *B* all the defects of the product.[17] *S* must disclose these defects in a straightforward, unambiguous manner.[18] If a defect is known to *S*, *B* has every legal right to expect *S* to forthrightly disclose the defect. Even if the sale item is of a type that frequently suffers from defects, the burden does not shift to *B* to insist that the validity of the transaction depends on the absence of defects. Instead, *B* has the right to rely on *S* to disclose whatever *S* knows regarding the defects.[19] Failure to disclose those defects makes *S*, according to R. Joshua b. Alexander ha-Kohen Falk (*Sema*, Poland, 1565–1614), guilty of both fraud and theft.[20]

B's right to be protected against product defects is preserved even if it is reasonable to assume that *S* was not aware of the defects when the parties entered into the transaction.[21] Moreover, Jewish law sets no statute of limitations defining the amount of time *B* has to lodge his product defect claim.[22] Nonetheless, *B*'s use of the article subsequent to his discovery of a defect creates the presumption that he desires to keep the transaction intact despite the defect.[23]

The remedy available to *B* upon discovery of a defect depends on the nature of the defect. In Jewish law, defects are categorized as either material or not material. For a defect to qualify as a material defect, "everyone in the country must agree that discovery of the defect would make the typical buyer want to cancel the transaction."[24] If the defect is a material defect, *B* has the right to cancel the transaction even if he paid a fair price for the defective item.[25] When the rescission right applies, *B* may reject *S*'s offer to satisfy his complaint with a price adjustment.[26] Moreover, in the material-defect case, *S* need not accept *B*'s offer to keep the transaction intact at a reduced price. Instead, *S* may insist that *B* either purchase the item "as is" at the contract price or accept a refund of the purchase price.[27]

If the defect is not material, discovery of the defect does not allow *B* to cancel the transaction under Jewish law. Nonetheless, because the defective item was not sold at its fair market price, *B* may be entitled to a price adjustment, depending on the magnitude of the discrepancy between the sales price and the fair market price of the item. The guidepost here is the law of *ona'ah* (price fraud),[28] as described below.

In the opinion of R. Asher b. Jehiel (*Rosh*, Germany, 1250–1327), *B*'s rescission right is not recognized when the defect can be repaired and the sale item can be made whole. In the specific case addressed by R. Asher, *S* sold his house to *B*. The house was located in a town called Kurtova, but the parties conducted the sale in a different town, Ashbalia. Subsequently, it became known that, before the transaction was concluded, vandals damaged the house. As a result of the damage, *B* sued to cancel the deal. *S* countered with an offer to keep the deal intact but reduce the sales price by an amount equal to the cost to repair the house. R. Asher ruled in favor of *S*. Since the house could be restored to its previous condition and the cost of the repairs was an insignificant portion of the sales price, the vandalism did not render the transaction a *mekah ta'ut* (transaction made in error). Instead, R. Asher ruled that the transaction stood, and the price was reduced by a repair allowance determined by a panel of experts.[29] The codifiers adopt R. Asher's position.[30]

A variation of the above case occurs when the house turns out to have unstable walls. *B* claims *mekah ta'ut* based on the unsuitable living conditions. *S*, however, wants to keep the transaction intact and replace the unstable walls with stable walls. On those facts, R. Moses Isserles (*Rema*, Poland, 1525 or 1530–1572) ruled that the transaction must be regarded as a *mekah ta'ut*. In his view, a house without stable walls is not simply a defective house, but rather no house at all. *S*'s offer to fix the house therefore would not be an offer to repair the specific house named in the transaction, but rather a house not yet in existence. Hence, the unstable condition of the walls that existed at the time the transaction was concluded renders the transaction a *mekah ta'ut*.[31]

Relying on both R. Asher and R. Isserles, R. Yehudah Itach (Israel, contemp.) avers that *B*'s rescission right remains intact, even when the sale item can be restored through repairs, if either (1) the repair bill amounts to a significant percentage of the sales price, or (2) the sale item is not functional until the repairs are completed.[32]

The discussion above should not be construed as implying that Jewish law places the entire burden on *S* to ensure the quality of the sale item. With respect to ensuring quality, Jewish law has certain expectations for *B* as well. If *B* fails to meet up to those expectations, *B* is guilty of a self-inflicted harm and *S* will not be responsible for *B*'s loss. *B*'s responsibilities to ensure quality include the following:

1. In a face-to-face transaction, *S* has no responsibility to point out to *B* the openly visibly defects of the item of sale. Because the defects are obvious, *B* is expected to discover them himself. Consequently, once the transaction is finalized, *B*'s silence must be taken as acceptance of the price and other terms of the deal, despite the defects. *B*'s demand to cancel or adjust a transaction based on defects that should have been obvious to him at the time of the face-to-face presentation is therefore not recognized.[33]

2. In certain instances, according to R. Asher, the discovery of a material defect will not allow *B* to cancel the transaction unless *B* stipulated in advance that the transaction would be cancelled if the defect is found. This rule applies when the good has a latent defect that *S* cannot possibly be aware of at the time of the sale but the probability that the defect will be discovered later is more than remote.

The sale of an animal for slaughter illustrates this point of Jewish law relating to latent defects. Preliminarily, let's note that a standard procedure after slaughtering an animal is to examine the animal's lungs for the presence of an adhesion in the lobes (*sirkha*). Discovery of a *sirkha* may render the animal organically defective and hence unfit for consumption under Jewish law. Suppose that upon slaughtering an animal, *B* discovers a disqualifying *sirkha*. If it can be ascertained that the disqualifying *sirkha* was already present before the sale was consummated, *B* may have a claim to recover the purchase price. Consider however that the occurrence of a disqualifying *sirkha* is an infrequent event, and most people would find it an acceptable risk to buy an animal with the chance that it would turn out to be unfit for consumption. In such a case, *B* is provided a remedy only if he stipulated in advance that the transaction would be cancelled if a *sirkha* is found.[34]

A contrary position is taken here by Nahmanides (*Ramban*, Spain, 1194–1270). In his view, *B* always has the right to cancel a transaction based on the discovery of a material defect. That right remains intact even if the defect is sufficiently common that *B* should have been concerned about it, and even if *S* could not have been aware of the defect before he entered into the sale.[35]

Taking note of these divergent views, R. Jehiel Michal Epstein (Belarus, 1829–1908) rules that the party to the contract who is holding the money at the time of discovery of the *sirkha* (the *muhzak*) will have the advantage. Accordingly, if *B* discovers a *sirkha* in the animal but has not yet made payment to *S*, the Jewish court (*Beit Din*) would not order *B* to pay. Instead, the court would allow *B* to declare that the transaction was a *mekah ta'ut* unless *S* can prove that no *sirkha* existed at the time of sale.[36]

3. If the defect is not an absolute defect but affects only the item's fitness for a particular purpose, *B* will be at a disadvantage. The vicious ox (*nag'han*) case illustrates this principle. In that case, *S* sells an ox to *B* but does not inform *B* that the ox is vicious. Because the ox is a menace to society, it must be destroyed and may not be used for plowing.[37] After the transaction is completed, *B* discovers that the ox is a *nag'han*. *B*'s intention was to purchase an ox for plowing, but he was silent on this point during his negotiations with *S*. *B* sues for a refund on the grounds that most people purchase oxen for plowing and not for slaughter.

Talmudic authorities dispute the scope of *B*'s rights in this case. Rav allows *B* to obtain a refund based on the type of use that a majority of people would have from the ox.[38] Samuel, whose opinion is considered normative, takes the view, however, that because majority practice is not decisive in monetary matters,[39] *B* will not prevail based on the argument that most people purchase oxen for plowing. What *B* needs to prove is that the circumstances of his transaction with *S* demonstrated that *S* was aware of *B*'s intention to use the ox for plowing. One possible way for *B* to prove this is to refer to the purchase price. If the purchase price of an ox suitable for plowing is higher than the purchase price of an ox suitable only for slaughter, *B*'s willingness to pay the higher price is deemed to have clearly communicated to *S* his intention to use the ox for plowing.

Another way for *B* to validate his claim is to show that he is known to *S* as a farmer, and in his past dealings with *S* had bought oxen only for plowing. Even if *B* was silent about his planned use for the ox in the present transaction, *S* should have reasonably understood *B*'s intention by assuming that *B* would follow his normal pattern of use.[40]

The *nag'han* case illustrates that Jewish law does not inherently assign *S* the role of counselor vis-à-vis *B*. Unless expressly requested to assume that role by

B, *S* is required only to make proper disclosure of absolute defects. Now, if the price of an ox suitable for plowing is higher than the price of an ox suitable only for slaughter, *nag'han* status is definitely an absolute defect, regardless of *B*'s intended use for the ox. If *B* intends to use the ox for plowing, the *nag'han* is useless for *B*'s purposes. If, by contrast, *B*'s intended use is for slaughter, the price *S* demands is excessive and violates the law of *ona'ah*.[41] When the price of the two types of oxen is the same, however, *nag'han* status can be considered a defect only if *B*'s intended use is for plowing. Because Jewish law does not inherently impose on *S* the role of counselor to *B*, it is *B*'s responsibility to speak up and inform *S* of his intended use. If *B* fails to do so, he has inflicted the harm on himself.

FITNESS FOR A PARTICULAR PURPOSE

As we have seen, American warranty law recognizes that *S* provides an implied warranty of fitness for a particular purpose under certain circumstances. Recall the illustration of this warranty discussed above: *S* is an appliance retailer and *B* asks for a washing machine that can handle 15 pounds of laundry in one load. If *S* recommends a particular model, and *B* buys that model on the strength of *S*'s recommendation, the law says that *S* has made a warranty of fitness for a particular purpose. If the model *S* recommended proves unable to handle 15-pound loads, the warranty is breached, even if the machine washes 10-pound loads well.

In the analogous case in Jewish law, *B* transacts with *S* for superior wheat but *S* delivers inferior wheat. Given the mistake, *B* has the right to cancel the deal and recoup the purchase price,[42] even if the transaction did not entail *ona'ah*.[43]

R. Shelomoh Kluger (Poland, 1783–1869) clarifies the wheat case in a way that shows its close affinity with the washing-machine case. In R. Kluger's opinion, the parties contemplate that *B* will grind the grain into flour. The difference between superior and inferior grain lies only in the amount of flour that can be extracted per measure of grain. The Talmud records that one-third less flour can be extracted from inferior grain than from superior grain.[44] Given this differential, if *B* had not specified that he wanted superior grain, but instead asked for only, say, $5 worth of grain, *S* would be within his rights to fill the order with either *Q* of inferior grain or 2/3*Q* of superior grain. But since it is undisputed that *B* requested $5 worth of superior grain, *B* can insist that *S* fill the order with superior grain or refund the purchase price.[45]

Because the issue is not *ona'ah*, the difference that the quality of the grain makes is that *B* will be required to devote more time to grinding the grain into flour if the flour is of an inferior quality. This is the same type of inconvenience that *B* would experience in the washing-machine case if the machine could not properly handle 15-pound loads. *B*'s right to cancel the deal is based on the idea that the transaction included an implicit warranty that *B* is entitled to obtain what he specifically requested.

SCOPE OF IMPLIED WARRANTIES

Despite the similarities between Jewish law and American law in their approaches to implied warranties, we can identify some important differences:

1. Since implied warranties in Jewish law proceed from the presumed intentions of the parties, the implied warranties should apply not only to the original seller, but to any seller along the distribution chain.[46] By the same logic, the warranties should be enforceable even if a transaction is oral and *S* is not a professional merchant.

UCC warranty law, by contrast, applies only to sales by merchants. A merchant is defined in the UCC as:

> a person that deals in goods of the kind or otherwise holds itself out by occupation as having knowledge or skill peculiar to the practices or goods involved in the transaction or to which the knowledge or skill may be attributed by the person's employment of an agent or broker or other intermediary that holds itself out by occupation as having the knowledge or skill.[47]

This definition does not cover all transactions, such as a sale by a lay person.[48] It does, however, cover virtually all transactions that take place in a store or dealership because it includes anyone who works for an employer.[49]

Similarly, under American law, oral warranties are recognized only in limited circumstances. The Magnuson-Moss Warranty Act protects *B* only when *S* is a merchant and the warranty *S* offers is written rather than oral.[50] To be sure, as under Jewish law, oral guarantees receive some level of protection under American law.[51] If a merchant affirms that "this is a new car" or displays a sample model,[52] the merchant has made an express warranty.[53] Similarly, if the merchant promises that "when the sale item arrives, it will be painted yellow" or "if it doesn't work, I'll fix it," the merchant has made an express warranty.[54]

Finally, the Magnuson-Moss Warranty Act does not apply to warranties of products sold for resale or for commercial purposes; the Act covers warranties only of consumer products.[55]

2. In contrast to American law, Jewish law recognizes implied warranties not only for merchantability and fitness for a particular use, but also for "fairness" of price.

In Jewish law, fairness of price is governed by the law of *ona'ah*.[56] The law of *ona'ah* prohibits one from concluding a transaction at a price more favorable to himself than the competitive norm.[57] A transaction involving *ona'ah* is regarded as a form of theft.[58] Depending on how widely the price of the subject transaction departs from the competitive norm, the injured party may have the right to void or adjust the transaction.

B's right to void a first-degree *ona'ah* transaction is recognized when the sales price is more than one-sixth higher than the market price.[59] When the differential is exactly one-sixth (i.e., second-degree *ona'ah*), neither party may void the transaction on account of the price discrepancy. The plaintiff is, however, entitled to full restitution of the *ona'ah*.[60] Lastly, third-degree *ona'ah* occurs when the sales price differs from the market price by less than one-sixth. In that case, the transaction not only remains binding, but the plaintiff also has no legal right to recoup the price differential.[61] In the case of third-degree *ona'ah*, however, the plaintiff's claim for the price differential is denied only when the transaction involves a non-standardized product. For a standardized product, such as milk, the plaintiff's claim for the price differential would be honored regardless of how small the differential is.[62] One caveat should, however, be noted. Remedy in an *ona'ah* claim is recognized only when the discrepancy in price does not exceed the margin of error the typical consumer could make regarding the fair market value of the item at hand.[63]

WAIVING IMPLIED WARRANTIES

Compared to American law, Jewish law protects *B* more comprehensively against *S*'s ability to negate implied warranties by issuing a disclaimer. Under American law, if *S* stipulates that he is selling a product "with all faults" or "as is," the stipulation allows *S* to escape responsibility if the product proves to be defective or unfit for the purpose for which *S* represented it could be used.[64] Moreover, even when the law does not permit *S* to issue an advance disclaimer, the automatic protection *B* obtains from implied warranties is narrow. To see this, it will be useful as a preliminary matter to examine the requirement under American law that any written warranty provided by *S* must be designated as either a "full" warranty or a "limited" warranty.

For a warranty to qualify as a "full" warranty, five conditions must be satisfied: (1) *S* may not limit the duration of the warranty; (2) the warranty must apply to anyone who owns the product during the warranty period, not just to the first purchaser; (3) the warranty service must be free of charge; (4) if *S* is unable to repair the product after a reasonable number of attempts, *S* must provide *B* with a replacement item or a refund, at *B*'s option; and (5) *S* may not require *B* to perform any duty as a prerequisite to receive service unless *S* can demonstrate that the duty is reasonable.[65]

By designating a warranty as a full warranty, *S* communicates to *B* that the coverage offered meets the federal minimum standards for comprehensive warranties under the Magnuson-Moss Warranty Act. *S* is, however, under no requirement to make the written warranty a full warranty. Instead, *S* may designate the warranty a limited warranty.

Prior to the enactment of the Magnuson-Moss Warranty Act, *S* had the legal right to disclaim the implied warranties that proceeded from a written warranty by making the disclaimer conspicuous in the warranty document that *S* showed or gave to *B*.[66] The Magnuson-Moss Warranty Act makes this practice illegal. Accordingly, even if the disclaimer is prominently displayed on the face of the warranty document, *B* remains protected if the item proves defective or unfit for the purpose for which *S* represented it could be used. The Act, however, provides *S* with a significant exception to this rule: *S* may limit the duration of the implied warranties, provided that the limitation is reasonable and "set forth in clear and unmistakable language and prominently displayed on the face of the warranty."[67]

In Jewish law, *B*'s upfront agreement not to cancel a sale if he discovers a defect in the sale item does not forfeit his rights. For the waiver to be effective, *B* must agree in advance to accept a specific defect or up to a certain specific amount of depreciation in the value of the sale item attributable to defects.[68] The law treats *S*'s advance disclaimer of an *ona'ah* claim similarly. *S*'s disclaimer is not valid unless *B* agrees not to file suit if the transaction price does not turn out to exceed the competitive norm by a specific sum specified in the agreement.[69]

S and *B* may also void the implied warranty of fair-market price by using the *nosei be-emunah* (selling on trust) mechanism. In the prototypical case of *nosei be-emunah*, *S* informs *B* that his cost base involved *ona'ah* and that after *S* purchased the item, he discovered that he could have purchased it for half the price he actually paid. *S* then proposes that *B* agree to buy the article for a certain percentage markup above *S*'s cost. If *B* agrees to these terms, he forfeits any right to cancel or modify the transaction on the grounds that *S*'s cost base involved *ona'ah*. This is so because the validity of the transaction is based on the circumstance that *S* and *B* agreed that the marketplace would not be the arbiter of the fairness of price for the article. Instead, their agreement called for a certain markup for *S* above his cost base. Accordingly, notwithstanding the *ona'ah* the transaction entailed, *B* has forfeited any *ona'ah* claim.

A variation of this case occurs when *S*'s upfront disclosure acknowledged only that the article was worth less than what he paid for it, but failed to specify by what amount. Here, some authorities regard the transaction price as subject to adjustment or cancellation if the amount of the *ona'ah* was very significant. Because *B* was not told upfront how much *ona'ah* was involved in the transaction, credibility is given to *B* that had he only known at the time of the transaction that *S*'s cost price entailed such a significant amount of *ona'ah*, he would have never entered into the transaction.

One more variation: If it can be established that *S* knew at the time of the transaction with *B* that his cost price entailed *ona'ah* but failed to disclose this to *B*, *B* would have a right to adjust or overturn the transaction based on the *ona'ah*, notwithstanding that *B* agreed to *S*'s stipulated markup.[70]

Compared to American law, the requirement in Jewish law that waivers must be very specific in order to be legally binding is more protective of *B*'s rights in two situations:

1. *S* stipulates to *B* that he is selling a product "with all faults" or "as is." In that case, the stipulation does not relieve *S* of his responsibility under Jewish law to make *B* whole if the product proves defective or unfit for a particular purpose.[71] Since this stipulation does not expressly waive any specific defect or specific amount of depreciation in value attributable to defects, *B*'s rights remain intact.

2. *S* sells a car to *B* and offers a three-year warranty. In the warranty, *S* stipulates that if the car is defective, *S* is responsible only for replacing parts free of charge, but *B* must bear the cost of the labor necessary to install the new parts. In evaluating the validity of this warranty, the salient point to note is that absent *S*'s stipulation, *B* is entitled to automatic remedies in the event of the product defect. Depending on the circumstances, these remedies will consist of either a rescission right or a right to insist upon repair or replacement of the defective part at no charge. *S* has no right to reduce these rights by merely informing *B* that he is offering only a limited warranty. *S*'s stipulation is valid only if *B* waives the implied warranty rights to which he is entitled. A proper waiver, in turn, requires that the specificity requirement for waivers be met. For the warranty at hand, the specificity standard is met with respect to *B*'s agreement to accept repair or replacement of defective parts instead of exercising his rescission right. The labor costs, however, are inherently *S*'s responsibility. Moreover, because the agreement is not formulated in terms of relieving *S* of up to some specific sum for labor costs, *B*'s waiver with respect to labor costs is invalid. Consequently, if the car has a defective part, *S* will be required to replace it free of charge.

MODIFYING THE IMPLIED WARRANTY

The Magnuson-Moss Warranty Act addresses the issue of whether *S* has a right to condition the implied warranty of a product through the tie-in sale mechanism. Let's use the following illustration of this stratagem, taken from the website of the Federal Trade Commission (FTC), to compare Jewish law and American law on this matter.

Suppose the Plenum Vacuum Cleaner Company stipulates the following in its written warranty:

> In order to keep your new Plenum Vacuum Cleaner warranty in effect, you must use genuine Plenum brand filter bags.

Plenum's tie-in sale warranty will not be binding on *B* unless the FTC gives its prior approval. To get approval, Plenum must demonstrate that use of filter bags other than Plenum bags will ruin its vacuum cleaner. If the company makes the above tie-in sale without prior approval from the FTC, the stipulation is not binding on *B* and the warranty remains intact, even if the customer uses a different brand of filter bags.[72]

In considering how Jewish law would treat the tie-in sale, let's consider a number of different scenarios. First, suppose comparable filter bags will do just as well, but *B* agrees to use Plenum bags only because he believes the company's representation that non-Plenum bags will ruin his vacuum cleaner. Because the company obtains *B*'s waiver of its warranty by deception, *B*'s waiver is a waiver made in error (*mehilah be-ta'ut*) and should therefore be invalid.[73]

Moreover, suppose the FTC approves Plenum's tie-in sale. Even though the tie-in sale is not a duping mechanism to make the customer use Plenum's bags, *B*'s waiver of Plenum's warranty is not binding. This is so because Plenum's agreement fails to meet one of Jewish law's technical requirements to make a conditional stipulation binding. This is the rule of *tenai kaful* (lit., double condition). The *tenai kaful* rule says that, in general, a condition stipulated by *S* at the time he enters into a transaction is binding on *B* only if *S* explicitly describes the consequences of alternative actions at that time.[74] In the case at hand, satisfaction of the *tenai kaful* rule requires *S* to state, "If you use filter bags other than the Plenum bags, your warranty is cancelled." Because *S* fails to make the stipulation in the *tenai kaful* form, the warranty remains in place, even if *B* violates the warranty condition.

Let's consider the possibility that even with the insertion of *tenai kaful* language, Plenum's FTC-approved tie-in sale may not pass muster under Jewish law because it would be characterized as *asmakhta* (equivocal commitment). What follows is an explanation of the principle of *asmakhta* and its relevance to the case at hand.

For an undertaking to become legally binding, two critical tests must be met. First, the commitment must be made with deliberate and perfect intent (*gemirat da'at*). Second, the commitment must generate reliance (*semikhat da'at*) by the party to whom it was made.[75] Both of these related conditions may be absent in a transaction that projects the finalization of an obligation into the future, becoming operative only upon the fulfillment of a specific condition. A transaction containing these elements is referred to in the Talmudic literature as *asmakhta*. With the undertaking becoming operative only when a condition is fulfilled, the person obligating himself may very well rely on the probability that the condition will not be fulfilled, and that he thus will not become obligated. Because the presumption of perfect intent is lacking at the time the commitment was made, the presumption that the commitment generated reliance is equally lacking.

A transaction characterized as *asmakhta* does not confer legal title.[76] Because the *asmakhta* transaction is regarded as invalid *ab initio*, a transfer made after the conditions are fulfilled is characteristically involuntary and hence a form of robbery.[77]

B's agreement to waive his rights to the warranty if he uses a non-Plenum filter bag apparently amounts to an *asmakhta* undertaking and is thus void. This is so because *B* agreed in advance to waive his rights only because he intends not to violate *S*'s stipulation and install only the approved filter bags. When, however, the time comes to replace the filter bags, *B* is surprised to find that Plenum bags are not conveniently accessible and therefore takes a chance on a different brand of filter bags. *B*'s agreement in advance to forgo the warranty if he uses the wrong bags was therefore not made with perfect resolve. Does *B*'s agreement amount to an *asmakhta* undertaking?

Let's take note that *Rishonim* have proposed various formulations of an *asmakhta* undertaking.[78] *B*'s undertaking here apparently satisfies the criteria R. Solomon b. Isaac (*Rashi*, France, 1040–1105) and others adopt for an *asmakhta* undertaking. In *Rashi*'s view, *asmakhta* obtains when an obligor (*R*) undertakes a conditional obligation to an obligee (*E*) but can escape the obligation entirely because *R* partially controls the condition that makes the obligation operative. Let's illustrate this principle with a case discussed in the Talmud: *R* agrees to buy current vintage wine for *E* at the low-price Zolshafat marketplace. *R* stipulates that if he misses the window of opportunity to buy the wine while it is still cheap, he will make good on the price differential to *E*. Now, if *R* acts quickly, he can obtain the wine at the low price. If, on the other hand, *R* is negligent and tarries, he will miss the window of opportunity. Since *R* relies on himself to act quickly and avoid liability to *E*, he lacks firm resolve to make payment to *E* if he misses the window of opportunity and faces the higher price. He will therefore not be ordered to pay *E* the price differential.[79]

While the tie-in sale and Zolshafat marketplace case share the feature that the triggering mechanism is partially in *R*'s control, the cases are essentially different. The Zolshafat case deals with the issue of whether *R* must affirmatively follow through with a compensatory payment if the sales price rises. Since *R*'s commitment lacks perfect resolve, *Beit Din* will not order *R* to make the payment. In sharp contrast, the issue in the tie-in sale case is whether *B*'s waiver is valid—that is, whether *B* has agreed to give up his right to force *S* to deliver a good. Consider that when *B* discovers the defect in the vacuum cleaner, the refund or replacement vacuum is in the hands of *S*. Because *B* will not be required to hand over anything to *S*, the concept of forcing a party to act on an agreement he made without firm resolve does not come into play.

Addressing the issue of whether a waiver can be rendered invalid on the basis of *asmakhta*, R. Vidal Yom Tov of Toloso (*Maggid Mishneh*, Spain, ca. 1300–1370) posits that the "majority of opinions" take the position that a waiver is not rendered invalid by reason of *asmakhta*.[80]

Based on these rulings, we may conclude that when the tie-in sale is not a deceptive ploy by *S* to get *B* to use a complementary product, *B*'s agreement to waive his warranty right if he uses a different brand of the complementary product is valid. If, however, *S* fails to use *tenai kaful* language in the stipulation,

B's agreement to the stipulation will not render the warranty nugatory if *B* violates the stipulation.

State Lemon Laws

State lemon laws, which were first enacted in Connecticut in 1982,[81] were intended to close an important gap in warranty law. Under the UCC and the Magnuson-Moss Warranty Act, auto manufacturers typically offered a limited warranty, which obligated them only to repair and replace defective parts.[82] This practice left the consumer without adequate recourse when a car turned out to be a lemon.[83] A lemon has been defined as "a chronically defective car that cannot be repaired with a reasonable effort."[84] A lemon typically experiences multiple or significant recurring problems. For example, the engine leaks oil, the electrical system shorts out, or the car vibrates at various speeds.[85]

In Jewish law, the lemon case arises when *B* agrees to a limited warranty for a new car. Let's assume that Jewish law's specificity requirements for waivers, as described above, are satisfied for the transaction. As matters turn out, the vehicle is plagued with multiple or significant recurring problems. The issue for Jewish law is therefore the same as it is in American law: Does the implied warranty of merchantability entitle *B* to make claims against *S* for defects beyond those covered by an express warranty provided by *S*?

State lemon laws present a number of issues for comparison with Jewish law: (a) the definition of a lemon; (b) the form the right of rescission takes; (c) whether the buyer or the seller controls the form the right of rescission takes; and (d) the availability of an arbitration procedure.

DEFINITION OF A LEMON

The definition of a lemon in American law, as Brian Shaffer and Daniel Ostas point out, has evolved as the result of political mediation between the conflicting interests of the manufacturer and the consumer. Indeed, the alliance between the consumer and the dealer against the manufacturer is what has made lemon laws possible.[86] The diversity of the criteria that the states have adopted to define a lemon supports Shaffer and Ostas' thesis. Consider this contrast: Kansas defines a lemon as a vehicle that experiences four repair attempts for the same problem, 10 repair attempts for separate problems, or 30 calendar days out of service.[87] Minnesota, on the other hand, defines a lemon as a vehicle that experiences one repair attempt in the braking or steering system, or four repair attempts or 30 business days out of service for other problems.[88] Many states define a car as a lemon more often when a safety feature is faulty than when the car has a defect that does not impair safety. Other states lump together all defects without making a distinction based on safety.[89]

By contrast, Jewish law's definition of a lemon is entirely consumer-driven. Recall that in a product defect claim, Jewish law recognizes a rescission right for *B* when the defect would cause the typical buyer to cancel the transaction. Consumer surveys should have the last word here on whether a defect is sufficiently severe to justify rescission. One strongly suspects that those surveys would confirm that a defect that impairs a car's safety, such as faulty brakes, renders the transaction a *mekah ta'ut* the first time the defect is discovered. We might also expect these surveys to show that consumers do not restrict their definition of a lemon to a car that exhibits the same problem at least three or four times after *S*'s repairs. Rather, we would expect that a typical consumer would consider a car a lemon if the car displays multiple problems over a short period of time.

The purpose of these surveys is to identify the mindset of the typical consumer at the time of the sales transaction. Accordingly, once the definition of a lemon is established, *B*'s rights in a lemon case are based on the implied warranty of merchantability that takes effect as soon as the sale is completed.

Jewish law recognizes that attitudes among consumers regarding the definition of a lemon may differ by geographic location.[90] Accordingly, instead of establishing a federal standard for defining a lemon, Jewish law would propose conducting consumer surveys in each state and allowing each state to specify the criteria for a lemon.

FORM OF RESCISSION REMEDY

Another issue that requires clarification is *B*'s rescission rights in the lemon case. Does *B* have a right to demand a replacement vehicle instead of a refund of the purchase price? Alternatively, if *B* desires a refund, does *S* have the right to force *B* to accept a replacement vehicle instead?

In assessing what form *B*'s rescission remedy takes under Jewish law in the lemon case, we look to the law that governs a sale where no express warranty is provided and *B* later discovers a defect that allows him to cancel the transaction. The *nag'han* case described above is relevant here. In that case, *B* believes that he is buying an ox suitable for plowing but subsequently discovers that the ox is a *nag'han* and is thus suitable only for slaughter. Since the status of the ox as a *nag'han* is a defect that cannot be repaired, the *nag'han* case is closely analogous to the lemon case.

Recall the dispute between Rav and Samuel regarding *B*'s rights in the *nag'han* case. Rav allows *B* to obtain a refund based on the type of use that a majority of people would have from the ox.[91] Samuel, however, takes the view that majority practice is not decisive in monetary matters.[92] According to Samuel, *B* will not prevail unless he can prove that the circumstances of his transaction with *S* demonstrated that *S* was aware of *B*'s intention to use the ox for plowing. One way for *B* to prove his intention is to refer to the purchase price. If the price of an ox suitable for plowing is higher than the price of an ox suitable only for slaughter, *B*'s willingness to pay the higher price is deemed to have clearly communicated to *S* his intention to use the ox for plowing.

Now suppose that the price of an ox that can be used for plowing is the same as the price of an ox that can be used only for slaughter. In that case, according to Rav's opinion, the sale would be overturned as a *mekah ta'ut* because a majority of users would purchase an ox for plowing, whereas *B* obtained an ox suitable only for slaughter. According to Samuel's opinion, by contrast, the sale would be upheld because we do not follow majority practice in monetary matters. In addition, *B* cannot point to the purchase price as proof that *S* was aware that *B* wanted to purchase an ox suitable for plowing because the price of the *nag'han* is the same as the price of an ox suitable for plowing.

Assessing these two views, the Talmud queries: What is the practical difference between Rav's and Samuel's opinions when the price of the two types of oxen is the same?[93] *B* appears to receive the same value regardless of whether the sale is upheld or overturned. Specifically, if the sale is upheld, *B* acquires an ox with the same market value as an ox suitable for plowing. If the sale is overturned and *B* obtains a refund, the amount of the refund is equal to the value of the ox that *B* would have acquired if the sale had been upheld.

Analyzing this case further, the Talmud explains that there is indeed a practical difference between the two opinions. The difference is with respect to *tirhah* (bother). What is meant here, according to R. Samuel b. Meir (*Rashbam*, France, ca. 1080–1174), is which party is burdened with the toil and effort to set things straight for *B* so he can acquire the plow ox he wanted. If the transaction is canceled, as Rav rules, *B* receives a refund and may use the refund to purchase an ox suitable for plowing. But if the transaction is upheld, as Samuel rules, *B* is left with the *nag'han* and bears the burden of both selling the ox for slaughter and buying an ox suitable for plowing.[94]

What can be inferred from *Rashbam*'s explanation, according to R. Yehudah Itach, is that Rav would find no objection with an offer by *S* to undertake the *tirhah* himself to provide *B* with a replacement ox. Consider that oxen are by no means interchangeable. Thus, if *S*'s offer to replace the *nag'han* with an ox suitable for plowing is valid, *S*'s offer to replace a lemon with a functional vehicle rather than provide a refund should certainly be valid for an item that is more standardized. Furthermore, avers R. Itach, *S*'s right to satisfy *B* with a replacement item instead of a cash refund should not be questioned because common custom has made this practice acceptable. Accordingly, if *S* remedies the breach of warranty by offering a suitable replacement item, the defect is no longer one that would drive the typical buyer to cancel the transaction.[95]

What emerges from the above analysis is that in the lemon case involving a new car, Jewish law would give *S* the option of either furnishing *B* with a refund or providing a suitable replacement item. American law, by contrast, gives *B* the choice of either obtaining a refund or requiring *S* to provide a replacement item.

Another scenario for *B*'s rescission rights obtains when the item of sale is a used car. In Jewish law, new cars and used cars should not be treated similarly if the item of sale is a lemon. If the product is brand new, it cannot reasonably be asserted that *B* was determined to buy only the car that he was shown in the showroom and a comparable car out of the factory would not do just as well. Accordingly, if the model *B* actually bought turns out to be a lemon, *S* satisfies his obligation to *B* by providing *B* with a comparable car. If, however, the product is a used car, *B* certainly focused exclusively on the car he actually bought. If the used car turns out to be a lemon, *B* should therefore have the right to demand a refund and reject *S*'s offer to provide him with a comparable used car.

Our conclusion that the option of choosing between a refund or a replacement vehicle in the used-car lemon case resides with *B* puts Jewish law in accord with the approach state lemon laws take on this issue.[96]

"EVERY PROBLEM IS MAJOR UNTIL PROVEN OTHERWISE" AND JEWISH LAW

While many assume that lemon laws do not cover minor defects, Vince Megna, a prominent lemon law attorney, contests this notion. Based on his success in litigation, Megna asserts that "every problem is major until proven otherwise."[97] Megna defends his position on the grounds that automobile companies should be held to the vision of automotive perfection that they project for their goods in their huge advertising campaigns. Megna cites a number of examples of how he won lemon law suits for his clients based on apparently minor defects.

Two of Megna's examples are particularly useful in illustrating a difference between Jewish law and American law in their respective approaches to minor defects. The first case involved an imperfection in the paint job of a new car. Initially, the salesperson recommended that buffing the car would correct the imperfection. When repeated buffing proved ineffective, the defect was diagnosed as a finish imperfection caused by silicone contamination. The dealership offered the owner, we'll call him Steven, $1,000 as "goodwill" for his inconvenience and told Steven that the defect was common and could not be fixed. Moreover, the company claimed that the defect was too minor to qualify for a replacement vehicle under the lemon law. Megna sued and won the case for Steven.

The second case involved a defective radio. Megna's client in that case, we'll call her Matilda, struggled with nine repair attempts over two years to get her defective radio in working order. The problem was particularly annoying for Matilda because she faced a two-hour commute to and from work each day and she looked forward to playing the radio to relieve her boredom. General Motors refused to buy back the vehicle under the lemon law. Instead, the company advised Matilda to go to Radio Shack and pick up a portable radio if she wanted a radio in her car. Megna sued General Motors to buy back Matilda's car under the lemon law and won the suit.[98]

Recall that in Jewish law, *B*'s right to overturn a transaction obtains only if the defect at issue is one that would drive a typical buyer to cancel the transaction. Megna's notion that "every problem is major until proven otherwise" falls far short of this standard because it presumes that minor defects will inconvenience or annoy all car buyers in the same way.

Basing liability on a mere discrepancy between what the automobile manufacturer "promised" in its promotional ads and what an individual customer actually received falls short of Jewish law's standard on two levels. First, the public may very well recognize that the promotion is puffery. Moreover, even if a consumer does not discount statements of "perfection" as puffery, his disappointment in the "defect" may simply make him conclude that the car is overpriced. In the unlikely event that the complaint can be quantified in the form of an *ona'ah* complaint, the applicable remedy will ordinarily be a price adjustment rather than an overturning of the transaction. The case involving a finish imperfection, for example, may very well qualify as an *ona'ah* complaint, rather than a case entitling the buyer to overturn the transaction. Accordingly, the initial duty of the manufacturer is to fix the finish and make the car look "perfectly" new. Once it becomes clear that this remedy will not work, the customer should be entitled to a reduction of the purchase price.

Moreover, in Jewish law, *B*'s credible claim that if he had known about the defect at the outset, he would not have purchased the car does not automatically make the car a lemon. *B* must also prove that the defect would cause the *typical* buyer to rescind the transaction. Given Matilda's long commute, the car radio was certainly very important to her. But for the typical customer who does not use his or her car for a long commute, a defective car radio would not render the car a lemon. Moreover, even for the subgroup of car buyers who are commuters, does a defective car radio always make a car a lemon?

An analogous case is discussed at *Kiddushin* 49b:

> A certain man sold his possessions with the intention to move to the Land of Israel. At the time of sale, however, the seller said nothing of these intentions. In the end, unforeseen circumstances prevented him from making the journey, and the seller wished to reclaim his property. Rava said [the seller's thoughts] of moving to the Land of Israel are unexpressed intentions (*devarim she-ba-lev*), and unexpressed intentions are not recognized in Jewish law. Thus, the sale remains valid despite the unfulfilled plans of the seller.

In a variation of this case, *S* indicates in the days before the sale that he intends to move to the Land of Israel. Does this circumstance allow *S* to the cancel the deal if his plans fall through? R. Nissim b. Reuben Gerondi (*Ran*, Spain, 1320–1376) rules in the negative. Because *S* did not mention his plans during the transaction itself, it is not objectively evident that *S* intends to make the sale contingent upon his move to the Land of Israel. If, however, *S* mentions during the sale that he plans to move to the Land of Israel, his intention to make the sale contingent on going forward with the move is objectively clear. A tacit understanding between *S* and *B* that the sale depends on the move should therefore be assumed because no one would reside in a country without having land or a house in which to live.[99]

However, the case of the land sale by the emigrating seller differs markedly from the case of the broken car radio. In the land-sale case, it is objectively evident that *S*'s acceptance of *B*'s offer is contingent on *S*'s moving to the Land of Israel, even if *S* does not explicitly make the sale conditional on this event. Letting *B* know about his plans during the sales transaction suffices to make *S*'s intentions clear. The same cannot be said for the car radio case. Most fundamentally, absent an explicit advance stipulation by Matilda, she has no right to cancel the transaction unless we can be certain that she reached a meeting of the minds with the salesperson that the deal would be cancelled if the radio proved to be incurably defective.

Arguing against the presumption that this mindset is present in the ordinary case is that commuters are by no means a homogeneous group. To be sure, during the pre-sale talk, Matilda identified herself as a commuter and told the salesperson that the car radio was important to her to relieve her boredom. But not all commuters who would make this very same declaration enter into the transaction with a mindset to cancel the deal if the car radio proves incurably defective. Instead, honest self-appraisal would tell them that at the time of the transaction, they never considered the possibility that the car radio would be incurably defective. If the "unthinkable" actually happens, the disappointed commuter copes with the boredom by using a portable radio in the car, or plays CDs during the trip.

We can certainly conjure up a scenario where Matilda made it clear that the possibility that the car radio would prove incurably defective was uppermost in her mind during the pre-sale talk. For example, suppose that Matilda spent extra money to order optional features for the car radio, or that the salesperson does not dispute Matilda's contention that in the pre-sale talk, Matilda offered a strong and reasoned opinion why a portable radio is not an acceptable substitute for a radio installed in the car's dashboard. Under those circumstances, the parties certainly reached a meeting of the minds before the transaction was concluded that the deal would be cancelled if the radio proved to be incurably defective. Absent these special circumstances, however, discovery that the car radio is incurably defective amounts to an *ona'ah* claim, not a lemon claim.

The discussion above illustrates that lemons-product area allows room for free-market negotiation. For purposes of illustration, let's assume again that in a Torah society, a car with an incurably defective radio does not qualify as a lemon. Now suppose a particular customer is not the typical consumer and would reject the purchase if the car had a defective radio. Nothing prevents that customer from stipulating in advance that the deal will be cancelled if the radio proves to be defective. Any concessions that the customer will be required to make to get this clause inserted in his or her contract will depend entirely on the parties' assessment of risk and the market forces of supply and demand. For the agreement to be valid, the various technical requirements that Jewish law prescribes for a conditional agreement must also be satisfied.

ARBITRATION PANELS SET UP BY MANUFACTURERS

State lemon laws encourage manufacturers to set up their own arbitration panels to settle customer claims of breach of warranty. The findings of these panels are final as far as the manufacturer is concerned. The customer, however, has a right to appeal the decision of these panels and litigate in court.[100]

From the perspective of Jewish law, the role for government in the area of breach-of-warranty disputes is to enforce the rights of the consumer. Jewish law contemplates such enforcement through an impartial panel of judges who are well versed in the law of warranty and are responsible for fact-finding and the application of the relevant law. Recall that in cases involving lemon-type defects, *S* has no right to deflect *B*'s complaint with an offer for a price discount. Encouraging the manufacturer to establish its own arbitration procedure for such cases does not protect consumer rights. Instead, it puts pressure on consumers to compromise their rights.

An examination of the record of the panels established by automobile manufacturers bears out this contention. Instead of giving lemon owners their due, these panels often try to placate the owners with cheap financial incentives to head off a claim. For example, the panels try gimmicks such as offering to extend the car's warranty or pay a few car payments, or even to give an "appreciation certificate" for one or two thousand dollars toward a trade-in purchase.[101]

LOSER PAYS ATTORNEYS' FEES OF WINNER

An essential feature of a good lemon law, as Vince Megna points out, is that the law requires the manufacturer to pay the consumer's attorneys' fees if the consumer wins a lemon law case. Consider that legal fees can run as high as $100,000 in contested lemon law cases. If the value of the refund or replacement vehicle the consumer seeks is only $20,000, the typical consumer would be very discouraged from pursuing his or her legitimate rights in court. The cost–benefit calculus changes radically when the law provides that the manufacturer must pay the consumer's attorneys' fees if the consumer wins. Consider also that the consumer can usually hire a lemon lawyer on a contingency basis pursuant to which the consumer is not required to pay the lawyer if the consumer loses the case.[102] Taken together, these factors produce a powerful incentive for the manufacturer not to tie up the lemon owner in litigation but instead to accommodate the lemon owner's legitimate claims. Although most state lemon laws require the manufacturer to pay the consumer's attorneys' fees if the consumer wins, eight states and the District of Columbia do not have this requirement.[103] To add insult to injury, Colorado's lemon law provides that if the consumer loses, the consumer pays the manufacturer's attorneys' fees.[104]

Jewish law generally does not subscribe to the notion that the loser in a court case must pay the attorneys' fees of the winner.[105] Imposing such a requirement applies only if the plaintiff's claim is fraudulent or the judge decides that the complaint had no merit and was lodged only to aggravate the defendant.[106] The no-fee rule applies in Jewish law, however, only to private proceedings, not to how lemon law legislation should be drafted. Since the purpose of lemon laws is to correct the injustice that lemon owners suffer, the issue of who pays the winner's attorneys' fees turns on how the goals of the legislation will be advanced. From the standpoint of Jewish law, Megna's analysis appears to be right on the mark. What follows as a corollary is that Jewish law would apply its general rule regarding attorneys' fees to deny the customer's claim for attorneys' fees when the customer is on the losing end of a lemon law case.

Jewish Warranty Law and the Environment of Trustworthiness

MORAL EDUCATION FOR THE YOUTH

In showing how Jewish warranty law counteracts the lemons problem, the legal discussion does not tell the whole story. Jewish law calls for educational efforts to create an environment of trustworthiness. If dishonesty is widespread, manufacturers and dealers will do their best to exploit naïve customers and give the runaround to customers who are persistent and well informed. The more dishonesty practiced by sellers and their agents, the more lemon owners will be required to resort to litigation to get satisfaction of their legitimate claims. An environment of trustworthiness is hence essential for the smooth operation of warranty law.

Let's begin by recasting a commercial transaction in theological terms as a setting that demands the fulfillment of moral duties by both *B* and *S*. Both parties must conduct themselves in a forthright manner and share information that the other side is entitled to know.[107] When *S* enjoys an informational advantage over *B*, and *B* relies on *S*, *S*'s moral fiber is tested more than *B*'s. As a merchant, *S* has the duty to be both conversant with and committed to the law of warranty. In practical terms, this translates into *S*'s duty to disclose defects in a full and forthright manner and make good on both explicit and implicit warranties if a defect is later discovered.

From the perspective of the Torah society, opportunistic behavior is an ever-present concern. In the asymmetric information case, *S* may be convinced that no adverse consequences will result from selective neglect of his responsibilities. The asymmetric information problem is hence an aspect of the phenomenon of veiled misconduct. In the veiled-misconduct scenario, an individual violates a prohibition involving interpersonal conduct because he is convinced that the violation will go undetected and, even if it is discovered, he will suffer no loss in social standing. For example, Jewish law prohibits the proffering of ill-suited advice.[108] In many instances, the violator may believe that he can profit from proffering ill-suited advice and, at the same time, suffer no adverse consequences, even if the victim eventually realizes that the advice was ill suited. A case in point is the brokerage practice of churning. In this practice, a broker recommends a trade, not because the broker thinks the trade is in the best interests of the client, but only to generate a sales commission. If the practice is used sparingly and selectively, and only on naïve clients, the client may never catch on.

From a Jewish theological perspective, overcoming the temptation to engage in veiled misconduct is accomplished by nurturing moral sensitivity. Whenever the Torah prohibits a particular action that constitutes veiled misconduct, the Torah adds the adjuration "And you shall fear your God." That phrase, *Rashi* explains, is reserved for instances where society's judgment regarding whether a deed is good or bad depends entirely on the actor's intentions. Because a perpetrator may have a plausible explanation to put a favorable spin on a particular action, the Torah forewarns the perpetrator that God knows one's true intent.[109] "And you shall fear your God" hence conveys the notion that overcoming a test of piety is a matter of strengthening one's ethical sensitivity.

Ethical sensitivity cannot be fostered in a vacuum: "A boor cannot be fearful of sin" (*Avot* 2:6). Knowledge of the law is hence the most basic prerequisite for fostering the moral personality. Knowledge of the law, however, is not enough to deter unethical conduct; overcoming a test of veiled misconduct also requires moral sensitivity.

Judaism's primary approach to preventing veiled misconduct is hence not to rely on the disciplinary forces of the marketplace but rather to prepare market participants to behave ethically. That preparation requires both knowledge of, and commitment to, the law with a rarified sensitivity. In the Torah society, this preparation begins very early in life in the form of compulsory religious education. It is a duty assigned to parents[110] and religious educational institutions.[111] There is no better evidence of its social importance than the requirement that society subsidize the education of the poor.[112] Elsewhere we have demonstrated that moral education is a vital component of the religious education of the youth.[113] Let's briefly summarize the essential components of this system and make the case that Judaism requires that moral education continue into adulthood as part of on-the-job training.

Standing at the core of moral education in both the family and school is a system of reward and punishment that emphasizes truth-telling and provides training against selfishness and greed. The sanctity of a promise is given special emphasis. In this system, fostering the character trait of gratitude is crucial. Its essential role is to make an individual equate his or her failing a test of piety with letting down and betraying his or her parents and moral educators. The challenge is therefore to put the family and school system on a solid financial footing so that these institutions can maximize their impact on the moral climate of society.

Opportunities to engage in veiled misconduct present themselves repeatedly in one's lifetime. It would therefore stand to reason that moral training should not be limited to the training of the youth, but rather should continue in the adult world of the workplace. As far as moral education is concerned, the workplace provides the ideal educational setting for ensuring that actual business practices conform to legal and ethical norms.

The case for on-the-job moral training begins with the *imitatio Dei* (imitation of God) principle. In Judaism, the guidepost for interpersonal conduct is the duty to emulate God's attributes of mercy in our interpersonal conduct. This behavioral norm is called *imitatio Dei*. As we have shown elsewhere, many of the nuances of the *imitatio Dei* principle are necessary for successful economic public policy.[114] The following exposition of the *imitatio Dei* principle touches directly on the asymmetric information problem:

> "To walk in all His ways" [Deuteronomy 10:12]. These are the "ways of the Lord," as it is written [Exodus 34:6–7], "The Lord, the Lord, God, merciful and gracious, long-suffering and abundant in goodness and truth, keeping mercy unto the thousandth generation, forgiving iniquity and transgression and sin, and cleansing."[115]

This passage tells us that God's thirteen attributes of mercy should serve as the guidepost for our interpersonal relationships. Let's focus on the eighth attribute, *emet*, or truth. To understand how the Divine attribute of *emet*, which ordinarily evokes the notion of strict, uncompromising justice, provides a guidepost for kindness in interpersonal relationships, it is necessary to identify the mercy aspect of God's attribute of *emet*. *Rashi* provides the key here by telling us that *emet* in the context of the thirteen attributes of Divine mercy means "to pay a good reward to those who perform His will."[116] *Rashi*'s interpretation clarifies the mercy element in *emet*. Preliminarily, consider that God endows humankind with free will. This means that neither virtue nor the avoidance of sin is for us compelling. If doing God's will would be compelling, we would not deserve a reward for virtue or for resisting sin.[117] The reward God promises us for doing His will (i.e., "so that you will benefit and you will live long"[118]) is infinite[119] and offers us a delight beyond human imagination,[120] a reward that one can experience only in the infinite world of the afterlife.[121]

But it is undeniable that human beings have a positive time preference: We are quite willing to trade off an indefinitely deferred reward, even an infinite one, for a lesser reward that we can enjoy here and now. Our eagerness and even desperation to make this tradeoff, however, is the result of our ignorance of the nature of the infinite reward that is awaiting us. Here, God displays His mercy element in *emet* and does not accept our willingness to trade our reward in the afterlife for an immediate reward. Instead, God is faithful in fulfilling His promise. Everyone who performs God's commandments will get his or her due in the form of an infinite reward.

What we have just said in theological terms about the mercy element of truth can be formulated in economic terms. Man's plea to God to trade his infinite reward in the afterlife for a lesser reward here and now is a situation of asymmetric information. God knows the nature of the infinite. We, by contrast, have no comprehension of the nature of this reward. Because we proffer our bargain out of foolishness and ignorance, God rejects our plea. In other words, God refuses to exploit our ignorance.

Recall that if *S* is remiss in his disclosure or fails to honor his implicit warranty, he is guilty of theft and price fraud. The implication of these prohibitions is to require *S*, if he is an employer, to organize his business so that these prohibitions are not violated. The *imitatio Dei* imperative frames these duties in positive terms, rather than in terms of negative duties. Since fulfillment of these duties entails overcoming a test of veiled misconduct, training in ethical sensitivity specifically relating to workplace conduct is therefore indicated.

MORAL ON-THE-JOB TRAINING AND LEMON LAW

Let's relate moral on-the-job training to lemon law. At times, a customer who seeks relief under the lemon law will encounter a runaround. For example, the owner may get shuffled back and forth between the manufacturer's customer service department and the dealership who sold the car. If the customer correctly sticks with the dealership to lodge a complaint, the dealer may respond with an assortment of lies. For example, the dealer may claim that the problem is not covered by the lemon law or that the state has no lemon law. Alternatively, the dealer's representative may promise to call back but never does.[122]

From the perspective of Jewish law, giving a runaround to a customer who claims a breach of warranty violates the prohibition against unlawfully withholding property to which another person is legally entitled (*oshek*). *Oshek* entails the misappropriation of property that comes into one's possession with the consent of the owner of the property. Maimonides (*Rambam*, Egypt, 1135–1204) formulates *oshek* in the following manner:

> Who is deemed guilty of unlawful withholding [*oshek*]? One who, having come into possession of another person's money with the latter's consent, withholds it forcibly and does not return it upon the other's demand. Such is the case if one who has a loan or wages due him from another, claims his due but cannot get it from his debtor because he is an overbearing and hard-hearted person. It is of this that Scripture says, "You shall not oppress [*lo ta'ashok*] your neighbor" [Leviticus 19:13].[123]

Note that in Maimonides' formulation, *oshek* is not violated on a Biblical level unless the misappropriating party (*M*) is overbearing or hard-hearted in resisting the original owner's (*O*'s) efforts to obtain what is lawfully his. In their formulations of *oshek*, R. Jacob b. Asher,[124] R. Joseph Caro,[125] and R. Jehiel Michal Epstein[126] all expand the ambit of the prohibition: *M* violates Jewish law even if he is not overbearing but only resists *O*'s demands that *M* is capable of meeting by telling *O* to go away and return. This type of conduct violates a rabbinic prohibition alluded to in the Biblical verse: "Say not to your neighbor, 'Go and come back (*lekh va-shuv*), and tomorrow I will give, when you have [it] with you'" (Proverbs 3:28).[127]

In the opinion of R. Yaakov Yeshayahu Bloi (Israel, contemp.), the rabbinic extension of the law of *oshek* (referred to as *lekh va-shuv*) applies to any *M* who unlawfully withholds *O*'s property and resists the demands of *O* to get his due by using dilatory tactics. Nonetheless, if *M* was preoccupied when *O* made his demand, *M* does not violate *lekh va-shuv*.[128]

Given that a sales transaction operates under an implied warranty, *S* owes his customer, at the very least, a duty to hear out a complaint. The complaint may entail a demand for a repair job covered by the warranty, or if the customer is convinced that he bought a lemon, a demand for a refund or replacement vehicle. Stonewalling or responding to the complaint with dilatory tactics withholds from the customer a repair job or refund to which he may be entitled. The tactic therefore violates the *oshek* interdict.

Another frustration a typical dissatisfied automobile customer encounters is when a dealer deflects a complaint about a flaw by producing a Technical Service Bulletin (TSB) issued by the manufacturer that claims that the flaw is trifling and cannot be corrected. As an example, Megna cites an official General Motor's TSB stating that its power engineering department determined that engine knocking on cold starts "is not detrimental to the performance, reliability, or durability of the engine."[129] Under Jewish law, a dealer has no right to dismiss a customer complaint by producing a TSB that says the defect is trifling and cannot be corrected. Rather, what constitutes a defect and therefore qualifies for a price reduction or a refund is determined by establishing the consensus of the users of the product.

Akerlof's Reformulation of the Lemons Problem in Terms of the Cost of Dishonesty to Society

At one point in his presentation of the lemons model, Akerlof reconfigures the model in terms of the impact of dishonesty on the marketplace:

> [T]here may be potential buyers of good quality products and there may be potential sellers of such products in the appropriate price range; however, the presence of people who wish to pawn bad wares as good wares tends to drive out the legitimate business. The cost of dishonesty,

therefore, lies not only in the amount by which the purchaser is cheated; the cost also must include the loss incurred from driving legitimate business out of existence.[130]

Reconfiguring the lemons model in this light suggests that religion has potentially a very useful role in mitigating the asymmetric information problem. Its most obvious role is to prescribe and promote integrity and honesty in commercial dealings. From an economist's standpoint, as Professor Jonas Prager points out, moral prohibitions relating to the lemons problem must be analyzed in terms of their deterrent effect.[131] In contradistinction to that approach, our focus has not been the deterrent effect of moral preaching per se, but instead the manner in which compliance with warranty law is fostered through the compulsory education of the youth and the continuation of moral training for adults. Because the main objective of moral education is to produce the trustworthy person, successful moral training during youth and adulthood can mitigate the lemons problem.

Creating an Environment of Trustworthiness

In the beginning of the chapter, a number of mechanisms to counteract the lemons problem were identified. In this section, we will demonstrate that each of these mechanisms must operate against a backdrop of trustworthiness to be effective.

COUNTERVAILING MECHANISMS

Let's begin with third-party product ratings. The work of *Consumer Reports*, published by the nonprofit organization Consumer Union (CU), exemplifies how a nonprofit can be a powerful force in mitigating the asymmetric information problem. The effectiveness of *Consumer Reports* in improving the information channels of the marketplace is predicated entirely on CU's independence and impartiality in performing its rating procedures. Toward this end, CU accepts no outside advertising or free test samples, and has no agenda other than the interest of consumers.[132]

While *Consumer Reports* illustrates the importance of integrity and trustworthiness in countervailing the asymmetric information problem, a flawed report the magazine issued in its January 2007 issue shows how fragile integrity and trustworthiness are. In that issue, the magazine reported that 10 infant car seats failed CU's safety test and urged that one seat be recalled. Within weeks, the magazine retracted the report, explaining that the tests on which it based its advisory were conducted by an outside company and were flawed. The magazine promised that in the future, it would disclose when it used outside labs and would double-check the results when they seemed unusual.[133] These promises tell us that *Consumer Reports* understood that it had disappointed the public, not only because the tests were flawed but also because the public widely believed that CU did its own testing. *Consumer Reports* knew it had lost the confidence of the public and was taking measures to restore it.

Another countervailing force is seller guarantees. Unless the seller's promise has credibility, however, it will do nothing to increase the efficiency of the marketplace. Moreover, even when government imposes implied warranties on the seller, consumers will often have to resort to litigation to enforce their rights unless an environment of trustworthiness is in place. In this regard, Steven Shavell has shown that litigation always entails a divergence between private and social costs and private and social benefits. On the cost side, the plaintiff considers only the cost to him of bringing a suit, but does not take into account the litigation costs that the suit imposes on the defendant and on society to run the court system. On the benefit side, the plaintiff considers only the probable benefit the suit will bring to him, but does not take into account the deterrent effect on other wrongdoers.[134] In the United States, legal services absorb approximately 1% of the labor force and 1.3% of gross domestic production.[135] The implication to be drawn from Shavell's work is that if society could become less litigious, economic efficiency would increase.

Brand names also counteract the asymmetric information problem. A critical element behind a brand name is not only a seller's reputation for the quality and superiority of its product, but also its reputation for honesty and reliability. In an environment devoid of trustworthiness, brand names will have no effect.

Consumer action is another way to counteract the asymmetric information problem. By collecting information themselves, consumers can overcome a seller's informational edge at least to a certain degree. To illustrate, a customer in the market to buy a used car can bring along a mechanic to check out the vehicle before buying it. If dishonesty is rampant, however, it will be more difficult and expensive for the customer to find a trustworthy mechanic who could give him the confidence to conclude the transaction.

The asymmetric information problem is also mitigated when the providers of a product or service form a professional association to regulate themselves in the public interest. Consider the American Medical Association (AMA). This organization includes in its mission statement the goals of enhancing the quality of medical care and the betterment of public health.[136] Yet, over the years, this organization has been subject to a barrage of attacks that it has not pursued this aspect of its mission statement with convincing vigor. Instead of regulating itself and lobbying the government to promote the public interest, the organization is biased towards promoting the welfare of its own members.[137] An early critic of the AMA, Milton Friedman, characterized the AMA as the strongest trade union in the United States and showed that the organization worked in various ways to promote the economic interests of its members by restricting supply relative to demand.[138]

CREATING AN ENVIRONMENT OF TRUSTWORTHINESS—AN EXPENDITURE ON BASIC RESEARCH

Notwithstanding that an environment of trustworthiness improves marketplace efficiency, we cannot rely on the profit motive to make investments to foster this character trait in society. One reason is that the goal of increasing trustworthiness faces a paradox. On the one hand, attaining an environment of increased trustworthiness is a goal in society's preference scale. On the other hand, if only the profit motive is operative, no one individual will be driven to invest to advance this goal because the economic return for any given expenditure is at best unknown and uncertain, and the steps required to be taken by the individual to achieve this goal are not known with any precision.

The distinction Richard R. Nelson draws between basic research and applied research is helpful in explaining why we cannot rely on the profit motive to create an environment of trustworthiness. By "basic research," Nelson refers to human activity directed toward the discovery of facts and data observed in reproducible experiments, and to the discovery of theories or relationships between facts. Applied research, on the other hand, is defined as "human activity directed toward the creation of new and improved practical products and processes."[139] Since basic research entails a general foray into the unknown, only monopoly firms with huge resources at their disposal can be expected to undertake this investment. They will do so, however, only if the government imposes no restrictions on their pricing policy so that the large profits they expect to earn will compensate for their risk-taking. The other alternative is for government to finance basic research. Once basic research has discovered some promising theory or data, the profit motive will drive the holder of the information to develop it further toward practical ends.[140]

Nelson's analysis leads to only one way to gain the resources necessary to create an environment of trustworthiness. The route of freeing private-sector companies from legal restrictions on profit will not work because expenditures to produce "trustworthiness" will, in all probability, never offer an investor the prospect of earning an identifiable economic return. Rather, it will take significant and persistent efforts by the government to raise the public's consciousness and convince members of society of the qualitative link between investment in trustworthiness and the good society. Expenditures on creating an environment of trustworthiness are thus investments in basic research.

CREATING AN ENVIRONMENT OF TRUSTWORTHINESS—ASPECTS OF A PURE PUBLIC GOOD

In this section, we will demonstrate that an environment of trustworthiness takes on aspects of what economists call a pure public good. It is for this reason that the private sector cannot be relied upon to create an environment of trustworthiness.

Let's define the pure public good case and show its application for fostering trustworthiness in society.

Within a market system of voluntary exchange, goods that are traded are characterized by two features: excludability and rivalry. Excludability means that the seller has the ability to exclude nonpayers from the benefit of the good. Rivalry means that the consumption of the good by any one person subtracts from the ability of any other person to consume the good.

An example of a good that exhibits both excludability and rivalry is any food item. Because the necessary conditions for the profit motive to work are in place, the food item, say a cake, will be traded in the marketplace, provided that the cake is valued by consumers at the price the seller demands.

A pure public good, by contrast, is a good that lacks excludability and rivalry. Illustrating the pure public good case is the problem of national defense. For the sake of simplicity, let's assume that country *A*'s national defense system consists of a standing army, navy, and air force, an anti-missile system, and an elaborate intelligence-gathering network. Once this system is set up, it will be well-neigh impossible to exclude nonpayers in the geographic boundaries of country *A* from the benefits of the system. Moreover, the benefits derived by those who financed the system are in no way diminished by the benefits derived by free riders.

Because excludability and rivalry do not characterize national defense, the profit motive breaks down and it becomes unlikely that this most vital good will emerge within a system of voluntary exchange. Ironically, the priority that everyone accords to national defense exacerbates the free-rider motive since everyone assumes that because of the indisputable importance of national defense, the collective action of "everyone else" will get the system running. The case for government taxation to set up the national defense system is clear. Given the paradox that national defense is a preferred item in everyone's budget, but the absence of the profit motive frustrates its emergence, government taxation brings into existence an economic good that everyone is willing to pay for. What government taxation does here is to eliminate the free-rider motive and make possible the provision of a good for which an effective demand exists.[141]

Let's now apply the concept of a pure public good to the goal of fostering an environment of trustworthiness. Integrity and trustworthiness take on both features of a pure public good—that is, the inability to exclude nonpayers from the good's benefits and nonrivalry in consumption. A person who has earned a reputation for trustworthiness (*T*) in the form of making proper disclosure and delivering on what he promises generates a reputation of trustworthiness for his future dealings. Because *T* carries his reputation from one transaction to another, the trust that *T* establishes is not depleted as he moves on to a new transaction. *T*'s trustworthiness therefore takes on a nonrivalrous character.

Consider, however, that *T* attracts all kinds of people who are very eager to transact with him in the marketplace. To be sure, people who are likewise committed to integrity are included in this group. But so too are immoral people who are looking to exploit *T*'s integrity through veiled misconduct. Still others may come to the transaction with no premeditated plan of evil, but may spontaneously engage in opportunistic conduct should the occasion arise.

While *T*'s reputation for trustworthiness makes him easy to discover, in seeking a trustworthy counterparty for his transactions, *T* may have little ability to distinguish between the good, the bad, and the amoral people who are eager to deal with him if they have no track record. Given that free riders may eagerly want to "consume" *T*'s trustworthiness but are not willing to reciprocate, the trustworthiness that *T* brings from transaction to transaction may take on the character of nonexcludability from the perspective of these free riders. If *T* is repeatedly exploited by those who do business with him in the marketplace, the disillusionment *T* experiences may very well change his attitude toward the duty of integrity. Unless society takes strong measures to foster and strengthen the practice of ethical behavior, the nonexcludability feature of the attribute of trustworthiness will significantly undermine this virtue.

A diminished degree of trust and integrity not only inhibits transactions, but also causes parties to attempt to address every imaginable contingency by contract, use short-term contracts, and break contracts more frequently. These measures increase transaction costs, inhibit wealth creation, and burden the justice system. Likewise, when integrity and trust are scarce, cynicism and suspicion reign supreme. The byproduct of this sinister environment is the attitude that acting unethically is nothing more than preempting someone who was planning the same for us.

The presumption that the creation and enhancement of the value of trustworthiness in society is a preferred item in everyone's budget is reinforced by the recognition that bequeathing an environment of greater trustworthiness to one's children is a goal few would dispute.

Once one understands that the goal of achieving increased trustworthiness in society takes on the features of both a pure public good and a project entailing an expenditure on basic research, government taxation for this goal is a win–win situation and thus a Pareto gain for society. In discerning the form that a government subsidy should take, the most important issue we must recognize is that integrity is a capital good with a long gestation period and production cycle. Fostering integrity and trustworthiness in society perforce must be done through parents and the school system. Toward this end, the government should require schools to implement programs to inculcate the values of integrity and trustworthiness. Government grants for devising curricular and extracurricular activities and programs to accomplish these objectives could be part of this thrust.

Conclusion

Our purpose here was to show how Jewish warranty law counteracts the lemons problem. The concept of implied warranties, consisting of the implied warranty of merchantability and the implied warranty of fitness for a particular purpose, finds wide expression in Jewish law. In the comparison with American law, we found that Jewish warranty law is generally far more consumer-friendly than American law, both in the scope of the implied warranties provided and in the limited ability of the seller to disclaim or modify the implied warranties in advance.

We also compared Jewish law's treatment of the lemons problem with current state lemon laws. In defining a lemon, Jewish law would resort to consumer surveys in each state. These surveys would identify the type of defects that would drive a typical buyer to cancel a transaction. Since the definition of a lemon is consumer-driven, the manufacturer has no right to ignore a customer's complaint by invoking the opinion of its engineers that the complaint is trifling. At the same time, the definition of a lemon is not a subjective matter for each customer to decide. Accordingly, the notion that "every problem is major until proven otherwise" as the criterion for defining a legitimate lemon complaint is rejected in Jewish law.

Once, however, the law defines a lemon, the law should be designed to discourage *S* from deflecting *B*'s legitimate complaint by giving *B* a runaround. Requiring *S* to pay *B*'s legal fees if *B* wins a lemon case accomplishes this objective because it encourages *S* to avoid litigation whenever possible when dealing with a legitimate complaint. Calling for *B* to pay *S*'s legal fees if *S* wins the case is warranted only if *B*'s claim was fraudulent or the complaint was meritless and was lodged only to aggravate *S*.

Lemon laws should be designed to make it easy for lemon owners to secure their legitimate rights. Any arbitration panel that *S* establishes will certainly represent *S*'s own interests well and will even have a bias in *S*'s favor. Given that such a panel is not impartial, encouraging *S* to set up an arbitration panel puts pressure on *B* to compromise his rights. Unless these arbitration panels are carefully monitored to ensure impartiality, they generally undermine the objective of helping lemon owners secure the rights to which they are entitled.

Our study noted one exception to the finding that Jewish warranty law is more consumer-friendly than American warranty law. This is with respect to which party is given control over the form the rescission remedy takes. American law grants *B* the right to choose between receiving a refund or replacement vehicle, regardless of whether the lemon is a new or used car. While Jewish law is consistent with American law in the used-car case, in the new-car case, Jewish law grants *S* the right to choose between providing a refund or replacement vehicle.

In showing how Jewish warranty law counteracts the lemons problem, the legal discussion does not tell the whole story. Jewish law calls for educational efforts to foster an environment of trustworthiness. The mandate consists of religious compulsory education, with the task assigned to parents and religious educational institutions. Moral education is a vital part of this education. Standing at the core of moral education in both the family and school is a system of reward and punishment that emphasizes truth-telling and provides training against selfishness and greed. The sanctity of a promise is given special emphasis. The principle of *imitatio Dei* tells us that moral education should continue into adulthood, particularly in the workplace setting.

Finally, we have demonstrated that all the mechanisms that countervail the lemons problem require the operation of an environment of trustworthiness to be effective. The goal of creating an environment of trustworthiness takes on aspects of a pure public good and is an expenditure on basic, rather than applied, research. Fostering trustworthiness is hence a form of social capital. Government investment to foster this environment is thus consistent with economic efficiency.

Notes

1. George A. Akerlof, "The Market for 'Lemons': Quality Uncertainty and the Market Mechanism," *Quarterly Journal of Economics* 84, no. 3 (1970): 488.
2. Jeffrey M. Perloff, *Microeconomics*, 5th ed. (Boston: Pearson Addison Wesley, 2009), 647–650. Perloff's list is standard. See also Akerlof, "The Market for 'Lemons,'" 499–500.
3. Akerlof's lemons problem has made its way into the standard Intermediate Microeconomics textbooks, but we will draw specifically upon Browning and Zupan's explication of Akerlof's theory. See Edgar K. Browning and Mark A. Zupan, *Microeconomics: Theory & Applications*, 10th ed. (Hoboken, NJ: John Wiley, 2009), 420–422; Steven E. Landsburg, *Price Theory and Applications*, 8th ed. (Mason, OH: South-Western, 2011), 300; Perloff, *Microeconomics*, 643–647.
4. Akerlof, "The Market for 'Lemons,'" 489.
5. Browning, *Microeconomics*, 420.
6. Ibid., 421.
7. The first draft of the UCC was published in the fall of 1951 by an editorial board consisting of representatives from the National Conference of Commissioners on Uniform State Laws and the American Law Institute. In 1953, Pennsylvania became the first state to adopt the draft as law. The UCC has been adopted by all the states (except Louisiana, which has adopted only certain parts) and the District of Columbia. Cindy Rhodes Victor, *Encyclopedia of Management: Uniform Commercial Code*, http://www.referenceforbusiness.com/management/Tr-Z/Uniform-Commercial-Code.html.
8. 15 U.S.C. § 2301 et seq. (2006).
9. U.C.C. § 2–314(2)(a), (c).
10. Federal Trade Commission, *A Businessperson's Guide to Federal Warranty Law* (December 2006), http://www.business.ftc.gov/documents/bus01-businesspersons-guide-federal-warranty-law [hereinafter *Businessperson's Guide*].
11. Ibid. Another example is shoes, which are usually used simply for walking. If a seller knows that a particular pair is to be used for mountain climbing, the seller warrants the fitness for that particular purpose. U.C.C. § 2–315, comment 2.
12. See *Shaffer v. Victoria Station, Inc.*, 588 P.2d 233, 234–235 (Wash. 1978).
13. U.C.C. § 2–315. Whether this warranty arises is determined on a case-by-case basis. If the circumstances of sale indicate that the goods are to be used for a particular purpose, it is reasonably assumed that the buyer is relying on the seller's advice that the goods are fit for that purpose. See ibid., comment 1.
14. *Businessperson's Guide*, loc. cit.
15. Maimonides (*Rambam*, Egypt, 1135–1204), *Mishneh Torah, Mekhirah* 15:6; R. Vidal Yom Tov of Tolosa (*Maggid Mishneh*, Spain, ca. 1300–1370), *Maggid Mishneh* to *Mishneh Torah*, ad loc.; R. Jacob b. Asher (*Tur*, Spain, 1270–1343), *Tur, Hoshen Mishpat* 232; R. Joseph Caro (Safed, 1488–1575), *Shulhan Arukh, Hoshen Mishpat* 232:7; R. Jehiel Michal Epstein (Belarus, 1829–1908), *Arukh ha-Shulhan, Hoshen Mishpat* 232:11.

16. R. Yehudah Itach, *Netiv Yosher: Hilkhot va-Halikhot Mekah u-Memkar* (Jerusalem, 1992), 136. *B*'s right to cancel the transaction proceeds from the presumption that had he only known of the defect (*mum*), he would not have entered into the transaction. When that presumption is operative, the transaction is referred to as a "*mekah ta'ut*" (a transaction entered into by error). R. Itach identifies two different understandings of how *mekah ta'ut* works in the *mum* case. In the first understanding, advanced by R. Akiva Eiger (Hungary, 1761–1837), we treat the transaction as if *B* had made a stipulation with *S* that discovery of the *mum* will allow *B* to cancel the transaction. In R. Eiger's understanding, an implicit stipulation is what triggers *mekah ta'ut* and is therefore no different from any other explicit stipulation made by *B* in advance of the sale. In both cases, the transaction is legally binding and becomes invalid only after *B* discovers that the condition was not fulfilled and *B* calls for the cancellation of the deal because of the nonfulfillment of his condition. If *B* is willing to accept the item despite his discovery of the defect, the original symbolic act (*kinyan*) remains intact and there is no need to perform a new *kinyan* to make the transaction binding. A different understanding of how *mekah ta'ut* works, however, is described by R. Ephraim b. Aaron Navon (Constantinople, 1677–1735). In his understanding, once *B* discovers a defect that renders the transaction a *mekah ta'ut*, the original *kinyan* becomes null and void. Consequently, if *B* desires to accept the item of sale as is, a new *kinyan* is necessary. Ibid., 137, n. 3.

    It would appear that all opinions agree that in a *mekah ta'ut* transaction, *B*'s right to cancel the transaction is not predicated on any explicit stipulation he was required to have made in advance. In R. Eiger's understanding, *B*'s rescission right is based on his implicit stipulation with *S* regarding the merchantability of the item. In R. Navon's understanding, *B*'s rescission right is more fundamental. Since the rescission right can be invoked only if the *mum* is of a type that the typical buyer would want to cancel the transaction, it is the mindset of the typical buyer and not *B*'s implicit condition that cancels the original transaction. Accordingly, *B*'s declaration that he wants the transaction to remain intact goes against a presumption of human nature. Consequently, a defect that causes a transaction to be a *mekah ta'ut* renders the original *kinyan* null and void, and a new *kinyan* must be performed if *B* wants to keep the transaction intact.
17. *Hullin* 94a; R. Isaac b. Jacob Alfasi (*Rif*, Algeria, 1013–1103), *Rif*, ad loc.; *Mishneh Torah*, *Mekhirah* 18:1; R. Asher b. Jehiel (*Rosh*, Germany, ca. 1250–1327), *Rosh*, *Hullin* 7:18; *Tur*, *Hoshen Mishpat* 228; *Shulhan Arukh*, *Hoshen Mishpat* 228:6; *Arukh ha-Shulhan*, *Hoshen Mishpat* 228:3.
18. *Bava Metzia* 80a; *Rif*, ad loc.; *Mishneh Torah*, op. cit., 15:7–10; *Rosh*, *Bava Metzia* 6:14; *Tur*, op. cit., 232; *Shulhan Arukh*, op. cit., 232:8–9; *Arukh ha-Shulhan*, op. cit., 232:12–15.
19. *Rosh*, *Hullin* 3:34.
20. R. Joshua b. Alexander ha-Kohen Falk, *Perishah* to *Tur*, *Hoshen Mishpat* 228, n. 5.
21. *Tur*, op. cit., 232; *Shulhan Arukh*, op. cit., 232:11; *Arukh ha-Shulhan*, op. cit., 232:17.
22. *Rif*, *Bava Metzia* 49b (quoting the authority of *Rabbeinu Hai Gaon*); *Mishneh Torah*, op. cit., 15:3; *Tur*, op. cit., 232; *Shulhan Arukh*, op. cit., 232:3.
23. *Mishneh Torah*, op. cit.; *Tur*, op. cit.; *Shulhan Arukh*, op. cit.
24. *Mishneh Torah*, op. cit., 15:5; *Tur*, op. cit., 232; *Shulhan Arukh*, op. cit., 232:6; *Arukh ha-Shulhan*, op. cit., 232:7.
25. *Tur*, op. cit., 233; *Shulhan Arukh*, op. cit., 233:1; *Arukh ha-Shulhan*, op. cit., 233:1.
26. *Mishneh Torah*, op. cit., 15:4; *Tur*, op. cit., 232; *Shulhan Arukh*, op. cit., 232:4; *Arukh ha-Shulhan*, op. cit., 232:6.
27. *Mishneh Torah*, op. cit.; *Tur*, op. cit., 232; *Shulhan Arukh*, op. cit.; *Arukh ha-Shulhan*, op. cit.
28. *Arukh ha-Shulhan*, op. cit., 232:7.
29. R. Asher b. Jehiel, *She'elot u-Teshuvot ha-Rosh*, *kelal* 96:6 (quoted in *Tur*, op. cit., 232).
30. *Tur*, op. cit., 232; *Shulhan Arukh*, op. cit., 232:5; *Arukh ha-Shulhan*, op. cit., 232:10.
31. R. Moses Isserles, *Rema* to *Shulhan Arukh*, op. cit., 232:5.
32. R. Yehudah Itach, *Netiv Yosher*, p. 146, ¶¶ 12–13.
33. *Kiddushin* 11a; *Mishneh Torah*, op. cit., 15:12; *Tur*, op. cit., 232; *Shulhan Arukh*, op. cit., 232:10; *Arukh ha-Shulhan*, op. cit., 232:16.

34. *Rosh, Hullin* 3:34.
35. Nahmanides, quoted in *Rosh, Hullin* 3:34.
36. *Arukh ha-Shulhan*, op. cit., 232:18.
37. R. Joshua b. Alexander ha-Kohen Falk, *Sema* to *Shulhan Arukh, Hoshen Mishpat* 232, n. 57.
38. Rav, *Bava Batra* 92a.
39. Samuel, *Bava Batra* 92a; *Rif*, ad loc.; *Rosh, Bava Batra* 6:2; *Tur*, op. cit., 232; *Shulhan Arukh*, op. cit., 232:23; *Arukh ha-Shulhan*, op. cit., 232:36.
40. *Tur*, op. cit.; *Shulhan Arukh*, op. cit.; *Arukh ha-Shulhan*, op. cit.
41. For the general parameters of the law of *ona'ah*, please refer to Chapter 2 of this volume.
42. Mishnah, *Bava Batra* 5:6; *Bava Batra* 83b; *Rif*, ad loc.; *Mishneh Torah, Mekhirah* 16:1; *Rosh, Bava Batra* 5:13; *Tur*, op. cit., 233; *Shulhan Arukh*, op. cit., 233:1; *Arukh ha-Shulhan*, op. cit., 233:1.
43. *Mishneh Torah*, op. cit.; *Tur*, op. cit.; *Shulhan Arukh*, op. cit.; *Arukh ha-Shulhan*, op. cit.
44. *Pesahim* 48a.
45. See R. Shelomoh Kluger, *Hokhmat Shelomoh* to *Shulhan Arukh, Hoshen Mishpat* 233:1.
46. *Rosh, Bava Metzia* 3:24; *Tur*, op. cit., 232; *Rema* to *Shulhan Arukh*, op. cit., 232:18; *Arukh ha-Shulhan*, op. cit., 232:26–28. In the specific Talmudic case addressing the implied warranty of merchantability, S_2 sold an animal to *B*. S_2, in turn, had purchased the animal from S_1. Relying on S_2 having properly inspected the animal for defects before the sale, *B* put the animal together with the rest of his herd and placed food in front of all the animals. Unbeknown to *B*, the new animal had no molars. Eventually, the animal starved to death because it could not chew food. According to R. Asher b. Jehiel, R. Jacob b. Asher, and R. Moses Isserles, the law of implied warranty of merchantability makes S_2 responsible for *B*'s loss. Based on this same principle, S_2 has a claim against S_1 for failing to inspect the animal for molars before selling the animal to S_2.

    In opposition to these authorities, Maimonides (*Mishneh Torah, Mekhirah* 16:11) and R. Joseph Caro (*Shulhan Arukh*, op. cit., 232:18) hold that S_2 bears no liability here. *B* has no one but himself to blame for the misfortune because he should have made sure that the animal had molars before setting food in front of it. In the opinion of R. Epstein (*Arukh ha-Shulhan*, op. cit., 232:26–27), Maimonides and R. Caro are in basic agreement with the principle that any seller, regardless of his position in the commercial distribution chain, operates under an implied warranty of merchantability. Holding a seller not liable is restricted to cases analogous to the molar case. The salient feature of the molar case is that S_2 was a trader who held onto his inventory for only a very brief period of time and therefore never inspected his stock of animals for defects. *B* should have known this and inspected the animal himself to make sure it had molars. For a seller whose inventory cycle is longer than that of the trader in the molar case, the warranty of merchantability fully applies, regardless of the seller's position in the commercial distribution chain.
47. U.C.C. § 2-104(1).
48. For instance, a deal between two friends, where the seller does not hold himself out as having knowledge or skill in the wares that he is selling, would not be considered a bargain with a merchant. This could be the case at a garage sale or if a lay person is selling his car.
49. In a store, we would assume that the person doing business is an agent of an employer and therefore has special knowledge about the goods or services he is selling. This holds true for a circumstance such as a car dealership. Anyone who works at the dealership is an agent who by his occupation is putting himself out as having skill or knowledge about cars.
50. Magnuson-Moss Warranty Act, 15 U.S.C. § 2302(a) (2006).
51. See U.C.C. § 2–313 (indicating an oral guarantee can be considered an express warranty).
52. By displaying a sample model, the merchant is essentially saying: "This is what it looks like."
53. U.C.C. § 2–313, comment 3 ("In actual practice affirmations of fact made by the seller about the goods during a bargain are regarded as part of the description of those goods; hence no particular reliance on such statements need be shown in order to weave them into the fabric of the agreement.").
54. Ibid.

55. 15 U.S.C. §§ 2302(e), 2303(d).
56. "When you make a sale to your fellow or when you buy from the hand of your fellow, do not victimize one another" (Leviticus 25:14).
57. *Baraita, Bava Metzia* 51a; *Rif*, ad loc.; *Mishneh Torah, Mekhirah* 12:1; *Rosh, Bava Metzia* 4:17; *Tur*, op. cit., 227; *Shulhan Arukh*, op. cit., 227:1; *Arukh ha-Shulhan*, op. cit., 227:1.
58. *Bava Metzia* 61a; *Tur*, op. cit.; *Sema* to *Shulhan Arukh*, op. cit., 227, n. 1.
59. *Mishneh Torah*, op. cit., 12:4; *Shulhan Arukh*, op. cit., 227:4; *Sema* to *Shulhan Arukh*, op. cit., 227:4, nn. 6–7. Expressing a minority opinion in this matter, however, is R. Jonah b. Abraham Gerondi (*Rabbeinu Yonah*, Spain, ca. 1200–1263). In his view, as long as the plaintiff does not uphold the transaction, the offender too is given the prerogative of voiding it. The offender's rights in this matter proceed from the magnitude of the price discrimination involved. Since the price at which the transaction was concluded diverged more than one-sixth from the market norm, the offender may insist that the original transaction be treated as an agreement consummated in error (*mekah ta'ut*). Once, however, the transaction is upheld by the plaintiff, the offender loses his right to void the sale. Denying the offender full nullification rights here follows from the fact that the offender enjoys no such rights when his offense consists of the less severe violation of contracting for a sales price involving second-degree *ona'ah*. Granting him full nullification rights when his offense is graver than second-degree *ona'ah* seems to run counter to all canons of equity. R. Jonah b. Abraham Gerondi, quoted in *Tur*, op. cit., 227, *Rema* to *Shulhan Arukh*, op. cit., 227:4, and *Arukh ha-Shulhan*, op. cit., 227:3. Ruling in accordance with R. Jonah is R. Asher b. Jehiel. See *Rosh, Bava Batra* 5:14.
60. *Bava Metzia* 50b; *Rif*, ad loc.; *Mishneh Torah*, op. cit., 12:2; *Rosh, Bava Metzia* 4:15; *Tur*, op. cit., 227; *Shulhan Arukh*, op. cit., 227:2; *Arukh ha-Shulhan*, op. cit., 227:3.
61. *Bava Metzia* 50b; *Rif*, ad loc.; *Mishneh Torah*, op. cit., 12:3; *Tur*, op. cit., 227; *Shulhan Arukh*, op. cit., 227:3; *Arukh ha-Shulhan*, op. cit.
62. *Arukh ha-Shulhan*, op. cit., 227:7.
63. *Bava Batra* 78a; R. Samuel b. Meir (*Rashbam*, France, ca. 1080–1174) to *Bava Batra* 78a; *Rif, Bava Batra* 78a; *Mishneh Torah*, op. cit., 27:5; *Rosh, Bava Batra* 5:7; *Tur*, op. cit., 220; *Shulhan Arukh*, op. cit., 220:8; *Arukh ha-Shulhan*, op. cit., 220:7.
64. See Magnuson-Moss Warranty Act, 15 U.S.C. § 2304(a)(3) (2006).
65. 15 U.S.C. § 2304(a), (b).
66. U.C.C. § 2–316(2). Further, U.C.C. § 2–316(3)(a) generally allows for the exclusion of all implied warranties with the use of expressions "as is," "with all faults," or other language that "in common understanding calls the buyer's attention to the exclusion of warranties [and] makes plain that there is no implied warranty."
67. 15 U.S.C. § 2308(b).
68. *Mishneh Torah*, op. cit., 15:6; *Tur*, op. cit., 232; *Shulhan Arukh*, op. cit., 232:7; *Arukh ha-Shulhan*, op. cit., 232:11.
69. *Mishneh Torah*, op. cit., 13:3–4; *Tur*, op. cit., 227; *Shulhan Arukh*, op. cit., 227:21; *Arukh ha-Shulhan*, op. cit., 227:22.
70. *Arukh ha-Shulhan*, op. cit., 227:22, 28.
71. *Mishneh Torah*, op. cit., 15:6; *Tur*, op. cit., 232; *Shulhan Arukh*, op. cit., 232:7; *Arukh ha-Shulhan*, op. cit., 232:11.
72. *Businessperson's Guide*, loc. cit.
73. The model case here is R. Nahman's ruling, recorded at *Bava Batra* 41a. In that ruling, a flood swept through R. Anan's land and washed away a fence that marked the boundary line between his land and his neighbor's land. R. Anan rebuilt the fence with his neighbor's assistance. Subsequently, the neighbor realized that the fence had inadvertently been built inside his own property and demanded that the fence be moved back to its original position. R. Nahman ruled in favor of the neighbor. The neighbor relinquished his land by mistake and consequently his action was not legally binding. Jewish law follows R. Nahman's ruling. See *Rif, Bava Batra* 41a; *Rosh, Bava Batra* 3:36; *Tur*, op. cit., 142; *Shulhan Arukh*, op. cit., 142:2; *Arukh ha-Shulhan*, op. cit., 142:3.

In his treatment of *mehilah be-ta'ut*, R. Yom Tov Ishbili (*Ritva*, Spain, ca. 1250–1330) points out that R. Nahman's ruling in a second case, recorded at *Bava Metzia* 66b, seems inconsistent with R. Nahman's ruling at *Bava Batra* 41a. See *Hiddushei ha-Ritva, Bava Metzia* 66b. In the second case, *S* sold the future produce of his date tree to *B* through a formal symbolic act of acquisition (*kinyan*). Since the produce did not yet exist at the time of the *kinyan*, *B* did not legally acquire the produce, even after it came into existence. The rule here is that one cannot effect a transfer of an item that has not yet come into existence (*ein adam makneh davar she-lo ba le-olam*). If, however, *B* removes the produce and eats it with *S*'s consent, the consent effects a waiver of *S*'s right to withdraw from the deal. Even if *S*'s waiver is made in error, R. Nahman regards the waiver as valid based on the presumption that the sale was valid.

In the opinion of R. Ishbili, R. Nahman's rulings do not contradict each other. In the case of the date tree, *S*'s intention is clearly to confer on *B* ownership of the future produce of the tree. *S*'s intention does not, however, become legally binding at the time of the sale because of the technicality of *ein adam makneh davar she-lo ba le-olam*. Even if *S* subsequently learns that the original *kinyan* was invalid, that does nothing to change his original intention to confer on *B* ownership of the future produce of his date tree. Given that *S*'s mistaken waiver does not frustrate his original intention, *B*'s subsequent *kinyan* of the produce is valid and the original terms of the deal remain operative. In contrast, R. Anan's neighbor assisted in rebuilding the fence only because he mistakenly believed that the fence was not being constructed inside his own property. Subsequent awareness that the fence was inadvertently built inside his own property makes the neighbor's original waiver a *mehilah be-ta'ut*.

The warranty case addressed in the text is analogous to R. Anan's case.

74. For the *tenai kafu'* condition, see *Mishneh Torah, Ishut* 6:1–7; *Rosh, Gittin* 6:9; *Tur, Even ha-Ezer* 38; *Shulhan Arukh, Even ha-Ezer* 38:2; *Arukh ha-Shulhan, Even ha-Ezer* 38:26–27.
75. For a development of Talmudic and *Rishonic* sources dealing with both the *gemirat da'at* and the *semikhat da'at* conditions, see Shalom Albeck, *Dinei ha-Mamonot ba-Talmud* (Tel Aviv: Dvir, 1976), 112–143.
76. *Bava Batra* 168a; *Rif*, ad loc.; *Mishneh Torah, Mekhirah* 11:5; *Rosh, Bava Batra* 10:19; *Tur, Hoshen Mishpat* 207; *Shulhan Arukh, Hoshen Mishpat* 207:9–13; *Arukh ha-Shulhan, Hoshen Mishpat* 207:22–53.
77. *Rashi* to *Sanhedrin* 24b, s.v. "*lo kanya*."
78. For a presentation of these views, see Aaron Levine, *Case Studies in Jewish Business Ethics* (Hoboken, NJ: Ktav, 2000), 271–274.
79. *Rashi* to *Sanhedrin* 24b; *Tosafot* to *Bava Metzia* 73b–74a; Nahmanides, *Hiddushei ha-Ramban, Bava Batra* 168a; *Rema* to *Shulhan Arukh, Hoshen Mishpat* 207:13.
80. *Maggid Mishneh* to *Mishneh Torah, Mekhirah* 11:18.
81. An Act Concerning Automobile Warranties, Conn. Pub. Acts 1982, No. 82–287 (June 4, 1982) (codified at Conn. Gen. Stat. § 42–179 (2011)). For a survey of substantive provisions of state lemon laws, see Joan Vogel, "Squeezing Consumers: Lemon Laws, Consumer Warranties, and a Proposal for Reform," *Arizona State Law Journal* (1985): 615–644.
82. Mary B. Kegley and Janine S. Hiller, "'Emerging' Lemon Car Laws," *American Business Law Journal* 24, no. 1 (Spring 1986): 91.
83. Ibid., 91–96.
84. Brian Shaffer and Daniel T. Ostas, "Exploring the Political Economy of Consumer Legislation: The Development of Automobile Lemon Laws," *Business and Politics* 3, no. 1 (2001): 65.
85. Ibid.
86. Ibid., 70–74.
87. See Kan. Stat. Ann. § 50–645(d)(1)–(3) (2011).
88. See Minn. Stat. § 325F.665, subd. 3(b), (c) (2010).
89. Car Lemon, "Lemon Law Summaries," http://www.carlemon.com/lemons.html.
90. R. Itach, *Netiv Yosher*, 140.
91. Rav, *Bava Batra* 92a.
92. Samuel, *Bava Batra* 92a; *Rif*, ad loc.; *Rosh, Bava Batra* 6:2; *Tur*, op. cit., 232; *Shulhan Arukh*, op. cit., 232:23; *Arukh ha-Shulhan*, op. cit., 232:36.

93. *Bava Batra* 92a.
94. *Rashbam* to *Bava Batra* 92a.
95. R. Itach, *Netiv Yosher*, 144–145, n. 18.
96. Not all states extend coverage of lemon laws to used cars. For a tabular comparison of state laws on this issue, see Car Lemon, http://www.carlemon.com. For an example of how the used-car lemon case is treated under state law, see N.Y. Gen. Bus. L. § 198–b (Consol. 2011).
97. Vince Megna, *Bring on Goliath: Lemon Law Justice in America* (Tucson: Ken Press, 2004), 177.
98. Ibid., 183–185.
99. R. Nissim b. Reuben Gerondi, *Ran* to *Kiddushin* 49b.
100. See, e.g., N.Y. Gen. Bus. L. § 198–a(g)–(l) (Consol. 2011).
101. Megna, quoted in Don Oldenburg, "Recourse for When That Sweet Ride Turns Sour; Car Buyers Who Get Clunkers Can Use Lemon Laws Against Automakers," *Washington Post*, February 26, 2006, F05.
102. Megna, *Bring on Goliath*, 94.
103. Ibid., 95. The eight states are Alaska, Illinois, Kansas, Montana, Nevada, North Dakota, Oklahoma, and Texas.
104. Conn. Gen. Stat. § 42–180 (2011).
105. *Rosh, Sanhedrin* 3:40; *Shulhan Arukh, Hoshen Misphat* 14:5.
106. R. Moshe Sternbuch (Israel, contemp.), *Teshuvot va-Hanhagot* 4:303 (Jerusalem, 2002), p. 376.
107. In a commercial transaction, not all information must be shared. For a treatment of this topic from the perspective of Jewish law, see Levine, *Case Studies*, 153–177.
108. Leviticus 19:14; *Torat Kohanim*, ad loc.; *Mishneh Torah, Rotzeah u-Shemirat Nefesh* 12:14.
109. *Rashi* to Leviticus 19:14. The Torah uses the phrase "And you shall fear your God" in connection with the following moral imperatives: (1) the prohibition against offering ill-suited advice (Leviticus 19:14); (2) the duty to bestow honor upon a Talmudic scholar (Leviticus 19:32); (3) the injunction against causing someone needless mental anguish (Leviticus 25:17); (4) the interdict against charging interest (Leviticus 25:36); and (5) the prohibition against working an Israelite bondman oppressively (Leviticus 25:43).
110. The father's moral educational role proceeds most directly from the *mitzvah* of *hinnukh*. This rabbinically mandated *mitzvah* requires the father to train his children in the performance of the *mitzvot* that they will be subject to when they reach adulthood. *Hagigah* 4a. Relatedly, this *mitzvah* assigns the father an interventionist role whenever he observes his children engaged in wrongdoing, with the additional duty to remonstrate with them for their misconduct. Cf. *Shulhan Arukh, Orah Hayyim* 343:1. The father's role of remonstrator continues even after his children reach adulthood by dint of the Pentateuchal *mitzvah* of *tokhahah* (reproof). Leviticus 19:17.

    The *hinnukh* a son receives in normative conduct is potentially reinforced by the father's Pentateuchal obligation to teach him Torah. *Kiddushin* 29a. This obligation requires the father to teach his son the entire *Torah she-bikhtav* (Written Law). *Shulhan Arukh, Yoreh De'ah* 245:6; R. David b. Samuel ha-Levi Segal (*Turei Zahav*, Poland, 1586–1667), *Turei Zahav* to *Shulhan Arukh*, ad loc., n. 2; R. Shabbetai b. Meir ha-Kohen (*Siftei Kohen*, Poland, 1621–1662), *Siftei Kohen* to *Shulhan Arukh*, ad loc., n. 5.

    For a glimpse at how the moral educational role of the father worked itself out in practice, see R. Israel ibn Al-Nakawa (Spain, 14th cent.), *Menorat ha-Ma'or*, ed. Hillel G. Enelow, vol. 4 (New York: Bloch, 1932), 145.

    For the mother's role as enabler in connection with the *mitzvah* of *talmud Torah*, see *Berakhot* 17a. For the mother's obligation to transmit the experience of Sinai to her children, see R. Aharon Soloveitchik, "The Fire of Sinai," in *Building Jewish Ethical Character*, eds. Joseph Kaminetsky and Murray I. Friedman (New York: Fryer Foundation, 1975), 12.

    Authorities dispute whether the Sages imposed the *mitzvah* of *hinnukh* on the mother. For opposing views, compare R. Abraham Abele b. Hayyim ha-Levi Gombiner (Poland, ca. 1637–1683), *Magen Avraham* to *Shulhan Arukh, Orah Hayyim* 343, n. 1, and R. Samuel b. Nathan ha-Levi Kolin (Bohemia, 1720–1806), *Mahazit ha-Shekel* to *Shulhan Arukh, Orah*

Hayyim 343, n. 1. In any case, Halakhah assigns a vital role to the mother as a moral educator of her children. One manifestation of this role is the mother's responsibility to remonstrate with her children for wrongdoing. In this regard, many authorities assign greater responsibility to the mother than the father. See R. Isaiah ha-Levi Horowitz (*Shelah*, Poland, 1565–1630), *Shenei Luhot ha-Brit*, *Sha'ar ha-Otiot*, s.v. "*derekh eretz*."

For a description of the vital role mothers historically assumed in the moral education of their daughters, see R. Moses b. Hanoch, *Sefer Brontshpiegel*, quoted and translated by Solomon Schimmel, "Ethical Dimensions of Traditional Jewish Education," in *Studies in Jewish Education*, vol. 1, ed. Barry Chazan (Jerusalem: Magnes Press, 1983), 94–95.

111. *Bava Batra* 21a.
112. *Arukh ha-Shulhan*, *Yoreh De'ah* 245:9, 27.
113. Levine, *Case Studies*, 1–32.
114. Aaron Levine, *Economic Public Policy and Jewish Law* (Hoboken, NJ: Ktav, 1993), 12–20.
115. *Sifrei* to Deuteronomy 10:12.
116. *Rashi* to Exodus 34:6.
117. *Mishneh Torah*, *Teshuvah* 5:1–5.
118. Deuteronomy 22:7.
119. In various Scriptural verses, the Torah does promise that adherence to the Divine commandments will be rewarded with physical and material recompense, and disobedience will be followed by punishment in this world. Addressing this issue, Maimonides avers that the material and physical rewards and punishments mentioned are not for compliance and disobedience. Rather, if we desire with gladness to perform God's will, God will remove all obstacles to the performance of *mitzvot*. These obstacles include war, disease, and poverty. If we fail to perform *mitzvot* with alacrity, we may not merit having these obstacles removed. But the reward for performing God's will and the punishment for disobedience are infinite in nature and therefore reserved for the world of the infinite. *Mishneh Torah*, *Teshuvah* 9:1.
120. The exception to this rule is that the person who is called "God's enemy" is given a reward for his good deeds in this world: "And He pays His enemy to his face to destroy him. He does not delay for his enemy; to his face does He pay him" (Deuteronomy 7:10). See *Rashi*, ad loc.
121. *Mishneh Torah*, *Teshuvah* 8:7–8; Nahmanides, *Kitvei Rabbeinu Mosheh ben Nahman*, vol. 1, ed. R. Chaim Dov Chavel (Jerusalem: Mossad HaRav Kook, 1963), 23–24.
122. Megna, *Bring on Goliath*, 67–72.
123. *Mishneh Torah*, *Gezeilah va-Aveidah* 1:4.
124. *Tur*, *Hoshen Mishpat* 359.
125. *Shulhan Arukh*, *Hoshen Mishpat* 359:8.
126. *Arukh ha-Shulhan*, *Hoshen Mishpat* 359:7.
127. R. Joseph, *Bava Metzia* 110b.
128. R. Yaakov Yeshayahu Bloi, *Pit'hei Hoshen*: *Likkutim u-Ve'urim ba-Halakhah be-Hilkhot Geneivah u-Gezeilah va-Hassagat Gevul, Ona'ah u-Mekah Ta'ut* (Jerusalem: Mechon L'Hoyroa, 1987), ch. 1, ¶ 5, n. 11.
129. Megna, *Bring on Goliath*, 73.
130. Akerlof, "The Market for 'Lemons,'" 495.
131. Jonas Prager, "Balancing the Scales: *Halakhah*, the Firm, and Information Asymmetries," in *Jewish Business Ethics: The Firm and Its Stakeholders*, eds. Aaron Levine and Moses Pava (Northvale, NJ: Jason Aronson, 1999), 123–124. In his study, Professor Prager identifies the Torah's admonishments regarding various opportunities for veiled misconduct and identifies both the direct and indirect penalties and enforcement mechanisms the Torah prescribes for these infractions. Ibid., 135–143.
132. See Consumers Union, http://www.consumersunion.org/about.
133. Katharine Q. Seelye, "Magazine Will Begin Consulting with Experts," *New York Times*, March 21, 2007, C1.
134. Steven Shavell, *Foundations of Economic Analysis of Law* (Boston: Harvard University Press, 2004), 391.

135. See U.S. Census Bureau, *Statistical Abstract of the United States 2011*, tbl. 631, "Nonfarm Industries—Employees and Earnings: 1990 to 2009," pp. 408–411; tbl. 669, "Gross Domestic Product in Current and Chained (2005) Dollars by Industry: 2000 to 2009," p. 437.
136. American Medical Association, "Our Mission," http://www.ama-assn.org/ama/pub/about-ama/our-mission.page?
137. Dale Steinreich, "100 Years of Medical Robbery," *Mises Daily* (June 10, 2004), http://www.mises.org/story/1547; Doug Bandow, "Doctors Operate to Cut Out Competition," *Business and Society Review*, no. 58 (Summer 1986): 4–9.
138. Milton Friedman, *Capitalism and Freedom* (Chicago: University of Chicago Press, 1962), 149–160.
139. Richard R. Nelson, "The Simple Economics of Basic Scientific Research," *Journal of Political Economy* 67, no. 3 (1959): 299.
140. Ibid., 302, 305.
141. For a discussion of externalities and public goods, see Paul A. Samuelson and William D. Nordhaus, *Economics*, 19th ed. (New York: McGraw-Hill, 2009), 36–38.

CHAPTER 7

The Living Wage and Jewish Law

Introduction

To afford the working poor a decent standard of living, many local governments have enacted living wage ordinances (LWOs). First adopted in Des Moines, Iowa, in 1988, LWOs have been enacted in over 100 localities to date.

Within the framework of LWOs, municipal workers and employees of businesses that have service contracts with the local government are entitled to receive wages at a rate above any prevailing federal or state minimum wage. In addition, the living wage is typically indexed to a price index so the required minimum will increase at the same rate as prices.

Because many households have more than one wage earner, even a poverty-level living wage would be high enough to lift a multiple-earner household out of poverty. The ultimate goal of the living wage movement is to elevate families two to four times above the poverty level.[1]

Our purpose here will be to analyze the living wage from the standpoint of both welfare economics and Jewish law. Since the living wage is essentially an anti-poverty measure, it relates to economic morality on two levels. The first is whether requiring employers to pay their workers a living wage is a legitimate interference with market forces. The second issue is whether the living wage accomplishes its anti-poverty objective. Resolution of the latter issue entails identification of all the consequences that are likely to proceed from this policy initiative.

THE LIVING WAGE AND WELFARE ECONOMICS

Standard economic theory demonstrates that despite the noble intent behind minimum wage legislation, this legislation sets into motion various distortions in the low end of the labor market. These distortions are so severe that the very people the legislation is designed to help actually become worse off. Insofar as proponents of the living wage aim to have government set the minimum wage at a level much higher than the federal minimum wage, the arguments against the minimum wage apply with even greater force to the living wage.

Let's use the supply and demand curves of Figure 7.1 to illustrate why economists are generally opposed to minimum wage legislation.

In the absence of government intervention, the wage rate for the low end of the labor market would tend toward the equilibrium wage rate. In Figure 7.1, the equilibrium wage rate is \$6.00 per hour. By increasing the wage rate to \$7.25 per hour, the workers who are hired will be better off, but fewer workers will be hired. The reduction in employment is illustrated in Figure 7.1 by the decrease in demand for labor from L_2 to L_1. Another measure of the negative side effect of raising the wage rate above equilibrium is that at the minimum wage of \$7.25, L_3 workers want to work, but only L_1 workers are in demand by employers. The imbalance between supply and demand that the minimum wage creates is an increase in unemployment by L_1L_3 workers.

These mixed effects of minimum wage legislation are considerably exacerbated when we take into account that the low end of the labor market is by no means homogeneous. Within this group are workers who, if left to their own devices, would command a wage nowhere near the minimum wage. For example, suppose that the free market wage rate for the lowest end of the labor market is \$4.00 per hour. Given this disparity in market power within the low end of the labor market, the brunt of the disemployment generated by the minimum wage would be borne by the least skilled workers in this group. Minimum wage legislation hence produces the irony that the very group that the legislation is designed to help is hurt the most. The legislation is therefore self-defeating.

Let's consider a number of additional negative side effects of minimum wage legislation:

Studies have shown that when government requires firms to pay a higher money wage, employers will respond by reducing pensions, health insurance, and

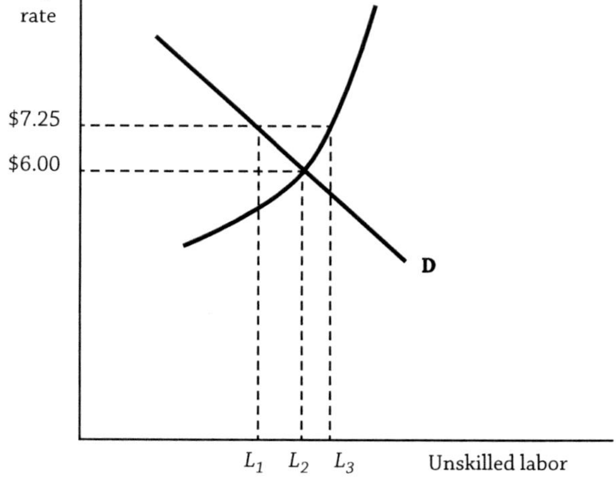

Figure 7.1 Disemployment Effect of the Minimum Wage

on-the-job training for their workers, if possible. Reducing fringe benefits means that the real wage employers pay rises by less than the money wage.

Another negative side effect is that the imbalance between supply and demand created by the minimum wage allows employers to be more selective about whom they hire. When employers are faced with a glut of applicants, they can more easily discriminate on the basis of gender, race, age, or religion.[2]

One more negative consideration is that minimum wage legislation targets the individual worker. But if the goal of this legislation is to alleviate poverty for the working poor, the unit that anti-poverty programs should target is the poor family rather than the individual worker. This is so because most people who are paid a low wage rate are members of families that are not poor, and most people in poor families who work are paid more than the minimum wage.[3]

THE LIVING WAGE AND JEWISH LAW

From the standpoint of Jewish law, we will look at the living wage both as a desideratum for the private employer and as a public policy measure.

Preliminarily, let's note that employers are bound by secular law concerning matters such as minimum wage and safety in the workplace. The operative principle is *dina de-malkhuta dina* (lit., the law of the kingdom is the law).[4] Those secular laws do not, however, guarantee a living wage for workers and their families. Our concern here is the extent to which Jewish law requires us to go beyond secular law. The issue is both a public policy one and, in the absence of such legislation, a question of whether the living wage is obligatory for the private employer.

The Living Wage and the Private Employer—Labor Law

We will consider whether Jewish law requires an employer to pay his workers a living wage from the standpoint of both labor law and charity law. We begin with labor law.

In Jewish law, the key moral principle in determining fairness of price in a commercial setting is the law of *ona'ah*.[5] The issue of the living wage therefore turns on the application of the law of *ona'ah* to the labor market.

The law of *ona'ah* gives validity to a plaintiff's complaint that a better marketplace opportunity was available to him at the time he entered into a particular transaction. In the terminology of economists, the *ona'ah* complaint would be called an opportunity cost claim. The plaintiff does not lose his right to transact at the market norm unless we can be certain that he waived this right at the time he entered into the transaction.[6]

Before applying the law of *ona'ah* to the labor market, we note that Halakhah classifies an employee as either a day laborer (*po'el*) or a piece-worker (*kabbelan*). What distinguishes the *po'el* from the *kabbelan* is the provision for fixed working hours in the labor contract. While the *po'el*'s labor contract obligates him to perform work at specified hours over a given period of time, no such clause is included in the *kabbelan*'s contract.[7] Given the controlling nature of the fixed-hours factor, an employee is considered a *kabbelan* if he is not required to work fixed hours, even if his employment agreement requires him to complete a project by a specified date.[8]

In his discussion of the law of *ona'ah* as it pertains to the labor market, Maimonides (*Rambam*, Egypt, 1135–1204) rules that *ona'ah* applies only to a *kabbelan* and not to a *po'el*.[9] Several strands of *ona'ah* law support this ruling. Exegetical interpretation of the source of the *ona'ah* prohibition, "When you make a sale to your fellow or when you buy from the hand of your fellow, do not victimize one another" (Leviticus 25:14), establishes that the prohibition applies only to something that is acquired (by being passed) from "hand to hand," excluding land. Because slaves are assimilated to land,[10] this exemption from *ona'ah* extends to transactions involving slaves.[11]

Another point of the law of *ona'ah* is that the prohibition applies not only to an outright permanent sale but also to a rental transaction. The rationale for this extension is that a rental transaction is in effect a sale of the rented property for the duration of the lease.[12] Consequently, whenever the law of *ona'ah* does not apply to a particular sales transaction, it does not apply to the corresponding rental transaction. Because a *po'el* is regarded in Halakhah as akin to a slave in certain respects,[13] the law of *ona'ah* does not apply to the hiring of a *po'el*.[14]

Another authority who formulates the exemption from *ona'ah* for a *po'el* in blanket terms is R. Israel b. Petahiah Isserlein (*Terumat ha-Deshen*, Germany, 1390–1460). Advancing his own rationale, R. Isserlein avers that the exemption is rooted in the impossibility of assigning a precise market value to the *po'el*'s services, as an employer would pay a premium for the services of a *po'el* when the work at hand requires immediate attention to avert a material loss (*davar ha-avud*). Similarly, finding himself in dire financial straits, a job seeker would presumably accept a below-market wage.[15]

While blanket exclusion of the *po'el* from the law of *ona'ah* follows from the views of both Maimonides and R. Isserlein, the issue is far from conclusive. Maimonides, as will be recalled, ultimately bases the exclusion for a *po'el* on the assimilation of slaves to immovable property. While Maimonides holds that the exclusion of immovable property from the *ona'ah* prohibition is absolute,[16] many other *Rishonim* do not share this view. R. Eliezer b. Samuel of Metz (France, ca. 1115–ca. 1198) and others, for instance, take the position that if the price of the immoveable-property transaction departs from the competitive norm by more than 100%, the plaintiff is allowed to void the transaction.[17] R. Jacob b. Meir (*Rabbeinu Tam*, Remerupt, ca. 1100–ca. 1171) vests the plaintiff with this right as long as the discrepancy is less than 100%.[18] Finally, other authorities, quoted by R. Isaac b. Jacob Alfasi (*Rif*, Algeria, 1013–1103) and R. Asher b. Jehiel (*Rosh*, Germany, 1250–1327), allow the plaintiff to rescind the transaction when the price discrepancy is more than one-sixth.[19] Thus, if the *ona'ah* exemption of the *po'el* ultimately rests on the immoveable-property exclusion, in the view of these other *Rishonim*, blanket exclusion for the *po'el* does not obtain.

However, Nahmanides (*Ramban*, Spain, 1194–1270), in his discussion of the immoveable-property exemption, asserts that the exemption pertains only to the restitution procedure normally prescribed for an *ona'ah* claim, but not to the prohibition against knowingly contracting into *ona'ah* in the first place.[20] Under this view, if the *ona'ah* exemption for the *po'el* is rooted in the immoveable-property exclusion, the prohibition against knowingly contracting into *ona'ah* will operate in this segment of the labor market.

Despite the diversity of opinion regarding whether an *ona'ah* claim is to be honored in the immoveable-property market, and if so, to what extent, R. Shabbetai b. Meir ha-Kohen (*Siftei Kohen*, Poland, 1621–1662) rules in accordance with Maimonides.[21] The import of this ruling is to deny the plaintiff judicial remedy for an *ona'ah* claim in the *po'el* labor market.

The law of *ona'ah* as it applies to the labor market shows that labor law does not require an employer to pay his workers a living wage. This is so because the *ona'ah* claim, as mentioned earlier, is essentially an opportunity cost claim. In the context of the labor market, a worker's claim of underpayment is therefore valid only if the same[22] job was reasonably available to him at the time he entered into his employment agreement. A *po'el* demonstrates this by showing that his own employer pays a higher wage to other workers for the same job, or that another local employer would have hired him for the same job at a higher wage.[23] A worker who cannot command a living wage in the marketplace cannot claim a living wage based on *ona'ah*. Moreover, given that the restitution procedure does not apply to the *po'el* labor market, even a worker who commands a living wage in the marketplace is not entitled to any judicially mandated wage adjustment because of his *ona'ah* claim.

Marketplace Rules Set aside the Living Wage

To further illustrate that Halakhah's marketplace rules reign supreme in the labor market and that the concept of the living wage does not interfere with these rules in setting wages, we consider three cases:

1. An employer (*E*) hires a *po'el* (*P*) to complete a specific task but fails to stipulate a wage rate. Suppose that for the specific task *P* was hired to perform, the local wage rate varies. Because the labor contract failed to specify a wage rate, according to Jewish law, *E* may pay *P* the *lowest* local wage workers receive for the type of work *P* performed. The general rule in Halakhah of placing the burden of proof on the party who sues for payment[24] applies here.[25] Now, if *E* were obligated to pay *P* a living wage under Jewish law, *P*'s entitlement to only the lowest local wage is not understandable.

2. Suppose an employer instructs an agent to hire a *po'el* on his behalf at a rate of three *dinarim* (silver coins) for a day's work. Instead of hiring the worker on terms consistent with the employer's instructions, the agent hires the *po'el* at a rate of four *dinarim* and tells the worker that the wage is the responsibility of the employer. Given that the agent's representation to the worker is a misstatement of the employer's instructions, the agency is null and void.[26] The employer's responsibility to the worker is to pay no more than the lowest prevailing wage for the type of work performed. Accordingly, if all the workers in the vicinity receive four *dinarim* for that type of work, the worker will get four *dinarim*. But if some workers receive four *dinarim* and others receive three *dinarim*, the employer is responsible to pay no more than three *dinarim*. Since the agency is null and void, the work is regarded as if done without any contract, which allows the worker to claim no more than the lowest[27] compensation accepted for this type of work.[28] This rule applies even if the complainant is known to work only at a rate of four *dinarim*. Certainly, had the complainant known that the employer would pay only three *dinarim*, he might have sought employment elsewhere for his usual compensation of four *dinarim*. But this argument serves only as a basis for the worker to have a legitimate grievance against the agent. It does not change the award, which remains at three *dinarim*.[29]

Now, if Jewish labor law required an employer to pay a living wage, the rule should not be that when a labor contract becomes null and void, the worker is entitled to only the lowest market wage for the type of work performed. Instead, the lowest-wage rule should apply only if the lowest wage is a living wage. If the lowest wage is below a living wage, the worker should be entitled to a living wage.

3. Suppose an employer hires a worker and the labor contract is silent on whether the employer obligates himself to provide food for his worker. Jewish law says that local custom must be followed. If it is not the local custom for employers to provide food, the worker will not be entitled to a food allowance in addition to his salary.[30] The rationale here is that, unless stipulated to the contrary, the mindset of workers is to hire themselves out on the basis of local custom.[31]

If Jewish law required an employer to pay a living wage, however, this rule should be modified. Even if the local custom is generally to provide no food allowance for the many types of work that command a market wage rate above subsistence, this should not imply that work that commands a wage rate below subsistence will not be accompanied by a food allowance. Unless the local custom is that no food allowance is provided for jobs that pay below subsistence, there is no presumption that these bottom-scale workers voluntarily waive their right to a food allowance.

If, however, we presume that Jewish law does not require a private employer to pay a living wage, the logic for considering the below-subsistence workers as a separate category is no longer compelling. To the contrary, out of fear of pricing themselves out of the market, these workers would naturally be reluctant to negotiate terms of employment that are more favorable than the terms they can command in the free market. What follows therefore from the assumption that Jewish law does not require private employers to pay their workers a living wage is that all workers are lumped together in ascertaining the local custom.

Sources that Appear to Indicate Jewish Law Requires a Living Wage

In a paper that was given recognition by the rabbinical membership organization of the Conservative Jewish movement, Rabbi Jill Jacobs proposed that Jewish law requires an employer to pay his workers a living wage.[32] She adduces a number of sources to prove her contention. Let's examine these sources.

One source is the formulation of the Biblical prohibition against withholding a worker's wages and Nahmanides' comment on this prohibition. In the rabbinic literature, this prohibition is commonly referred to as *lo talin*:

> You must not withhold the wages of a poor or destitute (*evyon*) hired worker, [regardless of whether he is] one of your brothers, one of your converts in your land, [or a resident alien] within your cities. You must give him his wages on the day they are due, and not let the sun set upon him, for he is poor, and he endangers his life [to work for you]. Do not cause him to cry out to God against you, for then [the punishment for] this sin will be upon you [more quickly]. (Deuteronomy 24:14–15).

Commenting on the Torah's formulation of the prohibition against withholding the wages of the poor and destitute worker, Nahmanides remarks:

> For he is poor, like the majority of hired laborers, and he depends on the wages to buy food by which to live. . . . If he does not collect the wages right away as he is leaving work, he will go home, and his wages will remain with you until the morning, and he will die of hunger that night.[33]

According to R. Jacobs, Nahmanides' comment that a person who does not receive his wages on time will "die of hunger that night" assumes that a person who *does* receive payment on time *will* be able to provide sufficiently for himself and his family and will not die of hunger. This inference leads R. Jacobs to find support for the notion that Jewish labor law requires an employer to pay a living wage.[34]

The inference is unwarranted. This can be seen by examining a number of the exemptions to this prohibition.

One such exemption obtains when an employer has no liquid assets at the time payment is due.[35] Besides cash, liquid assets, according to R. Yom Tov Ishbili (*Ritva*, Spain, 1250–1330), include merchandise the employer has for sale.[36] To ensure payment on time, the employer is not, however, required to sell off his personal assets.[37]

Consider that the presumed desperate need of the worker for his wages in no way changes if the employer has no liquid assets. Specifically, not having his wages will cause the worker to "die of hunger that night." If so, even if labor law exempts the employer from the prohibition against withholding wages in this circumstance, the employer still has a duty to ensure that his worker not perish as a result of not being paid on time. The principle here is "Do not stand idly by the blood of your neighbor" (*Lo ta'amod al dam re'ekha*) (Leviticus 19:16). On the basis of this verse, if *A*'s life is in danger and a bystander (*B*) is in position to extricate *A* from the danger, *B* must take timely action to do so.[38]

The above difficulty only increases once we consider that if the employer is exempt from *lo talin* during the original time frame when payment was due, the exemption, on a Biblical level,[39] remains even after the original window passes.[40] To illustrate, suppose a worker was hired for the entire night. Payment is due the worker at dawn and the employer has until sunset to make payment.[41] If the employer has no liquid assets during the time frame in which the wages should have been paid, the employer's exemption continues even past sunset.

The above difficulties suggest that Nahmanides never meant to read into Deuteronomy 24:14–15 that *every* violation of *lo talin* in connection with the *evyon* worker will cause the *evyon*'s death. Indeed, the instances where nonpayment actually causes the worker to perish should be rare. The instinct of self-preservation alone would tell the unpaid worker not to allow himself to sink into paralysis and perish, but instead to do something to relieve his hunger and even resort to begging, if necessary.

What then of the death imagery the Torah employs in describing the consequences of not paying the *evyon* worker on time? Consider that the *evyon* is inherently an embittered person. In pursuing his livelihood, he constantly puts his life on the line,[42] but ends up with but a pittance for his efforts. The pain and bitterness the *evyon* feels in his daily struggle is exacerbated when his employer withholds his wages. Because withholding his wages puts the *evyon*'s physical survival in a crisis mode and assuredly intensifies his feeling that he is a victim of exploitation, the Torah not only forewarns this conduct, but also exhorts the employer: "this sin will be upon you."[43]

Rabbinical interpretation of Deuteronomy 24:14–15 goes further and characterizes the sin: "Whoever withholds the wages of an employee is considered as if he took his life from him."[44] Since withholding the wages of an *evyon* will rarely result in the *actual* death of the *evyon*, the exegesis of Deuteronomy 24:14–15 should be taken in the same vein as R. Nahman b. Isaac's dictum: "If anyone makes his friend's face turn white from shame in public, he has spilled blood [i.e., murdered the friend]."[45] In both instances, the perpetrator's action does not result in the actual loss of life, but is so egregious that the Torah regards it *as if* the perpetrator took the victim's life.

Further evidence that Deuteronomy 24:14–15 does not mean that every violation of *lo talin* will result in the death of the *evyon* worker can be seen by examining several other *lo talin* exemptions.

First, if the worker does not make a claim for his wages during the time frame in which his wages are due, the employer does not violate the Biblical prohibition of *lo talin*.[46] This exemption is based on the lesson derived from the seemingly superfluous word "*itkha*" (lit. with you) in the phrase "*lo talin pe'ulat sakhir itkha*" (Leviticus 19:13). R. Solomon b. Isaac (*Rashi*, France, 1040–1105) explains that the prohibition applies only if the employer *ignores* the worker's claim, withholding the worker's wages *itkha*—that is, only with the employer's own consent, but not with the consent of the worker. But if the worker makes no claim, *itkha* no longer applies, as the employer is not withholding the wages against the express wishes of the worker.[47]

Second, if the employer hires the worker through an agent rather than directly, neither the employer nor the agent violates *lo talin* if the employer withholds the worker's wages.[48] This exemption is based on the consideration that when a worker is hired by an agent, the worker no longer relies on getting paid on time.[49]

These two exemptions provide a window into the subsistence needs of the *po'el evyon*. If we assume that the *po'el evyon* lives a daily "hand to mouth" struggle just to survive, the presumption that he waives his rights in the two cases mentioned above is unreasonable. Those exemptions make sense only if we assume that even the *po'el evyon* usually accumulates at least a small surplus. It is then reasonable to presume that he waives his right to timely payment under certain conditions.

Having established that Nahmanides does not understand from Deuteronomy 24:14–15 that the consequence of not paying the *evyon* worker on time is always to cause the worker's death,[50] no inference can be drawn from Nahmanides' comment regarding the level of wages the Torah requires the employer to pay an *evyon* worker. Not paying the *evyon* worker on time will, in the preponderance of instances, not cause the worker's death. However, because the moral duty of the employer is to pay his workers no more than a competitive wage, paying the *evyon* worker on time will not guarantee his survival either.

Communal Employees and the Living Wage

Another source R. Jacobs adduces to prove that Jewish law requires an employer to pay a living wage is Maimonides' treatment of the Jewish community's duty to provide adequate compensation for judges and correctors of holy books in Jerusalem:

> The judges who adjudicated cases of theft in Jerusalem would take their salary from these (*terumat ha-lishkah*, i.e., Temple) funds. And how much would they take? Ninety-nine *maneh* per year. And if this was not enough for them, [those responsible for distributing the money] would increase the amount. Even if [these communal workers] did not want to take more, they would increase the amount according to the needs of the workers, their wives and their families.[51]

Preliminarily, let's note that Maimonides' dictum is based on the Talmudic text at *Ketubbot* 105a. In evaluating whether Maimonides' text supports R. Jacobs' thesis, let's consider the question *Tosafot* pose with respect to this dictum: How can the taking of a salary by a judge be reconciled with the law that a judge may not accept compensation for taking on a case, even when the compensation is accompanied by the instruction that he should judge correctly?[52] The Torah calls this prohibited payment *shohad* (a bribe).[53]

Tosafot offer two answers. R. Jacob b. Meir posits that the prohibition against taking *shohad* applies only if the payment is offered by the litigants. If the payment is offered by the community, the prohibition does not apply. In their second answer, *Tosafot* legitimize the payment under the assumption that the judges agreed to devote themselves exclusively to their judicial duties. Because the payment is the only source of livelihood for the judges, it is legitimate for the community to pay the judges a salary.[54]

Recall that the judges' compensation was 99 *maneh* per year. Investigation into the rationale for this sum demonstrates that the two answers *Tosafot* offer are not mutually exclusive. Preliminarily, let's note the following dispute regarding how the sum of 99 *maneh* relates to a living wage.

In the opinion of R. Samuel Eliezer b. Judah ha-Levi Edels (*Maharsha*, Poland, 1555–1631), the 99 *maneh* was an annual allocation that was divided among the judges who headed three courts that promulgated decrees in Jerusalem. Since each court had 23 judges,[55] the annual allocation per court of 33 *maneh* was divided among its 23 judges. Given that a *maneh* equals 100 *zuz* (Roman denarius), each judge received approximately 143.5 *zuz* per year. In the opinion of R. Edels, 143.5 *zuz* constituted a living wage for a year. Accordingly, if the price level increased, the rabbis would insist that the judges accept a raise.[56]

R. Edels' contention that 143.5 *zuz* is a living wage runs counter to the poverty line Halakhah sets for eligibility to receive agricultural gifts in ancient Israel.[57] In this regard, a household was classified as poor if its net worth was below 200 *zuz*. When net worth consisted of capital invested in business transactions, the minimum net worth shrank to 50 *zuz*.[58] The underlying rationale behind these figures, according to R. Obadiah b. Abraham of Bertinoro (Italy, ca. 1456–ca. 1516), is that capital sums of these amounts generated subsistence for a year.[59]

If we understand salary to consist of both pecuniary and non-pecuniary benefits, R. Edels' view can readily be reconciled with Halakhah's notion that subsistence consists of 200 *zuz*. We need only postulate that the community did not hire judges with an exclusive claim on their time. Instead, the community hired them with the understanding that they would be free to pursue livelihood activities when these opportunities did not conflict with their judicial duties. With the judges free to earn outside income, the community felt no duty to set a salary for its judges that would cover their entire subsistence needs. Though this arrangement gave the judges the latitude to pursue outside work, we imagine the community could safely assume that, with the goal of maximizing their Torah study, the judges would engage in supplemental work only to make up their subsistence deficit. If we are correct here, it becomes clear why the community increased the judges' stipend when either the price level increased or the judge had to support another dependent; the increase in salary ensured that the judge would not feel compelled to spend additional time on outside work in order to subsist.

A different calculation of the portion each judge received from the 99 *maneh* allocated to the three courts proceeds from R. Jacob Emden's (*Ya'avetz*, Altona, 1697–1776) contention that the work of the three courts fell under the rubric of monetary matters and therefore each consisted of only three judges.[60] Since there were in total only nine judges, each received an allocation of 1,100 *zuz*, which is 5½ times the living wage.

Paying the judges a salary 5½ times above the subsistence wage is understandable only if the community hired its judges with the stipulation that they could not undertake outside employment, even if the employment did not conflict with their judicial duties. Instead, the judges were expected to spend their free time in Torah study.

This understanding of the generous salary the community paid its judges provides, as appears to this writer, a solid basis for R. Moses Sofer's (*Hatam Sofer*, Hungary, 1762–1839) ruling that communities should hire a rabbi with the stipulation that he make himself available on a standby basis to teach them Torah and attend to their spiritual needs. As a *quid pro quo* for these demands, the community should support its rabbi generously, beyond subsistence. In addition, if the price level rises or the rabbi's family grows, the community should increase his salary.[61]

The upshot of the above analysis is that the two opinions quoted in *Tosafot* are in basic agreement, but refer to different circumstances. If the community hires a judge with the stipulation that he should devote his time exclusively to his judicial duties and spend his free time in Torah study, the community must pay him a living wage, and a generous one at that. On the other hand, if the community allows the judge to take on outside employment when it does not conflict with his judicial duties, the community bears no responsibility to provide him with a living wage.

Private-Sector Full-Time Workers and the Living Wage

The above analysis identified an instance when the living wage is required. It obtains when the community hires a judge and stipulates that he may not take on outside employment.

Perhaps the public-sector case can be extended to the private sector. For the private-sector case to be analogous to the public-sector case, however, *P*'s terms of employment in the private sector must be very much akin to the terms of a judge's employment. Consider that the judge gives up not only outside employment, but also the free use of his leisure time. Specifically, when the judge is not occupied with his judicial duties, he must devote himself to Torah studies. Because the judge gives up the discretionary use of his time, it is only proper that the community provide him a generous living wage.

For the private-sector case to be analogous to the public-sector case, *P* must give up more than just outside employment. The two cases converge, as it appears to this writer, when the following elements are in place: *P* is the breadwinner of a poor household. *E* hires *P* for a full-time job and stipulates that *P* may not take on an outside job. Finally, the employment agreement calls for *P* to receive a wage that is in line with the competitive wage for the type of work *P* was hired to perform.

Does Halakhah require *E* to pay *P* a living wage instead of the competitive wage? No. In the halakhic system, as discussed earlier, the law of *ona'ah* is the arbiter of the issue of fairness of wages specified in a labor contract. Accordingly, *P*'s *ona'ah* claim does not even get off the ground unless he can demonstrate a number of things. First, he must show that for the job description and the hours he agreed to, other employers in the same job market do not stipulate a prohibition against outside work. In addition, the comparison job must be occupied by someone who is the sole breadwinner of a poor household. Now, even if *P* can prove these elements of his claim, the law of *ona'ah*, as will be recalled, pertains to the labor market only with respect to the prohibition against knowingly contracting into *ona'ah*, but not to the adjustment or cancellation of the contact that ordinarily accompanies the finding that the prohibition was violated.

Notwithstanding that the law of *ona'ah* provides no easy path, even on a moral level, to modify a labor contract that calls for a below-subsistence wage and also prohibits outside work, this contract is objectionable on a number of grounds. These objections, as we shall see, make this type of contract subject to remedy through legislation by the Jewish community. In monetary matters, Jewish law grants the Jewish community legislative authority. Provided the laws are enacted in a nondiscriminatory manner, such legislation becomes effective by majority rule.[62] We now turn to identifying the objectionable aspects of a labor contract that calls for a below-subsistence wage and at the same time prohibits outside work.

Let's put the first objectionable aspect of such a labor contract within the context of the prohibition in Jewish law for *P* to take on outside work. Consider that Halakhah imposes on *P* an obligation to exert himself on behalf of his employer with his *utmost* energy.[63] Proceeding from this requirement of energetic exertion is the prohibition against taking on outside night work while under contract as an employee during the day.[64] Similarly, a worker may not refuse to use his wages to provide himself with minimum nourishment, even if the money saved is used to support his family.[65] Similarly a school teacher may not stay up late at night or rise very early.[66] In all these instances, the conduct reduces the worker's productivity while performing his contracted work and is therefore prohibited.

In assessing whether *P*'s right to take on outside work should be denied, we must take into account the length of the workday that was common during the historical period when the interdict against outside work was promulgated. Let's first note that Jewish law provides that if a *po'el* hires himself out for a day, he must leave his home for the workplace at sunrise and continue to work at the workplace until nightfall.[67] Over time, the workday, of course, shortened.

Elsewhere we have demonstrated that the prohibition against taking on outside work generally applies only if the outside work causes *P*'s productivity at his full-time job to fall below the average productivity of those who hold the same full-time job.[68]

The only valid halakhic basis for *E* to object to *P*'s outside work is that the outside work robs *E* of his entitlement to *P*'s productivity. But consider that it takes a living wage to equip *P*, who is the breadwinner of a poor household, with the minimum physical and mental resources that would allow him to direct his utmost energy and concentration to his full-time job. Paying *P* a wage below a living wage and at the same time denying him the right to take on outside work is akin to equipping *P* with inferior tools yet demanding that he meet the same productivity standards that apply to co-workers equipped with proper tools.

Let's now turn to the second objectionable aspect of this labor contract. Denying *P* a right to moonlight inevitably induces *P* to violate Jewish law's code of ethics for a charity recipient. Why? Consider that if *P* does not earn a living wage, he is eligible to receive funds from the public coffers because he is the sole breadwinner of a poor household. By agreeing to *E*'s stipulation, *P* effectively abdicates his duty to engage in self-help before imposing his needs on the public as a charity case.

R. Ephraim Solomon b. Aaron Lunshits (*Keli Yakar*, Leczyca, 1550–1619) derives the duty of self-help from the Biblical obligation to come to the aid of a neighbor who requests assistance with unburdening his animal that is faltering under the weight of its load: "If you see the donkey of a man who hates you lying helpless under its load, you must refrain from deserting him; you must be sure to help him unburden the animal" (Exodus 23:5). Exegetical interpretation of the phrase "to help him" (*immo*) understands the obligation of the passerby to consist of *assisting* the owner in unloading the animal. Demanding that the passerby unload the animal himself, however, constitutes an unreasonable request on the part of the owner, and consequently need not be heeded. Under the assumption that the *immo* caveat applies to the charity obligation generally, *Keli*

Yakar derives the principle that before a supplicant qualifies for public assistance, he must be willing to do his part (i.e., exhaust his efforts to secure gainful employment).[69]

The two objections we have raised with respect to prohibiting a privately employed *P* who is the sole provider of a poor household from taking on outside work makes this case a primary candidate for regulation under the Jewish community's legislative authority.

The Living Wage and the Charity Duty

If Jewish labor law does not require an employer to pay a living wage, perhaps Jewish charity law does. Consider that Maimonides regards preventing someone from falling into the throes of poverty as the highest level of charitable giving. One of his examples of this type of charitable giving is to provide a needy person with a job.[70]

Maimonides' treatment of the job-offer example requires clarification. From the standpoint of self-interest, an employer should choose the candidate who would add the most value to his business at the least possible cost. Using instead the criterion of which candidate most desperately needs the job will, at times, entail making a suboptimal choice and hence incur an extra cost for the employer. Does the duty to provide a needy person with a job apply even when other candidates are more qualified? Consider that extending a loan to someone who is poor is another example Maimonides records as the highest level of charity. Because extending an interest-free loan, and a risky one at that, entails forgone opportunities to earn income from the capital over the entire loan period, Maimonides' other examples should also be understood as entailing some cost to the donor.

Hiring someone in need when more qualified candidates are available has limits. Most fundamentally, out of fear that over-generosity in charitable giving may subject the donor to a risk of falling into poverty himself, the Sages decreed that one should not give charity in excess of 20% of one's net worth.[71] Putting the viability of one's source of livelihood at risk is an example of this prohibition.

Let's show how hiring a person based on need can put a business at risk. Suppose the needy individual does not have the requisite skills for the job but can be trained. If labor costs are a significant component of cost for the employer, the higher labor cost the employer incurs by hiring the needy candidate puts the employer at a competitive disadvantage. The law of *ona'ah* tells the employer that, other things equal, he may not pass on his differential cost to his customers by raising prices, except through upfront disclosure.[72] To get customers to accommodate him and at the same time dispel their suspicions that he is either lying or inefficient, the employer would have to say: "My costs are higher because I hired a needy person who is unqualified for the job. These differential costs are the training cost I incurred and the ongoing cost of having a worker on staff with a below-par productivity level."

This disclosure is problematic, however. Consider that the ideal prescribed for the donor is to hide his identity and charitable intent,[73] and certainly not to cause the recipient needless mental anguish (*ona'at devarim*).[74] But *E*'s upfront disclosure may very well result in violation of these norms. A case in point is when *E*'s firm is located in the same community where the needy worker lives and the firm hires only a few people. Under those circumstances, *E*'s disclosure may easily expose the identity of the needy worker. If *P*'s poverty status was not previously known and *E*'s disclosure makes this information public, *P*'s privacy has been violated.[75] If the needy worker learns of the disclosure, the disclosure will not only have revealed *E*'s charitable motive, but also might shatter *P*'s self-esteem by conveying the message that *P* is not valuable to the firm and is instead just a charity case.

The problems outlined above are only compounded if the employer is also required to pay the "charity case" a living wage.

Moreover, from a practical standpoint, introduction of the living wage disrupts the entire pay structure of the employer. This is so because the unit of support in Jewish law, as we shall explain in the next section, is not the individual, but rather the household. Accordingly, a teenager who is member of a household that is not poor is not entitled to a subsidy. At the other extreme, if the wage earner is a head of a household and the household is poor, the wage subsidy should be geared to the number of dependents the head of the household must support. Paying market-driven wages to workers who are not poor while paying workers who are heads of a poor household wages according to household need is very disruptive. This system may have the effect of dragging down the morale and productivity of the labor force because of the resentment it generates.

If an employer has a duty of charity to pay a living wage, the source of that duty would be the Torah's mandate: "Grant him enough for his lack, whatever is lacking for him" (*dei mahsoro asher yehsar lo*) (Deuteronomy 15:8). But Halakhah has interpreted the *dei mahsoro* mandate as a collective responsibility rather than a duty for an individual to shoulder alone when he personally encounters a charity case.[76] Because the living wage mandate saddles the burden of relieving poverty for the working poor on employers alone, the *dei mahsoro* mandate is violated.

The thrust of the above discussion is not that employers have no ethical duty to their poor workers other than to pay them a competitive wage for the type of work they perform. An employer's interaction with his workforce makes his indigent workers priority candidates for some of his charity funds.[77] Giving these workers small bonuses before holidays, gifts to mark new additions to their families, and special consideration in the event of illness, is therefore appropriate. These gestures are not only good business, but also charity on the highest level.

Living Wage Ordinances and *Halakhah*

We now turn to the living wage as a public policy mandate. Preliminarily, let's note that in Jewish law, the duty to alleviate poverty is both a mandate for the private citizen and the responsibility of government.[78]

Elsewhere we have proposed that determining the appropriate allocation of responsibility between government and private citizens for discharging the anti-poverty duty is entirely a matter of ascertaining which sector best advances Halakhah's specific anti-poverty goals.[79]

Reducing poverty through job creation promotes Halakhah's anti-poverty goals on the noblest level because the Torah abhors idleness[80] and values work and gainful employment.[81] Consider also that giving a needy person a job, as mentioned earlier, *prevents* poverty and therefore falls under the rubric of the highest level of charitable giving. In advancing the goal of poverty reduction through job creation, government enjoys a decided advantage over the private citizen. The issue therefore is whether the living wage is the best means for government to foster gainful employment for those who cannot command a living wage on their own.

From the standpoint of Halakhah, LWOs are riddled with a number of debits:

1. In Jewish law, the target for anti-poverty efforts is not the indigent individual but rather the poor household. This approach can be seen from the ruling that public charity funds may not be used to support an indigent individual when the would-be public charge has a father of means. Instead, the father is forced to support his son. Coercion applies even when the father is not otherwise legally obligated to support his son (i.e., the son is not a minor).[82] Similarly, public charity funds may not be used to support an indigent individual who is known to have wealthy relatives in the local area. Since the wealthy relatives are expected to support their indigent kin from their own resources, public funds may not be used for this purpose, even if the wealthy relatives contributed to the public charity chest.[83]

LWOs fall short of the halakhic standard here. Instead of targeting the poor household, they target the individual wage earner. But family size and composition are widely acknowledged to have a major impact on the resources available to any individual family member and hence on economic well-being and poverty status.[84] In this regard, most minimum wage workers are between 16 and 24 years old and typically are not the family's sole breadwinner. Rather, they tend to live in middle-class households that do not rely on their earnings. Only one in five live in a family with earnings below the poverty line. Over three-fifths work part-time and only 6% are married.[85]

2. Halakhah requires public sector anti-poverty measures to be financed by a tax that is proportional to wealth.[86] LWOs do not meet this standard because the burden of directly financing the living wage falls only on employers. Depending on the coverage of these ordinances, these employers include the local government

itself and those that provide services or lease property from the municipality or one of its agencies. LWOs may also include employers who receive a benefit from a locality in the form of an economic development subsidy or tax break.[87] To be sure, employers might be successful in shifting part of their increase in labor costs to consumers and suppliers, but the financing of the living wage will in the final analysis fall far short of a broad-based tax proportional to wealth.

With respect to the effectiveness of LWOs as an anti-poverty measure, let's consider the following two additional criticisms:

3. Toikka, Yelowitz, and Neveu point out that many families living with earnings below the poverty line are enrolled in programs specifically designed to help lift them out of poverty. Phase-out rates of benefit programs are structured so that additional earnings from taking on gainful employment largely disappear through benefit reduction and increased taxation. These vanishing benefits reduce the ability of LWOs to alleviate poverty.[88]

4. Neumark and Wascher demonstrate that LWOs boost the wages of the lowest-wage earners, but at the cost of depriving these workers of employment opportunities.[89] According to these scholars, additional policies are needed to help those without jobs or strategies enhance skills and make them more employable at higher wages.[90]

Supply- and Demand-Side Anti-Poverty Policies and Jewish Law

To foster both job creation and job enhancement for low-wage workers, Halakhah would assign government the role of establishing policies that would advance these goals both from the supply and demand sides of the marketplace. In the next section, we will describe both supply-side and demand-side anti-poverty policies for government that meet Halakhah's standards and goals.

SUPPLY SIDE—THE EARNED INCOME TAX CREDIT

The Earned Income Tax Credit (EITC) is a U.S. federal wage subsidy program. First enacted in 1975, the program is administered by the Internal Revenue Service (IRS). One applies for the tax credit by filing a U.S. federal income tax return with the IRS, even if no taxes are owed. To qualify for the credit, a worker's adjusted gross income (AGI) and earned income must be below certain threshold amounts.[91]

For 2011, a taxpayer with two dependents is allowed a credit equal to 40% of earned income up to $12,780. The maximum credit for that taxpayer is thus $5,112. If the taxpayer is married and files a joint return, the maximum credit begins to phase out when AGI reaches $21,770. Specifically, for every dollar of AGI earned above $21,770, the tax credit is reduced by 21.06 cents. Consequently, the credit is completely phased out when AGI reaches $46,044. In addition, no credit is allowed if the taxpayer's investment income for the taxable year exceeds $3,150.[92]

From the standpoint of halakhic goals and standards, the EITC comports well as an anti-poverty measure because the targeted unit is the taxpaying household rather than the individual. In addition, the predominant source of financing for the EITC is the U.S. federal progressive income tax, which is the type of tax Halakhah prescribes for the financing of anti-poverty measures. Yet another advantage of the EITC is that it preserves the dignity of the poor by integrating the EITC with the filing of tax returns with the IRS. Finally, empirical evidence shows that the EITC has been successful in reducing poverty and increasing participation in the labor force.[93]

Given that the EITC comports well with halakhic standards as an anti-poverty measure, the adoption of an EITC on a local level to supplement the federal EITC program appears to be a promising direction to take.[94]

DEMAND SIDE—INCREASING EMPLOYMENT OPPORTUNITIES FOR POVERTY-LEVEL HOUSEHOLDS

By establishing incentives for low-income workers to increase their participation in the labor market, the EITC works through the supply side of the marketplace to increase work effort and hence alleviate poverty. Consider however that the highest level of charity consists of preventing an individual from falling into the throes of poverty. From the standpoint of government, this highest level of charity translates into a duty to implement the proper monetary–fiscal policy mix that fosters an economic environment where employment opportunities proliferate. On the microeconomic level, it requires the government to help the indigent find jobs. It also requires the government to subsidize the education and training of poverty households to make the wage earner in these households more attractive to hire.

Edmund S. Phelps' proposal that the government subsidize employers who hire low-wage workers[95] is consistent with halakhic goals. In Phelps' scheme, employers receive the highest subsidy for the lowest-paid jobs.[96] The wage rate subsidy spurs competition among employers to hire low-wage workers.[97] This competition can be expected not only to bid up the wages of low-wage workers, but also to encourage employers to provide these workers with job training and a promising career path.

Phelps' proposal does not limit eligibility to breadwinners of a household. This feature of his program is also consistent with Halakhah because his program is both a poverty-relief and a poverty-prevention measure. Accordingly, teenagers who are currently dependents should also qualify for the program. By training low-skilled teenagers, the program makes them attractive to hire when they set up their own households.

Conclusion

In this chapter, we compared the treatment of the living wage from the standpoint of both standard economic theory and Jewish law.

Standard economic theory demonstrates that the minimum wage has a mixed effect. As a result of minimum wage legislation, workers who get hired will earn a higher wage than they would have otherwise earned if left to their own devices. The higher wage will, however, cause employers to hire fewer workers. Since the intended beneficiary of minimum wage legislation is not homogeneous but instead consists of unskilled workers with various degrees of employability, minimum wage legislation will adversely affect the lowest echelons of the unskilled labor market the most. Minimum wage legislation hence produces the irony that the very group the legislation is intended to help is actually hurt the most by the legislation. The conclusion therefore is that minimum wage legislation is self-defeating.

The lesson of minimum wage legislation should apply with even greater force to the living wage proposal, which seeks to mandate a wage at a level much higher than the federal minimum wage.

Jewish law's deontological system of ethics proposes rules for the labor market. It also assigns an anti-poverty role for both the private citizen and the government. The issue the living wage presents for Jewish law is therefore whether the living wage is consistent with Jewish labor law or charity law. The conclusion of economic theory that the living wage concept is self-defeating would be readily adopted by Jewish law.

Beyond the notion that the living wage concept is self-defeating, we have demonstrated that in Jewish law, the living wage is generally neither a desideratum for the private employer nor a mandate for the government. One exception is that when a community hires a religious functionary full-time and stipulates that he may not take on outside employment, the community must pay him a living wage.

In determining the duty that a private employer owes his workers, both labor law and charity law must be satisfied. With respect to labor law, the operative principle is the equity rule of *ona'ah*. This rule requires the employer to pay his workers no more than the competitive norm for the type of work performed. For a worker who cannot command a living wage in the marketplace, a claim for a living wage based on *ona'ah* does not get off the ground. Moreover, given that the restitution procedure for *ona'ah* does not apply to the *po'el* labor market, even a worker who commands a living wage in the marketplace is entitled to no judicial relief in the form of a wage adjustment based on an *ona'ah* claim.

When an employer is not paying the head of a poor household a living wage, the employer has no right to prevent the worker from taking on outside work. Even an explicit clause to this effect in the worker's employment agreement will be null and void.

From the standpoint of charity law, if the living wage is required, it would be rooted in the *dei mahsoro* duty. But *dei mahsoro* is a collective rather than an individual responsibility. Consequently, no single individual is required to shoulder the entire burden of lifting a family out of poverty. Recommending a living wage on the supererogatory level without taking into account the consequences an employer may face from implementing a living wage in his workplace may very well court disaster for the employer by putting him out of business.

In the arena of public policy, we demonstrated that living wage ordinances fall far short of the halakhic criterion of an anti-poverty measure. Alternative policies would do the job much better. The EITC is one such policy. It works on the supply side of the labor market to increase both the income and work effort of the poor. The EITC must be augmented, however, with public-sector programs designed to help the poor find work and enhance their marketability by subsidizing their education and job training. Phelps' wage rate subsidy is one such proposal.

Notes

1. Bruce E. Kaufman and Julie L. Hotchkiss, *The Economics of Labor Markets*, 7th ed. (Mason, OH: Thomson South-Western, 2006), 286–287.
2. Edgar K. Browning and Mark A. Zupan, *Microeconomics: Theory & Applications*, 10th ed. (Hoboken, NJ: John Wiley, 2009), 514–518.
3. Bradley R. Schiller, "Just Getting By?: Income Dependence on Minimum Wage Jobs," *Employment Policies Institute* (March 2011): 11–12; Richard V. Burkhauser and Joseph J. Sabia, "Why Raising the Minimum Wage is a Poor Way to Help the Working Poor," *Employment Policies Institute* (July 2004): 3.
4. Samuel, *Gittin* 10b. R. Yosef Eliyahu Henkin (New York, 1881–1973) posits that in the absence of the *kehillah* organizational structure, government social welfare legislation is, according to all authorities, binding on the basis of *dina de-malkhuta dina*. See R. Yosef Eliyahu Henkin, *Kitvei ha-Gri'a Henkin*, vol. 2, *Teshuvot Ivra*, ed. R. Abraham Hillel Henkin (New York: Ezras Torah, 1989), no. 96, ¶ 1(4), p. 175.
5. "When you make a sale to your fellow or when you buy from the hand of your fellow, do not victimize one another" (Leviticus 25:14). For a general description of the law of *ona'ah*, please turn to Chapter 2 of this volume.
6. For the development of these points based on Talmudic sources, see Aaron Levine, "*Onaa* and the Operation of the Modern Marketplace," *Jewish Law Annual* 14 (2003): 225–258.
7. See R. Meir b. Barukh of Rothenburg (*Maharam me-Rotenburg*, Germany, ca. 1215–1293), *She'elot u-Teshuvot Maharam*, no. 247, and *Haggahot Maimuniyyot* to *Mishneh Torah*, *Sekhirut* 9:4, n. 5; R. Isaac b. Moses (*Or Zaru'a*, Vienna, ca. 1180–1250), *Or Zaru'a*, *Bava Metzia* 6, ¶ 242.
8. R. Jekutiel Asher Zalman Enzil Zausmir (*Mahariaz Enzil*, Volhynia, d. 1858), *She'elot u-Teshuvot Mahariaz Enzil*, *siman* 15, *amud* 14, *tur* 1.
9. *Mishneh Torah*, *Mekhirah* 13:15, 13:18.
10. The Talmud explicitly states only that heathen slaves are assimilated to land. *Megillah* 23b. Commentators, however, understand the assimilation to apply to Israelite slaves as well. See R. Israel b. Petahiah Isserlein (Germany, 1390–1460), *Terumat ha-Deshen*, *helek* 1, *She'elot u-Teshuvot*, no. 318, ed. Shemuel Avitan (Jerusalem, 1991), p. 258; R. Elijah b. Solomon Zalman (*Gra*, Vilna, 1720–1797), *Be'ur ha-Gra* to R. Joseph Caro (Safed, 1488–1575), *Shulhan Arukh*, *Hoshen Mishpat* 227, n. 48. See also R. Joshua b. Alexander ha-Kohen Falk (*Sema*, Poland, 1565–1614), *Sema* to *Shulhan Arukh*, *Hoshen Mishpat* 227, n. 60.

11. *Baraita, Bava Metzia* 56b.
12. Ibid.
13. See *Bava Metzia* 10a.
14. *Sema* to *Shulhan Arukh, Hoshen Mishpat* 227, n. 59.
15. R. Isserlein, *Terumat ha-Deshen*, no. 318.
16. *Mishneh Torah, Mekhirah* 13:3.
17. R. Eliezer b. Samuel of Metz, *Sefer Yere'im* 127; R. Moses Isserles (*Rema*, Poland, 1525 or 1530–1572), *Rema* to *Shulhan Arukh, Hoshen Mishpat* 227, as understood by R. Shabbetai b. Meir ha-Kohen (*Siftei Kohen*, Poland, 1621–1662), *Siftei Kohen* to *Shulhan Arukh*, ad loc., n. 17.
18. *Rabbeinu Tam*, quoted in *Rosh, She'elot u-Teshuvot ha-Rosh, kelal* 102 and *Tur, Hoshen Mishpat* 227; *Rema* to *Shulhan Arukh, Hoshen Mishpat* 227, as understood by *Sema* to *Shulhan Arukh*, ad loc., n. 50.
19. *Bava Metzia* 56b–57a (opinions of R. Ami and R. Yohanan); *Rif*, ad loc.; *Rosh, Bava Metzia* 4:21.
20. Nahmanides to Leviticus 25:14.
21. *Siftei Kohen* to *Shulhan Arukh, Hoshen Mishpat* 227, n. 50.
22. An *ona'ah* claim in the product market is entertained even when the reference product is slightly differentiated. See R. Jehiel Michal Epstein (Belarus, 1829–1908), *Arukh ha-Shulhan, Hoshen Mishpat* 227:7, based on *Rosh, Bava Metzia* 4:20. Accordingly, the complainant's job need not be identical to the reference job in all respects. To be analogous to the product market, the core duties of the two jobs must, however, be identical. After the validity of the comparison is established, the complainant's opportunity cost claim is evaluated on the basis of the offsetting advantages and disadvantages of the two jobs. The *ona'ah* claim may be disqualified if the higher-paying reference job compensates workers according to seniority or based on a productivity standard that the complainant has not achieved.
23. Lodging an *ona'ah* claim based on what employers pay for the same job in a different locale is not valid. The principle here is "*ein la-hekdesh ela mekomo ve-sha'to*." Mishnah, *Arakhin* 6:5. For discussion of this point, see Levine, "*Onaa* and the Operation of the Modern Marketplace," 243–248.
24. *Bava Kamma* 46a ("*ha-motzi me-havero, alav ha-re'ayah*"); *Bava Metzia* 2b.
25. R. Aryeh Leib b. Joseph ha-Kohen Heller (*Ketzot*, Poland, 1745–1813), *Ketzot ha-Hoshen* to *Shulhan Arukh, Hoshen Mishpat* 331, n. 3; *Arukh ha-Shulhan, Hoshen Mishpat* 331:8.
26. *Sema* to *Shulhan Arukh*, op. cit., 332, n. 8; *Siftei Kohen* to *Shulhan Arukh*, op. cit., 332, n. 12; *Arukh ha-Shulhan*, op. cit., 332:2.
27. *Rif, Bava Metzia* 76a; R. Yom Tov Ishbili (*Ritva*, Spain, ca. 1250–1330), *Hiddushei ha-Ritva, Bava Metzia* 76a, ed. R. Shiloh Raphael (Jerusalem: Mossad HaRav Kook, 1993), *tur* 742, s.v. "*lo tzerikha de-ikka de-mitaggar be-arba'ah*."
28. *Bava Metzia* 76a; *Rif*, ad loc.; *Mishneh Torah, Sekhirut* 9:3; *Rosh, Bava Metzia* 6:1; R. Jacob b. Asher (*Tur*, Spain, 1270–1343), *Tur, Hoshen Mishpat* 332; *Shulhan Arukh, Hoshen Mishpat* 332:1; *Arukh ha-Shulhan, Hoshen Mishpat* 332:1–2.
29. *Arukh ha-Shulhan*, op. cit. 332:2.
30. Ibid., 331:6.
31. Ibid., 331:7.
32. Rabbi Jill Jacobs, "Work, Workers and the Jewish Owner" (responsum adopted by the Committee on Jewish Law and Standards of the Rabbinical Assembly on May 28, 2008, with 13 members in favor, one opposed, and three abstaining). The resolution specifically said that "Jews should 'strive' to hire unionized workers and pay a living wage."
33. Nahmanides to Deuteronomy 24:14–15.
34. R. Jacobs, "Work, Workers and the Jewish Owner," 23.
35. *Baraita, Bava Metzia* 112a; *Rif*, ad loc.; *Mishneh Torah, Sekhirut* 11:4; *Rosh, Bava Metzia* 9:43; *Tur, Hoshen Mishpat* 339 *Shulhan Arukh, Hoshen Mishpat* 339:10; *Arukh ha-Shulhan, Hoshen Mishpat* 339:12.
36. R. Yom Tov Ishbili, *Hiddushei ha-Ritva, Bava Metzia* 111b.

37. Ibid.; R. Akiva Eiger (Hungary, 1761–1837) to *Shulhan Arukh*, op. cit., 339:10; R. Shneur Zalman of Liadi (Russia, 1745–1812), *Shulhan Arukh ha-Rav, Hoshen Mishpat, helek* 6, *Hilkhot She'elah, u-Sekhirut, va-Hasimah, se'if* 15 (Brooklyn: Otzar ha-Hasidim, 2005), p. 143.
38. *Baraita, Sanhedrin* 73a; *Mishneh Torah, Rotzeah u-Shemirat Nefesh* 1:14; *Tur, Hoshen Mishpat* 426; *Shulhan Arukh, Hoshen Mishpat* 426:1; *Arukh ha-Shulhan, Hoshen Mishpat* 426:1. The *lo ta'amod* duty, according to R. Menasheh Klein (New York, contemp.), applies even when the danger *A* faces threatens him only as a result of a transgression he is bent on committing. See R. Menasheh Klein, *"Hal'itehu la-Rasha ve-Yamut," Pa'amei Yaakov be-Sedei ha-Halakhah* (*Nisan* 2000): 115–116.
39. Delay in paying a worker beyond the initial window when the wages are due will, however, violate for the employer the rabbinical interdict of: "Say not to your neighbor, 'go and come back, and tomorrow I will give, when you have [it] with you'" (Proverbs 3:28). *Bava Metzia* 111a.
40. *Bava Metzia* 110b; *Shulhan Arukh, Hoshen Mishpat* 339:8; *Sema* to *Shulhan Arukh, Hoshen Mishpat* 339, nn. 16–17; R. Israel Meir ha-Kohen Kagan (*Hafetz Hayyim*, Radin, 1838–1933), *Ahavat Hesed* 9:12 and *Netiv ha-Hesed* 9:35.
41. *Bava Metzia* 110b; R. Kagan, *Ahavat Hesed* 9:1.
42. *Bava Metzia* 112a.
43. Deuteronomy 24:15.
44. *Bava Metzia* 112a.
45. R. Nahman b. Isaac, *Bava Metzia* 58b. For another instance of "as if," see *Nedarim* 40a.
46. *Bava Metzia* 112a. This conduct, however, violates a rabbinical prohibition, as discussed in note 39 above.
47. *Rashi* to *Bava Metzia* 112a, s.v. *"le-da'atekha."*
48. *Bava Metzia* 110b; *Shulhan Arukh, Hoshen Mishpat* 339:7.
49. *Tosafot Rid, Bava Metzia* 111a.
50. *Bava Metzia* 112a.
51. *Mishneh Torah, Shekalim* 4:7.
52. Exodus 23:8 and *Rashi*, ad loc.; Deuteronomy 16:19; *Sifrei*, Deuteronomy 16:19.
53. Exodus 23:8; Deuteronomy 16:19.
54. *Tosafot* to *Ketubbot* 105a, s.v. *"gozerei gezeirot she-bi-Yerushalayim."*
55. *Rashi* to *Ketubbot* 105a, s.v. *"batei dinin."*
56. R. Samuel Eliezer b. Judah ha-Levi Edels, *Maharsha, Ketubbot* 105a.
57. Biblically prescribed charities included *leket* (gleanings), *shikhehah* (forgotten sheaves), and *pe'ah* (the corner of the field), as well as the agricultural tithe. See Leviticus 19:9, Leviticus 23:22, and Deuteronomy 24:19. For a description of the operation of these agricultural gifts, see Menahem Haran, "Poor, Provisions for the," in *Encyclopedia Judaica*, 2nd ed., vol. 16, eds. Michael Berenbaum and Fred Skolnik (Detroit: Macmillan Reference, 2007), 371–372.
58. Mishnah, *Pe'ah* 8:8–9. R. Ephraim b. Isaac of Regensberg (Germany, d. 1175) and R. Isaac b. Moses of Vienna extend the Talmudic 200 *zuz* criterion for eligibility to modern times. See R. Joseph Caro, *Beit Yosef* to *Tur, Yoreh De'ah* 253.
59. R. Obadiah b. Abraham of Bertinoro, *Bartenura*, Mishnah, *Pe'ah* 8:8. For a discussion of whether the sum of 200 *zuz* represents the subsistence needs of a single individual or the collective needs of a husband and wife, see R. Shelomoh Adani (*Melekhet Shelomoh*, Yemen, b. 1567) to Mishnah, *Pe'ah* 8:8 (citing R. Samson b. Abraham of Sens [*Rash*, ca. 1150–ca. 1230]).
60. R. Jacob Emden on *Rashi* to *Ketubbot* 105a, reprinted in *Yalkut Mefareshim he-Hadash*, Babylonian Talmud, *Ketubbot*, *Oz ve-Hadar* ed. (Jerusalem, 2006), s.v. *"Rashi, dibbur ha-mat'hil 'batei dinin.'"*
61. R. Moses Sofer, *Hatam Sofer, Hoshen Mishpat*, nos. 22, 164, 166.
62. For a concise discussion of the parameters of Jewish communal legislation, see Aaron Levine, *Economic Public Policy and Jewish Law* (Hoboken, NJ: Ktav, 1993), 3–20.
63. *Mishneh Torah, Sekhirut* 13:7; *Shulhan Arukh, Hoshen Mishpat* 337:20; *Arukh ha-Shulhan, Hoshen Mishpat* 337:26.
64. *Mishneh Torah, Sekhirut* 13:6; *Shulhan Arukh*, op. cit., 337:19; *Arukh ha-Shulhan*, op. cit., 337:25.

65. *Shulhan Arukh*, op. cit.; *Arukh ha-Shulhan*, op. cit.
66. R. Mordekhai b. Hillel ha-Kohen (*Mordekhai*, Germany, ca. 1250–1298), *Mordekhai, Bava Metzia* 6:343.
67. *Rema* to *Shulhan Arukh, Hoshen Mishpat* 331:1; *Arukh ha-Shulhan, Hoshen Mishpat* 331:2. Opinions differ on the precise formulation of the Biblical standard for the workday. For a discussion of this point, see Shillem Warhaftig, *Dinei Avodah ba-Mishpat ha-Ivri*, 2nd ed., vol. 1 (Jerusalem: Machon Harry Fischel, 1982), 481–490.
68. Aaron Levine, *Free Enterprise and Jewish Law: Aspects of Jewish Business Ethics* (New York: Ktav, 1980), 57.
69. R. Ephraim Solomon b. Aaron Lunshits, *Keli Yakar* to Exodus 23:5. See also R. Aharon Lichtenstein, "*Sa'od Tis'od Immo: Hishtatfut ha-Mekabbel be-Gemilut Hasadim*" in *Sefer ha-Zikaron le-Avraham Spiegelman*, ed. Aryeh Morgenstern (Tel Aviv: Moreshet, 1979), 81–93.
70. *Mishneh Torah, Matanot Aniyyim* 10:7.
71. *Ketubbot* 50a.
72. Levine, "*Onaa* and the Operation of the Modern Marketplace," 229, 248.
73. *Mishneh Torah, Matanot Aniyyim* 10:8.
74. Leviticus 25:17.
75. *E*'s disclosure of *P*'s private information violates "You shall not go as a talebearer" (Leviticus 19:16). See *Mishneh Torah, De'ot* 7:2 and *Kesef Mishneh*, ad loc.
76. *Rema* to *Shulhan Arukh, Yoreh De'ah* 250:1; *Arukh ha-Shulhan, Yoreh De'ah* 250:4–5.
77. One of the categories of indigents that Jewish law considers a priority for the donor is *shekhenav* (lit., his neighbors). Decisors dispute whether *shekhenav* should be understood as indigents who live near the donor or indigents with whom the donor interacts. R. Abraham Danzig (Prague, 1748–1820), *Hokhmat Adam* 145:1, takes the latter position. What follows from R. Danzig's position is that if the owner of a business interacts with his employees, the employer, other things equal, must give his poor workers preferential treatment in the distribution of his charity funds.
78. Aaron Levine, "Welfare Programs and Jewish Law," in *Public Policy and Social Issues: Jewish Sources and Perspectives*, ed. Marshall J. Breger (Westport, CT: Praeger, 2003), 140–153.
79. Aaron Levine, *Economics and Jewish Law* (Hoboken, NJ: Ktav, 1987), 126–131.
80. R. Simeon b. Gamliel, Mishnah, *Ketubbot* 5:5.
81. *Pesahim* 113a; Mishnah, *Avot* 1:10; *Avot de-Rabbi Natan* 11:1.
82. R. Solomon b. Abraham Adret (*Rashba*, Spain, 1235–1310), *She'elot u-Teshuvot ha-Rashba* 3:292, quoted in R. Joseph Caro, *Beit Yosef* to *Tur, Yoreh De'ah* 251, n. 4; *Shulhan Arukh, Yoreh De'ah* 251:4; *Arukh ha-Shulhan, Yoreh De'ah* 251:9.
83. R. Eliezer b. Samuel of Metz to *Nedarim* 65a, quoted in *Beit Yosef* to *Tur, Yoreh De'ah* 257, n. 8; *Shulhan Arukh, Yoreh De'ah* 257:8; *Arukh ha-Shulhan, Yoreh De'ah* 257:16.
84. Richard V. Burkhauser, Kenneth A. Couch, and David C. Wittenburg, "'Who Gets What' from Minimum Wage Hikes: A Re-Evaluation of Card and Krueger's Distributional Analysis in *Myth and Measurement: The New Economics of the Minimum Wage*," *Industrial and Labor Relations Review* 49, no. 3 (April 1996): 548.
85. James Sherk and Rea S. Hederman, Jr., "Who Earns the Minimum Wage? Suburban Teenagers, Not Single Parents," *Heritage Foundation WebMemo*, no. 1320 (January 23, 2007), http://www.heritage.org/Research/Economy/wm1320.cfm.
86. R. Solomon b. Abraham Adret, *She'elot u-Teshuvot ha-Rashba* 3:381.
87. James A. Buss and Arthur Romeo, "The Changing Employment Situation in Some Cities with Living Wage Ordinances," *Review of Social Economy* 64, no. 3 (September 2006): 351.
88. Richard S. Toikka, Aaron Yelowitz, and Andre Neveu, "The 'Poverty Trap' and Living Wage Laws," *Economic Development Quarterly* 19, no. 1 (February 2005): 62–79.
89. David Neumark and William L. Wascher, *Minimum Wages* (Cambridge, MA: MIT Press, 2008), 37–106 (surveying selected studies on the employment effects of minimum wage and concluding that more than 80% of the studies reveal negative employment effects); David Neumark and William L. Wascher, "Minimum Wages and Employment," *IZA Discussion Paper Series*, no. 2570 (January 2007) (reviewing over 100 papers on minimum wage written since

the early 1990s and concluding that approximately two-thirds of the papers yield evidence of negative employment effects).

90. Neumark and Wascher, *Minimum Wages*, 294–295.
91. Kaufman and Hotchkiss, *Economics of Labor Markets*, 153; V. Joseph Hotz and John Karl Scholz, "The Earned Income Tax Credit," *NBER Working Paper Series*, no. 8078 (January 2001): 1, 8.
92. 26 U.S.C. § 32; Rev. Proc. 2011–12, § 2.04. For a single taxpayer or head of household with two dependents, the maximum credit of $5,112 begins to phase out when AGI reaches $16,690 and is completely phased out when AGI reaches $40,964. No EITC is allowed for a married taxpayer who files a separate return. 26 U.S.C. § 32(d).
93. Kaufman and Hotchkiss, *Economics of Labor Markets*, 155–156; Hotz and Scholz, "Earned Income Tax Credit," 18–20 (anti-poverty effects), 49–50 (labor participation effects).
94. As of June 3, 2011, 19 states had a fully refundable EITC, calculated as a percentage of the federal EITC. See Internal Revenue Service, "State and Local Governments with Earned Income Tax Credit," http://www.irs.gov/individuals/article/0,id=177866,00.html.
95. Edmond S. Phelps, *Rewarding Work: How to Restore Participation and Self-Support to Free Enterprise* (Cambridge, MA: Harvard University Press, 1997), 105–109.
96. Ibid., 112–116.
97. Ibid., 124.

CHAPTER 8

Short Selling and Jewish Law

Introduction

In short selling, an investor sells stock he does not own. Typically, the investor accomplishes the sale by either borrowing the stock from a brokerage firm's inventory or from the margin accounts of the firm's clients. The investor executes the short sale because he believes the price of the stock will go down. If that happens, the investor will buy back the stock at the lower price, return the stock to the lender, and profit from the difference in price. If instead the price of the stock rises, the short seller will be forced to buy back the stock at a higher price and suffer a loss.

In the context of the current severe economic downturn, the phenomenon of short selling has grabbed the public's attention. The failure of Lehman Brothers was a pivotal event in the downturn, and the CEO of the company, Richard Fuld, claimed that a particular variety of short selling, called "naked short selling," played an important role in the collapse of his company.[1]

Our purpose here will be to examine the ethics of short selling from the perspective of Jewish law. We will also address short selling from an efficiency standpoint and show that, as a matter of stabilization policy, Jewish law would approve of this phenomenon in the financial markets.

Short Selling and U.S. Federal Securities Law

We begin with a description of the mechanics of short selling and the related U.S. federal securities laws. Most fundamentally, a broker-dealer may not execute a short sale of a security for a client unless the broker-dealer has borrowed or arranged to borrow the security, or has reasonable grounds to believe that the security can be borrowed and delivered on the date delivery is due. This rule is called the "locate" requirement.[2]

Once the shares of stock are borrowed, the broker must actually deliver the shares to the short seller within three business days of the trade.[3] Delivery of the shares is effected through the Depository Trust Company (DTC). A financial service company, DTC processes most of the securities transactions in the United States. Its function is to provide an efficient and safe mechanism for buyers and sellers to make their exchanges without the burden of exchanging paper certificates every time a security is traded.

To illustrate the role of DTC in a short sale, suppose Avery Kurtz wants to sell short 1,000 shares of Citigroup stock. He arranges to borrow the shares through his brokerage firm, Merrill Lynch.[4] Merrill Lynch has three days to deliver the shares to Kurtz. If Merrill Lynch does not deliver the shares within the three-day period, the rules of DTC call for Merrill Lynch to create an IOU that it owes DTC 1,000 shares of Citigroup stock. Merrill Lynch must then send this IOU to DTC, which in turn records a debit against Merrill Lynch's account and calls it a "fails to deliver."[5] At the same time, Merrill Lynch credits Kurtz's account with 1,000 shares of Citigroup stock.

To be sure, in a matter of days, Merrill Lynch may erase the "fails to deliver" by sending a stock certificate to DTC for 1,000 shares of Citigroup stock. But it is also possible that the shares will never be delivered. Let's take note that when a broker-dealer sends "fails to deliver" into the system, the supply of stock increases significantly because the system views the "fails to deliver" as actual stock. The result is that shares of stock can be duplicated multiple times and can be owned by multiple investors, creating phantom shares of the stock and depressing the stock's price.[6]

Naked Short Selling

Let us first turn our attention to the illegal form of short selling known as naked short selling. This illegal practice consists of selling a stock short without first borrowing the stock or ensuring that the stock can be borrowed. The most abusive form of this type of trade occurs when the stock the seller wants to sell short is for all intents and purposes not available to borrow. These stocks are called "threshold securities."[7]

In analyzing the ethics of naked short selling in Jewish law, the most salient point to note is that a naked short sale of a company's stock increases the number of outstanding shares of the company's stock without the company's authorization. Moreover, consider that, other things remaining equal, an expansion of the number of outstanding shares increases the supply of the shares relative to demand and therefore lowers the price of the shares. Accordingly, the price of the company's stock may decline as a result of naked short selling, generating a loss to the company's shareholders. Proceeding from the above analysis is that naked short selling is conceptualized in Jewish law as conducting business in a company for one's own benefit without authorization from the owners of the company.

The analogue for the ethics of naked short selling is R. Yose's dictum, recorded in the Mishnah at *Bava Metzia* 3:2:

> [If] one rents a cow from another and lends it to someone else, and it dies naturally, the renter must swear that it died naturally, and the borrower must pay the renter. Said R. Yose: "How does that person [i.e., the renter] do business with another's cow? Rather, the cow should be returned to the owner."

In the view of the first opinion expressed, when the animal dies, the renter becomes exempt from paying the owner, and acquires the animal. Since the renter is not liable for accidents, he takes the oath that the animal died naturally merely to placate the owner. Therefore, the borrower—who is responsible for accidents—must pay the renter.[8] R. Yose, however, regards the renter who lends out the cow as an agent of the owner.[9] Therefore, the borrower's payment for the cow should be given to the owner, not the renter.[10]

While Talmudic decisors follow R. Yose's opinion,[11] authorities are in disagreement regarding the conditions necessary to trigger the prohibition against doing business with someone else's property.

The majority position calls for disgorgement whenever *A* makes commercial use of *B*'s property without having any right to do so. The circumstance that *B* suffers no loss thereby is not a saving factor according to this school of thought.

Exemplifying this point of view are the following two rulings of R. Solomon b. Abraham Adret (*Rashba*, Spain, 1235–1310):

In the first ruling, *A* rents *B*'s house to *C* without *B*'s authorization. Given that the property had not been up for rental, *B* suffers no loss thereby. Nevertheless, according to R. Adret, it would be unconscionable for *A* to keep the rent, as this would amount to doing business with another's property. R. Adret hedges, however, on a definitive ruling regarding the disposition of the rent *A* receives. It might be appropriate, he points out, to return the rent to *C* rather than to give it *B* on the grounds that *B* suffers no loss as a result of *C*'s use of the property.[12]

In the second application of R. Yose's dictum, R. Adret rules that if *A* builds up *B*'s ruin and rents it to *C*, *A* must surrender the rent to *B*. Since the ruin is not rentable without *A*'s improvements, this too is a case where *A*'s commercialization of *B*'s property entails no loss for *B*, yet *A* is not entitled to keep the rent.[13]

A final example of a ruling that follows the above line of reasoning is the subletting case that came before R. Joseph ibn Habiba (*Nimmukei Yosef*, Spain, early 15th cent.). *A* rents an apartment from *B* and then sublets it to *C* at a higher rent. With respect to the disposition of the rent differential, *Nimmukei Yosef* finds the critical factor to be whether *A* was within his rights to sublet the apartment. If *A*'s subletting was legal, he bears no responsibility to surrender the differential to *B*. *B*'s unjust enrichment claim against *A* is dismissed on the grounds that *A*'s gain causes *B* no harm (*zeh neheneh ve-zeh lo haser*). The circumstance that *B* suffers no loss as a result of *A*'s subletting activity, however, is not a saving factor when *A* did not have permission to sublet the apartment to *C*, as would be the case when *C*'s household was larger than *A*'s. In that case, *A* must surrender the rent differential to *B* based on the principle that it is unconscionable to do business with someone else's asset.[14]

A minority interpretation of R. Yose's dictum is expressed by R. Ephraim b. Aaron Navon (Constantinople, 1677–1735). Disgorgement, in R. Navon's view, is called for only when the following two conditions obtain: (1) the defendant's commercialization of the plaintiff's property was unauthorized; and (2) the plaintiff suffered a loss as a result of the unauthorized use of his property. Understanding this to be the position of *Nimmukei Yosef*, R. Navon posits that the subletting case speaks of the instance where *A* rents an apartment from *B* below its market value and then sublets it to *C* at a higher price. Here, *A* bears a responsibility to surrender the differential to *B* if the subletting was illegal. If *A* was, however, within his rights to sublet the apartment to *C*, Halakhah does not compel *A* to surrender the rent differential to *B*, even though *A* makes a profit by conducting business with *B*'s asset.[15]

What proceeds from the mainstream explication of R. Yose's view is that the prohibition against doing business with someone else's asset applies even when the owner of the asset sustains no loss on account of the unauthorized use. The critical factor underlying the prohibition is that the owner did not give permission to use his asset. Application of R. Yose's dictum to the practice of naked short selling indicates that naked short selling of a company's stock is prohibited even if we cannot point to a definite loss that the shareholders of the company will suffer as a result of the practice.

Vanilla Variety of Short Selling

In contrast to naked short selling, in the vanilla variety of short selling, the seller borrows stock from a brokerage firm's inventory or the margin accounts of the firm's clients. Since the obligation of the short seller to the owner of the stock is only to return the stock that was borrowed, selling the stock does not constitute doing business with someone else's asset. Nevertheless, in evaluating the ethics of short selling, the motive of the short seller is most relevant. Let's consider a number of scenarios.

OVERVALUED STOCK

In one scenario, the seller believes that the stock of the company he is selling short is overvalued. Examination of the company's financial statements may convince the seller that the earnings of the company are not sustainable and are headed lower. The red flags may include a growth in accounts receivable at a rate much faster than the growth in revenue, the listing of nonrecurring earnings as ordinary revenue, capitalization of routine expenses, the failure of the company to meet its strategic goals as set out in its previous financial reports, and the arrival of new competition on the scene.[16]

In this scenario, the short sale is consummated because the counterparties have opposing opinions regarding the prospects of the stock. To be sure, one party may have superior information, but if the relevant information is publicly available, the ethics of the transaction should not be put to question.[17]

PROFITING ON THE DISCOVERY OF FRAUD BY SELLING SHORT—U.S. LAW

The motivation for short selling is not always the conviction that the stock that is sold short is overvalued. The driving force behind the transaction might instead be a conviction that the issuer of the stock is guilty of outright fraud. What follows is a description of a famous insider trading case, *Dirks v. SEC*, 463 U.S. 646 (1983). Our discussion will be confined to the aspects of the case that involve short selling.

Raymond Dirks, an investment analyst who specialized in the insurance industry, discovered that Equity Funding Corporation of America (Equity Funding), a publicly traded insurance company, was engaged in massive fraud. The fraud consisted of selling partnerships in non-existent real estate and writing fictitious insurance policies that vastly overstated the company's assets. Dirks first learned of the fraud from a former employee of Equity Funding, Ronald Secrist. Dirks then investigated Secrist's allegations by interviewing officers and employees of Equity Funding, several of whom corroborated the fraud charges. Although Dirks did not personally trade on the insider information, he shared it with his clients and other investors.[18] Those who took advantage of Dirks' tip by selling short or purchasing put options on Equity Funding stock profited handsomely when the scandal broke and the price of the stock plummeted.[19]

Invoking the parity of information doctrine, the Securities and Exchange Commission (SEC) censured Dirks for selectively disclosing the insider information he had obtained.[20] Under that doctrine, any person who knows or should know that the information he possesses is insider information must either publicly disclose the information or abstain from both personally trading on it and tipping others.[21] The censure was upheld by the Court of Appeals for the D.C. Circuit.[22]

On appeal, the Supreme Court reversed the censure. In rejecting the SEC's judgment, the Supreme Court insisted that the disclose-or-abstain rule cannot be invoked when its operation would exert an inhibiting influence on the role of market analysts. Holding Dirks culpable for his behavior would discourage other analysts from conducting similar investigations in the future. One way to encourage investigations to ferret out fraud is to afford investment analysts a property right in their disclosures, thereby permitting them to reap the profits of their labor.[23]

Proceeding from the *Dirks* case is the notion that U.S. federal securities law finds no fault with short selling when the transaction is motivated by the seller's desire to profit from the discovery of fraud.

PROFITING ON THE DISCOVERY OF FRAUD BY SELLING SHORT—JEWISH LAW

From the standpoint of Jewish law, the key issue for analyzing the ethics of short selling when the motive is to profit from the discovery of fraud is the disclosure duty. In Jewish law, the seller is obligated to disclose in a forthright manner[24] all the flaws of his product or service.[25] Short selling stock in a company that the seller knows is guilty of fraud is in every way identical to selling merchandise that the seller knows is defective without disclosing the defects upfront to the buyer. The rule here is that if an undisclosed flaw is material, the transaction is null and void.[26]

In the case of short sales of Equity Funding stock, if the counterparties to the sellers in those transactions had been aware of the widespread fraud in Equity Funding, they would never have entered into the transactions. Those short sales should therefore be declared null and void.

Since trading on the knowledge of fraud in Equity Funding is in every way identical to selling defective merchandise, advising an investor to unload or sell short Equity Funding stock based on insider information amounts to advising the investor to defraud the counterparty to the sale. Dirks' conduct hence violates the Biblical prohibition against proffering ill-suited advice (*lifnei ivver*).[27]

Because selective disclosure here entails the violation of a Biblical prohibition,[28] Halakhah, unlike the Supreme Court in the *Dirks* case, would not afford Dirks a property right in his discovery. The determination of the permissible course of conduct for Dirks requires an analysis of the parameters for engaging in whistle-blowing in both Jewish and non-Jewish society. Elsewhere we have dealt with these issues.[29]

Short Selling a Competitor's Stock

In his treatment of short selling, Karl Muth points out that there are no laws that prohibit a short sale of a competitor's stock.[30] Because the practice is rare and the business community finds it reprehensible, Muth believes that legislating against the practice is unnecessary.[31]

From the perspective of Jewish law, short selling a competitor's stock is not just a matter of public opinion, but rather is prohibited by law. The case against this practice begins with the following explication of the parameters of "fair competition" in Jewish law:

> R. Huna [d. 296] said: "If a resident of an alley sets up a hand mill [for commercial purposes] and another resident of the alley wants to set up one next to him, the first has the right to stop him, because he can say to him: 'You are interfering with my livelihood.'"
>
> R. Huna b. Joshua said: "It is quite clear to me that the resident of one town can prevent the resident of another town [from establishing a competing outlet in his town]. But if he [i.e., the outsider] pays the poll tax to that town, one cannot prevent him [from establishing a competing outlet in the town]. A resident of an alley cannot prevent another resident of the same alley [from establishing a competing outlet in the alley]."

> R. Huna b. Joshua then raised the question: "Can the resident of one alley prevent the resident of another [alley in the same town from competing with him]?" This question remains unresolved.[32]

Talmudic decisors rule in accordance with R. Huna b. Joshua's view.[33] What follows from this advocacy of freedom of entry is that an established firm is entitled to protection against intrusion into its territory only when the potential entrant is an out-of-town tradesman who does not pay taxes in the complainant's town. Given the unresolved entry status of a resident of a different alley in the same town, the Jewish court would not enjoin that resident from entering the complainant's alley.[34] In contemporary society, rabbinical courts in Israel have understood the modern "neighborhood" to correspond to the Talmudic "alley."[35]

To ascertain the position Jewish law takes with respect to short selling a competitor's stock, we need only probe into the underlying rationale behind R. Huna b. Joshua's normative view. Preliminarily, let's note that the Talmud finds support for R. Huna b. Joshua's freedom of entry position in an earlier anonymous *Tannaic* opinion recorded in a *Baraita*.[36]

Commenting on this *Tannaic* position, R. Meir b. Todros ha-Levi Abulafia (*Ramah*, Spain, ca. 1180–1244) offers two different rationales for why an established firm (S_1) cannot block a resident of its neighborhood (S_2) from setting up a competing business in the same neighborhood. One rationale is that S_2 can "turn the tables" on S_1 and say: "You operate your business on your premises, and I operate my business on my premises; I need not be concerned about your livelihood, and you need not be concerned about my livelihood." In the second rationale R. Abulafia offers, S_2's argument begins the same way but disarms S_1's claim of loss by saying that S_2 takes away nothing from S_1: "Whatever Heaven has decided for each of us in the form of livelihood we will get [and no more]."[37]

Notice that the common denominator of the two rationales is that S_2 is generating livelihood activities for himself on *his own premises*. What can be inferred is that S_2's competition with S_1 is not legitimate if S_2 generates livelihood activities for himself on S_1's premises. Consider that short selling is accomplished when S_2 borrows the shares of one of the owners of S_1 and immediately sells these shares with the expectation of buying them back at a lower price. The short sale hence generates profit for S_2 not by increasing sales on S_2's own premises, but rather by using an asset of S_1. S_2's short sale is therefore tantamount to competing with S_1 by operating on S_1's premises.

R. Yaakov Yeshayahu Bloi dealt with an analogous case: S_2 marketed his product by making use of S_1's trademark. Given that the trademark is an economic asset of S_1, albeit an intangible one, S_2's infringement of the trademark makes him guilty of effectively conducting business on S_1's premises.[38]

One could argue that the analogy is valid only if the volume of S_2's short selling is sufficiently large to affect S_1's stock price. Refuting this argument, however, is the recognition that what makes for the prohibition against conducting business on a competitor's premises or infringing a competitor's trademark is not the success or failure of the tactic to generate additional revenues for S_2 but rather the utilization of a rival's asset to generate income for oneself. Accordingly, suppose S_2 assesses that a new product that he developed will enable him to capture additional market share at the expense of S_1. To further capitalize on his predicted increase in market share, S_2 sells S_1's stock short. Notwithstanding that market forces are responsible for driving down S_1's share price, S_2 may not use S_1's assets to gain additional revenue in his competition with S_1.

Short Selling that Entails Creating a False Impression or Proffering Ill-Suited Advice

Another ethical issue for short selling obtains when a broker advises a client to buy a particular security when the broker's firm is simultaneously taking a short position in a derivative of that security. A case in point is a trading strategy that the Goldman Sachs Group, Inc. (Goldman) adopted in 2007. The strategy consisted of a trading activity conducted by two departments at the firm that reflected opposite expectations regarding the direction of housing prices.

In 2007, Goldman's mortgage department promoted collateralized debt obligations (CDOs) to its clients. These CDOs were entitlements to the income generated by a pool of subprime mortgages. If home prices would rise or interest rates would fall, the price of the CDOs would rise. At the same time, the firm's structured products trading group purchased credit default swaps (CDSs). These financial instruments entitled insurers to collect a premium in exchange for guaranteeing payment on mortgage-backed securities if the borrowers defaulted on their obligations. When the rate of foreclosures increased in 2007, insurers naturally demanded a higher premium to insure mortgage-backed securities, and the value of the CDSs held by Goldman rose.

In a nutshell, Goldman's mortgage division was essentially predicting to its customers that home mortgage prices would rise, while the firm's structured products group was betting on a decline in housing prices. In 2007, Goldman suffered losses of approximately $2 billion on its CDO portfolio, but earned a sizable profit for the year because it made a $4 billion profit on its trading in CDSs.[39]

This trading strategy of Goldman violates Jewish business ethics. Consider that investors were naturally attracted to CDOs because the credit rating agencies assigned a triple-A rating to 80% of the tranches of the CDOs.[40] Goldman's brokers presumably emphasized this point to any hesitant investor. In addition, the issuer of a CDO typically retains the equity tranche, and thereby absorbs the "first hit" if default rates exceed expectations.[41] These factors convincingly communicate to the investing public that Goldman truly believes in its own recommendation to invest in CDOs and that home prices will continue to rise. But the public's reasonable expectations are dashed because Goldman's structured products division is at the same time betting that housing prices will decline. Accordingly, Goldman's sale of CDOs to the investing public amounts to proffering ill-suited advice (*lifnei ivver*).[42] In addition, Goldman's brokers are guilty of making sales based on the creation of a false impression (*geneivat da'at*).[43]

Short Selling and the Prohibition of *Avak Ribbit*

Jewish law forbids the exaction of interest by a creditor and the payment of interest by a debtor in a loan between Jews. These laws are called the prohibition against *ribbit* (interest payments). The prohibition on a Biblical level, called *ribbit ketzutzah* (lit., prearranged *ribbit*), is violated only in the context of a loan transaction, and here only if the *ribbit* is stipulated in advance[44] or as a condition to extend the maturity date.[45]

By rabbinical enactment, the *ribbit* interdict is considerably expanded. These extensions are called *avak ribbit* (lit., the dust of *ribbit*).[46] The *avak ribbit* law that is relevant here is Jewish law's treatment of a commodity loan that calls for repayment in kind rather than in cash. The prohibition against entering into this type of commodity loan is referred to in the rabbinical literature as *se'ah be-se'ah*.[47] What follows are the details of this prohibition.

Out of fear that the market value of the commodity that is lent may increase by the time of repayment, the Sages prohibited commodity loans in kind.[48] The prohibited agreement places the creditor at a disadvantage. Specifically, if the price of the commodity appreciates by the time repayment is due, the debt may not be discharged through payment in kind. Instead, a cash payment is required, with the debtor's obligation set equal to the value of the commodity at the time the loan was entered into. If, on the other hand, the commodity depreciates in value, payment must be made in kind rather than in cash.[49]

Since the *se'ah be-se'ah* transaction is prohibited only by dint of the rabbinical law of *avak ribbit* rather than Biblical law, the Sages suspended their interdict under certain conditions.

One circumstance that may suspend the *se'ah be-se'ah* interdict occurs when the commodity trades at a definite market price (*yatza ha-sha'ar*). With repayment in kind possible at any time, the borrower is regarded as being capable of discharging his debt by purchasing the requisite commodity before it appreciates in value above its value at the time the transaction was entered into.[50] Legitimacy is given to this mechanism even when the borrower lacks the necessary cash to make the commodity purchase because the borrower is regarded as capable of making the purchase by establishing a line of credit.[51]

Another circumstance that frees the commodity loan from *avak ribbit* is the mechanism of *yesh lo* (lit., he has). If the borrower has in his possession some amount of the commodity he is borrowing, the commodity loan is permissible. The rationale here is that we regard the amount of the commodity in the borrower's possession as if it were given immediately to the lender as payment at the time the loan was entered into. Any subsequent appreciation in the value of the commodity is therefore regarded as having occurred while the commodity was in the domain of the lender.[52]

The *yesh lo* leniency extends even to the case where the quantity of the commodity in the debtor's possession at the time of the loan amounts to only a small portion of the loan. Since the *se'ah be-se'ah* loan is prohibited only because of *avak ribbit*, the *yesh lo* exemption is available even when the factual predicate for its rationale is only partially satisfied.[53]

Another aspect of the above leniency is that the "small portion" criterion is met even if the borrower acquires the small amount of the commodity just before the commodity loan is entered into, and acquires this small portion from the very person who will be extending the loan.[54]

When the *se'ah be-se'ah* transaction is legitimized by the *yesh lo* mechanism, ideally both parties should be aware that the borrower has some amount of the loan commodity in his possession at the time the transaction is entered into and that this circumstance is what legally validates their agreement. If, however, the parties entered into the transaction without awareness of either of these facts, the borrower may still return the loan commodity, even if it has appreciated in value.[55]

Since a short sale entails a commitment on the part of the borrower to pay back the stock loan in kind and not in cash, the short sale falls clearly within the ambit of the *se'ah be-se'ah* transaction. The issue therefore becomes whether the short sale can be legitimized by either the *yatza ha-sha'ar* or *yesh lo* mechanism. Let's begin with *yatza ha-sha'ar*.

Because securities are actively traded in the financial markets today, the *yatza ha-sha'ar* mechanism apparently provides a ready means of freeing the short sale from the *se'ah be-se'ah* prohibition. The interpretation of *yatza ha-sha'ar* by the *Rishonim*, however, casts doubt on the applicability of this approach to the problem at hand.

Clarification of the concept of *yatza ha-sha'ar* is found in connection with the futures contract. *A*'s commitment to deliver a commodity to *B* over a period of time in exchange for *B*'s prepayment of the order is ordinarily prohibited. Out of fear that the market price of the commodity will increase over the delivery period, the commitment to deliver is viewed as a disguised interest premium in exchange for the prepayment. Accepting prepayment for future delivery when the market price of the commodity is established at the time the contract is entered into is, however, permitted. With the commodity available in the market for purchase at the stipulated price, *A* is regarded as capable of making immediate delivery to *B* before the commodity has a chance to appreciate in value. Subsequent delivery of the commodity at a time when the commodity is traded at a higher price is therefore not regarded as a disguised interest premium.[56]

The operation of the grain market in Talmudic times illustrates *yatza ha-sha'ar*. In the beginning of the harvest season, only a few producers put their grain on the market. At this very early stage, the preponderance of the current crop of grain was not yet on the market, and the price obtained by the few sellers who placed their grain on the market was not stable. The market price for grain was not established until the entire supply was on the market.[57] This occurred sometime later and was identified with *dormus*, the price of the central market located in a big city where large quantities of grain were sold.[58] In this vein, R. Josiah b. Joseph Pinto (Damascus, 1565–1648) posits that the salient feature of *yatza ha-sha'ar* is stability. An established price, according to R. Pinto, is a price that holds for two or three months.[59] R. Hananel b. Hushiel (*Rabbeinu Hananel*, North Africa, 11th cent.) and R. Yom Tov Ishbili (*Ritva*, Spain, ca. 1250–1330) also define *yatza ha-sha'ar* in terms of price stability, though without mention of a specific time window.[60]

Thus, *yatza ha-sha'ar* is not a validating mechanism unless the stability test is met. Given the daily volatility of the prices of current financial instruments, it is doubtful whether *yatza ha-sha'ar* is operative in any of the financial markets today.

Technological advances in transportation and communications have considerably widened the marketplace. Consequently, hardly any price is free from the possibility of sudden change on account of the vicissitudes of aggregate supply and demand factors. Noting this phenomenon, R. Ezra Batzri (Israel, contemp.) posits that all prices today, with the exception of those under government control, are inherently unstable and should therefore not be considered well defined.[61]

While the *yatza ha-sha'ar* mechanism does not work to free the short sale from the *se'ah be-se'ah* prohibition, the *yesh lo* mechanism, discussed earlier, accomplishes this objective. What is needed to free the short sale from *avak ribbit* is for the short seller to be in possession of some small number of shares of stock of the company he wants to sell short before executing his trade. Given that the "small portion" criterion is met even if the portion is acquired from the very person who will be making the commodity loan, this condition can easily be satisfied in the organized financial markets today.

In addition, to satisfy the requirements of *yesh lo*, ideally both the short seller and the shareholder that is lending the short seller the stock should be aware that the short seller is in possession of some number of shares of the company and that this factor legitimizes the short sale. As discussed earlier, however, this condition is not indispensable.[62]

Short Selling and Efficient Markets

In this section, we present the economic case that short selling fosters stability and efficiency in the financial markets. We then proceed to show that the establishment of stabilization policy is a role Jewish law assigns to the government. Proposals to limit the types of short selling that Jewish law does not find objectionable should therefore be evaluated on the basis of whether those proposals help or hinder stabilization policy.

The case that short selling promotes efficiency begins with the notion that an efficient market is defined as a market in which prices fully reflect all available information. The efficient price of a security hence reflects the fundamental value of the security. Under the assumption that individual investors hold different beliefs about a security's prospects, the price of the security will be determined in the open market by investor bets that are driven by heterogeneous expectations. Optimists ("bulls") bet by taking long positions, while pessimists ("bears") bet by taking short positions. Consider that counted among the bears are those who do not own a particular security because they believe that the prospects of the security are dim. Prohibiting or imposing constraints on short selling hence obstructs the ability of relatively pessimistic investors to place their bets in the marketplace.[63]

Moreover, it may very well be that bears derive their pessimism from better information than the investing public as a whole. If this is so, average bear expectations would most efficiently reflect all available information.[64]

Constraints on short selling are hence likely to inflate prices of securities above their fundamental value. Under the assumption that markets cannot sustain inaccurate prices, constraints against short selling would likely lead to undue volatility. In addition, evidence shows that constraints on short selling decrease the speed at which prices adjust to reflect bad news. Finally, consider the impact that constraints on short selling have on the influence of "noise traders" on market price. Noise traders, who are much more likely to be bulls rather than bears, act on market momentum, misinformation, or poor strategy. Because noise traders are activated based on momentum, their trading contributes very significantly to the formation of market bubbles. Sophisticated short sellers are therefore needed to rein in noise traders and prevent bubbles.[65]

Underscoring the importance of having in place mechanisms to tame bubbles is the recognition that the bursting of a bubble in a particular market can at times ramify into a pandemic condition for financial markets in general and bring on a severe recession. A case in point is the global recession that began in December 2007, which, as of this writing, continues. Standing at ground zero of this severe downturn was the bursting of the housing bubble. When the housing bubble began in 2003, an investor who perceived that a bubble was in progress had no way to express this opinion other than by selling his home, which is a drastic step. In the opinion of Robert Shiller, a leading economist, if a home-price futures market had existed, the housing bubble would have been tamed and the ensuing catastrophic consequences would have been avoided. The availability of a futures market in home prices of single-family residences would have given any skeptic anywhere in the world the ability to sell real estate short. A declining home-price futures market would have signaled home builders to scale back construction and thus avert the huge construction boom and bust that accompanied the housing bubble.

The potential for the development of a home-price futures market has existed since 1987 with the introduction of the S&P/Case-Shiller Home Price Index. This index provides a measure of price appreciation across 20 different metropolitan areas. In May 2006, the Chicago Mercantile Exchange created a single-family home-price futures market and made the S&P/Case-Shiller Home Price Index the trading instrument.[66]

Short Selling and the Stabilization Role Jewish Law Assigns Government

From the standpoint of Jewish law, the introduction of a futures market for home prices is a very welcome event. This is so because Jewish law assigns government the role of crafting and implementing stabilization policy.

The case for assigning government a stabilization role begins with an analysis of the charity duty in Jewish law. We begin by taking note that the charity duty is set out twice, first in Leviticus and again in Deuteronomy:

> If your brother near you becomes poor and cannot support himself, you shall maintain him; and he shall live with you, even when he is a resident alien (Leviticus 25:35).
>
> If one of your brothers is in need in any community of yours within your country that the Lord your God is giving you, you must not harden your heart nor close your hand against your needy brother. Rather, open, you shall open your hand to him, and grant, you shall grant him, enough for his lack that is lacking for him. . . . Give, you shall give him, and let your heart not feel bad when you give him, for because of this matter, Hashem, your God, will bless you in all your deeds and in your every undertaking (Deuteronomy 15:7–8, 10).

The repetition of the charity duty is taken by R. Hayyim Soloveitchik (Russia, 1853–1918) to convey that the duty has a dual aspect. In R. Soloveitchik's view, the passage from Deuteronomy is directed to the individual, while the passage from Leviticus is directed to society as a collective.[67] Within the dual system, the public sector uses its coercive powers to establish social welfare programs.[68]

If the public sector's anti-poverty role is rooted in the Leviticus passage, its function extends beyond poverty relief. Consider that *Torat Kohanim* interprets the phrase "you shall maintain him," which appears in the Leviticus passage, to establish that charity in its noblest form consists of aiding a struggling individual from falling into the throes of poverty. The position of such an individual must be stabilized, with his dignity preserved, by conferring upon him a gift, extending him a loan, entering into a business partnership with him, or creating a job for him.[69]

The lesson of *Torat Kohanim* can be generalized to say that poverty prevention stands at a higher priority than poverty relief. The implication for the public sector's management of the economy can best be seen by the distinction between automatic stabilizers[70] and discretionary monetary and fiscal policy.

Automatic stabilizers entail the adoption of a program that will automatically act as a countervailing force when the economy either goes into a tailspin or becomes overheated. One example of an automatic stabilizer is the progressive income tax. In a progressive income tax, the tax rate increases as income increases. On the aggregate level, this means that as income rises, the government will take an increasingly larger fraction of the economy's income in the form of taxes. This increased taxation reduces the inflationary pressures otherwise engendered by the additional spending that accompanies a rise in income. Similarly, if the economy experiences a downturn, the government will take an increasingly smaller percentage of the economy's income in the form of taxes, reducing the drop in spending that would otherwise occur as a result of the decline in income.

Another example of an automatic stabilizer is government unemployment benefits. Once this program is in place, it will automatically result in increased benefits as a downturn worsens. At the same time, if the economy is expanding and the ranks of the unemployed are diminishing, the spending emanating from government unemployment benefits will diminish and hence moderate inflationary pressures.

Discretionary policies are new government initiatives designed to stimulate or slow down the economy, depending on whether the predominant economic condition is recession or inflation. On the fiscal side, if the malaise is inflation, the government will legislate an increase in taxes or a reduction in spending. On the monetary side, for these same conditions, the Federal Reserve will engineer either an increase or decrease in interest rates, as conditions require. More often than not, automatic stabilizers will prove unequal to the task and must be supplemented with discretionary fiscal and monetary policies.

Given that the practice of short selling has the effect of taming bubbles in the financial markets, legalizing short selling is an aspect of the government's arsenal of anti-bubble mechanisms, which is part of its duty to adopt measures to prevent poverty.

One practical implication of Jewish law's favorable attitude toward short selling, other than the abusive types discussed above, is that proposals to curtail short selling should be evaluated only on the basis of efficiency. In this vein, let's consider the SEC's former "uptick rule," Rule 10a–1.

Rule 10a–1 provided that traders may sell a security short only at a price that is above the last sale price for that security (an "uptick") or at a price equal to the last sale price for the security if that last price was itself an uptick.[71] The rule was designed to allow short selling in an advancing market but prevent short selling from either driving prices downward or accelerating downward price moves in a declining market.

From the standpoint of promoting efficient pricing in the financial markets, the uptick rule fails as a regulatory measure. This is so because even during a declining market, short selling in a security increases efficiency by facilitating price movements towards the market's perception of the true value of the security.

In light of both the general inefficiency of the uptick rule and the growing sentiment that short selling generally does not pose unique risks to the market, the SEC adopted a pilot program in 2004 to test repealing the uptick rule,[72] and eliminated the rule in 2007.[73]

Conclusion

Our investigation of the phenomenon of short selling has demonstrated that Jewish law generally finds no moral issue with this type of trade in the financial markets. The key here is that the short seller accomplishes the sale by first borrowing the shares that he sells, hoping to make a profit by buying them back at a lower price. Nonetheless, when motivated by the seller's desire to capitalize on the discovery of fraud in the company whose stock is sold short, the short sale is unethical because it amounts to selling defective merchandise without apprising the buyer upfront of the defects in the merchandise. Disgorgement of the ill-gotten profits is indicated in that case.

Another objectionable case is short selling a competitor's stock. This conduct amounts to conducting business for oneself on the premises of the competitor.

Yet another objectionable case obtains when a broker advises a client to buy a particular security while the broker's firm is taking a short position in a derivative of that security. What is objectionable here is not the short trade per se, but the lack of proper disclosure in the broker's dealings with his customer.

Finally, in inter-Jewish transactions, the short sale violates *avak ribbit* law. Legitimizing the transaction can easily be achieved through the *yesh lo* mechanism.

In both secular and Jewish law, naked short selling is prohibited. Since the naked short sale is accomplished without first borrowing the stock that is sold, the basis of the objection to this type of trade in Jewish law is the prohibition against conducting business for oneself with someone else's assets.

Lastly, we considered an argument in favor of allowing the practice of short selling in the financial markets. This is the argument that short selling accelerates the integration of bad news into the pricing of financial assets. Short selling hence keeps the emergence of bubbles under control. A case in point is the desirability of having in place an organized exchange where a trader can sell real estate short. Had a financial futures market for home prices been in place when the housing bubble started in 2003, the housing bubble might not have grown to the huge levels it did. Accordingly, the severity of the downturn when the bubble finally burst could have been modulated.

Notes

1. Statement of Richard S. Fuld, Jr. before the U.S. House of Representatives Committee on Oversight and Government Reform, October 6, 2008, 9–11.
2. SEC Regulation SHO, 17 C.F.R. § 242.203(b)(1) (2011).
3. Ibid., § 242.204.
4. In executing the short sale, Kurtz will have to pay a fee for borrowing the shares and reimburse the lender for any dividends he receives on the shares.
5. See Rules, By-Laws and Organization Certificate of the Depository Trust Company (June 2011), Rule 9(B).
6. Alexis Brown Stokes, "In Pursuit of the Naked Short," *New York University Journal of Law and Business* 5 (Spring 2009): 7.
7. The organized exchanges, such as the New York Stock Exchange and NASDAQ, compile a list of threshold securities. These lists are available on the websites of these organizations. Technically speaking, threshold securities are equity securities that have an aggregate fail-to-deliver position for five consecutive settlement days at a registered clearing agency of 10,000 shares or more, and that is equal to at least 0.5% of the issue's total shares outstanding. SEC Regulation SHO, 17 C.F.R. § 242.203(c)(6) (2011).
8. *Bava Metzia* 35b; R. Solomon b. Isaac (*Rashi*, France, 1040–1105), ad loc.
9. R. Asher b. Jehiel (*Rosh*, Germany, 1250–1327), *Bava Metzia* 3:5.
10. Mishnah, *Bava Metzia* 3:2.
11. R. Isaac b. Jacob Alfasi (*Rif*, Algeria, 1013–1103), *Bava Metzia* 35b–36a; Maimonides (*Rambam*, Egypt, 1135–1204), *Mishneh Torah, Sekhirut* 1:6; *Rosh, Bava Metzia* 3:5; R. Jacob b. Asher (*Tur*, Spain, 1270–1343), *Tur, Hoshen Mishpat* 307; R. Joseph Caro (Safed, 1488–1575), *Shulhan Arukh, Hoshen Mishpat* 307:5; R. Jehiel Michal Epstein (Belorus, 1829–1908), *Arukh ha-Shulhan, Hoshen Mishpat* 307:5.
12. *Rashba, Hiddushei ha-Rashba, Bava Kamma* 21a, ed. R. Eliyahu Lichtenstein (Jerusalem: Mossad HaRav Kook, 2008), 110.
13. *Rashba, Hiddushei ha-Rashba, Bava Metzia* 101a, ed. R. Eliyahu Lichtenstein (Jerusalem: Mossad HaRav Kook, 2006), 734–735.
14. R. Joseph ibn Habiba, *Nimmukei Yosef* to *Rif, Bava Kamma* 21a.
15. R. Ephraim b. Aaron Navon, *Mahaneh Ephraim, Sekhirut* 19.
16. Kathryn F. Staley, *The Art of Short Selling* (New York: John Wiley, 1997), 257–264.
17. For the ethics of trading on superior information when that information is publicly available, see Aaron Levine, *Case Studies in Jewish Business Ethics* (Hoboken, NJ: Ktav, 2000), 153–177.
18. *Dirks v. SEC*, 463 U.S. 646, 649–650 (1983).
19. Jonathan R. Macey, *Insider Trading: Economics, Politics, and Policy* (Washington, DC: AEI Press, 1991), 56.
20. Opinion of the Commission, Broker-Dealer Proceedings, Exchange Act Release No. 17480, 21 SEC Docket 1401 (January 22, 1981).
21. Securities Exchange Act of 1934, § 10(b); SEC Rule 10b–5; *SEC v. Texas Gulf Sulphur, Co.*, 401 F.2d 833, 848 (2d Cir. 1968).
22. *Dirks v. SEC*, 681 F.2d 824 (D.C. Cir. 1982).
23. *Dirks v. SEC*, 463 U.S. 646, 658–659 (1983).
24. For an exposition of this principle in general terms, see *Shulhan Arukh, Hoshen Mishpat* 232:8–9.
25. The seller's duty of disclosure applies even when the flaws are not material and the price is "fair" with respect to what the buyer actually receives. In the latter instance, the rationale behind the disclosure requirement is that nondisclosure causes the buyer to feel an unwarranted sense of indebtedness to the seller for the bargain that the buyer mistakenly thinks he received. A slight exception to this rule obtains in a face-to-face transaction where the defects can be ascertained through visual inspection. This would be the case, for example, if the object of transfer were an animal. Here, the seller is required to point out only the latent

defects, and the buyer is expected to detect the obvious defects himself. Accordingly, if the buyer demands cancellation of the deal based on his discovery of an obvious defect subsequent to the closing of the transaction, his claim lacks credibility. Instead, we take his silence at the close of the deal as acceptance of the defect. See *Shulhan Arukh, Hoshen Mishpat* 228:6, 232:4, 6–7; *Arukh ha-Shulhan, Hoshen Mishpat* 232:6–7; R. Yehudah Itach (Israel, contemp.), *Netiv Yosher: Hilkhot va-Halikhot Mekah u-Memkar* (Jerusalem, 1992), pp. 139–140.

26. *Tur, Hoshen Mishpat* 233; *Shulhan Arukh*, op. cit., 233:1; *Arukh ha-Shulhan*, op. cit., 233:1.
27. Leviticus 19:14; *Torat Kohanim*, ad loc.; *Mishneh Torah, Rotzeah u-Shemirat Nefesh* 12:14.
28. In addition to proffering ill-suited advice, Dirks' conduct violates the Biblical prohibition against talebearing (*rekhilut*) (Leviticus 19:16). For a discussion of this point, see Levine, *Case Studies*, 171–172.
29. See Aaron Levine, "Whistleblowing as Treated in Jewish Law," in *Whistleblowing: In Defense of Proper Action; Praxiology: The International Annual of Practical Philosophy and Methodology*, vol. 18, eds. Marek Arszułowicz and Wojciech W. Gasparski (New Brunswick, NJ: Transaction Publishers, 2011), 69–81.
30. Karl T. Muth, "The Fragile Armistice: The Legal, Economic, and Policy Implications of Trading in a Competitor's Stock," *Loyola University Chicago Law Journal* 40 (Spring 2009): 612–614.
31. Ibid., 621, 624, 641–642.
32. *Bava Batra* 21a.
33. *Rif, Bava Batra* 21b; *Tosafot, Bava Batra* 21b; *Mishneh Torah, Shekhenim* 6:8; *Rosh, Bava Batra* 2:12; *Tur, Hoshen Mishpat* 156; *Shulhan Arukh, Hoshen Mishpat* 156:5; *Arukh ha-Shulhan, Hoshen Mishpat* 156:6.
34. *Rif, Bava Batra* 21b; *Mishneh Torah, Shekhenim* 6:8; *Rosh, Bava Batra* 2:12; *Tur, Hoshen Mishpat* 156; *Shulhan Arukh, Hoshen Mishpat* 156:5; *Arukh ha-Shulhan, Hoshen Mishpat* 156:6.
35. See *Piskei Din shel Batei ha-Din ha-Rabbaniyyim bi-Yisrael*, vol. 6, ed. R. Dov Katz (Jerusalem: Weiss, 1966), 93; R. Nahum Rakover, *Halikhot ha-Mis'har: Hassagat Gevul Mis'harit be-Piskei ha-Din ha-Rabbaniyim, Sidrat Mehkarim u-Sekirot ba-Mishpat ha-Ivri* 41 (Jerusalem: Misrad ha-Mishpatim, 1976), 12.
36. *Tanna Kamma, Baraita, Bava Batra* 21b.
37. R. Meir b. Todros ha-Levi Abulafia, *Yad Ramah, Bava Batra* 21b.
38. R. Yaakov Yeshayahu Bloi, *Pit'hei Hoshen: Likkutim u-Ve'urim ba-Halakhah be-Hilkhot Geneivah u-Gezeilah va-Hassagat Gevul, Ona'ah u-Mekah Ta'ut* 9:11 (Jerusalem: Mechon L'Hoyroa, 1987), p. 280, n. 26.
39. Kate Kelly, "How Goldman Won Big on Mortgage Meltdown: A Team's Bearish Bets Netted Firm Billions; A Nudge from the CFO," *Wall Street Journal*, December 14, 2007: A1.
40. Mark Zandi, *Financial Shock: A 360° Look at the Subprime Mortgage Implosion, and How to Avoid the Next Financial Crisis* (Upper Saddle River, NJ: Pearson, 2009), 115.
41. See Sivan Mahadevan et al., *Structured Credit Insights: Instruments, Valuation and Strategies*, 3rd ed. (Morgan Stanley, 2007), 16. The size of the equity tranche relative to the total size of the transaction varies by the type of CDO issued. See ibid., 18; Douglas J. Lucas, Laurie S. Goodman, and Frank J. Fabozzi, *Collateralized Debt Obligations: Structures and Analysis*, 2nd ed. (Hoboken, NJ: Wiley, 2006), 34–35. As a result of U.S. federal securities legislation enacted in 2010, securitizers of CDOs are now generally required to retain at least 5% of the credit risk of the assets underlying the CDOs. See Dodd-Frank Wall Street Reform and Consumer Protection Act, Pub. L. No. 111–203, § 941, 124 Stat. 1891 (2010) (to be codified at 15 U.S.C. § 78o–11).
42. Leviticus 19:14; *Torat Kohanim*, ad loc.; *Mishneh Torah, Rotzeah u-Shemirat Nefesh* 12:14.
43. *Hullin* 94a. The Biblical source of the *geneivat da'at* interdict is disputed by Talmudic decisors. R. Jonah b. Abraham Gerondi (*Rabbeinu Yonah*, Spain, ca. 1200–1263) places this conduct under the rubric of falsehood (*sheker*). *Sha'arei Teshuvah* 3:184. R. Yom Tov Ishbili (*Ritva*, Spain, ca. 1250–1330), however, subsumes it under the Torah's admonition against theft (*lo tignovu*) at Leviticus 19:11. *Hiddushei ha-Ritva, Hullin* 94a, ed. R. Shiloh Raphael (Jerusalem: Mossad HaRav Kook, 2008), *tur* 127, s.v. "*ke-de-amar Shemuel.*" *Lo tignovu*

enjoins both theft of property and "theft of the mind" by means of deception. *Rashi* to *Hullin* 94b. For a discussion of the application of the *geneivat da'at* interdict to the subprime mortgage crisis, see Aaron Levine, "The Global Recession of 2007–2009: The Moral Factor and Jewish Law," in *The Oxford Handbook of Judaism and Economics*, ed. Aaron Levine (New York: Oxford University Press, 2010), 407–408.

44. R. Abraham Danzig (Prague, 1748–1820), *Hokhmat Adam* 131:1–2.
45. R. Shabbbetai b. Meir ha-Kohen (*Siftei Kohen*, Poland, 1621–1662), *Siftei Kohen* to *Shulhan Arukh, Yoreh De'ah* 166, n. 8; *Hokhmat Adam* 131:2.
46. R. Moses Isserles (*Rema*, Poland, 1525 or 1530–1572), *Rema* to *Shulhan Arukh, Yoreh De'ah* 161:1; *Hokhmat Adam* 131:3.
47. A *se'ah* is a unit of dry volume equal to 7.33 liters.
48. Mishnah, *Bava Metzia* 5:9; *Bava Metzia* 75a; *Rif*, ad loc.; *Mishneh Torah, Malveh ve-Loveh* 10:3; *Rosh, Bava Metzia* 5:75; *Tur*, op. cit., 162; *Shulhan Arukh*, op. cit., 162:1; *Hokhmat Adam* 134:1.
49. R. Sheshet, *Bava Metzia* 75a; *Rif*, ad loc.; *Mishneh Torah*, op. cit., 10:4; *Rosh*, op. cit., 5:74; *Tur*, op. cit.; *Shulhan Arukh*, op. cit.; *Hokhmat Adam*, op. cit.
50. *Bava Metzia* 72b; *Mishneh Torah*, op. cit., 10:1; *Rosh*, op. cit., 5:61; *Tur*, op. cit.; *Shulhan Arukh*, op. cit., 162:3; *Hokhmat Adam* 134:5.
51. *Mishneh Torah*, op. cit., 10:1; *Siftei Kohen* to *Shulhan Arukh*, op. cit., n. 10; *Hokhmat Adam*, op. cit.
52. R. Isaac, *Bava Metzia* 75a; *Rif*, ad loc.; *Mishneh Torah*, op. cit., 10:2; *Rosh*, op. cit., 5:75; *Tur*, op. cit.; *Shulhan Arukh*, op. cit., 162:2; *Hokhmat Adam* 134:2.
53. *She'elot u-Teshuvot ha-Rosh, kelal* 108:15; R. Vidal Yom Tov of Tolosa (*Maggid Mishneh*, Spain, ca. 1300–1370), *Maggid Mishneh* to *Mishneh Torah, Malveh ve-Loveh* 10:2, s.v. "*va-afilu hayesah*."
54. *Shulhan Arukh*, op. cit., 162:2; *Siftei Kohen* to *Shulhan Arukh*, ad loc., n. 8.
55. R. David b. Samuel ha-Levi Segal (*Turei Zahav*, Poland, ca. 1586–1667), *Turei Zahav* to *Shulhan Arukh*, op. cit., 162:2, n. 3; *Siftei Kohen* to *Shulhan Arukh*, op. cit., n. 7; R. Yaakov Yeshayahu Bloi, *Berit Yehudah: Likkutim u-Ve'urim la-Halakhah be-Hilkhot Ribbit ve-Iska*, 2nd ed. (Jerusalem, 1979), p. 317, ¶ 13.
56. Mishnah, *Bava Metzia* 5:7; *Bava Metzia* 72b; *Rif*, ad loc.; *Mishneh Torah, Malveh ve-Loveh* 9:1; *Rosh, Bava Metzia* 5:60; *Tur, Yoreh De'ah* 175; *Shulhan Arukh, Yoreh De'ah* 175:1; *Hokhmat Adam* 141:1–2.
57. *Rashi* to *Bava Metzia* 62b, s.v. "*ein poskin al ha-peirot*."
58. R. Assi, *Bava Metzia* 72b; *Rif*, ad loc.; *Mishneh Torah*, op. cit., 9:4; *Shulhan Arukh*, op. cit., 175:1. Another view in this matter is that a farmer may enter into a forward contract as soon as a market price becomes established in the local town. This price appears earlier than the *dormus* price, but is less stable. The latter view is taken by *Tur*, op. cit., 175, and *Rema* to *Shulhan Arukh*, op. cit., 175:1.
59. R. Josiah b. Joseph Pinto, quoted in R. Bezalel Ashkenazi (Egypt, 1520–ca. 1594), *Shitah Mekubbetzet, Bava Metzia* 72b.
60. R. Hananel b. Hushiel and R. Yom Tov Ishbili, quoted in *Shitah Mekubbetzet, Bava Metzia* 72b.
61. R. Ezra Batzri, *Dinei Mamonot*, 2nd ed., vol. 1 (Jerusalem: Machon ha-Ketav, 1990), p. 127, ¶ 3. R. Batzri's formulation is apparently identical to the criterion R. Yom Tov Ishbili's teachers set forth in the 13th century. R. Ishbili rejected this formulation. See *Shitah Mekubbetzet, Bava Metzia* 72b.
62. The *yesh lo* caveat yields a ready halakhic mechanism to engage in one type of short sale, called a "short against the box." In this short sale, the seller is in actual possession of the security that is sold short. Before 1997, both the desire to hedge an investment and defer tax on a gain in the investment provided the motivation for this type of transaction. See David M. Schizer, "Frictions as a Constraint on Tax Planning," *Columbia Law Review* 101 (2001): 1340–1345.

To illustrate a short sale against the box, suppose Phillip Safe purchased 1,000 shares of ASL stock on January 1, 2005, at a price of $50 per share. On December 31, 2005, the stock was trading at $70 per share. At this point, Safe feared that the price of the stock would decline and wanted to liquidate his investment. Safe had two choices: sell the stock immediately, or sell the stock short.

If Safe sold the stock immediately, his gain of $20 would have been subject to tax for the 2005 taxable year. If, however, Safe sold the shares short in 2005 and closed out both his long and short positions simultaneously in 2006, he would have locked in the $20 gain regardless of the movement in the price of the stock after the date of the short sale. Specifically, if the price of the stock increased, the loss Safe would have suffered on the short sale would have been offset by the gain on the sale of the ASL shares that Safe owned, producing a net gain of $20. For example, if the stock price rose to $80, Safe would have been required to cover the short position with stock worth $80, thereby suffering a loss of $10. At the same time, Safe would have sold his ASL shares with a cost basis of $50 for $80, recognizing a $30 gain. The net gain would thus have been $20. Similarly, if the price of the stock declined after the short sale, the loss Safe would have suffered on selling the ASL shares that he owned would have been offset by the gain he would have recognized on closing out the short sale.

Through the short sale against the box, Safe would have locked in the $20 gain in 2005 and, under prior law, shifted the related tax liability to 2006. The Taxpayer Relief Act of 1997 generally eliminated this tax deferral technique by treating the short sale against the box as an actual sale. See 26 U.S.C. § 1259.

63. Kevin A. Crisp, "Giving Investors Short Shrift: How Short Sale Constraints Decrease Market Efficiency and a Modest Proposal for Letting More Shorts Go Naked," *Journal of Business and Securities Law* 8 (Spring 2008): 140.
64. Lynn A. Stout, "Are Takeover Premiums Really Premiums? Market Price, Fair Value, and Corporate Law," *Yale Law Journal* 99 (1990): 1249.
65. Crisp, "Giving Investors Short Shrift," 141–142.
66. Robert J. Shiller, *The Subprime Solution: How Today's Global Financial Crisis Happened, and What to Do about It* (Princeton, NJ: Princeton University Press, 2008), 149–150.
67. Talmudic sources differ on whether the 10% charity obligation imposed by the Torah on agricultural produce applies to income as well. Opinions in the matter range from an income tithe requirement arising from Biblical law to one established by rabbinical edict. In his survey of the responsa literature, R. Ezra Batzri concludes that the majority opinion regards the 10% level as a definite obligation, albeit by dint of rabbinical decree. See *Dinei Mamonot*, vol. 1, p. 403. In any case, devoting less than 10% of one's income to charity is considered by the rabbis to reflect an ungenerous nature.

    An issue that requires clarification is the extent to which an individual may count government anti-poverty measures as fulfilling part of his 10% charity duty.
68. R. Hayyim Soloveitchik, quoted in the name of R. Joseph B. Soloveitchik by R. Daniel Lander, "*Be-Inyan Hiyyuv Dei Mahsoro*," in *Sefer Kevod ha-Rav: Kovetz Meyuhad le-Hiddushei Torah ve-Inyanei Halakhah*, eds. R. Moshe Sherman and R. Yosef Wolf (New York: Student Organization of Yeshiva Rabbi Isaac Elchanan Theological Seminary, 1984), 202–203.

    In Talmudic times, the public charity duty consisted of weekly collections for the communal charity box (*kuppah*) and daily collections for the communal charity plate (*tamhui*). In addition, a special charity drive was conducted before Passover to enable the poor to purchase unleavened bread for the holiday (*ma'ot hittin*). Another dimension of the public subsidy to the poor consisted of a compulsory hospitality scheme pursuant to which the townspeople were required to take turns providing lodging for guests.

    Widespread poverty forced many Jewish communities in the period of the *Rishonim* (mid-11th to mid-15th cent.) to abandon most of the above elements of public philanthropy in favor of private philanthropy. For a discussion of the public charity duty and related halakhic sources, see Aaron Levine, *Economics and Jewish Law* (Hoboken, NJ: Ktav, 1987), 125–126.

69. *Torat Kohanim* at Leviticus 25:35; *Mishneh Torah, Matanot Aniyyim* 10:7; *Arukh ha-Shulhan, Yoreh De'ah* 249:15.
70. The stabilization policies the Biblical Joseph implemented in Egypt may very well represent the first recorded instance of government use of an automatic stabilizer. Joseph predicted that the Egyptian economy would experience a period of seven years of plenty followed by seven years of famine. To survive the famine, Joseph imposed a 20% tax on the grain that was produced in the years of plenty and stored it in government granaries for future distribution when needed.

    To ensure an adequate food supply for the years of famine, a much more popular approach would have been to call for the government to purchase and store 20% of the crop in each of the years of plenty and sell this surplus during the years of famine. Herein lies Joseph's genius. Buying the grain, instead of taxing it, would have enormously increased the money supply during the years of plenty. This enormous increase in the money supply held in private hands would translate into a frenzied bidding up of the price level fueled by the many panic-stricken buyers. Compounding the depression, there would be inflation as well.
71. 17 C.F.R. § 240.10a–1(a)(1)(i).
72. SEC Regulation SHO, 17 C.F.R. § 242.202T, Exchange Act Release No. 50104 (July 28, 2004), 69 Fed. Reg. 48032 (August 6, 2004) (providing that the pilot would commence on January 3, 2005, and terminate on December 31, 2005); Exchange Act Release No. 50747 (November 29, 2004), 69 Fed. Reg. 70480 (December 6, 2004) (re-setting the pilot to commence on May 2, 2005, and end on April 28, 2006); Exchange Act Release No. 53684 (April 20, 2006), 71 Fed. Reg. 24765 (April 26, 2006) (extending the termination date of the pilot to August 6, 2007).
73. Exchange Act Release No. 55970 (June 28, 2007) (eliminating Rule 10a–1 and adding Rule 201). In response to the financial turmoil in 2008 and 2009, the SEC received comments requesting reinstatement of the uptick rule. In 2010, the SEC adopted an alternative uptick rule that imposes restrictions on short selling a security only when the price of the security declines in one day by 10% or more from the prior day's closing price. At that point, a short sale would be prohibited unless the sales price is above the current national best bid for the security. The restriction would apply only for the remainder of the day in which the restriction is triggered and the following day. SEC Regulation SHO, 17 C.F.R. § 242.201, Exchange Act Release No. 61595 (February 26, 2010).

GLOSSARY

ADAM HASHUV. Lit., a distinguished person. A locally recognized religious authority and communal leader.

ADJUSTED GROSS INCOME (AGI). Total gross income less certain deductions. Taxable income for U.S. federal income tax purposes is equal to AGI less personal exemptions and itemized deductions.

AGGADAH, (PL.) AGGADOT, (ADJ.) AGGADIC. Hebrew designation of a particular genre of rabbinic literature consisting mainly of exegesis of specific books of the Bible.

AMMA, (PL.) AMMOT. Common measure used in the Torah and the Talmud that is equivalent to 18 inches according to some scholars, and 22.9 inches according to others.

AMORA, (PL.) AMORAIM. Aramaic for "spokesman" or "interpreter." Generic terms for the rabbis of the post-Mishnaic period but prior to the redaction of the Gemara (ca. 200–500 C.E.).

APPLIED RESEARCH. Activity directed toward the creation of new and improved practical products and processes.

ASHKENAZ, (ADJ.) ASHKENAZI. Designation of the first area of settlement of Jews in Northwest Europe, initially on the banks of the Rhine. The term has evolved to take on the broader connotation of a cultural complex that had its beginnings in France and Germany in the second part of the 10th century, spread later to Poland-Lithuania, and in modern times finds adherents all over the world.

ASMAKHTA. An agreement that lacks the presumption of firm resolve on the part of the obligor or fails to generate a presumption of reliance on the part of the party to whom the commitment was made.

ASYMMETRIC INFORMATION. Unequal knowledge that each party to a transaction has about the other party.

AUTOMATIC STABILIZERS. Government spending, taxation, and transfer programs that automatically increase aggregate spending during economic downturns and decrease aggregate spending during periods of prosperity, without legislative action.

AVAK RIBBIT. Lit., the dust of *ribbit*. Violation of one of the rabbinical extensions of the Biblical prohibition against charging or receiving interest on a loan between Jews.

BA'ALEI BATIM. Householders.

BAIT AND SWITCH. The practice of enticing or "baiting" a potential customer with a misleading advertisement for a product and then persuading the customer to purchase a more expensive substitute product.

BARAITA. A teaching or tradition of the *Tannaim* that was excluded from the Mishnah and incorporated in a later collection complied by R. Hiyya and R. Oshaia.

BARZANYATA. Lit., announcer. A person hired by a wine merchant in Talmudic times to take barrels of wine into the street and announce that they were for sale.

BASIC RESEARCH. Activity directed toward the discovery of facts and data observed in repeated experiments. Also refers to the discovery of theories or relationships between facts.

BEAR. An investor or trader who expects prices to fall.

BEHEMAH DAKKAH. Lit., small cattle. Sheep and goats.

BEIT DIN. Jewish court of law.

BILATERAL MONOPOLY. A market that has only one seller and one prospective buyer. In this market, price and output will be determined based on the relative bargaining power of the two parties.

BLACK MARKET. An illegal market that violates rationing or price-control laws.

BULL. An investor or trader who expects prices to rise.

CARTEL. An agreement, often in writing, among independent producers to restrict output or prices, or to divide territories.

CHOLENT. Traditional Jewish stew, usually made of potatoes, meat, beans, and barley.

COASE THEOREM. The idea that, as long as property rights are clearly defined and enforced, bargaining between two parties can produce an efficient outcome without any further government intervention.

COLLATERALIZED DEBT OBLIGATION (CDO). A structured finance instrument consisting of a bond or note backed by a pool of fixed-income assets. Rights to cash flow from this pool, along with different levels of credit risk, are allocated to different classes or "tranches" of the instrument. Specific types of CDOs include collateralized bond obligations, collateralized loan obligations, and collateralized mortgage obligations.

COMPETITION. A market situation in which multiple sellers of a standardized product compete with each other for customers and in which free entry and complete information are available to all parties.

CONSEQUENTIALISM. The view that the value of an action derives entirely from the value of its consequences. Compare "Deontology."

CONSUMER SURPLUS. The difference between the maximum amount a consumer is willing to pay for a given quantity of a good and the amount actually paid.

COST–BENEFIT ANALYSIS. An appraisal analysis method that places values on all the benefits arising from a project and then compares the total value of the benefits with the total cost of the project.

CREDIT DEFAULT SWAP (CDS). A credit derivative pursuant to which a buyer agrees to pay a premium to a seller, who in return contracts to pay the buyer a much larger sum if a specified loan or bond defaults. A CDS is a form of insurance that protects the buyer of the CDS in the event of a loan default.

DARKHEI SHALOM. Lit., the ways of peace. Refers to the duty to end discord. To achieve this result, the use of lies is permitted under certain circumstances.

DARSHAN. One who delivers sermons.

DAVAR HA-AVUD. Circumstance in which a worker would cause a loss to his employer if the worker fails to give immediate attention to the job at hand.

DAVSHAH. Lit., treading. A Jewish law that provides that if one constructs a wall on his property, and his neighbor wants to build a wall nearby, the neighbor must distance his wall at least four *ammot* from the first wall. The rationale for the law is that if the distance between the walls is at least four *ammot*, pedestrians will not hesitate to walk between the walls, and this pedestrian traffic will harden the earth and thereby strengthen the foundations of the walls.

DEADWEIGHT LOSS. A measure of the aggregate loss in well-being of participants in a market attributable to an inefficient level of output in the market.

DEI MAHSORO. Lit., sufficient for his need. Judaism's charity obligation at Deuteronomy 15:8 to provide for the entire needs of the poor, both physical and psychological.

DEMAND. Desired quantity of a good or service by consumers in a market, usually dependent on price.

DEMAND CURVE. A graph illustrating the quantity of a good or service demanded at various prices, with all other variables held constant. Price is usually shown on the vertical axis, and quantity demanded on the horizontal axis. A demand curve typically slopes downward, reflecting that the number of units demanded declines as price rises.

DEONTOLOGY. A system of ethics under which the morality of an action is evaluated based on the action's adherence to a set of rules or duties, rather than on the consequences of the action. Compare "Consequentialism."

DERASHAH, (PL.) DERASHOT. Sermon.

DERIVED DEMAND. Demand for an input by producers that is determined by the demand for the final product the input is used to produce. For example, demand for grain is derived from the demand for bread.

DEVARIM SHE-BA-LEV. Unexpressed intentions.

DINA DE-MALKHUTA DINA. Lit., the law of the kingdom is the law. The halakhic rule that the secular law of the country is binding for disputes between Jews in civil matters.

DINAR, (PL.) DINARIM. A silver coin equivalent in value to a *zuz*.

DISEQUILIBRIUM PRICE. A price that is inherently unstable. At the disequilibrium price, supply exceeds demand, or demand exceeds supply.

DOMINANT FIRM MODEL. A market model in which the leader or dominant firm sets prices for the industry and the firm's rivals follow. Also referred to as the "price leadership model."

DORMUS. The price of grain in the central market of a big city where large quantities of grain are sold.

DTC. The Depositary Trust Company. A central depository institution that holds certificates on behalf of its members and facilitates the transfer of ownership by reducing the exchange of physical certificates between the parties.

EASEMENT. A right to use real property owned by another person.

ECONOMIC RENT. Return earned by a seller above opportunity cost when the good or service offered is temporarily in fixed supply.

ECONOMIES OF SCALE. The increase in efficiency of production as the number of goods produced increases. A firm that achieves economies of scale usually reduces its average cost per unit through increased production because fixed costs are spread over an increased number of goods.

EFFICIENCY. Achieving the maximum value of output from a given set of inputs, or achieving the desired output with a minimum cost of inputs.

EHAD BA-PEH VE-EHAD BA-LEV. Insincere speech. Concealing the true desires of one's heart in conversations with others.

ELASTIC DEMAND. Market demand that is relatively responsive to changes in price. The degree to which a firm's total revenue changes as a result of a change in price provides a measure of this responsiveness. If a reduction in price causes the number of units demanded to increase to a degree that the firm's total revenue increases, or an increase in price reduces the number of units demanded to a degree that the firm's total revenue decreases, the demand is characterized as "elastic."

EMET. Truth. One of the thirteen Divine attributes of mercy.

EPHAH. A measure of grain equal to approximately one bushel.

EQUILIBRIUM PRICE. The market price that clears the market. At the equilibrium price, the number of units suppliers want to offer for sale is equal to the number of units demanders want to buy. When factors influencing supply and demand other than price are stable, the market price will tend toward the equilibrium price.

EVYON. A destitute person.

EXCLUDABILITY. The ability to exclude those who do not pay for a good or service from consuming the good or service.

EXTERNALITY. A side effect of the action of an individual or entity on another individual or entity. An externality may be positive or negative.

FAIL TO DELIVER. A transaction that does not clear or effect settlement because the seller has not delivered the security to be sold.

FEDERAL RESERVE. The central bank of the United States.

FEDERAL TRADE COMMISSION (FTC). A U.S. federal agency that regulates interstate commerce. The FTC is responsible for formulating competition policy and maintaining competitive enterprise.

FISCAL POLICY. Government's efforts to use its spending, taxing, and debt-issuing authority to smooth out the business cycle and maintain full employment without inflation.

FORWARD CONTRACT. Risk-shifting technique by which a party sells a specified quantity of a product at the current price for future delivery.

FREE ENTERPRISE. A market characterized by limited government regulation of commercial activity.

FREE ENTRY. The ability for companies to enter an industry with relative ease; a condition of a competitive marketplace.

FREE RIDER. Anyone who receives a benefit from a good or service without having to pay for it.

FULL EMPLOYMENT. A situation in which everyone who is willing and able to work can find a job.

FUNDAMENTAL VALUE. The value of a security that is intrinsic to the security itself, rather than the book value or market value of the security. Fundamental value is ordinarily calculated by determining the present value of the future cash flows from the security. Also called "intrinsic value."

GEMARA. Aramaic for "completion" or "tradition." This term is popularly applied to the Talmud as a whole, or more particularly to the discussions and elaborations by the *Amoraim* on the Mishnah.

GEMIRAT DA'AT. A firm resolve to conclude an agreement.

GENEIVAT DA'AT. Conduct designed to deceive or create a false impression.

HALAKHAH, (PL.) HALAKHOT. Jewish law.

HANUPPAH. Flattery.

HAYYEI NEFESH. Essential food.

HAYYEI OLAM. Eternal life. The *hayyei olam* status of Torah study makes every lost moment of Torah study an irretrievable loss.

HAYYEI SHA'AH. Temporal life.

HAZAKAH. Prescriptive right. Generally refers to conduct that is presumed to continue because it has already occurred three times.

HAZAN. Term used in the Mishnah to refer to a *melammed tinokot*. In modern usage, the term means a cantor.

HEZEK RE'IYAH. Visual penetration of privacy.

HILLUL HA-SHEM. Lit., disgrace of the Name. Refers to an action that brings dishonor and disgrace to God.

HINNUKH. Education.

IMITATIO DEI. Lit., imitation of God. A behavioral ideal in Judaism to emulate God's attributes of mercy in our interpersonal conduct.

IMPERFECT COMPETITION. A market situation characterized by the existence of only a few sellers, with each seller enjoying a degree of leverage over its customers.

INELASTIC DEMAND. Market demand that is unresponsive to changes in price. If a firm's total revenue changes in the same direction as changes in its pricing, the demand the firm faces for its product is characterized as "inelastic."

INPUTS. Factors of production of goods and services. Inputs consist of land, labor, capital, and entrepreneurial ability.

INSIDER INFORMATION. Confidential relevant information about a company that has not yet been made public.

INVENTORY CYCLE. The amount of time it takes for a firm to generate earnings from the current stock of its product.

INVISIBLE HAND. The notion that when individuals pursue economic gain for their own self-interest, their actions are directed by an unseen force (an "invisible hand") to promote the general good of society. The expression is derived from Adam Smith's economic treatise, *An Inquiry into the Nature and Causes of the Wealth of Nations* (1776), and is a basis for *laissez-faire* economics.

IR. Town.

KABBELAN. A piece-worker hired to perform a specific task, with no requirement to work fixed hours.

KALDOR-HICKS CRITERION. State *A* is preferred to state *B* if those who gain from *A* can compensate those who lose and still be better off. Compensation here is hypothetical; the Kaldor-Hicks criterion suggests that *A* is preferable to *B* even if compensation is not actually paid.

KEHILLAH. Autonomous Jewish community.

KEREN. Lit., horn. Damage inflicted through an aberration in an animal's normal behavior, such as when the animal bites, kicks, or attacks with its horns.

KIDDUSH. Lit., sanctification. A blessing recited over wine or grape juice to sanctify the Sabbath and Jewish holidays. The term is also used to refer to a reception held in the synagogue or a congregant's home after the morning Sabbath or holiday prayers where the blessing over wine is recited and refreshments are served.

KIM LI. Lit., I am certain. A rule under Jewish law that allows a defendant in a civil proceeding to insist that the judges consider the merits of his case based on the opinion of a substantial minority legal opinion.

KINAT SOFERIM TARBEH HOKHMAH. Lit., jealousy between scribes increases wisdom. This dictum serves as a basis for allowing free entry of new teachers into a religious elementary school system.

KINKED DEMAND CURVE. A demand curve that is more elastic for an increase in price than for a decrease in price. A firm that expects its rivals to follow its pricing strategy only when it cuts price, but not when it increases price, faces a kinked demand curve.

KINYAN. Acquisition of legal rights by the performance of a symbolic act.

KINYAN SUDAR. A legal form of acquisition of objects or confirmation of agreements, executed by the handing of a scarf or any other article by one of the contracting parties (or one of the witnesses to the agreement) to the other contracting party as a symbol that the object itself has been transferred or the obligation assumed.

KOFIN. Lit., compel or force. Refers to the Jewish court's ability under certain circumstances to compel individuals to act in a particular manner.

KOHEN GADOL. High Priest.

KUPPAH. Communal charity box.

LAISSEZ FAIRE. An environment in which transactions between private parties are free from government intervention.

LASHON HA-RA. Lit., evil speech. Tale-bearing in which *A* delivers a damaging but truthful report regarding *B* to *C*, when *C* is neither the object of *B*'s mischief nor the intended target of *B*'s evil designs.

LEKH VA-SHUV. Lit., go and come back. Rabbinical extension of the Biblical prohibition of *lo ta'ashok* pursuant to which one may not unlawfully withhold another's property by using dilatory tactics.

LEKET. Gleanings. Biblical commandment at Leviticus 19:9 that if one or two stalks of grain slip out of the reaper's hand while harvesting them, they must be left to the poor. If three stalks fall together, the owner may retrieve them.

LEMON. A poor investment. Typically refers to a chronically defective car that cannot be repaired with a reasonable effort.

LIFNEI IVVER. Lit., before a blind person. Refers to the prohibition against proffering ill-suited advice. Also refers to the prohibition against causing those who are morally blind to stumble by giving them the means to sin.

LIVING WAGE. A minimum wage that is set above the prevailing federal or state wage and is typically indexed to a price index.

LIVING WAGE ORDINANCE (LWO). A local ordinance requiring city governments and firms doing business with city governments to pay workers a living wage.

LO TA'AMOD. Biblical commandment at Leviticus 19:16 that a bystander not remain idle when another individual is in a life-threatening situation.

LO TA'ASHOK. Biblical prohibition at Leviticus 19:13 against unjustly withholding that which is due one's fellow.

LO TALIN. Biblical prohibition at Deuteronomy 24:14–15 against withholding payment of a worker's salary.

LOCATE. Legal requirement that before executing a short sale of a security, a broker-dealer must borrow or arrange to borrow the security, or have reasonable grounds to believe that the security can be borrowed and delivered on the date delivery of the security is due.

LONG POSITION. A position held in securities, derivatives, commodities, or currencies that increases in value as the market price rises.

LONG RUN. A period of time in which a firm can vary all its inputs.

MA'OT HITTIN. Lit., wheat monies. Charitable collections made before Passover in Talmudic times to enable the poor to purchase unleavened bread for the holiday. In modern times, the term denotes collections of charitable donations to provide for all the needs of the poor at Passover.

MACROECONOMICS. Analysis dealing with the behavior of the economy as a whole with respect to output, income, prices, and unemployment. Compare "Microeconomics."

MAKHSHEREI OKHEL NEFESH. Food additives, such as cumin, spices, and pepper.

MANEH. A unit of currency equal to 100 *zuz*.

MARGIN ACCOUNT. An account established with a broker that allows the investor to purchase stock on margin by paying cash for part of the cost and borrowing the remainder from the broker.

MARGINAL COST. The additional cost incurred by producing one more unit of a good.

MARGINAL REVENUE. The addition to total revenue that will result from selling one more unit of a good.

MARGINAL UTILITY. The change in total utility from consuming an additional unit of a good.

MARKET BUBBLE. A systemic overvaluation of a market beyond that implied by historical precedent and fundamental analysis.

MAZEL TOV. Lit., good luck. Congratulations.

MEHILAH BE-TA'UT. Waiver made in error.

MEHUSAR EMUNAH. Untrustworthy person. Refers to a person who reneges on his commitment.

MEKAH TA'UT. Transaction concluded in error.

MEKOMO VE-SHA'TO. Lit., its place and its time. The requirement that property dedicated to the Sanctuary be sold for the benefit of the Sanctuary in the geographic area and the time period in which the dedication was made. According to the Sages, the *mekomo ve-sha'to* principle applies to monetary matters generally, such as in establishing the reference price for adjudicating an *ona'ah* claim.

MELAMMED TINOKOT. Teacher of Torah to children. Also called a "*hazan*" in the Mishnah.

MI SHE-PARA. A judicial imprecation imposed on a buyer or seller who retracts before a transaction is legally consummated but after the sales price has been paid. The formula for the imprecation is: "He who exacted punishment from the generation of the Flood and the generation of the Dispersion will exact punishment from one who does not stand by his word."

MICROECONOMICS. Analysis dealing with the behavior of individual elements of the economy, such as the price of a single product or the behavior of single consumer. Compare "Macroeconomics."

MIKRA. Scripture.

MIKVEH. Ritual bath house.

MINYAN. A quorum of ten men necessary for public synagogue services and certain other religious ceremonies.

MISHKAL HA-HASIDUT. Lit., weighing saintliness. The mental process of weighing each contemplated deed against its expected result and the circumstances surrounding its anticipated performance to determine whether the action is meritorious and therefore should be performed.

MISHNAH. Designates the collection of rabbinic traditions redacted by R. Judah ha-Nasi at the beginning of the 3rd century. The purpose of the Mishnah is to elaborate, systematize, and concretize the commandments of the Torah.

MITKABBED BE-KALON SHEL HAVERO. Elevating oneself at the expense of another person's degradation. A person who acts in such a manner is said to lose his share in the World to Come.

MITZVAH, (PL.) MITZVOT. A religious act or duty.

MONETARY POLICY. The policy of the central bank in exercising its control over money, interest rates, and credit conditions.

MONOPOLY. An industry in which there is only one supplier of a product for which there are no close substitutes.

MORTGAGE-BACKED SECURITIES. Securities that represent a claim on the cash flows from a pool of mortgage loans.

MOTZI SHEM RA. The utterance or spreading of a false statement harmful to another's character or reputation.

MU'AD. A forewarned animal. An animal that has demonstrated that it is habituated to attack people by attacking on three occasions. The owner of a forewarned animal that inflicts damage is liable for the full amount of the damages.

MUHZAK. The party to a dispute over an entitlement to money or property who is in possession of the money or property at the time of the dispute.

MULTIPLIER EFFECT. The process by which an increase in expenditure generates a disproportionately larger increase in national income as result of several rounds of consumption and investment.

MUM. Defect.

NAG'HAN. A vicious ox. Because the ox is a menace to society, it must be destroyed and may not be used for plowing.

NAKED SHORT SELLING. The practice of selling a security short without first borrowing the security or ensuring that the security can be borrowed.

NASDAQ. An American stock exchange. "NASDAQ" originally stood for National Association of Securities Dealers Automated Quotations.

NATURAL MONOPOLY. A market situation in which one firm can satisfy the entire demand of the economy at a lower cost than can a combination of multiple firms as a result of decreasing average long-run costs based on continued economies of scale.

NAZIR. A person who voluntarily took the vow described in Numbers 6:1–21. The vow required one to abstain from drinking wine, refrain from cutting the hair on one's head, and avoid coming into contact with a corpse.

NEGATIVE EXTERNALITY. An adverse side effect of economic activity.

NOISE TRADER. A trader whose investment decisions are irrational and erratic.

NORMAL PROFIT. The profit that obtains when total revenue equals total cost.

NOSEI BE-EMUNAH. Lit., doing business on trust. An exemption from the prohibition of *ona'ah* that generally obtains when the seller discloses upfront his cost and desired markup, and the buyer agrees to the markup.

NUISANCE. A use of property or course of conduct that interferes with the legal rights of others by causing damage, annoyance, or inconvenience.

OLIGOPOLY. A market model characterized by a small number of firms that produce either a homogeneous product or differentiated products, and that are strategically interdependent.

ONA'AH. Price fraud involving selling above or below the competitive norm.

ONA'AT DEVARIM. Conduct that causes needless mental anguish to others.

OPPORTUNITY COST. The value of the best alternative sacrificed when a choice is made.

OSHEK. Misappropriation of property that comes into one's possession with the consent of the owner of the property.

OUTPUT. Goods and services produced by a firm.

PARETO OPTIMALITY. A situation in which no reorganization or trade could increase the utility or satisfaction of one individual without reducing the utility or satisfaction of another individual. Compare "Kaldor-Hicks Criterion."

PARTY WALL. A wall that divides two adjoining, separately owned properties and is shared by the neighboring property owners.

PE'AH. Lit., corner. Biblical commandment at Leviticus 19:9 that the corner of the field be left unharvested as a gift for the poor.

PESEIDA DE-LO HADRA. Irretrievable loss. In Jewish law, an employer may dismiss an employee who causes him an irretrievable loss. A teacher of Torah who idles on the job is considered to cause an irretrievable loss.

PIGOVIAN TAX; PIGOUVIAN TAX. A tax levied on a market activity associated with negative externalities to correct the market outcome. In the presence of negative externalities, the social cost of a market activity generally exceeds the private cost of the activity. In that case, the market outcome is not efficient and the market tends to oversupply the product. A Pigovian tax in an amount equal to the negative externality is thought to correct the market outcome to be efficient.

PO'EL. A day laborer required to work fixed hours.

PRICE. The money cost of a good, service, or asset.

PRICE CONTROLS. The setting of maximum or minimum prices by law.

PRICE LEADERSHIP MODEL. See "Dominant Firm Model."

PRICE SETTER. A firm that sets the price of a good or service rather than accepting the market price as a given. A monopolist seller is typically a price setter. Also called a "price maker."

PRICE TAKER. A firm that treats market price as a given and beyond its control.

PROBEH. Tryout sermon.

PROGRESSIVE TAX. A tax whose rate increases as income increases. Under this system, those with a high income pay a greater percentage of their income as tax than do those with a lower income.

PURE PUBLIC GOOD. A good that lacks excludability and rivalry.

PUT OPTION. A right, but not the obligation, to sell a specific amount of an underlying security at a specified price within a specified period of time.

RATIONING. A system of distributing goods and services that limits the quantity of a good or service that a consuming unit may purchase or obtain.

REBBE. Religious teacher.

REGEL. Lit., foot. Damage inflicted by an animal through its natural movement, such as when the animal steps on and breaks an article in its path.

REISH DUKHNA. An assistant appointed to help a teacher when the class reaches a certain size.

RESERVATION PRICE. The minimum price a seller would accept for a good or service.

RESHUT HA-RABBIM. Public domain.

RESPONSA. Exchanges of letters in which one party consults another on a halakhic matter.

RIBBIT. The prohibition against charging or receiving interest on a loan between Jews.

RIBBIT KETZUTZAH. Lit., prearranged *ribbit.* Stipulated and agreed-upon interest payment in a loan between Jews in violation of the Biblical prohibition against charging interest. A Jewish court has the authority in this case to force the lender to pay back the prohibited interest payments to the borrower.

RISHONIM. Early rabbinic authorities. The period of the *Rishonim* extended from the middle of the 11th century to the middle of the 15th century.

RIVALRY. A situation in which one person's consumption of a good or service subtracts from the ability of any other person to consume the good or service.

RUINOUS COMPETITION. An economically unhealthy form of competition in which prices do not cover costs of production, usually for the purpose of driving competitors out of the market.

SE'AH. A unit of dry volume equal to 7.33 liters.

SE'AH BE-SE'AH. A commodity loan that requires repayment in kind rather than in cash.

SEKHAR SHIMMUR. Lit., compensation for watching. Refers to the salary paid to a religious teacher of children.

SELA. Coin equal to four Roman denarii.

SELLING SHORT. The sale of securities that are borrowed, with the intention of buying equivalent securities to repay what was borrowed.

SEMIKHAH. Lit., learning. Refers to the process of rabbinic ordination. Traditionally, ordination was passed down through generations by an individual with *semikhah* placing his hands on the head of the appointee and conferring upon him the authority to judge.

SEMIKHAT DA'AT. Mental reliance. Without the presumption of mental reliance on the part of the principals to an agreement, the transaction lacks validity in Jewish law.

SHA'AR HA-LAKOTOT. Lit., the gleaners' price. The price at which the first market transactions for a new crop are concluded. These transactions are sales by paupers of a portion of the gleanings they collect at harvest time as their mandatory agricultural gifts.

SHA'AR SHE-EINO YADU'A. Indeterminate price.

SHABBAT. Sabbath.

SHALOM BAYIT. Domestic peace.

SHEN. Lit., tooth. Damage inflicted through an animal's pleasure-seeking activities, such as eating or scratching itself against a wall.

SHEMA. Lit., hear. Refers to the passage at Deuteronomy 6:4, "Hear, O Israel: The Lord is our God, the Lord is One." The term is used more generally to refer to the entire portion of the daily prayers that consist of Deuteronomy 6:4–9, Deuteronomy 11:13–21, and Numbers 15:37–41.

SHIKHEHAH. Forgotten sheaves. Biblical commandment at Deuteronomy 24:19 that if one or two bundles of wheat are forgotten in the field when other bundles are collected, the forgotten sheaves must be left to the poor.

SHOHAD. Bribe. Prohibited payment offered to a judge by litigants as compensation for taking on a case.

SHOR HA-MAZIK. An ox that inflicts damage.

SHORT AGAINST THE BOX. A short sale of a security that is owned by the seller at the time of sale. Also called a "covered short."

SHORT POSITION. A position held in securities, derivatives, commodities, or currencies that increases in value as the market price declines.

SHORT RUN. A period of time in which a firm cannot change one or more of its inputs.

SHUL. Synagogue.

SIRKHA. An adhesion in the lobes of the lungs of animal. Discovery of a *sirkha* may render the animal organically defective and thus unfit for consumption under Jewish law.

SOFER MATA. A head teacher who appoints *melammedim* and supervises their work.

SPONTANEOUS HARMONY. A doctrine of classical economic theory pursuant to which private interests are essentially consistent and harmonious with social welfare.

SUPPLY SHOCK. In macroeconomics, a sudden change in production costs or productivity that has a large and unexpected impact on the level of output and price.

SUPPLY. Quantity of a good or service available from suppliers in a market, usually dependent on price.

TAKKANOT HA-KAHAL. Lit., ordinances of the community. Legislation enacted by a Jewish community.

TALMUD. The record of discussions of scholars on the laws and teachings of the Mishnah. The Talmud consists of the Babylonian Talmud, codified in ca. 500 C.E., and the Palestinian Talmud, codified in ca. 400 C.E.

TALMUD TORAH. Learning of Torah.

TAM. An innocuous animal. An animal that has not demonstrated that it is habituated to attack people. The owner of an innocuous animal that damages is liable to pay for half the damages.

TAMHUI. Communal charity plate.

TANNA, (PL.) TANNAIM, (ADJ.) TANNAIC. Aramaic *teni*, "hand down orally." The term designates a teacher dating from the Mishnaic times. The *Tannaic* period covers five generations of rabbinic authorities, spanning from 20 to 200 C.E.

TEFAH, (PL.) TEFAHIM. Lit., a handsbreadth. A measure of length equal to the width of four thumbs.

TENAI KAFUL. Lit., double condition. A technicality of Jewish contract law that makes a conditional clause unenforceable unless the stipulations expressly spell out the consequences of both fulfillment and nonfulfillment of the clause.

TERUMAT HA-LISHKAH. Temple funds. Judges in Jerusalem who adjudicated cases of theft would be paid their salary from these funds.

TIE-IN SALE. An arrangement pursuant to which a sale of one good (the "tying good") is conditioned on the buyer's purchase of a different good (the "tied good") from the seller.

TINOK HARIF. Perspicacious child.

TIRHAH. Toil and effort.

TORAH. Lit., instruction. Refers to the Bible as a whole.

TORT. A private or civil wrong or injury, not involving breach of a contract.

TOSAFOT. French commentators on the Talmud who lived during the 12th to 14th centuries.

TOSEFTA. Aramaic for "additional" or "supplementary." Originally, the term was used to describe teachings of the rabbinic authorities who lived in the Mishnaic era that were not quoted by R. Judah ha-Nasi in the Mishnah. Subsequently, the term came to denote a particular literary work, the "*Tosefta*," a collection of teaching of Mishnaic-era authorities. This collected work served as a companion volume to the Mishnah.

TOTAL COST. The number of units sold multiplied by cost of production per unit.

TOTAL REVENUE. The number of units sold multiplied by the price charged per unit.

TRANSACTION COSTS. The costs of time and other factors required to carry out market exchange.

UCC. See "Uniform Commercial Code."

UNIFORM COMMERCIAL CODE. Standardized set of U.S. business laws that has been adopted by all the states (except Louisiana, which has adopted only certain parts) and the District of Columbia.

UPTICK RULE. Former SEC Rule 10a–1 that provides that a security may be sold short only at a price above the price for the last sale of the security (an "uptick"), or at the price of the last sale if that price was itself an uptick.

UTILITY. A quantitative measure of pleasure or satisfaction obtained from consuming a good or service.

VE-SHINNANTAM. Lit., and you shall thoroughly teach them. Biblical requirement at Deuteronomy 6:7 for a father to teach his son Torah.

VOLATILITY. The rate at which a financial variable, such as stock price, moves up or down over time.

VOUCHER. A certificate that may be used instead of money, but only for a specific purpose. For example, in certain school districts in the United States, parents receive vouchers to cover the cost of educating their children in the school of their choice. The system is intended to promote healthy competition among schools.

VSL. Value of statistical life. An estimate of the monetary benefits of preventing the death of an unidentified person. VSL is the maximum amount that government agencies will pay to save a life.

WELFARE ECONOMICS. The branch of economics concerned with the effects of economics on how well off people are or perceive themselves to be under different states of affairs. Welfare economics adopts a consequentialist approach to morality. Under that approach, the measure for evaluating the worthiness of an economic action is whether it increases society's wealth in the long run, regardless of how that wealth is distributed among individual members of society.

WILLINGNESS TO PAY. The amount that an individual is willing to pay to acquire a particular good or service.

YATZA HA-SHA'AR. Lit., the price went out. Stability of market prices. A basis for an exemption from Jewish law's prohibition against entering into a forward contract that obtains when the price of the commodity to be delivered under the contract is well established at the time the parties enter into the contract.

YESH LO. Lit., he has it in his possession. A basis for an exemption from Jewish law's prohibition against entering into a forward contract that obtains when the forward seller of a commodity has a sufficient amount of the commodity in stock at the time he enters into the contract to cover the entire order under the contract.

YESHIVAH, (PL.) YESHIVOT. Jewish religious school for boys.

ZUZ. A coin the value of a Roman denarius.

BIBLIOGRAPHY

Aaron ha-Levi of Barcelona, R. *Sefer ha-Hinnukh*.

Abramsky, R. Yehezkel. *Tosefta im Perush Hazon Yehezkel. Seder Nezikin*. Vol. 2. Jerusalem, 1986.

Abulafia, R. Meir b. Todros ha-Levi. *Yad Ramah. Bava Batra*.

Adani, R. Shelomoh. *Melekhet Shelomoh* to Mishnah.

Adret, R. Solomon b. Abraham. *Hiddushei ha-Rashba*.

Akerlof, George A. "The Market for 'Lemons': Quality Uncertainty and the Market Mechanism." *Quarterly Journal of Economics* 84, no. 3 (1970): 488–500.

Albeck, R. Shalom. *Dinei ha-Mamonot ba-Talmud*. Tel Aviv: Dvir, 1976.

Alfasi, R. Isaac b. Jacob. *Rif* to *Bava Kamma*; *Bava Metzia*; *Bava Batra*.

Al-Nakawa, R. Israel ibn. *Menorat ha-Ma'or*. Edited by Hillel G. Enelow. New York: Bloch, 1932.

Ariav, David. *Le-Re'akha Kamokha*. Vol. 1. *Halakhot u-Ve'urim be-Mitzvot: Lo Tahmod, Lo Tit'aveh, Lo Tahanifu, Issur Genevat Da'at, Lo Tikallel, Lo Tikkom ve-Lo Tittor*. Jerusalem, 2000.

Asher b. Jehiel, R. *Rosh*, *Bava Kamma*; *Bava Metzia*; *Bava Batra*.

———. *She'elot u-Teshuvot ha-Rosh*.

Ashkenazi, R. Tzvi Hirsch. *Hakham Tzvi*.

Assad, R. Judah. *Teshuvot Mahari*.

Attar, R. Hayyim b. Moses. *Or ha-Hayyim*. Commentary on the Pentateuch.

Bahya b. Asher, R. *Rabbeinu Behaye*. Commentary on the Pentateuch.

Bandow, Doug. "Doctors Operate to Cut Out Competition." *Business and Society Review*, no. 58 (Summer 1986): 4–9.

Batzri, R. Ezra. *Dinei Mamonot*. 2nd ed. Jerusalem: Machon ha-Ketav, 1990.

Baumol, William J. "On Taxation and the Control of Externalities." *American Economic Review* 62, no. 3 (1972): 307–322.

Baumol, William J. and Alan S. Blinder. *Economics: Principles and Policy*. 11th ed. Mason, OH: South-Western, 2009.

Beny, Laura Nyantung. "Insider Trading Laws and Stock Markets Around the World: An Empirical Contribution to the Theoretical Law and Economics Debate." *Journal of Corporation Law* 32 (Winter 2007): 237–300.

Berlin, R. Naftali Tzvi Yehudah. *Ha'amek She'elah*.

Blaser, R. Isaac. *She'elot u-Teshuvot Peri Yitzhak*.

Bleich, J. David. "The Infinite Value of Human Life." In *The Value of Human Life: Contemporary Perspectives in Jewish Medical Ethics*, edited by Refoel Guggenheim, Leonardo Leupin, Yves Nordmann, and Raphael Patcas, 15–30. New York: Feldheim, 2010.

Bleich, Moshe. "Class Size—A Halakhic Perspective." *Tradition* 38, no. 4 (Winter 2004): 29–47.

Bloi, R. Yaakov Yeshayahu. *Berit Yehudah: Likkutim u-Ve'urim la-Halakhah be-Hilkhot Ribbit ve-Iska*. 2nd ed. Jerusalem, 1979.

———. *Pit'hei Hoshen: Likkutim u-Ve'urim ba-Halakhah be-Dinei Kinyanim, Mekhirah u-Matanah*. Jerusalem, 1994.

———. *Pit'hei Hoshen: Likkutim u-Ve'urim ba-Halakhah be-Hilkhot Geneivah u-Gezeilah va-Hassagat Gevul, Ona'ah u-Mekah Ta'ut*. Jerusalem: Mechon L'Hoyroa, 1987.

———. *Tzedakah u-Mishpat*. 2nd ed. Jerusalem, 2000.

Brady, Kevin L. "The Value of Human Life: A Case for Altruism." *Natural Resources Journal* 48 (Summer 2008): 541–65.

Browning, Edgar K. and Mark A. Zupan. *Microeconomics: Theory & Applications*. 10th ed. Hoboken, NJ: John Wiley, 2009.

Burkhauser, Richard V., Kenneth A. Couch and David C. Wittenburg. "'Who Gets What' from Minimum Wage Hikes: A Re-Evaluation of Card and Krueger's Distributional Analysis in *Myth and Measurement: The New Economics of the Minimum Wage*." *Industrial and Labor Relations Review* 49, no. 3 (April 1996): 592–623.

Burkhauser, Richard V. and Joseph J. Sabia. "Why Raising the Minimum Wage is a Poor Way to Help the Working Poor." *Employment Policies Institute* (July 2004).

Buss, James A. and Arthur Romeo. "The Changing Employment Situation in Some Cities with Living Wage Ordinances." *Review of Social Economy* 64, no. 3 (September 2006): 349–67.

Butler, Richard R. and Robert P. Garnett. "Teaching the Coase Theorem: Are We Getting it Right?" *Atlantic Economic Journal* 31, no. 2 (June 2003): 133–45.

Caro, R. Joseph. *Beit Yosef* to *Tur*.

———. *Kesef Mishneh* to *Mishneh Torah*.

———. *Shulhan Arukh*.

Coase, Ronald H. "The Problem of Social Cost." *Journal of Law and Economics* 3 (October 1960): 1–44.

Craswell, Richard. "Interpreting Deceptive Advertising." *Boston University Law Review* 65, no. 4 (July 1985): 657–732.

Crisp, Kevin A. "Giving Investors Short Shrift: How Short Sale Constraints Decrease Market Efficiency and a Modest Proposal for Letting More Shorts Go Naked." *Journal of Business and Securities Law* 8 (Spring 2008): 135–156.

Culi, R. Jacob. *Me-Am Lo'ez*. Translated by R. Shemuel Yerushalmi. *Yalkut Me-Am Lo'ez*. Jerusalem: Mossad Yad Ezra, 1968.

Danzig, R. Abraham. *Hokhmat Adam*.

Dill, David D. "Allowing the Market to Rule: The Case of the United States." *Higher Education Quarterly* 57, no. 2 (April 2003): 136–157.

Duran, R. Simeon b. Tzemach. *Sefer ha-Tashbetz*.

Duran, R. Solomon b. Simeon. *She'elot u-Teshuvot ha-Rashbash*.

Edels, R. Samuel Eliezer b. Judah ha-Levi. *Maharsha* to *Makkot* and *Ketubbot*.

Eisenstadt, R. Abraham Hirsch b. Jacob. *Pit'hei Teshuvah* to *Shulhan Arukh, Hoshen Mishpat*.

Eliezer b. Samuel of Metz, R. *Sefer Yere'im*.

Elijah b. Solomon Zalman, R. *Be'ur ha-Gra* to *Shulhan Arukh*.

Emden, R. Jacob. Commentary on *Rashi* to *Ketubbot* 105a. Reprinted in *Yalkut Mefareshim he-Hadash*. Babylonian Talmud, *Ketubbot*. *Oz ve-Hadar* ed. Jerusalem, 2006.

Epstein, R. Jehiel Michal. *Arukh ha-Shulhan*.

Eybeschuetz, R. Jonathan. *Urim ve-Tummim*.

———. *Ya'arot Devash*.

Falk, R. Joshua b. Alexander ha-Kohen. *Perishah* to *Tur*.

———. *Sema* to *Shulhan Arukh, Hoshen Mishpat*.

Feinstein, R. Mosheh. *Iggerot Mosheh*.

Fisch, R. Yaakov Yehezkiyah. *Titen Emet le-Yaakov*. Jerusalem, 1981.

Fried, Aharon Hersh. "The Respect We Owe Each Other—For the Sake of Our Children." *Hakirah: Flatbush Journal of Jewish Law and Thought* 9 (Winter 2010): 139–171.

Friedman, Milton. *Capitalism and Freedom*. Chicago: University of Chicago Press, 1962.

———. "The Role of Government in Education." In *Economics and the Public Interest*, edited by Robert A. Solo, 123–144. New Brunswick, NJ: Rutgers University Press, 1955.

Gaustad, Joan. "Nongraded Education: Mixed-Age, Integrated, and Developmentally Appropriate Education for Primary Children." *Oregon School Study Council* 35, no. 7 (March 1992).

Gerondi, R. Jonah b. Abraham. *Sha'arei Teshuvah.*

Gerondi, R. Nissim b. Reuben. *Ran* to *Kiddushin.*

Gershuni, R. Yehudah. "*Ha-Shevitah le-Or ha-Halakhah.*" In *Torah she-be-al Peh*, vol. 19, edited by Isaac Raphael, 82–93. Jerusalem: Mossad HaRav Kook, 1977.

Gombiner, R. Abraham Abele b. Hayyim ha-Levi. *Magen Avraham* to *Shulhan Arukh.*

Goodlad, John I. and Robert H. Anderson. *The Nongraded Elementary School.* Rev. ed. New York: Teachers College Press, Columbia University, 1987.

Gottlieb, R. Dov Berish. *Yad ha-Ketanah.*

Hahn, Robert W. and James E. Prieger. "The Impact of Driver Cell Phone Use on Accidents." *Advances in Economic Analysis and Policy* 6, no. 1 (2006): 1–37.

Hallion, Andrea M. "Strategies for Developing Multi-Age Classrooms." Paper presented at the annual convention of the National Association of Elementary School Principals Association, Orlando, FL, March 4–9, 1994.

Hananel b. Hushiel, R. *Rabbeinu Hananel.* Quoted by R. Joseph ibn Habiba. *Nimmukei Yosef* to *Rif, Bava Metzia* 58b.

———. Reprinted in R. Bezalel Ashkenazi. *Shitah Mekubbetzet. Bava Metzia* 72b.

Hanushek, Eric A. "The Failure of Input-Based Schooling Policies." *Economic Journal* 113 (February 2003): F64–F98.

Hausman, Daniel M. and Michael S. McPherson. *Economic Analysis, Moral Philosophy and Public Policy.* 2nd ed. Cambridge: Cambridge University Press, 2006.

Heller, R. Aryeh Leib b. Joseph ha-Kohen. *Ketzot ha-Hoshen* to *Shulhan Arukh, Hoshen Mishpat.*

Henkin, R. Yosef Eliyahu. *Kitvei ha-Gri'a Henkin.* Vol. 1. *Edut le-Yisrael.* New York: Ezras Torah, 1981.

———. *Kitvei ha-Gri'a Henkin.* Vol. 2. *Teshuvot Ivra.* Edited by R. Abraham Hillel Henkin. New York: Ezras Torah, 1989.

Hezekiah b. Manoah, R. *Hizkuni.* Commentary on the Pentateuch.

Hicks, J. R. "The Foundations of Welfare Economics." *Economic Journal* 49, no. 196 (1939): 696–712.

Horowitz, R. Isaiah ha-Levi. *Shenei Luhot ha-Brit.*

Horowitz, R. Pinhas ha-Levi. *Sefer ha-Makneh.*

Hotz, V. Joseph and John Karl Scholz. "The Earned Income Tax Credit." *NBER Working Paper Series*, no. 8078 (January 2001).

Hoxby, Caroline Minter. "Rising Tide," *Education Next* (Winter 2001): 69–74.

Isaac b. Moses of Vienna, R. *Or Zaru'a.*

Ishbili, R. Yom Tov. *Hiddushei ha-Ritva.*

Isserlein, R. Israel b. Petahiah. *Terumat ha-Deshen. Helek* 1. *She'elot u-Teshuvot.* Edited by Shemuel Avitan. Jerusalem, 1991.

Isserles, R. Moses. *Darkhei Mosheh* to *Tur.*

———. *Rema* to *Shulhan Arukh.*

Itach, R. Yehudah. *Netiv Yosher: Hilkhot va-Halikhot Mekah u-Memkar.* Jerusalem, 1992.

Jacob b. Asher, R. *Arba'ah Turim.*

Jacobs, R. Jill. "Work, Workers and the Jewish Owner." Responsum adopted by the Committee on Jewish Law and Standards of the Rabbinical Assembly on May 28, 2008.

Jaffe, R. Mordecai b. Abraham. *Levush Malkhut. Levush Ir Shushan, Hoshen Mishpat.*

Joseph ibn Habiba, R. *Nimmukei Yosef* to *Rif.*

Judah b. Samuel he-Hasid, R. *Sefer Hasidim.*

Kagan, R. Israel Meir ha-Kohen. *Ahavat Hesed.*

———. *Likkutei Halakhot.*

———. *Sefat Tamim.*

———. *Sefer Hafetz Hayyim.*

Kagan, Shelly. *Normative Ethics.* Boulder, CO: Westview Press, 1998.

Kaidanover, R. Aaron Samuel b. Israel. *She'elot u-Teshuvot Emunat Shemuel.*

Kaldor, Nicholas. "Welfare Propositions of Economics and Interpersonal Comparisons of Utility." *Economic Journal* 49, no. 195 (1939): 549–552.

Kamenetsky, R. Yaakov. *Emet le-Yaakov.*

Kanarfogel, Ephraim. *Jewish Education and Society in the High Middle Ages*. Detroit: Wayne State University Press, 1992.

Karelitz, R. Abraham Isaiah. *Hazon Ish al Inyanei Emunah, Bitahon, ve-Od*. Jerusalem: S. Greineman, 1954.

———. *Hazon Ish. Hoshen Mishpat; Yoreh De'ah*.

Kaufman, Bruce E. and Julie L. Hotchkiss. *The Economics of Labor Markets*. 7th ed. Mason, OH: Thomson South-Western, 2006.

Kegley, Mary B. and Janine S. Hiller. "'Emerging' Lemon Car Laws." *American Business Law Journal* 24, no. 1 (Spring 1986): 87–103.

Kelly, Kate. "How Goldman Won Big on Mortgage Meltdown: A Team's Bearish Bets Netted Firm Billions; A Nudge from the CFO." *Wall Street Journal*. December 14, 2007: A1.

Kirschenbaum, Aaron. *Equity in Jewish Law: Halakhic Perspectives in Jewish Law*. Hoboken, NJ: Ktav, 1991.

Klein, R. Menasheh. "*Hal'itehu la-Rasha ve-Yamut*." In *Pa'amei Yaakov be-Sedei ha-Halakhah* (*Nisan* 2000): 114–116.

Kluger, R. Shelomoh. *Hokhmat Shelomoh* to *Shulhan Arukh*.

Kolin, R. Samuel b. Nathan ha-Levi. *Mahatzit ha-Shekel* to *Shulhan Arukh*.

Kotler, R. Aaron. *Mishnat Rabbi Aharon*. Jerusalem: Machon Mishnas Rabbi Aaron, 2003.

Lander, R. Daniel. "*Be-Inyan Hiyyuv Dei Mahsoro*." In *Sefer Kevod ha-Rav: Kovetz Meyuhad le-Hiddushei Torah ve-Inyanei Halakhah*, edited by R. Moshe Sherman and R. Yosef Wolf, 202–206. New York: Student Organization of Yeshiva Rabbi Isaac Elchanan Theological Seminary, 1984.

Landsburg, Steven E. *Price Theory and Applications*. 8th ed. Mason, OH: South-Western, 2011.

Leight, Robert L. and Alice D. Rinehart. "Revisiting Americana: One-Room School in Retrospect." *Educational Forum* 56, no. 2 (Winter 1992): 133–151.

Levi ibn Habib, R. *She'elot u-Teshuvot Ma-ha-Ralbach*.

Levine, Aaron. "Aspects of the Firm's Responsibility to Its Customers: Pharmaceutical Pricing and Consumer Privacy." In *Jewish Business Ethics: The Firm and Its Stakeholders*, edited by Aaron Levine and Moses Pava, 75–121. Northvale, NJ: Jason Aronson, 1999.

———. *Case Studies in Jewish Business Ethics*. Hoboken, NJ: Ktav, 2000.

———. *Economic Public Policy and Jewish Law*. Hoboken, NJ: Ktav, 1993.

———. *Economics and Jewish Law*. Hoboken, NJ: Ktav, 1987.

———. *Free Enterprise and Jewish Law: Aspects of Jewish Business Ethics*. New York: Ktav, 1980.

———. *Moral Issues of the Marketplace in Jewish Law*. Brooklyn, NY: Yashar Books, 2005.

———. "*Onaa* and the Operation of the Modern Marketplace." *Jewish Law Annual* 14 (2003): 225–258.

———. "The Global Recession of 2007–2009: The Moral Factor and Jewish Law." In *The Oxford Handbook of Judaism and Economics*, edited by Aaron Levine, 404–428. New York: Oxford University Press, 2010.

———. "Welfare Programs and Jewish Law." In *Public Policy and Social Issues: Jewish Sources and Perspectives*, edited by Marshall J. Breger, 140–153. Westport, CT: Praeger, 2003.

———. "Whistleblowing as Treated in Jewish Law." In *Whistleblowing: In Defense of Proper Action; Praxiology: The International Annual of Practical Philosophy and Methodology*, vol. 18, edited by Marek Arszułowicz and Wojciech W. Gasparski, 69–81. New Brunswick, NJ: Transaction Publishers, 2011.

Lichtenstein, R. Aharon. "*Sa'od Tis'od Immo: Hishtatfut ha-Mekabbel be-Gemilut Hasadim*." In *Sefer ha-Zikaron le-Avraham Spiegelman*, edited by Aryeh Morgenstern, 81–93. Tel Aviv: Moreshet, 1979.

Liebermann, Yehoshua. "The Coase Theorem in Jewish Law." *Journal of Legal Studies* 10, no. 2 (June 1981): 293–303.

Loew b. Bezalel, R. Judah. *Hiddushei Aggadot Maharal mi-Prague*.

Lorberbaum, R. Jacob Moses. *Netivot ha-Mishpat* to *Shulhan Arukh*.

Lucas, Douglas J., Laurie S. Goodman, and Frank J. Fabozzi. *Collateralized Debt Obligations: Structures and Analysis*. 2nd ed. Hoboken, NJ: Wiley, 2006.

Lunshits, R. Ephraim Solomon b. Aaron. *Keli Yakar*. Commentary on the Pentateuch.

Luria, R. Solomon b. Jehiel. *Yam shel Shelomoh*.

Luzzatto, R. Moses Hayyim. *Mesilat Yesharim.*

Macey, Jonathan R. "Getting the Word out About Fraud: A Theoretical Analysis of Whistleblowing and Insider Trading." *Michigan Law Review* 105 (2007): 1899–1940.

———. *Insider Trading: Economics, Politics, and Policy.* Washington, DC: AEI Press, 1991.

Mahadevan, Sivan, Vishwanath Tirupattur, Peter Polanskyj, Phanikiran Naraparaju, and Andrew Sheets. *Structured Credit Insights: Instruments, Valuation and Strategies.* 3rd ed. Morgan Stanley, 2007.

Maimonides. *Mishneh Torah.*

Manne, Henry G. *Insider Trading and the Stock Market.* New York: Free Press, 1966.

———. "Insider Trading: Hayek, Virtual Markets, and the Dog that Did Not Bark." *Journal of Corporation Law* 31 (Fall 2005): 167–186.

Megna, Vince. *Bring on Goliath: Lemon Law Justice in America.* Tucson: Ken Press, 2004.

Meir b. Barukh of Rothenburg, R. *Haggahot Maimuniyyot* to *Mishneh Torah.*

———. *She'elot u-Teshuvot Maharam.*

Meir Simhah ha-Kohen of Dvinsk, R. *Meshekh Hokhmah.*

———. *Or Sameah* on *Mishneh Torah.*

Meiri, R. Menahem b. Solomon. *Beit ha-Behirah.*

Meltzer, R. Isser Zalman. *Even ha-Ezel.*

Midrash. *Bereishit Rabbah.*

———. *Midrash Yelammedenu.* Quoted in R. Simeon ha-Darshan. *Yalkut Shimoni, Kuntras Aharon.* Reprinted in *Yalkut Shimoni ha-Shalem.* Jerusalem: Wagschal, 2003.

Mishnah. *Arakhin*; *Avot*; *Bava Batra*; *Bava Kamma*; *Bava Metzia*; *Ketubbot*; *Pe'ah*; *Shabbat.*

Mordekhai b. Hillel ha-Kohen, R. *Mordekhai. Bava Metzia.*

Moses ha-Kohen of Lunel, R. *Ramach* to *Bava Metzia* 58b. Quoted by R. Bezalel Ashkenazi. *Shitah Mekubbetzet. Bava Metzia* 58b.

Muth, Karl T. "The Fragile Armistice: The Legal, Economic, and Policy Implications of Trading in a Competitor's Stock." *Loyola University Chicago Law Journal* 40 (Spring 2009): 611–642.

Nahmanides. *Ha-Emunah ve-ha-Bitahon.*

———. *Hiddushei ha-Ramban.*

———. *Kitvei Rabbeinu Mosheh ben Nahman.* Edited by R. Chaim Dov Chavel. Jerusalem: Mossad HaRav Kook, 1963.

———. *Ramban.* Commentary on the Torah.

Nathansohn, R. Joseph Saul ha-Levi. *Yad Shaul.*

Navon, R. Ephraim b. Aaron. *Mahaneh Ephraim.*

Nelson, Richard R. "The Simple Economics of Basic Scientific Research." *Journal of Political Economy* 67, no. 3 (1959): 297–306.

Neumark, David and William L. Wascher. *Minimum Wages.* Cambridge, MA: MIT Press, 2008.

Obadiah b. Abraham of Bertinoro, R. *Bartenura* to Mishnah.

Oppenheimer, Steven. "Confronting Child Abuse." *Journal of Halacha and Contemporary Society* 44 (Fall 2002): 31–50.

Palaggi, R. Hayyim. *Lev Hayyim.*

Papo, R. Eliezer. *Pela Yoetz.*

Perloff, Jeffrey M. *Microeconomics.* 5th ed. Boston: Pearson Addison Wesley, 2009.

Phelps, Edmond S. *Rewarding Work: How to Restore Participation and Self-Support to Free Enterprise.* Cambridge, MA: Harvard University Press, 1997.

Pigou, Arthur C. *The Economics of Welfare.* 4th ed. London: Macmillan, 1932.

Pinto, R. Josiah b. Joseph. Commentary on *Bava Metzia* 72b. Reprinted in R. Bezalel Ashkenazi. *Shitah Mekubbetzet. Bava Metzia* 72b.

Pollack, R. David. *Be-Torato Yehgeh.* Jerusalem: Mahon Minhat Israel, 1997.

Posner, Richard A. *Economic Analysis of Law.* 7th ed. New York: Aspen, 2007.

Prager, Jonas. "Balancing the Scales: *Halakhah*, the Firm, and Information Asymmetries." In *Jewish Business Ethics: The Firm and Its Stakeholders*, edited by Aaron Levine and Moses Pava, 123–146. Northvale, NJ: Jason Aronson, 1999.

Rakover, R. Nahum. *Halikhot ha-Mis'har: Hassagat Gevul Mis'harit be-Piskei ha-Din ha-Rabbaniyim, Sidrat Mehkarim u-Sekirot ba-Mishpat ha-Ivri* 41. Jerusalem: Misrad ha-Mishpatim, 1976.

Reischer, R. Jacob b. Joseph. *Iyyun Yaakov*.

Richards, Jef I. and Ivan L. Preston. "Proving and Disproving Materiality of Deceptive Advertising Claims." *Journal of Public Policy and Marketing* 11, no. 2 (Fall 1992): 45–56.

Rubin, Paul H. "The Economics of Regulating Deception." *CATO Journal* 10, no. 3 (Winter 1991): 667–690.

Samuel b. Aaron of Joinville, R. *Tosafot* to *Bava Batra* 91a.

Samuel b. Meir, R. *Rashbam* to *Bava Batra*.

Samuelson, Paul A. and William D. Nordhaus. *Economics*. 19th ed. New York: McGraw-Hill, 2009.

Schepansky, R. Israel. *Ha-Takkanot bi-Yisrael*. Jerusalem: Mossad HaRav Kook, 2004.

Schiller, Bradley R. "Just Getting By?: Income Dependence on Minimum Wage Jobs." *Employment Policies Institute* (March 2011).

Schimmel, Solomon. "Ethical Dimensions of Traditional Jewish Education." In *Studies in Jewish Education*, vol. 1, edited by Barry Chazan, 91–111. Jerusalem: Magnes Press, 1983.

Schizer, David M. "Frictions as a Constraint on Tax Planning." *Columbia Law Review* 101 (2001): 1312–1409.

Segal, R. David b. Samuel ha-Levi. *Turei Zahav* to *Shulhan Arukh*.

Segal, R. Shalom Mordekhai. *Mishkan Shalom*. Jerusalem: Zihron Aharon, 2002.

Shabbetai b. Meir ha-Kohen, R. *Siftei Kohen* to *Shulhan Arukh*.

Shaffer, Brian and Daniel T. Ostas. "Exploring the Political Economy of Consumer Legislation: The Development of Automobile Lemon Laws." *Business and Politics* 3, no. 1 (2001): 65–76.

Shavell, Steven. *Foundations of Economic Analysis of Law*. Boston: Harvard University Press, 2004.

Sherk, James and Rea S. Hederman, Jr. "Who Earns the Minimum Wage? Suburban Teenagers, Not Single Parents." *Heritage Foundation WebMemo*, no. 1320 (January 23, 2007), http://www.heritage.org/Research/Economy/wm1320.cfm.

Shiller, Robert J. *The Subprime Solution: How Today's Global Financial Crisis Happened, and What to Do about It*. Princeton, NJ: Princeton University Press, 2008.

Shilo, Shmuel. *Dina de-Malkhuta Dina*. Jerusalem: Hebrew University Press, 1974.

———. "*Kofin al Midat S'dom*: Jewish Law's Concept of Abuse of Rights." *Israel Law Review* 15, no. 1 (1980): 49–78.

Shkop, R. Shimon Yehudah ha-Kohen. *Hiddushei Rabbi Shimon Yehudah ha-Kohen*.

Shneur Zalman of Liadi, R. *Shulhan Arukh ha-Rav*. Brooklyn: Otzar ha-Hasidim, 2004.

Sirkes, R. Joel. *Bah* to *Tur*.

Smith, Adam. *An Inquiry into the Nature and Causes of the Wealth of Nations*. 1776. Reprint, New York: Modern Library, 1937.

Sofer, R. Moses. *Hiddushei Hatam Sofer*.

———. *She'elot u-Teshuvot Hatam Sofer*.

Solomon b. Isaac, R. *Rashi*. Commentary on the Bible and Talmud.

Soloveitchik, R. Aharon. "The Fire of Sinai." In *Building Jewish Ethical Character*, edited by Joseph Kaminetsky and Murray I. Friedman, 11–18. New York: Fryer Foundation, 1975.

Staley, Kathryn F. *The Art of Short Selling*. New York: John Wiley, 1997.

Sternbuch, R. Moshe. *Teshuvot va-Hanhagot*. Jerusalem, 2002.

Stokes, Alexis Brown. "In Pursuit of the Naked Short." *New York University Journal of Law and Business* 5 (Spring 2009): 1–61.

Stout, Lynn A. "Are Takeover Premiums Really Premiums? Market Price, Fair Value, and Corporate Law." *Yale Law Journal* 99 (1990): 1235–1296.

Strashun, R. Samuel b. Joseph. *Rashash, Ketubbot* 17a.

Sunstein, Cass R. "Lives, Life-Years, and Willingness to Pay," *Columbia Law Review* 104 (2004): 205–252.

Sweezy, Paul M. "Demand under Conditions of Oligopoly." *Journal of Political Economy* 47, no. 4 (August 1939): 568–573.

Talmud (Babylonian). *Arakhin*; *Bava Batra*; *Bava Kamma*; *Bava Metzia*; *Berakhot*; *Gittin*; *Hullin*; *Ketubbot*; *Kiddushin*; *Makkot*; *Megillah*; *Pesahim*; *Sanhedrin*; *Shabbat*; *Yevamot*.

Talmud (Palestinian). *Berakhot*; *Hagigah*; *Shabbat*.

Teitelbaum, R. Joel. *Va-Yoel Mosheh. Ma'amar Lashon ha-Kodesh*. Brooklyn: Sender Deutsch, 1961.

Toikka, Richard S., Aaron Yelowitz, and Andre Neveu. "The 'Poverty Trap' and Living Wage Laws." *Economic Development Quarterly* 19, no. 1 (February 2005): 62–79.

Vidal Yom Tov of Tolosa, R. *Maggid Mishneh* to *Mishneh Torah*.

Vogel, Joan. "Squeezing Consumers: Lemon Laws, Consumer Warranties, and a Proposal for Reform." *Arizona State Law Journal* (1985): 589–675.

Wahrmann, R. Abraham David. *Kesef ha-Kadashim* to *Shulhan Arukh, Hoshen Mishpat*.

Warhaftig, Shillem. *Dinei Avodah ba-Mishpat ha-Ivri*. 2nd ed. Jerusalem: Machon Harry Fischel, 1982.

Weil, R. Nethanel b. Naftali Tzvi. *Korban Netanel* to *Rosh, Ketubbot*.

Weinberger, R. Moshe. "On Studying Secular Subjects." *Journal of Halacha and Contemporary Society* 11 (Spring 1986): 88–128.

Weiss, R. Yitzhak Yaakov. *She'elot u-Teshuvot Minhat Yitzhak*. Jerusalem, 1993.

Yalkut Shimoni. Edited by Dov Hyman. *Yalkut Shimoni al Nevi'im le-Rabbeinu Shimon ha-Darshan: Nevi'im Aharonim*. Jerusalem: Mossad HaRav Kook, 2009.

Yavruv, R. Nahum. *Niv Sefatayyim*. 4th ed. Jerusalem, 2005.

Zamir, Eyal and Barak Medina. *Law, Economics, and Morality*. New York: Oxford University Press, 2010.

Zandi, Mark. *Financial Shock: A 360° Look at the Subprime Mortgage Implosion, and How to Avoid the Next Financial Crisis*. Upper Saddle River, NJ: Pearson, 2009.

Zausmir, R. Jekutiel Asher Zalman Enzil. *She'elot u-Teshuvot Mahariaz Enzil*.

Ziegler, Edward H., Arden H. Rathkopf, and Daren A. Rathkopf. *Rathkopf's The Law of Zoning and Planning*. 4th ed. St. Paul, MN: Thomson Reuters, 2011.

NAME INDEX

SUBJECT INDEX